Fundamentals of Early Childhood Education

THIRD EDITION

George S. Morrison
University of North Texas

Merrill
Prentice Hall

Upper Saddle River, New Jersey
Columbus, Ohio

Library of Congress Cataloging in Publication Data

Morrison, George S.
    Fundamentals of early childhood education / George S. Morrison.--3rd ed.
        p. cm.
    Includes bibliographical references and index.
    ISBN 0-13-097512-5
    1. Early childhood education--United States.

    LB1139.25.M67 2003
    372.21'0973--dc21   2001059179

Vice President and Publisher: Jeffery W. Johnston
Executive Editor: Kevin M. Davis
Associate Editor: Christina M. Tawney
Editorial Assistant: Autumn Crisp
Development Editor: Gianna Marsella
Production Editor: Linda Hillis Bayma
Production Coordination: Tiffany Kuehn, Carlisle Publishers Services
Design Coordinator: Diane C. Lorenzo
Photo Coordinator: Kathleen Kirtland
Cover Designer: Thomas Borah
Cover photo: Corbis Stock Market
Production Manager: Laura Messerly
Director of Marketing: Ann Castel Davis
Marketing Manager: Amy June
Marketing Coordinator: Tyra Cooper

This book was set in Palatino by Carlisle Communications, Ltd. It was printed and bound by
R.R. Donnelley & Sons Company. The cover was printed by Phoenix Color Corp.

Photo Credits: David Buffington/PhotoDisc, p. 23; Tim Cairns/Merrill, p. 154; James Carroll/PH College, p. 84;
Scott Cunningham/Merrill, pp. 5, 7, 19, 33, 41, 57, 78, 95, 111, 133, 142, 189, 223, 253, 263, 276, 285, 293, 301, 330,
336, 351; Robert E. Daemmrich/Tony Stone Images, p. 12; Laima Druskis/PH College, p. 361; Richard Frear/
U.S. Department of Interior, p. 365; Ken Karp/PH College, p. 123; Lynchburg Police Department, p. 259;
Anthony Magnacca/Merrill, pp. 171, 251, 307, 321; National Institute on Aging, p. 345; Mike Peters/Silver
Burdett Ginn, p. 3; Rhoda Sidney/PH College, p. 37; Barbara Schwartz/Merrill, pp. 72, 107, 148, 229, 254, 319;
Anne Vega/Merrill, pp. 46, 65, 100, 128, 145, 159, 161, 162, 175, 182, 190, 214, 225, 226, 234, 323, 343; Tom Watson/
Merrill, p. 281; Todd Yarrington/Merrill, pp. 196, 209, 211, 240; Shirley Zeiberg/PH College, p. 29.

Pearson Education Ltd.
Pearson Education Australia Pty. Limited
Pearson Education Singapore Pte. Ltd.
Pearson Education North Asia Ltd.
Pearson Education Canada, Ltd.
Pearson Educación de Mexico, S.A. de C.V.
Pearson Education—Japan
Pearson Education Malaysia Pte. Ltd.
Pearson Education, *Upper Saddle River, New Jersey*

10 9 8 7 6 5 4 3 2 1
ISBN 0-13-097512-5

For Betty Jane—as always

About the Author

George S. Morrison, Ed.D., is professor of early childhood education and holder of the Velma E. Schmidt Endowed Chair in early childhood education at the University of North Texas. Professor Morrison's accomplishments include a Distinguished Academic Service Award from the Pennsylvania Department of Education, an Outstanding Alumni Award from the University of Pittsburgh School of Education, and Outstanding Service and Teaching Awards from Florida International University.

Dr. Morrison is the author of many books on early childhood education, child development, curriculum, and teacher education, including *Early Childhood Education Today*, Eighth Edition, and *Teaching in America*, Third Edition.

Dr. Morrison is a popular author, speaker, and presenter. He writes an ongoing column for the *Public School Montessorian* and contributes his opinions and views to a wide range of publications. His speaking engagements and presentations focus on the future of early childhood education, the changing roles of early childhood teachers, and the influence of contemporary educational reforms, research, and legislation on teaching and learning.

Dr. Morrison's professional interests also include the application of neuroscience and developmental research to early childhood programs. He has developed Success For Life, a research-based program for children from birth to six years of age. Success For Life helps children achieve success in school and daily life. The curriculum is an interdisciplinary approach and applies theory and research to practice for the education and optimum development of children and families.

Currently, 250 teachers in child care and early childhood education sites involving 4,000 children collaborate in the implementation of Success For Life. In addition, over 40 teachers and 1,000 children are involved in the Success For Life Thailand Project.

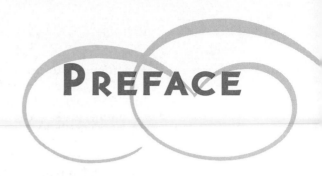

PREFACE

The field of early childhood education is undergoing significant change and transformation. In fact, early childhood education has changed more in the last five years than in the previous fifty years. Some of these changes include:

* New knowledge and ideas about how children grow and develop, and the conditions that support optimal learning.
* New views about how best to teach young children.
* Changing roles and responsibilities of early childhood professionals.
* Increasing demands from the public and politicians for accountability in ensuring that all children will learn to their fullest capacity.

This third edition of *Fundamentals of Early Childhood Education* captures the important changes occurring in early childhood education today and shows how they apply to teaching young children and collaborating with their parents and families.

As you, other early childhood professionals, scientists, and the public respond to the changing field of early childhood education, more opportunities arise for new programs and curricula to meet the ever-changing needs of children and families. These changes and opportunities create an aura of excitement in the field of early childhood education. As a result, we are in what I call a "Golden Age" of early childhood education. This Golden Age provides you and other early childhood educators with unprecedented opportunities and challenges. How well we respond to these opportunities and challenges will determine, to a large extent, whether or not this Golden Age continues into the next decade. I hope and believe it will.

Themes and Goals

The primary goal of *Fundamentals of Early Childhood Education,* Third Edition, is to help you respond positively and professionally to the opportunities of early childhood education today and to help you be the best early childhood professional you can be. This edition gives you the knowledge, skills, and insights necessary to confidently and appropriately achieve your goal of being a leader in educating children, parents, and families.

When I ask early childhood educators how I can help them be better professionals, they repeatedly express their desire for an early childhood book that is user-friendly and applies theory to practice. *Fundamentals of Early Childhood*

Education, Third Edition, meets this need for a book that is both practical and based on current research and thinking about how young children learn and how best to teach them.

In this book, eight core themes serve as an organizing framework:

* Professionalism—Being a professional is the foundation of high-quality programs for young children. Professionalism is the compass that guides and directs you throughout your work with children and families. In Chapter 1, "You and Early Childhood Education: What Does It Mean to Be a Professional?" you will encounter a Professional Development Checklist that consists of thirteen core professional outcomes consistent with NAEYC and CDA professional guidelines. The checklist and its core outcomes create a professional profile that will guide your professional thinking, reflection, and development throughout your career. Each chapter of this text begins with one or more of these thirteen professional outcomes and serves as an advance organizer for chapter content, "Professionalism in Practice," and "Program in Action" vignettes. As you read and engage in the activities in this book, you will be well on your way to becoming an accomplished professional.

* Theory to Practice—This text helps you understand how teachers and programs translate theories of learning and educating young children into practice. The "Program in Action" and "Professionalism in Practice" features provide real-life insights into how teachers in programs across the United States endeavor to apply early childhood theories to their everyday practices. These features personalize the practice of early childhood education by adding faces, names, and authentic voices of practicing professionals and high-quality programs to chapter content. You will read firsthand about professional colleagues who make theories come alive in concrete ways that truly help children succeed in school and life.

* Diversity—The United States is a nation of diverse people, and this diversity is reflected in every early childhood classroom and program. You and your colleagues must have the knowledge and sensitivity to teach all students well, and you must understand how culture and language influence teaching and learning. Chapter 10, "Educating Children with Diverse Backgrounds and Special Needs: Ensuring All Children Can Learn," helps you understand how all children are unique individuals with special strengths and challenges and emphasizes how all children, regardless of their multicultural, physical, mental, and emotional needs, can be included and fully taught in all early childhood classrooms. In addition, every chapter of this edition emphasizes the theme of diversity through narrative examples and program descriptions.

* Family-Centered, Community-Based Practice—To effectively meet children's needs, you and other early childhood professionals must collaborate with families and communities. Today, teaching is not an isolated endeavor in which one seeks to practice the craft of early childhood education removed

from colleagues and others in the school and community. Successful partnerships at all levels are essential for effective teaching and learning. Chapter 12, "Cooperation and Collaboration with Parents, Families, and the Community: Building a Partnership for Student Success," emphasizes the importance of family-centered practice, while every other chapter provides examples of successful partnerships and their influences on teaching and learning.

* Timeliness—This is a book for the twenty-first century. The information it contains is timely and reflects the very latest in trends and research. Every chapter has been thoroughly revised to reflect the changes in the field.

* Developmentally Appropriate Practice—The theme of developmentally appropriate practice is integrated and emphasized throughout this text. Developmentally appropriate practice is the foundation for all that early childhood professionals do. It is important, therefore, that you, as an early childhood education professional, understand developmentally appropriate practice and become familiar with how to implement it in your teaching. Every chapter provides examples and illustrations to show you how to apply developmentally appropriate practice to the teaching of young children.

* Technology Applied to Teaching and Learning—Technological and information literacy is essential for living and working in contemporary society. This edition provides you with the information and skills you need to integrate technology effectively into the curriculum and use new teaching and learning styles enabled by technology. Each chapter has a "Technology Tie-In" designed to enable you to become more technologically proficient. Teachers and all professionals in education are expected to use technology in a number of ways and for multiple purposes; today's professional cannot plead technological ignorance.

* Literacy Development—Currently, there is a great deal of emphasis on promoting children's early literacy development and helping children learn how to read. This emphasis will continue well into the future. Therefore, it is imperative for early childhood educators to know how to support and promote children's literacy development. For this reason, Chapters 6, 7, 8, and 9 place a special emphasis on literacy development, and knowledge, information, and activities about literacy development are integrated throughout the text.

Organization and Coverage of the Third Edition

Fundamentals of Early Childhood Education, Third Edition, provides a thorough introduction to the field of early childhood education in a straightforward and engaging style. The text is comprehensive in its approach to the profession and is divided into four large areas:

* Area I—Consists of Chapter 1, "You and Early Childhood Education: What Does It Mean to Be a Professional?" and Chapter 2, "Early Childhood

Education Today: Understanding Current Issues." Chapter 1 has been extensively revised to emphasize the importance of becoming a professional. It identifies four dimensions of professionalism and discusses each of these dimensions in detail. The Professional Development Checklist is introduced in this first chapter to emphasize that professional practice is at the heart of good teaching. Chapter 2 immerses you in contemporary practice and helps you understand how current issues and trends are influencing the practice of early childhood education.

* Area II—Consists of Chapter 3, "History and Theories: Foundations for Teaching and Learning," Chapter 4, "Implementing Early Childhood Programs: Applying Theories to Practice," and Chapter 5, "Observing and Assessing Young Children: Guiding, Teaching, and Learning." Chapter 3 enables you to become familiar with your profession's history and enables you to use knowledge of past practices to inform your current practice. Chapter 4 discusses major models of early childhood education today, familiarizes you with high-quality programs for young children, and identifies essential model features. Chapter 5 provides you with the knowledge and skills necessary to assess your students' achievement and behaviors with authentic measures and helps you understand how to apply assessment information to guide your teaching.

* Area III—Consists of Chapter 6, "Infants and Toddlers: Foundation Years for Learning," Chapter 7, "The Preschool Years: Getting Ready for School," Chapter 8, "Kindergarten Today: Meeting Academic and Developmental Needs," Chapter 9, "The Primary Grades: Preparation for Lifelong Success," and Chapter 10, "Educating Children with Diverse Backgrounds and Special Needs: Ensuring All Children Can Learn." In each of these chapters, a new focus on curriculum illustrates what to teach young children and how to teach it. This new focus is in keeping with the new professional emphasis on providing experiences and activities that support and promote children's learning. Chapter 6 provides an in-depth discussion of infant and toddler programs and supplies you with the knowledge and skills necessary to provide high-quality programs for children in these critical years. Chapter 7 addresses the important preschool years and discusses the changes occurring in the teaching and education of three- and four-year-olds and focuses on how to implement programs that will help children get ready for learning and school. Chapter 8 is devoted to kindergarten children and provides you with the most recent developments affecting five- and six-year-old children and the tools for advancing their intellectual, social, and emotional development. Chapter 9 discusses the development of young children in grades one to three and outlines curricula and effective teaching practices that will help children learn and be successful in school and in life. Chapter 10 emphasizes how to effectively teach and provide for children with diverse backgrounds and special needs and how to provide for these needs in inclusive and multiculturally sensitive and appropriate ways.

* Area IV—Consists of Chapter 11, "Guiding Children's Behavior: Helping Children Act Their Best," and Chapter 12, "Cooperation and Collaboration with Parents, Families, and the Community: Building a Partnership for Student Success." Chapter 11 focuses on guiding the behavior of children so they can become independent and motivated, responsible learners. Guiding children's behavior is a cooperative effort with parents and families and serves as a bridge to the next chapter. Chapter 12 emphasizes treating parents with dignity and respect and outlines ways to collaborate, encourage, and engage parents in their roles as their children's primary teachers.

The Appendix, "The NAEYC Code of Ethical Conduct," provides the basis for teaching in an ethical and professional manner.

Special Features

* Programs in Action—One of the hallmarks of the third edition of *Fundamentals of Early Childhood Education* is its practical nature and its ability to translate theory into practice. The "Program in Action" features in every chapter enable you to experience actual programs designed for children in real-life classrooms and early childhood programs throughout the United States. These real examples of schools, programs, classrooms, and teachers enable you to explore the best practices of early childhood education and see "up close and personal" what teaching is really like. They also offer special opportunities to spotlight current topics such as helping children resolve conflicts, high-quality infant care and education, educating children of diverse backgrounds, applying brain research to early childhood practice, bilingual education, gifted education, inclusion, multicultural education, early literacy, and improving children's mental and physical health. This approach enables you to make the transition from thinking about being a teacher to becoming a competent professional.

* Professionalism in Practice—I believe it is important for the teacher's voice to be heard in and throughout this edition of *Fundamentals of Early Childhood Education*. "Professionalism in Practice" provides experienced teachers with the opportunity to explain their philosophies, beliefs, and program practices. These teachers mentor you as they relate how they practice early childhood education. The majority of the "Professionalism in Practice" feature boxes are contributed by national, *USA Today*, and state Teachers of the Year. Combined, these words from award-winning teachers provide you with outstanding role models and mentors to guide your professional practice.

* Video Viewpoints—*Fundamentals of Early Childhood Education*, Third Edition, is a contemporary book. The "Video Viewpoint" boxes, linked to the ABC News/Prentice Hall video library, provide opportunities to interact with current child, family, and early childhood issues. These videos encourage

engagement, reflection, and problem solving and promote professional development.

* Electronic learning—Today, learning about early childhood education involves the use of a wide range of learning tools. One of the most important of these "tools for learning" involves the Internet. This text provides you with many opportunities to learn via the Internet.

* Margin and text notes direct readers to related information on the Companion Website for this textbook, located at *www.prenhall.com/morrison*. In this way, you and others are supported in using the Internet and new technologies as sources of professional growth and development.

New to This Edition

A number of new features have been added to this third edition. These new features make the book even more user-friendly and useful. They add value to the content and expand and enrich your understanding.

Technology Tie-Ins are included in each chapter. These are designed to help you be technologically literate and incorporate technology of all kinds into your teaching. Each of the "Technology Tie-In" boxes provide you with specific examples related to chapter content. They bridge theory and classroom practice and enable you to be a connected teacher. Collectively, the "Technology Tie-In" features help you to:

* Apply technology to your teaching of young children. Every day you will want to explore the opportunities the curriculum provides for using technology to help young children learn.

* Understand the full range of technology options. Technology includes more than computer hardware and software. Technology also includes digital cameras, overhead projectors, tape recorders, and hand-held electronic devices.

* Empower young children with appropriate technology skills that will promote, enhance, and enrich learning.

* Enhance collaboration with parents. E-mail is a good way to stay in touch with parents and keep them informed. You can also help parents use the technology they have in their homes to help them assist their children and themselves in learning.

The Professional Development Checklist, introduced in Chapter 1, provides a graphic tool enabling you to assess your professional practice and gauge your professional development. Each chapter opens with one or more of the thirteen essential professional goals that constitute professional practice. Each chapter concludes with "Activities for Professional Development" designed to help you achieve the professional development goals emphasized in the chapter. In this way, professionalism is integrated throughout each chapter and the entire book.

A new Chapter 4, "Implementing Early Childhood Programs: Applying Theories to Practice," combines coverage of theories about how children develop and learn with models of early childhood education designed to help children grow and develop to their fullest. In this chapter, theories are directly connected to program practices, allowing you to see how theories are applied to developing and implementing programs for young children.

Supplements to the Text

* Instructor's Manual—The *Instructor's Manual* provides professors with a variety of useful resources, including chapter overviews, teaching strategies, and ideas for classroom activities, discussions, and assessment that will assist them in using this text. The manual also includes a comprehensive printed test bank containing multiple-choice and essay questions.

* Computerized Test Bank Software—The computerized test bank software gives instructors electronic access to the test questions printed in the Instructor's Manual, allowing them to create and customize exams on their computer. The software can help professors manage their courses and gain insight into their students' progress and performance. Computerized test bank software is available in both Macintosh and PC/Windows versions.

* ABC News/Prentice Hall Video Library—Available free to instructors upon adoption of the text, *Current Issues in Early Childhood Education, volumes 1 and 2,* contain a total of eleven video segments. Video segments cover a variety of topics and vary in length for maximum instructional flexibility. The "Video Viewpoint" boxes in the book can be used to link the segments to the text and to promote thoughtful classroom discussion of current issues in early childhood education. A special table of contents identifies topics discussed and their locations in the text.

* Companion Website—Located at *www.prenhall.com/morrison,* the Companion Website for this text includes a wealth of resources for both students and professors. The Syllabus Manager™ enables professors to create and maintain the class syllabus online while also allowing the student access to the syllabus at any time from any computer on the Internet. "Focus Questions" help students review chapter content. Students can test their knowledge by taking interactive "Self-Tests" (multiple-choice quizzes that provide immediate feedback with a percentage score and correct answers) or by responding to essay questions that can be submitted to instructors or study partners via e-mail. The "Linking to Learning" feature contains hot links to all the websites mentioned in the text and assists students in using the Web to do additional research on chapter topics and key issues. The "Programs in Action" module provides hot links to many of the Web pages of the "Program in Action" boxes featured in the text and extends students' learning via Web-based activities. The "Glossary" helps students familiarize themselves with key vocabulary. Both the "Message Board" and

"Chat" features encourage student interaction outside the classroom. The "Professional Development" module provides students with readings for professional enrichment, activities to enhance professional development, and a "Professional Development Checklist" to assist students in monitoring their progress toward becoming accomplished early childhood educators. Finally, the "Resources" module links to Merrill Education's Early Childhood Education Supersite and provides special chapter resources.

* Student Study Guide—The *Student Study Guide* provides students with additional opportunities to review chapter content and helps them learn and study more effectively. The study guide leads readers through each chapter and helps them identify key concepts and information. Each chapter of the guide contains a number of helpful review resources, including a self-check quiz.

Acknowledgments

In the course of my teaching, service, and consulting, I meet and talk with many professionals who are deeply dedicated to doing their best for young children and their families. I am always touched, heartened, and encouraged by the openness, honesty, and unselfish sharing of ideas that characterize these professional colleagues. I thank all the individuals who contributed to "Professionalism in Practice," "Program in Action," and other program descriptions. They are all credited for sharing their personal accounts of their lives, their children's lives, and their programs.

I value and respect the feedback and sound advice that the following reviewers provided for me: Audrey Beard, Albany State University; Deborah J. Hess, Xavier University; Frank Miller, Pittsburg State University (Kansas); and Beth Nason Quick, Tennessee State University. In addition, I want to acknowledge the outstanding help and support of Jaime Thomson, Jesse Jones, and Larry Barroso.

My editors at Merrill are the best in the industry. It is a pleasure to work with Ann Davis and Christina Tawney. They are astute and visionary and continually develop ways to keep *Fundamentals of Early Childhood Education* a leader in the field. Gianna Marsella is creative, facilitative, and cheerful. As the development editor, she brings a can-do attitude to the developmental process. Linda Bayma is patient, persistent, and helpful. I greatly appreciate her attention to detail in her role as production editor. She always smoothes out the bumps of the production process. Together, Ann, Christina, Gianna, and Linda have made this third edition one of exceptional quality.

CONTENTS

Special Features

FUNDAMENTALS OF EARLY CHILDHOOD EDUCATION

FOCUS QUESTIONS

1. Who is an early childhood professional?
2. What can you do to demonstrate the *personal* dimensions of professionalism?
3. What can you do to demonstrate the *educational* dimensions of professionalism?
4. What can you do to demonstrate the practice of professionalism?
5. What can you do to demonstrate the *public* dimensions of professionalism?

chapter 1

You and Early Childhood Education

WHAT DOES IT MEAN TO BE A PROFESSIONAL?

To review the chapter focus questions online, go to the Companion Website at *http://www.prenhall.com/ morrison* and select Chapter 1.

 # PROFESSIONAL DEVELOPMENT GOALS

PHILOSOPHY OF TEACHING

I have thought about and written my philosophy of teaching and caring for young children. My actions are consistent with this philosophy.

PROFESSIONAL DEVELOPMENT

I have a professional career plan for the next year. I engage in study and training programs to improve my knowledge and competence, I belong to a professional organization, and I have worked or am working on a degree or credential (CDA, A.A., B.S.). I strive for positive, collaborative relationships with parents, my colleagues, and employer.

PERSONAL DEVELOPMENT

I try to improve myself by engaging in a personal program of self-development. I practice in my own life and model for others good moral and physical habits as well as ethical and lawful behavior.

Maria Cardenas is excited about her new assignment as a pre-K teacher. After years of study and serving as an assistant teacher, Maria now has her own classroom of three and four year olds. "I can't believe this day has finally come! I've worked so hard, and now my dream has come true! I can't wait to get started! I want my children to learn and be all they can be!"

I hope you are as excited as Maria about your opportunity to teach young children.

Today, more than ever, the public and politicians are creating a lot of excitement by seeking ways to improve the quality of early childhood education and teaching. As a result, you and other early childhood professionals have a wonderful opportunity to work with young children and their families, develop new and better programs, and advocate for the best practices. You can be a leader in helping the early childhood profession make a high-quality education a reality for all children. You can help ensure a high-quality education for all children by being a high-quality early childhood professional.

WHO IS AN EARLY CHILDHOOD PROFESSIONAL?

You are preparing to be an early childhood professional, to teach children from birth to age eight. You will work with families and the community to bring high-quality education and services to all children. You are touching the future through the lives of the children you teach. How do you explain the term *early childhood professional* to others? What does it mean to be a professional?

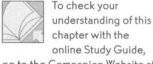

To check your understanding of this chapter with the online Study Guide, go to the Companion Website at *http://www.prenhall.com/ morrison*, select Chapter 1, then choose the Study Guide module.

An **early childhood professional** has the personal characteristics, knowledge, and skills necessary to teach and conduct programs so that all children learn, and the ability to inform the public about children's and family issues. Professionals promote high standards for themselves, their colleagues, and their students. They are continually improving and expanding their skills and knowledge. They are multidimensional.

THE FOUR DIMENSIONS OF PROFESSIONALISM

Early childhood professionals demonstrate competence in four dimensions: *personal characteristics, educational attainment, professional practice,* and *public presentation*. These dimensions are illustrated in Figure 1.1. Each dimension plays a powerful role in determining who professionals are and what they do. Let's review each of these dimensions and see how you can apply them to your professional practice.

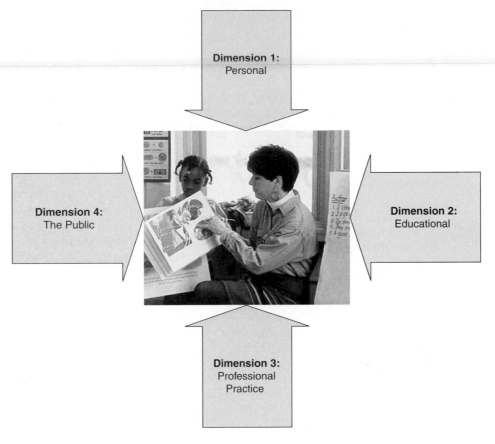

Dimension 1:
Personal

Dimension 4:
The Public

Dimension 2:
Educational

Dimension 3:
Professional
Practice

⌒ FIGURE 1.1   The Four Dimensions of Professionalism

Attainment of these four dimensions is essential for being a high-quality professional. Think of these four dimensions as the four legs of a table. If one leg is missing, the table is no good. You can't be an exemplary professional without practicing all four of these dimensions of professionalism. Reflect for a moment on how you can start now to prepare yourself in each of these dimensions.

Dimension 1: The Personal

The personal dimension includes the qualities, behaviors, and attitudes you demonstrate as a professional. Let's focus on four important areas of the personal dimension that are of the highest importance: *personal character, emotional qualities, physical health,* and *mental health.*

PERSONAL CHARACTER.   One crucial quality of your personal character is ethical behavior and having high morals and values. Professionals want to do what is right in their relationships with students, colleagues, and parents. They base their

For more information about NAEYC and similar professional organizations, go to the Companion Website at *http://www.prenhall.com/ morrison*, select Chapter 1, then choose the Linking to Learning module.

To review the NAEYC Code of Ethical Conduct, visit the Companion Website at *http://www.prenhall.com/ morrison*, select Chapter 1, then choose the Linking to Learning module.

knowledge on a code of professional ethics. Professional organizations, such as the National Association for the Education of Young Children (NAEYC), have developed codes of ethics that help inform and guide professional practice. Now would be a good time to review the NAEYC Code of Ethical Conduct, reprinted in Appendix. As you read about professional ethical conduct, reflect about how you will apply it to your practice.

A second important personal characteristic is civility, which includes compassion, patience, and acts of kindness and helpfulness. An example of civil behavior is mannerly and courteous interactions with children, parents and families, colleagues, and others.

Early childhood professionals also demonstrate the following personal character traits: dedication, respect, enthusiasm, honesty, intelligence, and motivation. Home and early school experiences are critical for developing these character qualities. If we want these qualities in our future citizens and teaching professionals, we need to promote them now, in our teaching of young children.

EMOTIONAL QUALITIES.   Emotion plays a powerful role in social relations and in learning. Some emotional qualities that are critical to being a successful early childhood professional are love and respect for children, understanding of children and their families, compassion, empathy, friendliness, kindness, sensitivity, trust, tolerance, warmth, and caring.

For early childhood professionals, caring is the most essential of these emotional qualities. High-quality professionals care deeply about children. They acknowledge and respect all children and their cultural and socioeconomic backgrounds. As the United States continues to become more diverse, you will teach children and work with families whose backgrounds and ways of life are not the same as yours.

Caring means you will lose sleep trying to find a way to help children learn to read, that you will seek creative ways to ensure all children learn, and you will spend long hours planning and gathering materials. Caring means you will employ your intelligence, enthusiasm, and talents in the center, classroom, administration offices, boards of directors' meetings, and wherever you can make a difference in the lives of children and their families. Because you care, the world will be a better place for children.

PHYSICAL HEALTH.   Health and physical fitness are important parts of life and professional practice. When you are healthy, you can do your best and be your best. When you practice good health habits, such as eating a well-balanced diet and staying physically fit, you also set a good example for children and families. Wellness and healthy living are vital for the energy, enthusiasm, and stamina teaching demands.

MENTAL HEALTH.   Mental health is as important as physical health. Good mental health includes having a positive outlook on life, the profession, and the future. Some

Health and wellness are critical components of development and learning. Good early childhood programs help children and their families stay healthy. Programs also should lead the way in preventing the major childhood diseases of asthma, lead poisoning, and obesity.

positive mental health characteristics are optimism, attentiveness, self-confidence, and self-respect. Good mental health means you continue to try and try again, and you maintain a can-do outlook. When you possess and demonstrate these attitudes, you will also instill them in young children. Helping children look on the bright side of things is one of the most important life lessons you can convey—this lesson begins with you.

Dimension 2: Education

The educational dimension of professionalism involves knowing about and demonstrating essential knowledge of the profession and professional practice. This knowledge includes the history and ethics of the profession, understanding how children develop and learn, and keeping up to date on public issues that influence early childhood and the profession.

Training and certification is a major challenge facing all areas of the early childhood profession and those who care for and teach young children. Training and certification requirements vary from state to state, and more states are tightening personnel standards for child care, preschool, kindergarten, and primary professionals. Many states have mandatory training requirements that individuals must meet before being certified. The curriculum of these training programs frequently specifies mandatory inclusion of such topics as:

* state and local rules and regulations governing child care;
* health, safety, and nutrition;
* identification and reporting of child abuse and neglect; and
* child growth and development.

Many states have career ladders that specify the requirements for progressing from one level of professionalism to the next. Figure 1.2 outlines the early childhood practitioner's professional pathway for Oklahoma. What two things do you find most informative about this career pathway?

To review the course offerings of the Massachusetts Bay Community College, visit the Companion Website at *http://www.prenhall.com/ morrison*, select Chapter 1, then choose the Linking to Learning module.

ASSOCIATE DEGREE PROGRAMS.   Many community colleges provide training in early childhood education that qualifies recipients to be child care aides, primary child care providers, and assistant teachers. For example, Massachusetts Bay Community College offers a two-year associate's degree in Early Childhood Education. Courses in the program include child development, early childhood education, children's literature, art and music for young children, health and emergency care, diagnosis and interventions for children with disabilities, and computers and technology.

BACCALAUREATE PROGRAMS.   Four-year colleges provide programs that result in early childhood teacher certification. The ages and grades to which the certification applies vary from state to state. Some states have separate certification for prekindergarten programs and nursery schools; in other states, these certifications are "add-ons" to elementary (K–6, 1–6, 1–4) certification. At the University of South Florida, the age three through grade three teacher certification program includes course work and extensive field experiences in early childhood settings to enable students to integrate theory with teaching practice.

MASTER'S DEGREE PROGRAMS.   Depending on the state, individuals may gain initial early childhood certification at the master's level. Many colleges and universities offer master's programs for people who want to qualify as program directors or assistant directors or may want to pursue a career in teaching. Mary Ladd graduated with a bachelor's degree in business and worked for five years in a high-tech company. However she felt a call to teach after 2½ years of working. Mary earned a master's degree and teacher certification. She now teaches second grade.

THE CDA NATIONAL CREDENTIALING PROGRAM.   The **Child Development Associate (CDA)** National Credentialing Program offers early childhood professionals the opportunity to develop and demonstrate competencies for meeting the needs of young children. A CDA is one who is "able to meet the specific needs of children and who, with parents and other adults, works to nurture children's physical, social, emotional, and intellectual growth in a child development framework."[1]

The CDA program is a major national effort to evaluate and improve the skills of caregivers in center-based preschool settings, center-based infant/toddler settings, family day care homes, home visitor settings, and programs that have specific goals for bilingual children. Persons seeking a CDA demonstrate national standards that are divided into six goals common to all child care settings and thirteen functional areas. The CDA National Credentialing Program is operated by the Council for Early Childhood Professional Recognition, which offers two options for obtaining the CDA credential. One option, the CDA Professional Preparation

Advanced degrees—M.S., M.A., Ph.D., Ed.D., J.D., M.D., R.N.

TRADITIONAL
- Occupational Child Care Instructor at technology centers
- Teacher Educator at a two-year college or four-year university
- Teacher/Administrator/Special Educator in a public or private elementary school—certification required
- Instructor/Curriculum Specialist in the armed services
- Child Development Specialist
- Child Guidance Specialist
- Researcher/Writer

RELATED
- Social worker
- Child Advocate/Lobbyist
- Librarian
- Pediatric Therapist—occupational and physical
- Human Resources Personnel in industry
- Child Life Specialist in a hospital
- Speech and Hearing Pathologist—Health Department, public/private school, private practice, university teaching
- Early Childhood Consultant
- Entertainer/Musician/Song Writer for children

- Author and Illustrator of children's books
- Physician/Pediatrician
- Pedodontist (works only with children)
- Dietitian
- Counselor
- Child Psychologist
- Psychiatrist
- Dietetic Assistant
- Recreation Supervisor
- Children's Policy Specialist
- Dental Hygienist
- Scouting Director

- Child Care Center or Playground/Recreation Center Designer
- Probation Officer
- 4-H Agent or County Extension Director
- Adoption Specialist
- Child Care Resource and Referral Director
- "Friend of the Court" Counselor
- Psychometrist
- Attorney with primary focus on children
- Religious Educator
- Certified Child and Parenting Specialist
- Family Mediator

Baccalaureate Level

TRADITIONAL
- Early Childhood Teacher in public school, Head Start or child care settings
- Special Education Teacher
- Family Child Care Home Provider
- Nanny
- Administrator in Head Start program
- Child Care Center Director/Owner/Coordinator
- Child Care Center Director in the armed services

- Parents as Teachers Facilitator
- Director of school-age (out-of-school time) program

RELATED
Some positions will require additional coursework at the baccalaureate level which will be in a field other than early childhood:
- Child Advocate/Lobbyist
- Recreation Director/Worker/Leader
- Web Master

- Journalist/Author/Publisher/Illustrator of children's books
- Children's Librarian
- Retail Manager of children's toy or book stores
- Licensing Worker
- Human Resource Personnel in industry
- Music Teacher, Musician/Entertainer for children
- Recreation Camp Director
- Camp Counselor/Scouts Camp Ranger

- Resource and Referral Trainer/Data Analyst/Referral Specialist/Child Care Food Program Consultant
- Childbirth Educator
- Gymnastic or Dance Teacher
- Pediatric Nurse Aide
- Child and Parenting Practitioner
- Producer of children's television shows and commercials
- Faith Community Coordinator and Educator

Associate Level

TRADITIONAL
- Head Start Teacher
- Child Care Teacher
- Family Child Care Home Provider
- Nanny
- Child Care Center Director

- School-Age Provider
- Early Intervention/Special Needs Program
- Para-Teacher/Aide

RELATED
In addition to those listed at the core level:

- Family and Human Services Worker
- LPN—specialized nurse training
- Entertainer for children at theme restaurants and parks
- Social Service Aide

- Playground Helper
- Physical Therapy Assistant
- Nursing Home Aide/Worker/Technician
- Faith Community Coordinators for families and children

Credential Level

- Head Start Teacher
- Child Care Teacher

- Family Child Care Home Provider
- Nanny

- Child Care Center Director
- Home Visitor

- Nursing Home Aide/Worker

Core Level
These positions require minimum education and training depending on the position

TRADITIONAL
- Child Care Teaching Assistant
- Family Child Care Home Provider
- Head Start Teacher Assistant
- Nanny
- Foster Parent
- Church Nursery Attendant

- Related positions which involve working with children in settings other than a child care center, family child care home, Head Start or public school program.

RELATED
Positions may require specialized pre-service training.

- Children's Storyteller, Art Instructor or Puppeteer
- Recreation Center Assistant
- Salesperson in toy, clothing or bookstore
- School Crossing Guard
- Children's Party Caterer
- Restaurant Helper for birthday parties
- Van or Transportation Driver
- Children's Art Museum Guide

- Receptionist in pediatrician's office
- Camp Counselor
- Special Needs Child Care Aide
- Live-in Caregiver
- Respite Caregiver
- Cook's Aide, Assistant Cook, Camp Cook, Head Start or Child Care Center Cook

FIGURE 1.2 Early Childhood Practitioner's Professional Pathway for Oklahoma

Source: Reprinted with permission from the Center for Early Childhood Professional Development, College of Continuing Education, University of Oklahoma, 2000.

Program allows candidates to work in postsecondary institutions as part of the credentialing process. The second option is the direct assessment method, which is designed for candidates who have child care work experience in combination with some early childhood education training.

A candidate for the CDA credential in any setting must be eighteen years or older, hold a high school diploma or equivalent, and be able to speak, read, and write well enough to fulfill the responsibilities of a CDA. To obtain the CDA national credential, candidates under the direct assessment option must meet these additional eligibility requirements:

* 480 hours of experience working with children from birth to three years of age.
* 120 clock hours of training within the last five years of formal education with at least ten hours in each of eight CDA training areas, with an emphasis in either infant/toddler or preschool concerns:
  * Health and safety
  * Physical and intellectual development
  * Social and emotional development
  * Relationships with families
  * Program operation
  * Professionalism
  * Observing and recording children's behavior
  * Child growth and development

The candidate must then demonstrate competence in the six CDA competency areas as outlined in Table 1–1.

THE CDA PROFESSIONAL PREPARATION PROGRAM.   To obtain credentialing by means of this option, the candidate must meet the two general eligibility requirements of age and education and also identify an advisor whom they work with during the year of study, which is made up of three phases: fieldwork, course work, and final evaluation.

Fieldwork involves study of the council's model curriculum, *Essentials for Child Development Associates Working with Young Children.* This curriculum includes the six competency areas listed in Table 1–1. In the second phase, course work, the candidate participates in seminars offered in community colleges and other postsecondary institutions. These seminars are designed to supplement the model curriculum and are administered by a seminar instructor. The third phase is the final evaluation, which takes place in the candidate's work setting or field placement.

For more information on the CDA Professional Preparation Program, visit the Companion Website at *http://www.prenhall.com/ morrison*, select Chapter 1, then choose the Linking to Learning module.

The results of all three phases are sent to the council office for review and determination of whether the candidate has successfully completed all aspects of the CDA Professional Preparation Program. To date, more than 50,000 persons have been awarded the CDA credential. The CDA program has played a major role in enhancing the quality of education for young children.

TABLE 1–1

CDA COMPETENCY GOALS AND FUNCTIONAL AREAS

CDA COMPETENCY GOALS	FUNCTIONAL AREAS
I. To establish and maintain a safe, healthy learning environment	1. Safe: Candidate provides a safe environment to prevent and reduce injuries.
	2. Healthy: Candidate promotes good health and nutrition and provides an environment that contributes to the prevention of illness.
	3. Learning environment: Candidate uses space, relationships, materials, and routines as resources for constructing an interesting, secure, and enjoyable environment that encourages play, exploration, and learning.
II. To advance physical and intellectual competence	4. Physical: Candidate provides a variety of equipment, activities, and opportunities to promote intellectual competence.
	5. Cognitive: Candidate provides activities and opportunities that encourage curiosity, exploration, and problem solving appropriate to the development levels and learning styles of children.
	6. Communication: Candidate actively communicates with children and provides opportunities and support for children to understand, acquire, and use verbal and nonverbal means of communicating thoughts and feelings.
	7. Creative: Candidate provides opportunities that stimulate children to play with sound, rhythm, language, materials, space, and ideas in individual ways and to express their creative abilities.
III. To support social and emotional development and to provide positive guidance	8. Self: Candidate provides physical and emotional security for each child and helps each child to know, accept, and take pride in himself or herself and to develop a sense of independence.
	9. Social: Candidate helps each child feel accepted in the group, helps children learn to communicate and get along with others, and encourages feelings of empathy and mutual respect among children and adults.
	10. Guidance: Candidate provides a supportive environment in which children can begin to learn and practice appropriate and acceptable behaviors as individuals and as a group.
IV. To establish positive and productive relationships with families	11. Families: Candidate maintains an open, friendly, and cooperative relationship with each child's family, encourages their involvement in the program, and supports the child's relationship with his or her family.
V. To ensure a well-run, purposeful program responsive to participant needs	12. Program management: Candidate is a manager who uses all available resources to ensure an effective operation. The candidate is a competent organizer, planner, record keeper, needs communicator, and a cooperative coworker.
VI. To maintain a commitment to professionalism	13. Professionalism: Candidate makes decisions based on knowledge of early childhood theories and practices; promotes quality in child care services; and takes advantage of opportunities to improve competence, both for personal and professional growth and for the benefit of children and families.

Source: The Council for Professional Recognition. *Essentials for Child Development Associates Working with Young Children* (Washington, DC Author, 1991), p. 415. Used by permission.

Early childhood educators are professionals who, in addition to teaching and caring for children, plan, assess, report, collaborate with colleagues and families, and behave in ethical ways.

Dimension 3: Professional Practice

For more information about becoming an early childhood professional, go to the Companion Website at *http://www.prenhall.com/ morrison,* select Chapter 1, then choose Topic 1 of the ECE Supersite module.

To review NAEYC's position statement on "Developmentally Appropriate Practice in Early Childhood Programs Serving Children from Birth Through Age Eight," visit the Companion Website at *http://www.prenhall.com/ morrison,* select Chapter 1, then choose the Linking to Learning module.

The professional dimension includes knowing children; developing a philosophy of education; planning; assessing; reporting; reflecting and thinking; teaching; collaborating with parents, families, and community partners; engaging in ethical practice; and seeking continued professional development opportunities.

These items represent the heart and soul of professional practice. Professionals should be committed to increasing their knowledge in these areas throughout their careers.

KNOWING CHILDREN. Every professional must have and demonstrate an understanding of child development. Child development knowledge enables you to understand how children grow and develop across all developmental levels—the cognitive, linguistic, social, emotional, and physical. Professionals also really know the children in their care. Knowledge of individual children, combined with knowledge of child growth and development, enables you to provide care and education that is developmentally appropriate for each child. **Developmentally appropriate practice (DAP)** means basing your teaching on how children grow and develop. Such knowledge is essential for knowing how to conduct developmentally appropriate practice, the recommended teaching practice of the profession. Ideas for how to conduct developmentally appropriate practice are found throughout this book. These guidelines will serve as your roadmap of teaching. As you review the guidelines, consider how you can begin to apply them to your practice.

Developmentally and Culturally Appropriate Practice (DCAP).   Appropriate professional practice includes being sensitive to and responding to children's cultural and ethnic backgrounds and needs. The United States is a nation of diverse people and this diversity will continue. Children in early childhood programs represent this diversity. When children enter schoolhouses and programs, they do not leave their uniqueness, gender, culture, socioeconomic status, and race at the door. Children bring themselves and their backgrounds to early childhood programs. As part of your professional practice you will embrace, value, and incorporate multiculturalism into your teaching.

Developing a Philosophy of Education.   Professional practice entails teaching with and from a philosophy of education, which acts as a guidepost to help you base your teaching on what you believe about children.

A **philosophy of education** is a set of beliefs about how children develop and learn and what and how they should be taught. Your philosophy of education is based in part on your philosophy of life. What you believe about yourself, about others, and about life determines your philosophy of education. For example, we previously talked about optimism. If you are optimistic about life, chances are you will be optimistic for your children and we know that when teachers have high expectations for their children, they achieve at higher levels. Core beliefs and values about education and teaching include what you believe about children, what you think are the purposes of education, how you view the teacher's role, and what you think you should know and be able to do.

In summary, your philosophy of education guides and directs your daily teaching. The following guidelines will help you develop your philosophy of education.

Read.   Read widely in textbooks, journals, and other professional literature to get ideas and points of view. A word of caution: When people refer to philosophies of education, they often think of historical influences. This is only part of the information available for writing a philosophy. Make sure you explore contemporary ideas as well, for these will also have a strong influence on you as a professional. The "Activities for Professional Development" section at the end of the chapter will help you get started. In addition, chapter 3, "History and Theories," provides helpful information for you to use in developing your philosophy.

Reflect.   As you read through and study this book, make notes and reflect about your philosophy of education. The following prompts will help you get started:

* I believe the purposes of education are . . .
* I believe that children learn best when they are taught under certain conditions and in certain ways. Some of these are . . .
* The curriculum of any classroom should include certain "basics" that contribute to children's social, emotional, intellectual, and physical development. These basics include . . .

* Children learn best in an environment that promotes learning. Features of a good learning environment are . . .
* All children have certain needs that must be met if they are to grow and learn at their best. Some of these basic needs are . . .
* I would meet these needs by . . .
* A teacher should have certain qualities and behave in certain ways. Qualities I think important for teaching are . . .

Talk.   Talk with successful teachers and other educators about their philosophies and practices. The personal accounts in the "Professionalism in Practice" boxes in each chapter of this text are evidence that a philosophy can help you be a successful, effective teacher. They also serve as an opportunity to "talk" with successful professionals.

Write.   Once you have thought about your philosophy of education, write it down, and have other people read it. Writing and sharing helps you clarify your ideas and redefine your thoughts, because your philosophy should be understandable to others (although they do not necessarily have to agree with you).

Evaluate.   Finally, evaluate your philosophy using this checklist:

* Does my philosophy accurately relate my beliefs about teaching? Have I been honest with myself?
* Is it understandable to me and others?
* Does it provide practical guidance for my teaching?
* Are my ideas consistent with one another?
* Does what I believe make good sense to me and others?

A well-thought-out philosophy will be like a compass throughout your career. It will point you in the right direction and keep you focused on doing your best for children.

PLANNING.   Planning is an essential part of practicing the art and craft of teaching. Planning consists of setting goals for what children will learn, selecting materials, and developing activities to help you achieve your teaching goals. Without planning you can't be a good teacher. Planning will help ensure that all children will learn, which is one of the most important and meaningful challenges you will face as an early childhood professional. Some essential steps in the planning process are:

* State what your children will learn and be able to do. These objectives can come from a number of sources. Currently, forty-nine states have developed or are developing standards regarding what students should know and be able to do in kindergarten through grade three. It is essential that you use state guidelines when planning for instruction. Many children, beginning in kindergarten, will have to pass tests based on state and district standards. In addition to state standards for kindergarten through grade three, many states have now adopted standards for prekindergarten. Program goals represent a second source of objectives. These goals are carefully thought out by

staff and families and provide direction for what and how children will learn. Local and program goals make education unique to each community.

* Select developmentally appropriate activities and materials and ones that are based on children's interests.
* Decide how much time to allocate to an activity.
* Decide how to assess activities and the knowledge and skills children have learned.

"Professionalism in Practice," a feature that appears in every chapter, lets you experience firsthand what award-winning teachers believe and how they translate theory into practice. Linda Luna DeMino, the 2001 Texas State Teacher of the Year, shares with you her philosophy of teaching and stresses how sucessful teachers must search for new and better ways in this first "Professionalism in Practice" box on pages 16 and 17.

ASSESSING.   Assessment is the process of gathering information about children's behavior and achievement and, on the basis of this data, making decisions about how to meet children's needs. Chapter 5, "Observing and Assessing Young Children," provides you with practical skills and ideas for how to conduct developmentally appropriate assessment.

REPORTING.   Reporting to parents and others in an understandable and meaningful way serves several purposes. First, it answers every parent's question, "How is my child doing?" and, every parent has a right to an honest and accurate answer. Second, information about children's achievement helps you, as a professional, be accountable to the public in fulfilling your role of helping children learn and be successful. Today, many school districts issue report cards on how well schools are doing in educating all children well. You in turn want to inform your parents about how well their children are achieving as a result of your teaching.

REFLECTING AND THINKING.   Professionals are always thinking about and reflecting on what they have done, are doing, and will do. A good guideline for thinking and reflecting is this: Think about what and how you will teach before you teach, think about your teaching while you are teaching, and think about what you have taught after you teach. This constant cycle of **reflective practice** will help you be a good professional.

TEACHING.   Ask teachers what they do, and they will tell you they have a job description that requires them to wear many hats and that their jobs are never done. Teachers' responsibilities and tasks are many and varied. Teaching involves making decisions about what and how to teach, planning for teaching, engaging students in learning activities, managing learning environments, assessing student behavior and achievement, reporting to parents and others, collaborating with colleagues and community partners, and engaging in ongoing professional development. You might feel a little overwhelmed from what teaching involves. However, you will have a lot of help and support from others on your journey to becoming a good teacher.

Professionalism in Practice

PHILOSOPHY ON EARLY CHILDHOOD EDUCATION

Linda Luna DeMino

2001 Texas State Teacher of the Year

My philosophy for teaching young children has remained fairly constant and has allowed me to remain enthusiastic and successful through the years. What have evolved are the methods used to support my philosophy. A successful teacher cannot stay stagnant and must always search for new and better ways to have the most productive year possible. Teachers must adapt to each new group of students. I believe that being a teacher is so much more than teaching content.

Teaching is a critical and challenging profession. If I were to write down the traits that a good teacher should cultivate, I would include: determination, responsibility, enthusiasm, self-confidence, tolerance, communication, trust, curiosity, creativity, selflessness, self-respect, and accountability. However, the most essential traits are self-confidence, self-respect, determination, and tolerance. In my opinion, combining these characteristics with knowledge is the formula for success. To instill these four traits in children is the ultimate gift we can bestow upon them.

Children need guidance. I help children to value success internally, and not just for what it will help them gain from someone else. Children usually come to school wanting to be praised for their work or good deeds. Slowly, I wean them from this need and get them to think about how their actions make them feel. "How

did it make you feel when you helped Claire?" "How do you feel when you work so hard and do a good job?" Learning can be made fun but sometimes it just requires hard work and determination. Children need help realizing that a failure is a good thing if you learn from your mistakes. Failure makes successes better and can help them strive to do better if they choose to persevere. I never embarrass a child for a mistake; instead, I help them think about things they can do to have a more successful outcome. To be human is to be imperfect. To ridicule a child for being human is unproductive.

Tolerance prepares them for an imperfect world. We are all different. No two people are exactly alike, and it is important to give children an opportunity to think about why this is so. Just telling them how they should treat each other because it is the right thing to do is not enough. To experience is to have better understanding. I have a program that I developed, called "I'm Special. You're Special," which helps children do just that. We discuss differences and experience certain types of disabilities. We observe how we are all disabled at different times during our lives and discuss how a disability does not make one incapable. Rather it necessitates the need to become creative so we can learn or do things a different way.

Teachers must also possess a communication process that serves to maximize parental involvement.

COLLABORATING WITH PARENTS, FAMILIES, AND COMMUNITY PARTNERS. Parents, families, and the community are essential partners in the process of schooling. Knowing how to collaborate effectively with these key partners will serve you well throughout your career. Chapter 12, "Cooperation and Collaboration with Parents, Families, and the Community," will help you learn more about this important topic.

Engaging in family education and support is an important role of the early childhood professional. Children's learning begins with parents and continues within the context of the family unit, whatever that family unit may be. Learning how to comfortably and confidently work with parents is as essential as teaching young children. You are a teacher of children and families.

Just as religious beliefs are not isloated to the confines of a church or temple, education is not isolated to the confines of a school. I give parents essential insight into their child's school day and provide them with ideas on how to not only expand concepts at home but also raise the realistic expectations they have for their child. I find communication between home and school critical.

I send home monthly calendars that map out what we will be studying each week and call attention to special events. I also send home daily notes that specifically state what concepts we covered that day. These are often accompanied by a rebus picture sentence that parents can have the child point to while they read or the child reads to them so that they can practice relaying an experience from school to home. Parents are also encouraged to send me notes about happenings at home so that we can discuss them at school. When children realize there is so much open communication between their parents and their teacher, it fosters their desire to be all that they can be.

This enables parents to develop effective communication between themselves and their children, and it facilitates a partnership with me, their child's teacher. This relationship must be based on trust and common goals. For this reason, I also have a "Parent's Night Out"

program where parents are invited to come and have dinner with me at a local restaurant once a month (Dutch treat). It is a great way for me to get to know them and for them to get to know me. It also provides a way for parents to talk to each other so they can find comfort knowing that they are not alone. They often provide great support for each other and develop unexpected friendships.

Teaching young children and facilitating their growth is such a rewarding experience. Ralph Waldo Emerson said it best, "To appreciate beauty, to find the best in others: to leave the world a bit better . . . to know even one life has breathed easier because you have lived. That is to have succeeded."

Linda Luna DeMino is a teacher of a Preschool Program for Children with Disabilities at the Howard Early Childhood Center, Alamo Heights Independent School District, San Antonio, Texas.

 To review the Professional Development Checklist and complete a Professionalism in Practice activity, visit the Companion Website at *http://www.prenhall.com/ morrison,* select Chapter 1, then choose the Professional Development module.

 To review the NAEYC Code of Ethical Conduct, visit the Companion Website at *http://www.prenhall.com/ morrison,* select Chapter 1, then choose the Linking to Learning module.

ENGAGING IN ETHICAL PRACTICE.   Ethical conduct is the exercise of responsible behavior with children, families, colleagues, and community members. Ethical practice enables you to confidently engage in exemplary professional practice. A professional is an ethical person in all that they do and say both on and off the job.

Revisit NAEYC's Code of Ethical Conduct and begin to incorporate professional ethical practices into your interactions with children and colleagues. Always engaging in ethical practice is never easy. The more you try to base all your behaviors on ethical principles, however, the easier it becomes.

SEEKING ONGOING PROFESSIONAL DEVELOPMENT OPPORTUNITIES.   When, if ever, does a person become a "finished" professional? A professional is never a "finished" product; you will always be involved in a process of studying, learning, changing, and becoming more professional.

Becoming a professional means you will participate in training and education beyond the minimum needed for your present position. You will also want to consider your career objectives and the qualifications you might need for positions of increasing responsibility. Also, the field of early childhood education is changing so rapidly that it takes constant reading and study to keep up. And keep up you must! Children deserve an up-to-date teacher.

Dimension 4: The Public

The public is the fourth dimension of professional practice. This is where many of your professional roles and responsibilities are demonstrated in the public spotlight. The public dimension includes advocacy, articulation, and representation.

ADVOCACY.   Advocacy is the act of promoting the causes of children and families to the profession and the public. There is no shortage of issues to advocate for in the lives of children and families. Some issues in need of strong advocates include providing and supporting quality programs, preventing abuse and neglect, promoting children's health and wellness, and promoting early literacy development. Some things you can do to advocate include the following:

For more information about NAEYC and similar organizations, go to the Companion Website at *http://www.prenhall. com/morrison*, select Chapter 1, then choose the Linking to Learning module.

* Join an early childhood professional organization such as the NAEYC, the Association for Childhood Education International (ACEI), and the Southern Early Childhood Association (SECA). These organizations have student and local affiliates. They are very active in advocating for young children, and you can serve on a committee or be involved in some other way. The Companion Website lists websites for these and other organizations.

* Organize an advocacy group in your program or as a part of your class. Select a critical issue to study, and develop strategies for increasing public awareness about this issue. Your voice needs to be clear and strong for young children. If not you, who? If not now, when?

ARTICULATION.   Articulation means you are able to communicate about your role and that of the profession when speaking to parents and the public. Early childhood professionals must be knowledgeable and informed about the profession and the issues it faces. At the same time, they must be able to discuss these issues with the public, the media, families, and others in the community. Writing a letter to the editor of your local newspaper about the importance of reading to children would be one good way to articulate the importance of early literacy.

REPRESENTATION.   Representation is the process of acting in the best possible ways on behalf of children and families. It involves being a role model for the profession. Representation includes how you dress, how you groom, and how you

Early childhood professionals are advocates for young children and their families. In reality, advocacy is a never-ending process. This is because the needs of children and families are ongoing.

talk and act. Professionals make a good impression. We cannot practice our profession well or expect and receive the respect of parents and the public if we don't always put our best foot forward. How we look and how we behave does make a difference. Like it or not, first impressions count with many people. How we appear to others often sets the tone for interpersonal interactions. You should always look your best, do your best, and be your best. You are a professional. You teach children.

These, then, are the four dimensions of professionalism: personal, educational, professional, and public. If you add these dimensions to whom and what you are now, you should be able to represent yourself and the profession very well. You can enhance your professional development by completing the Professional Development Checklist shown in Figure 1.3 as you read through this text.

USING THE PROFESSIONAL DEVELOPMENT CHECKLIST

To monitor your progress toward professionalism using the online version of the Professional Development Checklist, go to the Companion Website at *http://www.prenhall.com/morrison*, select Chapter 1, then choose the Professional Development module.

My basic purpose for writing this book is to support your professional development from the stage where you are—novice or mid-level to highly skilled expert. The Professional Development Checklist is a powerful tool you can begin to use now to achieve this goal. Each chapter emphasizes one or more professional outcomes from the checklist for you to consider and master. For each professional outcome on the checklist, I have asked nationally recognized Teachers of the Year to share their personal thoughts and experiences with you. These "Professionalism in Practice" accounts are inspiring and provide helpful ideas you can immediately put into practice. These accounts also demonstrate that early childhood educators are willing to help their colleagues attain true professional status.

FIGURE 1.3   Thirteen Steps to Becoming a Professional: A Development Checklist

Topic Number	Desired Professional Outcome
1	**Philosophy of Teaching** I have thought about and written my philosophy of teaching and caring for young children. My actions are consistent with this philosophy.
2	**Professional Development** I have a professional career plan for the next year. I engage in study and training programs to improve my knowledge and competence, belong to a professional organization, and have worked or am working on a degree or credential (CDA, A.A., B.S.). I strive for positive, collaborative relationships with parents, my colleagues, and employer.
3	**Personal Development** I try to improve myself as a person by engaging in a personal program of self-development. I practice in my own life and model for others good moral and physical habits as well as ethical and lawful behavior.
4	**Keeping Current in an Age of Change** I am familiar with the profession's contemporary development, and I understand current issues in society and trends in the field. I am willing to change my ideas, thinking, and practices based on study, new information, and the advice of colleagues and professionals.
5	**Historical Knowledge** I am familiar with my profession's history, and I use my knowledge of the past to inform my practice.
6	**Theories of Early Childhood Education** I understand the principles of each major theory of educating young children. The approach I use is consistent with my beliefs about how children learn.
7	**Delivering Education and Child Care** I am familiar with a variety of models and approaches for delivering education and child care, and I use this knowledge to deliver education and child care in a safe, healthy learning environment.
8	**Observation and Assessment** I pay attention to my students' actions and feelings. I evaluate students using appropriate and authentic measures. I use observation and assessment to guide my teaching.
9	**Developmentally Appropriate Practice** I understand children's developmental stages and growth from birth through age eight, and use this knowledge to implement developmentally appropriate practice. I do all I can to advance the physical, intellectual, social, and emotional development of the children in my care to their full potential.
10	**Educating All Students** I understand that all children are individuals with unique strengths and challenges. I embrace these differences, work to fulfill special needs, and promote tolerance and inclusion in my classroom. I value and respect the dignity of all children.
11	**Guiding Behavior** I understand the principles and importance of behavior guidance. I guide children to be peaceful, cooperative, and in control of their behavior.
12	**Collaborating with Parents and Communtiy** I am an advocate on behalf of children and families. I treat parents with dignity and respect. I involve parents and community members in my program and help and encourage parents in their roles as children's primary caregivers and teachers.
13	**Technology** I am technologically literate and integrate technology into my classroom to help all children learn.

Note: These professional development outcomes are consistent with the core values of the NAEYC and the competencies of the CDA.

LEVEL OF ACCOMPLISHMENT? (CIRCLE ONE)	IF HIGH, PROVIDE EVIDENCE OF ACCOMPLISHMENT	IF NEEDS IMPROVEMENT, SPECIFY ACTION PLAN FOR ACCOMPLISHMENT	TARGET DATE FOR COMPLETION OF ACCOMPLISHMENT	SEE THE FOLLOWING FOR MORE INFORMATION ON HOW TO MEET THE DESIRED PROFESSIONAL OUTCOME
High Needs Improvement				Chapter 1, "Professionalism in Practice" boxes
High Needs Improvement				Chapter 1
High Needs Improvement				Chapter 1
High Needs Improvement				Chapter 2
High Needs Improvement				Chapter 3
High Needs Improvement				Chapter 3
High Needs Improvement				Chapter 4, "Programs in Action" boxes
High Needs Improvement				Chapter 5
High Needs Improvement				Chapters 6, 7, 8, and 9, "Programs in Action" boxes
High Needs Improvement				Chapter 10
High Needs Improvement				Chapter 11
High Needs Improvement				Chapter 12
High Needs Improvement				"Technology Tie-In" Boxes

What Is the Terminology of Early Childhood Education?

For a complete online glossary of early childhood education terms, go to the Companion Website at *http://www.prenhall.com/ morrison,* select Chapter 1, then choose the Glossary module.

As an early childhood professional, you will need to know and use the terminology of the profession. The following paragraphs discuss key terms.

Professional refers to all who work with, care for, and teach children between birth and age eight. Using this term avoids the obvious confusion of trying to distinguish between *caregiver* and *teacher.* A **caregiver** provides care, education, and protection for very young children in and outside the home. Parents, relatives, child care workers, and early childhood teachers are all caregivers. The care-giving and teaching roles are now blended, so a person who cares for infants is teaching them as well. However, in the preschool, kindergarten, and primary years, the term **teacher** will continue to be used to designate these professionals. Also, the early childhood profession is trying to upgrade the image and role of all those who work with young children. Referring to everyone with the designation *professional* helps achieve this goal.

Early childhood is the period from birth to age eight. The term also frequently refers to children who have not yet reached school age, and the public often uses it to refer to children in any type of preschool program.

Early childhood programs provide "services for children from birth through age eight in part-day and full-day group programs in centers, homes, and institutions; kindergartens and primary schools; and recreational programs."[2]

Early childhood education consists of the services provided by early childhood professionals. It is common for professionals to use the terms *early childhood* and *early childhood education* synonymously. **Preschool** generally means any education program for children prior to their entrance into kindergarten. *Preschool programs* for three- and four-year-old children are rapidly becoming a part of the public school system, particularly those designed to serve low-income children and their families. For example, in 2000 the Dade County, Florida, public schools operated approximately 220 preschool programs for three- and four-year-old children.

Kindergarten is for five- and six-year-old children prior to their entry into first grade. Public school kindergarten is now almost universal for five-year-old children (see chapter 8) and is now part of the elementary grades.

Prekindergarten refers to programs for four-year-olds attending programs prior to kindergarten. Another term, *transitional kindergarten,* designates a program for children who are not ready for kindergarten and who can benefit from another year of educational and other experiences. *Transitional* also refers to grade school programs that provide additional opportunities for children to master skills associated with a particular grade. Transitional programs do not usually exist beyond the second and third grades.

Junior first grade, or *pre-first grade,* is a transitional program between kindergarten and first grade designed to help five-year-olds get ready to enter first grade. Not all children are equally ready to benefit from typical first grade because of their range of mental ages and experiential backgrounds; these children frequently benefit from such special programs. The goal of many early childhood professionals is to have all children learning at levels appropriate for them.

Preprimary refers to programs for children prior to their entering first grade; **primary** means first, second, and third grades. In some school districts, primary grade children are taught in classes that include two grade levels. In these **split,** or nongraded, **classes,** first and second graders or second and third graders are taught in a single class. Split classes are seldom composed of upper-elementary children. Reasons for split classes include increasing or decreasing school enrollments and teacher contracts that limit class size.

The term **child care** encompasses many programs and services for preschool children. The primary purpose of child care programs is to care for and educate young children who are not in school and for school-age children before and after school hours. Many programs have a sliding-fee schedule based on parents' ability to pay. Quality child care programs are increasingly characterized by comprehensive services that address children's total physical, social, emotional, linguistic, creative, and intellectual needs.

A large number of **family day care** programs provide child care services in the homes of caregivers. This alternative to center-based programs usually accommodates a maximum of four to five children in a family day care home. Formerly custodial in nature, there is a growing trend for caregivers to provide a full range of services in their homes.

Head Start is a federally sponsored program for children from low-income families. Established by the Economic Opportunities Act of 1964, Head Start is intended to help children and their families overcome the effects of poverty. **Follow Through** extends Head Start programs to children in grades one through three and works with school personnel rather than apart from the schools. **Early Head Start**

Early childhood professionals are often role models for the children they teach. Therefore, if we want children to be kind, caring, tolerant, and sensitive individuals, the adults in their lives should model those behaviors.

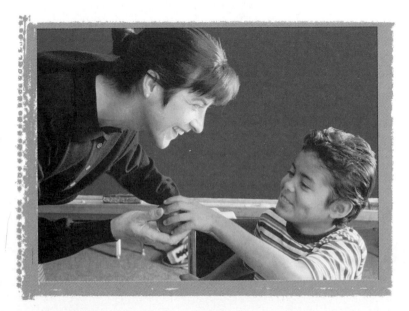

(EHS) is a federally funded community-based program for low-income families with infants and toddlers and pregnant women. Its mission is simple: to promote healthy prenatal outcomes for pregnant women, enhance the development of very young children, and promote healthy family functioning.

These are some of the professional terms with which you will need to be familiar. You will learn other terms for programs and services throughout the following chapters and in the glossary.

Involvement in the early childhood profession can be a joyful experience. The profession demands, and young children deserve, the best teachers have to offer. Becoming a good professional requires a lot of hard work and dedication. All who call themselves "professional" must accept the challenges and responsibilities that are part of the title.

WHY TECHNOLOGY TIE-INS?

In each chapter of this book there is a "Technology Tie-In" feature. Perhaps you are wondering "why?" I use these technology-focused features because they will:

* enable you to become more technologically proficient. As the technology tie-in for this chapter illustrates, teachers and all educational professionals are expected to use technology in a number of ways and for multiple purposes. Today's professional cannot plead technological ignorance.

* help you apply technology to your teaching of young children. Every day you will want to consider and explore the opportunities the curriculum provides for you to use technology to help young children learn. Technology includes more than computers. Technology also includes digital cameras, overhead projectors, tape recorders, and hand-held electronic devices.

* help you empower young children with appropriate technology skills that will promote, enhance, and enrich learning.

* enhance collaboration with parents. E-mail is a good way to stay in touch with parents and keep them informed. You can also help parents use the technology they have in their homes to help them and their children learn.

Technology Tie-In

Today, thousands of early childhood teachers use desktop and laptop computers with built-in modems, faxes, and CD-ROM drives; camcorders and digital cameras; optical scanners; and laser printers. They also use software for e-mail, word processing, desktop publishing, presentation graphics, spreadsheets, databases, and multimedia applications. You can begin now to prepare yourself to use technology to enhance your teaching and your students' learning. Colorado teachers are now required to demonstrate a broad usage of technology skills in these twelve areas. In which of these areas are you competent? Quiz yourself on which of the competencies you possess. Access the entire set of competencies on the website provided. Based on your self-analysis, develop a plan for how you will develop the competencies you need to be technologically proficient.

Technology Competencies	YES	NO
1. Computer Operation **a.** Start and shut down computer systems and peripherals		
b. Identify and use icons, windows, menus		
2. Setup, Maintenance, and Troubleshooting **a.** Protect and care for storage media		
b. Make backup copies of documents and files		
3. Word Processing/Introductory Desktop Publishing **a.** Enter and edit text		
b. Cut, copy, and paste text		
4. Spreadsheet/Graphing **a.** Interpret and communicate information in an existing spreadsheet		
b. Enter data into an existing spreadsheet		
5. Databases **a.** Interpret and communicate information in an existing database		
b. Add and delete records		
6. Networking **a.** Use a file server		
b. Share files with others on a network		
7. Telecommunications **a.** Connect to the Internet or an online service		
b. Use Internet search engines		

(Continued)

TECHNOLOGY COMPETENCIES	YES	NO
8. Media Communications and Integration a. Set up and operate video media		
b. Connect video output devices and other presentation systems to computers and video sources for large screen display		
9. Curriculum a. Select and create learning experiences that are appropriate for curriculum goals, relevant to learners, and based upon principles of effective teaching and learning; incorporate the use of media and technology for teaching where appropriate		
10. Design and Management of Learning Environments and Resources a. Develop performance tasks that require students to (1) locate and analyze information as well as draw conclusions and (2) use a variety of media to communicate results clearly		
11. Child Development, Learning, and Diversity a. Use media and technology to address differences in children's learning and performance		
b. Use media and technology to support learning for children with special needs		
12. Social, Legal, and Ethical Issues a. Follow school district policies, procedures, and federal law to ensure compliance with copyright law and fair-use guidelines.		

Source: *Colorado Department of Education (1999). Colorado Technology Competency Guidelines for Classroom Teachers and School Library Media Specialists. Available Online.*

 To complete this Technology Tie-In activity and for more information on the Technology Competencies, visit the Companion Website at *http://www.prenhall. com/morrison*, select Chapter 1, then choose the Technology Tie-In module.

ACTIVITIES FOR PROFESSIONAL DEVELOPMENT

In this chapter, we have stressed the importance of what it means to be a professional and how you can now begin to develop a plan for being a professional and a sense of professionalism. Refer again to the "Professional Development Goals" at the beginning of this chapter, the "Professional Development Checklist" on pages 20 and 21, and the "Professionalism in Practice: Philosophy on Early Childhood Education," by Linda Luna DeMino, 2001 Texas State Teacher of the Year, on pages 16 and 17. After you have reviewed these for ideas, complete the following exercises.

1. Recall the teachers who had a great influence on you. Which of their characteristics do you plan to incorporate into your philosophy of education?

2. Write your philosophy of education and share it with others. Ask them to critique it for comprehensiveness, clarity, and meaning. How do you feel about the changes they suggested?

3. Use a daily/monthly planner to develop your career development plan for the next year. First list your career development goals and then on a monthly basis specify activities, events, and other ways that you will achieve these goals. For example, in addition to attending classes at a local community college, preschool teacher Rosa Vaquerio plans to read a book a month on a topic related to teaching.

4. Many local schools and school districts elect and honor their teachers of the year. Contact these teachers and have them share with you their core ideas and beliefs that enabled them to be selected as a teacher of the year. Ask them to provide specific examples of how they apply ethical practice to their teaching. How do you plan to integrate these qualities into your professional development plan?

5. To a great extent, your ongoing professional development is your responsibility. As a result, you should constantly be on the alert for ways to grow professionally. Interview five pre-K to third grade teachers. Ask them to identify specific things they do to promote their own professional development.

6. Metaphors are an effective way of expressing meanings and ideas that are your part of a philosophy. They are also a good way to think about yourself, your beliefs, and your teaching role. For example, some of the metaphors my students use to describe their roles as teachers are leader, coach, and facilitator. Add to this list and then identify the one metaphor that best describes your role as teacher. Incorporate this metaphor and others into your philosophy of education.

For additional chapter resources and activities, visit the Companion Website at *http://www.prenhall.com/morrison*, select Chapter 1, then choose the Professional Development, Resources, or Linking to Learning modules.

FOCUS QUESTIONS

1. What critical issues do children, families, and early childhood professionals face today?

2. How do contemporary issues influence curriculum, teaching, and the life outcomes of children and families?

3. How can early childhood professionals respond to contemporary social problems for the betterment of children and families?

4. What are some ways you can keep current in the rapidly changing field of early childhood education?

chapter 2

Early Childhood Education Today

UNDERSTANDING CURRENT ISSUES

To review the chapter focus questions online, go to the Companion Website at *http://www.prenhall.com/morrison* and select Chapter 2.

 PROFESSIONAL DEVELOPMENT GOAL

KEEPING CURRENT IN AN AGE OF CHANGE

I am familiar with the profession's contemporary development, and I understand current issues in society and trends in the field. I am willing to change my ideas, thinking, and practices based on study, new information, and the advice of colleagues and professionals.

ISSUES INFLUENCING THE PRACTICE OF EARLY CHILDHOOD EDUCATION

Life is full of changes and so is early childhood education. These changes have and will continue to influence what and how you teach.

Many contemporary social issues affect decisions families and early childhood professionals must make about the education and care of young children. Child abuse, poverty, low-quality care and education, inequality of programs and services, and society's inability to meet the needs of all children are perennial sources of controversy and concern to which society continues to seek solutions. These problems dramatically and permanently affect the development and life outcomes of children. New ideas and issues relating to the education and care of young children and the quest to provide educationally and developmentally appropriate programs keep the field of early childhood education in a state of continual change. In fact, change is one constant of the early childhood profession. Early childhood professionals are constantly challenged to determine what is best for young children and their families given the needs and political demands of society today.

To check your understanding of this chapter with the online Study Guide, go to the Companion Website at *http://www.prenhall.com/ morrison*, select Chapter 2, then choose the Study Guide module.

Issues facing children and families are of concern to everyone. Daily newspapers provide ample evidence of the nation's interest in young children. Figure 2.1 shows newspaper headlines that call attention to young children, parents, families, and child service agencies.

The issues that we will discuss in this chapter will have an influence on the profession and you as you pursue your professional career. You cannot ignore these issues. You must be part of the solution to making it possible for all children to achieve their full potential. Education is political and those who ignore this reality do so at their own risk. Politicians and the public look to early childhood professionals to help develop educational solutions to social and political problems.

Agencies serving children and families, such as the Children's Defense Fund (CDF), offer "a voice for children" by expressing their views. For example, Marian Edelman, founder of CDF, says, "It is time for all U.S. adults to become angels who help children mature into compassionate human beings and productive citizens. We must change the odds against children so they don't have to struggle so hard to succeed."[1] Part of your professional role as a children's advocate will be to help change the odds against children.

Changing Families

Families are in a continual state of change as a result of social issues and changing times. The definition of what a family is varies as society changes. Consider the following ways families changed in the twentieth century:

1. *Structure.* Families now include arrangements other than the traditional nuclear family. Some of these contemporary families include single-parent

⌐☞ FIGURE 2.1   Examples of Recent Newspaper Headlines Relating to Early Childhood Issues

Newspapers are full of articles relating to children and family news. These are just a few representative headlines that show the enormous range of topics. A good way to keep informed about such issues is to read daily newspapers. You will be well informed and you can talk knowledgeably with parents and colleagues.

- "Early Head Start Yields Benefits, HHS Study Says" *Washington Post*, January 13, 2001
- "How to Read a Child's Anger" *Chicago Tribune,* January 14, 2001
- "Cultivating Family Role, Carefully" *Washington Post*, January 16, 2001
- "Burdened Families Look for Child-Care Aid" *Washington Post*, July 6, 2000
- "Bush Signs Bill to Expand Programs for At-Risk Children" *Baltimore Sun*, January 18, 2002
- "Study Shows Importance of Early Learning" *Chicago Tribune*, January 14, 2001
- "Full-day Kindergardens Boom" *Milwaukee Journal Sentinel*, January 13, 2002
- "Un Dia Nuevo for Schools" *Education Week*, November 8, 2000
- "New Event Making Case for Better After-School Options" *Education Week*, October 11, 2000
- "Where Homeless Children Do Homework" *Dallas Morning News*, October 17, 2000
- "Now a Majority: Families with Two Parents Who Work" *New York Times*, October 24, 2000
- "New Moms with Jobs Hit Record High" *USA Today*, October 24, 2000
- "Chicago Parents Get Report Cards on Involvement" *Education Week*, November 8, 2000
- "Bush, Kennedy work on Preschool Plan" *Boston Globe*, January 22, 2002
- "Administrators Say Technology Calls for Range of Skills" *Education Week*, November 29, 2000

families, headed by mothers or fathers; stepfamilies, including individuals related by either marriage or adoption; heterosexual, gay, or lesbian partners living together as families; and extended families, which may include grandparents, uncles, aunts, other relatives, and individuals not related by kinship. Grandparents as parents are growing in numbers and represent a fast-growing "new" family arrangement.

2. *Roles.* As families change, so do the roles that parents and other family members perform. More parents work and have less time for their children

and family affairs. Working parents must combine roles of both parents and employees. The number of hats that parents wear increases as families change. As grandparents assume the role of parenting their children's children, they must learn new roles and ways of relating to today's children.

3. *Responsibilities.* As families change, many parents find it difficult to afford quality care for their children. Some parents find that buffering their children from social ills such as drugs, violence, and delinquency is more than they can handle. Other parents are consumed by problems of their own and have little time or attention for their children. Nonetheless, the responsibilities of parenthood remain and increasingly, parents seek help from early childhood professionals to meet the demands and challenges of child rearing.

Families will certainly continue to change. As they do, you and other early childhood professionals must develop creative ways to provide services to children and families of all kinds.

Families and Early Childhood

Early childhood professionals agree that a good way to meet the needs of children is through their families, whatever the family units may be. Review Figure 2.2, which shows processes for educating both children and families. Providing for children's needs through and within the family system makes sense for a number of reasons.

First, the family system has the primary responsibility for meeting many children's needs. Parents are children's first teachers, and the experience and guidance they do or do not provide shapes their children for life. It is in the family that basic values, literacy skills, and approaches to learning are set and reinforced. This is why it is important to work with families and help them get a good start on parenting.

∞ **FIGURE 2.2**
Meeting the Needs of Children and Families

As families change, early childhood professionals have to develop new and different ways of meeting parents' needs.

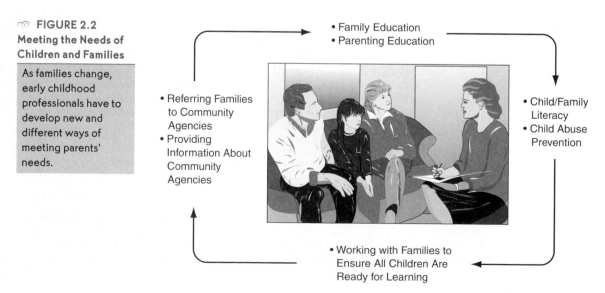

- Family Education
- Parenting Education

- Referring Families to Community Agencies
- Providing Information About Community Agencies

- Child/Family Literacy
- Child Abuse Prevention

- Working with Families to Ensure All Children Are Ready for Learning

Second, professionals frequently need to address family problems and issues before they can help children effectively. For example, helping parents gain access to adequate, affordable health care means that the whole family, including children, will be healthier. Just as we seek to meet children's basic needs, so too must we help parents meet their basic needs.

For more information about families and early childhood education, go to the Companion Website at *http://www.prenhall.com/morrison*, select Chapter 2, then choose Topic 10 of the ECE Supersite module.

Third, early childhood professionals can do many things concurrently with children and their families that will benefit both. Literacy is a good example. Early childhood professionals are taking a family approach to helping children, their parents, and other family members learn to read and write. Supporting parents' efforts to read helps them and their children. Children who are read to achieve much better when they come to school.

Fourth, a major trend in early childhood education is that professionals are expanding the family-centered approach to providing for the needs of children and families. Programs that provide education and support for literacy, health care, nutrition, healthy living, abuse prevention, AIDS education, and parenting are examples of this family-centered approach.

Families matter in the education and development of children. Working with parents becomes a win-win proposition for everyone. You are the key to making family-centered education work.

WORKING PARENTS.   An increasing percentage of mothers with children under age six are currently employed (nearly 65 percent in 2000; see Figure 2.3). This creates a greater demand for early childhood programs. Unfortunately, much of child care in the United States is of poor quality. Early childhood professionals are constantly partnering with parents to raise the quality of child care and to make it affordable and accessible.

Children's development begins in the family system. The family system, with the help and support of early childhood programs, provides for children's basic needs. It makes sense for early childhood professionals to work with and through the family system to deliver their services.

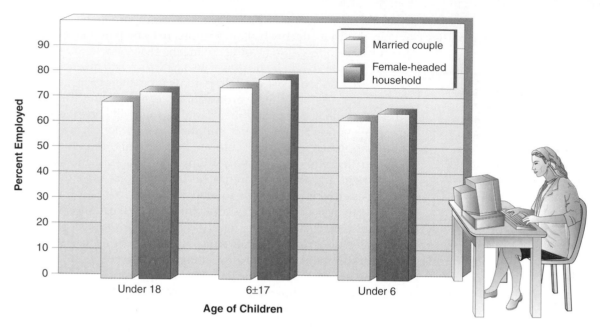

FIGURE 2.3   Mothers in the Workforce

Source: Data from National Bureau of Labor Statistics, 2000.

FATHERS.   Fathers are rediscovering the joys of parenting and working with young children. At the same time, early childhood educators have rediscovered fathers! Men are playing an active role in providing basic care, love, and nurturance to their children. Increasingly, men are more concerned about their roles as fathers and their participation in family events before, during, and after the birth of their children. Fathers want to be involved in the whole process of child rearing.

You are about to read the first of many "Program in Action" feature boxes that are integrated throughout the text. These features enable you to experience actual programs designed for real-life children in many different programs. They also are designed to support your professional development as you transition from thinking about being a professional to becoming one! This first "Program in Action: Los Padres" shows you how men are working hard at becoming connected and reconnected with their children.

Men are becoming single parents through adoption and surrogate childbearing. Also increasing in number are stay-at-home dads. Estimates of the number of fathers who stay home with their children are as high as 2 million.[2] Fathers are also receiving some of the employment benefits that have traditionally gone only to women, such as paternity leaves, flexible work schedules, and sick leave for family illness.

Program in Action

LOS PADRES

Jaime di Paulo thought he was a good dad. He worked twelve to fourteen hours a night as a cab driver, paid the rent and put food on the table.

"I was supporting my family like a good Latino dad should do. On my days off, I would say to my kids, 'Don't bother me. It's my day off.'"

Now he knows what he missed. As a founding member of Los Padres, a group of dads devoted to improving communication with their children, he is trying to persuade others to pay attention to their kids early, before they grow up.

Since 1996, Los Padres has helped more than 170 dads in Denver, Boulder, Adams County, and Grand Junction, Colorado. Most classes are held in Spanish. Child care is provided, and participants and trainees get a modest stipend. Trainees like di Paulo help recruit and train subsequent groups.

Francisco Guerro says the course saved his marriage by giving him better ways to communicate with his wife and four children. "I've learned to listen, to take turns, to wait five seconds after I've asked a question before expecting a response so they have a chance to think." Through Los Padres, di Paulo has learned "to talk to my kids, to play with my kids, to discipline my kids, to understand my kids . . . You're not born with the knowledge of being a dad. But you can learn."*

_____

*Bingham, J. "Latino fathers redefine roles," The Denver Post, May 27, 2001, p. 1B, 5B.

 To complete a Program in Action activity, visit the Companion Website at *http://www. prenhall.com/morrison*, select Chapter 2, then choose the Programs in Action module.

 For more information on the Fatherhood Project, visit the Companion Website at *http://www.prenhall.com/ morrison*, select Chapter 2, then choose the Linking to Learning module.

The **Fatherhood Project** is the longest running national initiative on fatherhood. It is a national research and education project that examines the future of fatherhood and develops ways to support men's involvement in child rearing.

SINGLE PARENTS. The number of one-parent families, both male and female, continues to increase. Certain ethnic groups are disproportionately represented in single-parent families. These increases are due to several factors. First, pregnancy rates are higher among lower socioeconomic groups. Second, teenage pregnancy rates in poor white, Hispanic, and African American populations are sometimes higher because of lower education levels, economic constraints, and fewer life opportunities. In 2000, 26 percent of single-parent families were headed by females and 5 percent were headed by males.

People become single parents for a number of reasons. Half of all marriages end in divorce, which immediately leads to single parenthood, changed lifestyles, and in many cases to lower standards of living. Single parenthood by choice is a growing option for increasing numbers of women, and some, including teenagers, become single parents by default. In addition, liberalized adoption procedures, artificial insemination, surrogate childbearing, and increasing public support for single parents make this lifestyle an attractive option for some people.

Video Viewpoint

CHILDREN GROWING UP WITHOUT FATHERS

Living in homes without fathers is a reality that affects the lives of growing numbers of children in the United States. In 25 percent of American households, mothers are raising 40 million children alone. These are children that may never see or have contact with their biological fathers.

REFLECTIVE DISCUSSION QUESTIONS

Why are we as a society so concerned about the absence of fathers in children's formative years? From your own background and experiences, what are some consequences for children being reared in homes without fathers? What does research show are some outcomes for children who are reared in homes without fathers? Why

is having two parents in the home important for children? What are some critical behaviors that fathers model for their children? In what ways do fathers make a critical difference in the lives of children? Why is it important for mothers and fathers to tell their children "I love you"?

REFLECTIVE DECISION MAKING

What can you as an early childhood professional do to make a difference in the lives of the children and their mothers living in homes without fathers? Make a list of community-based services that would be of help to families without fathers. How could you as an early childhood professional link children and their mothers to community-based services?

The reality is that more women are having children without marrying. In fact, 33 percent of all births today are to unmarried women.[3]

The growing extent of single parenthood has tremendous implications for early childhood professionals. For example, early childhood programs are developing curricula to help children and their single parents. In addition to needing assistance with child care, single parents frequently seek help in child rearing, especially in regard to discipline. Early childhood professionals are frequently asked to conduct seminars to help parents gain these skills. How well early childhood professionals meet the needs of single parents can make a difference in how successful parents are in providing for the needs of their children and other family members.

Integrated throughout this book are "Video Viewpoints," feature boxes that engage you in reflective thought and decision making. All of the video viewpoints, address current issues to help you connect theory to practice, and they relate important topics to your work with children and families. This first "Video Viewpoint: Children Growing Up Without Fathers" encourages you to think about ways you can support the education of young children who are without a father in the home.

TEENAGE PARENTS.   Although teenage pregnancies have declined over the past decade, they still continue to be a societal problem. Each year, one out of ten, or 1.1 million, teenagers becomes pregnant. The following facts about teenage pregnancy dramatically demonstrate its extent and effects:[4]

  * In 2001, for women aged fifteen through nineteen, there were 48.7 births per 1,000, down from 56.8 in 1995.

Teenage pregnancies continue to be a problem for a number of reasons. The financial costs of teenage childbearing are high, including costs to young mothers and their children. Teenage parents are less likely to complete their education and more likely to have limited career opportunities. How might early childhood programs help teenage parents meet their needs and the needs of their children?

* As a group, Latino teenagers have the highest birthrate, with 94.4 births per 1,000, down from 106.7 in 1995.
* Among states, Mississippi has the highest birthrate for teenagers, with 72.5 births per 1,000, down from 80.6 in 1995.

Concerned legislators, public policy developers, and national leaders view teenage pregnancy as a loss of human potential for young mothers and their children. From an early childhood point of view, teenage pregnancies create greater demand for infant and toddler child care and for programs to help teenagers learn how to be good parents.

Wellness and Healthy Living

As you know, when you feel good, life goes much better. The same is true for children and their families. One major goal of all early childhood programs is to provide for the safety and well-being of children. A second goal is to help parents and other family members provide for the well-being of themselves and their children. Poor health and unhealthy living conditions are major contributors to poor school achievement and life outcomes. A number of health issues facing children today put their chances for learning and success at risk.

For more information about children's health and well-being, go to the Companion Website at *http://www.prenhall. com/morrison*, select Chapter 2, then choose the Linking to Learning module.

Lack of sufficient exercise and poor nutrition are often cited as two reasons for young children's poor health status. As you read the "Program in Action: The Healthy Kids Program" on page 38, think about how you might apply their ideas to your program practices. Remember also that a healthy lifestyle and habits are part of professional practice.

Program in Action

THE HEALTHY KIDS PROGRAM

The purpose of "Education for Healthy Kids" is twofold: to engage very young children in increased physical activity and better nutrition choices and to integrate health/physical education into the core curriculum to help children avoid health-risk behavior choices, including tobacco and drug use, alcohol abuse, and sedentary lifestyles.

K–3 children are the target population for this comprehensive school wellness program. Specific interventions include:

* Thirty minutes of daily fitness activity and instruction for first, second, and third graders, twenty minutes three times a week for kindergarten students. These sessions are led by trained professional fitness educators.
* Integration of physical and health education into the core K–6 curriculum; participation of entire teaching and administrative staff in Healthy Kids.
* Regular opportunities for family involvement in health-related activities.
* Nutritious snack choices.
* Review and revision of schoolwide practices as they relate to a healthy school climate.
* Staff wellness activities.

A healthy lifestyle encompasses life in and out of school. The family is a major influence on the attitude of children. The Healthy Kids Program extends outside of the school environment, educating and promoting healthy lifestyles within the home among all family members. Activities involving parents and children are regularly held to promote healthy family fun together. Annual events such as the Mustang Mile Walk/Run and American Education Week Healthy Family Breakfast are two such examples of school-sponsored activities for families. Parent Barb Lincoln is enthusiastic about Healthy Kids. "Since our children have been in the Healthy Kids Program, we can really tell a difference in their eating and exercise habits. When asking for a snack, they choose fruits or vegetables. They prefer to take a walk or play basketball instead of watching TV. As parents, we are reminded daily by our children to make healthy choices."

Results of Healthy Kids are impressive. They include:

* Reduction in the number of playground conflicts referred to the principal or guidance staff for resolution.
* Significant improvements in fitness levels.
* Reports from teachers of improved focus in the classroom.
* Improved self-esteem among high-risk children.
* Healthy snacks replacing candy and sweets in lunch bags.
* Reports from parents of improved eating habits at home by children.

As children's health status becomes more of a national issue, it is likely that more programs such as Healthy Kids will become a regular part of the early childhood curriculum.

The Healthy Kids Program seeks to protect and improve the health status of low-income children in Oklahoma.

 To learn more about the Healthy Kids Program visit the Companion Website at *http://www.prenhall.com/morrison*, select Chapter 2, then choose the Programs in Action module.

ILLNESSES. When you think of children's illnesses, you probably think of measles, rubella, and mumps. Actually, asthma, lead poisoning, and obesity are the three leading childhood diseases.

Asthma. Asthma, a chronic inflammatory disorder of the airways, is the most common chronic childhood illness in the United States. An estimated 1.3 million children under age five suffer from asthma. Asthma is caused in part by poor air quality, dust, mold, animal fur and dander, allergens from cockroaches and rodent

For more information about asthma, visit the Companion Website at *http://www.prenhall.com/ morrison*, select Chapter 2, then choose the Linking to Learning module.

feces, and strong fumes. Many of these causes are found in poor and low-quality housing. You will want to reduce asthma-causing conditions in your early childhood programs and work with parents to reduce the causes of asthma in their homes. Some things you can do to reduce the causes of asthma are: prohibit smoking around children, keep the environment clean and free of mold, reduce or eliminate carpeting, have children sleep on mats or cots, and work with parents to ensure that their children are getting appropriate asthma medication.[5]

Lead Poisoning.   Lead poisoning is also a serious childhood disease. The Centers for Disease Control (CDC) estimates that approximately 1 million children between birth and age five have elevated blood lead levels. These children are at risk for lower IQs, short attention spans, reading and learning disabilities, hyperactivity, and behavioral problems.[6] The major source of lead poisoning is from old lead-based paint that still exists in many homes and apartments. Other sources of lead are from car batteries and dust and dirt from lead-polluted soil. Approximately 80 percent of homes built before 1978 have lead-based paint in them. Since then, lead has no longer been used in paint. Currently, the state of Rhode Island is suing five paint manufacturers who made lead-based paint. The state is trying to recover the medical costs of treating children with lead poisoning and the cost of removing lead-based paint from homes. Lead enters the body through inhalation and ingestion. Young children are especially vulnerable since they put many things in their mouths, chew on windowsills, and crawl on floors. The Grace Hill Neighborhood Health Centers in St. Louis treat children for lead poisoning and send health coaches into homes of children with high levels of lead. These health workers cover peeling windowsills and provide vacuum cleaners with high-efficiency filters.

For more information about how to prevent lead poisoning at home and school, visit the Companion Website at *http://www.prenhall.com/ morrison*, select Chapter 2, then choose the Linking to Learning module.

Obesity.   Today's generation of young children is often referred to as the "Super-size Generation." Many contend that one of the reasons they are overweight is because of their tendency to supersize burgers, fries, and colas. The percentage of children who are overweight has more than doubled in the last three decades.

What can you do as an early childhood professional to help children and parents win the Obesity War?

* Provide parents with information about nutrition. For example, send home copies of the Food Guide Pyramid for Young Children (Figure 2.4 page 41) and other nutritional information.
* Counsel parents to pull the plug on the television. TV watching at mealtime is associated with obesity because children are more likely to eat fast foods such as pizza and salty snack foods. Also, children who watch a lot of television tend to be less physically active, and inactivity tends to promote weight gain.
* When cooking with children, talk about foods and their nutritional values. Cooking activities are also a good way to eat and talk about new foods.

FIGURE 2.4   Good Nutrition for Young Children

Source: *U.S. Department of Agriculture.*

Readiness is now viewed as promoting children's learning and development in all areas. Readiness includes general health such as being well rested, well fed, and properly immunized. The United Nations estimates that worldwide more than 8 million children a year die from five major diseases: pneumonia, diarrhea, measles, tetanus, and whooping cough.

* Integrate literacy and nutritional activities. For example, reading and discussing labels is a good way to encourage children to be aware of and think about nutritional information.
* Provide opportunities for physical exercise and physical activities in your program.
* If your school or program does not provide breakfast for children, be an advocate for starting it. School breakfasts can be both a nutritional and educational program.

You can do a lot to promote children's health. Do not blame the parents. Work with them to enable them and their children to lead healthy lives. Continuing the theme of wellness and healthy living, the next "Video Viewpoint: They Are What They Eat," on page 42, looks at how marketing and advertising influences the food preferences and eating habits of young children. Children of today are often referred to as the "Super-size" generation and some complain that the first words children learn as they relate to food is "super-size it!" Think about some ways that you could help children eat better and healthier.

POVERTY. Poverty has serious negative consequences for children and families. Children account for approximately 40 percent of the poor population, even though they make up only one-quarter of the population. Nearly 22 percent of children under six—more than 4 million children—live in poverty.

Poverty is a greater risk for children living in single-parent homes with female heads of household. More than one-half of these children (59.1 percent) live in poverty. Approximately 40 percent of African American children under the age of six live in poverty; this figure climbs to 61 percent in single-mother households. Poverty rates for Hispanic American children under the age of six are 38.3 percent

Video Viewpoint

THEY ARE WHAT THEY EAT

Children are not born with a taste for high-fat foods. It is a learned behavior. But, often, children are not given better choices. When children are let loose in a supermarket to make their own choices, parents are appalled at what their children do not know about good nutrition—and at food manufacturers who do not necessarily offer the healthiest of choices in their kid-attractive packages.

REFLECTIVE DISCUSSION QUESTIONS

Why do you think that when given the opportunity, children select high-calorie, high-fat foods rather than "healthy foods"? Why do you think manufacturers produce and sell foods with higher-fat content for children than adults? How are children's cartoons and cartoon characters used to market children's foods? How does television advertising steer children toward "bad food choices"? What are some reasons that children are eating more "unhealthy" foods? What is your reaction to the comment that "there are no good or bad foods; that eaten in moderation, any food is part of a well-balanced diet"?

REFLECTIVE DECISION MAKING

Visit a local supermarket and read the fat, salt, and sugar content for foods marketed specifically for children. Make a list of the top fat, salt, and sugar foods for children. How can you work with parents to help them provide good nutritional meals for their children and other family members? What can you do in preschool and other early childhood settings to help children learn good nutritional practices? Conduct a survey of the foods that young children eat during the day. How many total grams of fat do you estimate they eat during a typical day? How does this compare with the 50 to 60 grams of fat recommended by nutritionists? Give specific examples of how manufacturers use food to promote and sell a particular product. What could you do as an early childhood educator to get children to eat more fruits and vegetables rather than fatty snacks?

overall and about 68 percent for those in single-mother homes.[7] Figure 2.5 shows the extent of family poverty.

Living in poverty means children and their families don't have the income that allows them to purchase adequate health care, housing, food, clothing, and educational services. In 2001, poverty for a nonfarm family of four meant an income of less than $17,650.[8] The federal government annually revises its poverty guidelines, which are the basis for distribution of federal aid to schools and student eligibility for academic services such as Head Start, **Title I** (a federal program that provides low-achieving students additional help in math and reading), and free and reduced-price school breakfasts and lunches.

Living in a rural community and in a rural southern state increases the likelihood that families will live in poverty. Cities with the highest school-age poverty rate are in the South and East. In Mississippi, one-third of all children are poor, well above the national average of 27%.[9]

Also, living in urban cities increases the chances of being poor. With increases in rural and urban poverty go decreases in wealth and support for education. This in turn means that, as a whole, children living in poverty will attend schools that have few resources and poorly prepared teachers.

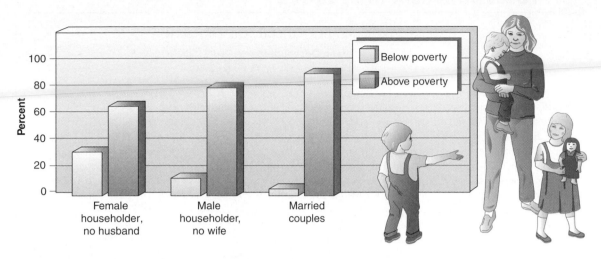

⌒ FIGURE 2.5   Families with Children Living in Poverty, 2000

Source: Data from U.S. Bureau of the Census, Historical Time Series, *Families (FM-2), May 1998.*

The effects of poverty are detrimental to students' achievement and life prospects. For example, children and youth from low-income families are often older than others in their grade level, move more slowly through the educational system, are more likely to drop out, and are less likely to find work.[10] Poor children are more likely to be retained in school, and students who have repeated one or more grades are more likely to become school dropouts.[11] Poverty affects students' health prospects as well. For example, more than one-half of all children who lack insured health care come from poor families.[12]

Children in poverty are more likely to have emotional and behavioral problems and are less likely than others to be "highly engaged" in school.[13] Also, parents of low-income families are less likely to help their children complete homework assignments.

Poverty negatively influences other areas of children's lives. More than one-third of all poor children have untreated dental cavities.[14] So improving the conditions that surround children of poverty is a major way teachers, politicians, and the public can collaborate to help children do better in all areas of life, including schooling.

Finally, teachers of low-income children must have high expectations for them and truly believe they can and will learn. Unfortunately, some teachers and care providers believe children cannot learn because they are poor. We cannot and must not tolerate such attitudes. Low achievement is not embedded in the DNA of poor children. Children's futures and America's future depend on how well we teach them.

In Chapter 1, we stressed the need for ongoing professional development. In the "Professionalism in Practice" feature on page 44, 2000 Disney's American Teacher Joann DesLauriers continues that theme and tells why she places students at the center of all she does.

Professionalism in Practice

PERSPECTIVE ON EARLY CHILDHOOD EDUCATION

Joann DesLauriers
Disney's American Teacher Award Honoree 2000

After twenty plus years as an educator I continue to be excited each August when I know it is time to meet a new class of first graders. I am acutely aware that I am one of the principal players in ensuring that the children who are placed under my care become readers and writers. This responsibility has led me to think constantly about my practice and to hold high standards for my own performance daily in my classroom. I have found that continued professional growth is the key to maintaining my love and passion for the teaching profession.

I have continued to grow and learn because I keep current through professional reading. Teachers are often so busy that reading of any sort is put "on the back burner." It is my strong belief that developing a habit of staying current through educational journals and books is essential. Through membership in professional organizations such as the International Reading Association, I receive a monthly journal and brochures of recently published books. A group of early childhood educators voluntarily gets together to discuss our readings and think about our practice. This group becomes my support group as I become more self-reflective. The dialogue that results from our readings creates significant changes in my classroom. If I had to name the one professional pursuit that has impacted my teaching most, it would be the discussions that come as a result of reading research-based text.

I have been so fortunate throughout my career to have other teachers who were willing to help me improve. In each school I teach I have looked for the most effective teachers on the staff. I make it a point to establish a relationship with them. Teachers become like those with whom they associate. My advice to any beginning teacher is to locate the "thinking" teachers in their buildings and make them their model. You will begin to take on their characteristics. I try to surround myself with strong, effective educators so that I, too, can become strong and effective.

Participating in professional development opportunities has also helped me maintain a high degree of interest and enthusiasm for teaching. Often attending a national conference or a local workshop gives fresh ideas for teaching basic curriculum and for extending present classroom practice. It also provides a way to meet people outside my campus who shed new light on challenges we all face daily. Quality professional development is sometimes difficult to find but is worth the effort.

It has been my great fortune to work with new teachers through mentoring. Whether these teachers have been new to the profession or completing their training, I have learned so much as we work together to think about what makes a lesson worthwhile. I view myself as a co-learner and welcome the chance to watch others teach. It always make me think about myself. As we discuss what went well and what needs to be improved, I take those ideas back to my own classroom.

I learned to be self-reflective during my pursuit of National Board Certification. The National Board for Professional Teaching Standards has developed a set of standards that describe what a teacher should know and be able to do. After nineteen years of teaching, I was rejuvenated as I thought about my teaching in relation to these standards. I received certification in 1999, and my teaching practice has improved as a result. I have worked with others pursuing their certification, which has provided endless opportunities for analysis of the choices I make in my classroom.

The primary motivation I have to continue to learn more about children and how they learn is the students. As teachers we must enter the doors of our classrooms prepared to meet the needs of each one. This is our calling. They each deserve our best. Professional growth and development falls squarely on the teacher's shoulders. It is a choice we make. The day I no longer want to grow is the day I should leave the classroom. My students are looking to me to give the foundation that will support their learning for the rest of their formal education. If I lay a weak and wobbly foundation, I have harmed them. If I lay a deep and strong foundation, I have given them endless opportunities.

Joann DesLauriers is a first grade teacher at Hoover Elementary, Bartlesville, Oklahoma.

 To review the Professional Development Checklist and complete a Professionalism in Practice activity, visit the Companion Website at *http://www.prenhall. com/ morrison,* select Chapter 1, then choose the Professional Development module.

Brain Research

Although the field of neuroscience has contributed to brain research for approximately twenty-five years, public interest in the application of this research to early childhood education has recently intensified.

What specifically does brain research tell us about early childhood experiences? In many cases it affirms what early childhood educators have always intuitively known: Good parental care, warm and loving attachments, and positive age-appropriate stimulation from birth onward make a tremendous difference in children's cognitive development for a lifetime.[15]

Brain research also tells us a great deal regarding stimulation and the development of specific areas of the brain. For example, brain research suggests that listening to music and learning to play musical instruments at very early ages stimulate the brain areas associated with mathematics and spatial reasoning. Brain research also suggests that gross motor activities and physical education should be included in a child's daily schedule throughout the elementary years.

New early childhood curricula are being developed based on the findings of brain research, and these programs strive to apply research findings in a practical way. Finding ways to apply research in practical ways is an important part of becoming a professional.

For more information about the Zero to Three organization, visit the Companion Website at *http://www.prenhall.com/morrison,* select Chapter 2, then choose the Linking to Learning module.

For example, **Zero to Three,** a national, nonprofit organization, focuses on the healthy development of infants, toddlers, and families by supporting and strengthening families, communities, and all who work on behalf of young children. Advocates of Zero to Three believe that a child's first three years are crucial for developing intellectual, emotional, and social skills. If these skills are not developed, the child's lifelong potential may be hampered. The organization supports professionals, parents, and policy makers and strives to increase public awareness, inspire leaders, and foster professional excellence through training, always emphasizing the first three years of a child's life.

Current brain research influences our ideas about how children learn, how to teach them, and what they should learn. As a result, there is a major shift in basic educational premises concerning what children can achieve. Early childhood professionals have arrived at the following conclusions about young children:

1. The period of most rapid intellectual growth occurs before age eight. The notion of promoting cognitive development implies that children benefit from enriched home environments that are conducive to learning and from early school-like experiences, especially for children in environments that place them at risk for learning problems.

2. Children are not born with fixed intelligences. This outdated concept does not do justice to children's tremendous capacity for learning and change. The extent to which individual intelligence develops depends on many variables, such as experiences, child-rearing practices, economic factors, nutrition, and the quality of prenatal and postnatal environments.

Inherited genetic characteristics set a broad framework within which intelligence develops. Heredity sets the limits, while environment determines the extent to which individuals achieve these limits.

3. Children reared in homes that are not intellectually stimulating may also lag intellectually behind their counterparts reared in more advantaged environments. Implications concerning the home environment are obvious. Experience shows that children who lack an environment that promotes learning opportunities may be at risk throughout life. On the other hand, homes that offer intellectual stimulation and a print-rich environment tend to produce children who do well in school.

4. Good parental care, warm and loving attachments, and positive, age-appropriate stimulation from birth onward make a difference in children's overall development for a lifetime. Even during the fetal stage, the kind of nourishment and care children receive affects neural development (i.e., the development of brain nerve cells). The majority of recent research shows that much of children's learning capacity is developed during the earliest years.

5. Positive interactions with caring adults stimulate children's brains profoundly in terms of establishing new synaptic connections and strengthening existing ones. For example, cuddling and singing to infants and toddlers stimulate brain connections and lay the foundation for learning throughout life. Those connections used over time become permanent, and those that are not used wither and become dormant. Increasingly, researchers are showing how early stimulation sets the stage for future

As a result of new research, we are learning more about children than ever before. This new research accounts for the tremendous popularity of early childhood programs and curriculum. List several ways that teaching young children has changed as a result of brain research.

cognitive processes. In addition, positive emotional interactions and formations of secure attachments lay the foundation for healthy emotional development. As you know from your experiences, learning is emotional as well as cognitive. Your emotional state sets the tone for learning in your classroom.

6. Early experiences during critical/sensitive periods and "windows of opportunity" are so powerful that they can completely change the way children develop.[16] The right input at the right time is crucial for children to fully develop cognitive potential. For example, the circuit for vision has a neuron growth spurt at two to four months of age, thus helping children begin to notice the shape of objects.[17] This neuron growth spurt peaks at eight months, suggesting the importance of providing appropriate visual stimuli early in life necessary to establish important neuron connections.

Violence

On March 5, 2001, a fifteen-year-old Santee, California, high school student walked into the high school restroom and courtyard and engaged in a shooting spree that left two students dead and thirteen injured. Increasing acts of violence such as this lead to proposals for how to provide violence-free homes and educational environments; how to teach children to get along nonviolently with others; and how to reduce violence on television, the movies, and in video games. Reducing violence on television, for example, in turn leads to discussions and proposals for ways to limit children's television viewing. Such proposals include "pulling the plug" on television; using the V-chip, which enables parents to block out programs with violent content; boycotting companies whose advertisements support programs with violent content; and limiting violence shown during prime-time viewing hours for children. Early childhood professionals play important roles in these and other debates and decision-making processes. Advocacy is a critical role of the professional. You can play a major role in reducing violence by being an advocate for reducing the media violence that negatively influences children's lives.

Programs to prevent and curb bullying are another example of how educators are combating the effects of violence on children. Although in the past bullying has been dismissed as "normal" or "kids' play," this is no longer the case, because bullying is related to school and other violence. Bullying includes teasing, slapping, hitting, pushing, unwanted touching, taking personal belongings, name-calling, and making sexual comments and insults about looks, behavior, and culture. Now, schools are starting to fight back against bullies and bullying.

The following "Program in Action: Teaching Conflict Resolution" on page 48, will help you understand how one school is making progress toward helping children put a stop to bullying practices.

Program in Action

POLITICS AND EARLY CHILDHOOD EDUCATION

The more early childhood is in the news, the more it generates public interest and attention; this is part of the political context of early childhood education. Whatever else can be said about education, one point is this—it is political. Politicians and politics exert a powerful influence in determining what is taught, how it is taught, to whom it is taught, and by whom it is taught. Early childhood education is no exception.

 For more information about public policy and early childhood education, go to the Companion Website at *http://www.prenhall.com/ morrison,* select Chapter 2, then choose the Linking to Learning module.

An important political and educational event occurred in 1989 when President George H. W. Bush and the governors of all fifty states met and set national education goals. One result of this meeting was the release in 1991 of *America 2000: An Education Strategy,* which outlined six educational goals, or national standards. These, and two additional goals, were passed as part of the Goals 2000: Educate America Act in 1994. The eight goals, which were to be achieved by the year 2000, are listed in Figure 2.6. Although still going by the name Goals 2000, politicians and educators remain dedicated to achieving them now and in the years to come.

 For a comprehensive review of work toward the national goals, go to the Companion Website at *http://www.prenhall. com/morrison,* select Chapter 2, then choose the Linking to Learning module.

These goals have generated a great deal of debate, particularly concerning what they mean and how best to achieve them. Goals 1, 2, 6, 7, and 8 will continue over the next decade to influence early childhood education. Goal 1 has implications for children's readiness for school. Goal 2 is pertinent because the early childhood years are seen as the place to prevent school dropout. Many public school programs for three- and four-year-old children are funded specifically as beginning efforts to keep children in school at a later age. Goal 6 has

👁 **FIGURE 2.6   Goals 2000**

Source: *U.S. Department of Education, 1994.*

The Goals 2000: Educate America Act includes these eight goals to be achieved by 2000.

1. All children in America will start school ready to learn.

2. The high school graduation rate will increase to at least 90 percent.

3. All students will leave grades four, eight, and twelve having demonstrated competency over challenging subject matter . . . and [all students will be] prepared for responsible citizenship, further learning, and productive employment.

4. The nation's teaching force will have access to programs for the continued improvement of their professional skills.

5. U.S. students will be first in the world in mathematics and science achievement.

6. Every adult American will be literate.

7. Every school in America will be free of drugs and violence and will offer a disciplined environment conducive to learning.

8. Every school and home will engage in partnerships that will increase parental involvement and participation in promoting the social, emotional, and academic growth of children.

encouraged many intergenerational literacy and family literacy programs in which children, their parents, and other family members are taught to read. Goal 7 supports the drug prevention programs implemented in early childhood programs, again on the premise that early prevention is much more effective than later treatment. Finally, Goal 8 makes implicit as part of national policy the importance of home-school partnerships. Implementation of Goal 8 is treated in detail in Chapter 12, "Cooperation and Collaboration with Parents, Families, and the Community."

Progress to Date toward Achieving the National Educational Goals

Regarding Goal 1, Ready to Learn, the National Education Goals Panel is seeking ways to adequately measure children's readiness to learn, which it broadly defines as children's physical health, social and emotional development, language use, and general knowledge. The panel cites Florida and Massachusetts as the highest performing states in reducing the percentage of infants born with health risks.[18]

 For more information about Healthy Start, visit the Companion Website at *http://www.prenhall.com/morrison*, select Chapter 2, then choose the Linking to Learning module.

In Florida, the Healthy Start program relies on a team of registered nurses and social workers to provide a wide variety of services. These include home visits by a nurse and/or social workers; nursing and developmental assessments; parent education and support; nutrition education and smoking cessation counseling; educational materials pertaining to prenatal care, birth, and infant care; and information and referral to other community services and programs. Services are provided in the clinic or in the parents' home.

FEDERAL AND STATE INVOLVEMENT IN EARLY CHILDHOOD PROGRAMS

Over the past decade there has been increased federal and state funding of early childhood programs. This trend will continue for a couple of reasons. First, politicians and the public recognize that the early years are the foundation for future learning. Second, spending money on children in the early years is more cost effective than trying to solve problems in the teenage years.

The Florida Department of Education, for example, has an office dedicated to early intervention and school readiness. One of its programs is Florida First Start, a home-school partnership designed to give children at risk of future school failure the best possible start in life and to support parents in their role as their children's first teachers. Emphasis is on enabling families to enhance their children's intellectual, physical, language, and social development by involving them in their children's education during the critical first three years of life. Through early parent education and support services, the program lays the foundation for later learning and future school success, while fostering effective parent-school relationships.

Many federal dollars are consolidated into what are known as *block grants*, money given to states to provide services according to broad general guidelines. In essence, the states control the way the money is spent to achieve certain federal goals such as increasing preschool children's readiness for school and learning.

Expanded Federal Support for Early Childhood Programs

One of the dramatic changes occurring in society is the expanded role of the federal government in the reform of public education. President George W. Bush made education reform a major part of his election campaign. We are currently witnessing more federal dollars allocated for specific early education initiatives than ever before. For example, the Bush administration through increased federal funding wants to reform Head Start by making it more academic and to emphasize the development of early literacy skills. The critics of federal support for such programs argue that the federal government should not allocate dollars for specific targeted programs. However, the number and size of federal allocations for reform initiatives will continue.

Keeping current in the profession is an important part of professional practice. There are many ways to keep yourself on the cutting edge. As you read how six kindergarten teachers keep themselves up to date in the "Professionalism in Practice" feature that follows, think about how you can apply their practices to your plans for keeping current.

Professionalism in Practice

Here is how six kindergarten teachers at Seneca Elementary School in Seneca, Missouri, keep current in the profession:

Glenna Whitehead: "I attend professional development workshops and teacher in-services, belong to the state teacher organization, read current education literature, periodicals and education websites."

Teresa Trone: "Workshops, in-services, talking with new teachers, and college courses."

Amy Cook: "This is my first year, so I haven't had the opportunity to participate in professional development workshops, etc., but I try to communicate with colleagues to see what they have learned that works best."

Kristy Padgett: "I look for a variety of ideas to use in my classroom. I use teacher magazines, the Internet, and other teachers to draw ideas from."

Pam Ward: "I read early childhood magazines and articles and attend workshops that are beneficial to me in the classroom."

Addie Gaines: "I frequently read professional literature to keep up with the world of early childhood education. I am active in the online community of educators at Teachers.Net and frequently exchange ideas and advice with teachers from all across the country. I enjoy attending teacher workshops and in-services and learning new ideas."

To review the Professional Development Checklist and complete a Professionalism in Practice activity, visit the Companion Website at *http://www.prenhall. com/ morrison,* select Chapter 2, then choose the Professional Development module.

Public Schools and Early Education

Traditionally, the majority of preschool programs were operated by private agencies or agencies supported wholly or in part by federal funds to help low-income families. But times have changed. All parents exert great pressure on public school officials and state legislatures to sponsor and fund additional preschool and early childhood programs.

Increasingly, preschool programs are part of the public schools: 42 of the 50 states offer free or subsidized preschools. The states spend more than $1.5 billion on preschool education. In Georgia, 70 percent of children attend preschool. Nationwide, about 500,000 preschool children are enrolled in public school programs. As preschool programs admit more three- and four-year-olds nationwide, opportunities for teachers of young children will grow. Recall from chapter 1 how Florida offers certification.

The spread of private and public preschools reflects changing family patterns, especially the rise in single-parent families and families with two adult wage earners. This later group creates a demand for "high-end" preschools. Demand for preschools also underscores the importance of their use in early childhood intervention programs and to the popular belief that three- and four-year-old children

Technology Tie-In

IS THE USE OF TECHNOLOGY IN EARLY CHILDHOOD PROGRAMS "FOOLS' GOLD"?

I want to be up-front with readers: I am a strong advocate of using technology in the home and classroom—in appropriate ways. My answer to the title of this article is an unequivocal "No!" I support the use of technology with young children for a number of reasons. First, today's children are the generation.com. They have a great deal of involvement with technology and have spent many years playing with and learning from technology. Children as young as nine months are using the computer, while nestled securely in their parents' laps. Programs such as Reader Rabbit and Jump-Start Baby are designed for the lapware set. These software programs and others like them constitute the fastest growing software on the market today. They are easy and fun to use, and children learn from them.

A second reason I support the use of technology with children is that the use of technology in early childhood programs can begin to level the educational playing field and close the digital divide that exists between the haves and have-nots of technology. Children from minority and low-income families have less access to computers and the Internet than do their more advantaged classmates. Having access to and use of computers and other technology at school can help all children get the knowledge and skills they need to be successful in school and life.

I recommend that all early childhood classrooms have a technology center that includes a computer, access to the Internet, a printer, a digital camera, and appropriate learning software.

However, you need to answer the "fools' gold" question for yourself. You can begin your process of decision making by reading "Fools' Gold: A Critical Look at Computers in Childhood," a report of the Alliance for Childhood, which advocates for the developmental needs of young children.

 To download this report and find resources to help answer this question, go to the Companion Website at *http://www.prenhall.com/morrison*, select Chapter 2, then choose the Technology Tie-In module.

are ready, willing, and able to learn. Read the "Technology Tie-In" on the use of technology in early childhood programs to see how classrooms can close the digital divide between the haves and have-nots.

Parents support public school programs for young children for a number of reasons. First, many working parents cannot find quality child care for their children. They look to the public schools to provide the solution to their child care needs. Second, the public believes that young children should have important educational and social services early in life to avoid future school and learning problems. Third, many people believe that early public schooling, especially for children from low-income families, is necessary if the United States is to promote equal opportunity for all. They argue that low-income children begin school already far behind their more fortunate middle-class counterparts and that the best way to keep them from falling hopelessly behind is for them to begin school earlier. Fourth, parents believe preschools, funded at the public's expense, are a reasonable, cost-efficient way to meet child care needs. Finally, today's parents are the best educated in U.S. history. They want preschool programs that emphasize earlier and more comprehensive education for their children at earlier ages.

Despite the support of many parents for early childhood programs, the movement toward universal preschool remains controversial. First, for some parents, *universal* preschool means mandatory. Many parents believe they should have the option to send their three- to five-year-old children to school. Generally the public supports universal and accessible, but not mandatory, preschool. Second, money is an issue. Universal preschools would involve a considerable expenditure of local, state, and federal funds. Understandably, poorer communities and states worry about how to pay for expanded preschool programs. Nonetheless, preschool is well on its way to becoming universal.

In short, early childhood education and young children have captured the attention of the nation. This increased attention in turn creates many issues and controversies. Consequently, early childhood professionals must learn more about how to care for, educate, and rear children so they can advise parents, legislators, and others in determining what is best for the nation's children.

NEW DIRECTIONS IN EARLY CHILDHOOD EDUCATION

Because of the changing needs of society and families, and because new research provides new directions, the field of early childhood education is constantly changing. Following are some important changes occurring in early childhood education today that will influence how you and others practice the profession of early childhood education:

* *Full-day, full-year services.* Parents want full-day, full-year services for a number of reasons. First, it fits in with their work schedule and lifestyle. Working parents, in particular, find it difficult to patch together child care and other arrangements when their children are not in school. Second, parents believe that full-day, full-year services support and enhance their children's learning. As a result, we will see more full-day, full-year services. Half-day, half-year programs do not meet the needs of parents or children.

* *Readiness for learning.* There is and will be an increase in programs designed to provide families with child development information and suggestions on parenting skills and other resources that will help them get their children ready for schools and learning. Working with parents to help them get their children ready for learning and school is an important and growing part of early childhood services.

* *Two-generation programs.* Intergenerational programs will become more common. As an early childhood professional you will work with children and their parents, and in many cases grandparents, to develop literacy, parenting, and other skills.

* *Wrap-around services.* Collaborative efforts in the form of wrap-around services (also referred to as an ecological approach) with professionals from other agencies and disciplines better use resources and avoid duplication of efforts. For example, many school districts work with social workers to help children and families meet their needs regarding nutrition, clothing,

counseling services, and other means of support. Collaboration is all about working together to help make life better for children and families.

* *Support for intellectual development.* Early childhood professionals have always acknowledged that they must educate the whole child—physical, social, emotional, and cognitive. However, sometimes the intellectual has not received enough emphasis. A recent trend is a greater emphasis on supporting children's cognitive development. A report released by the National Institute of Child Health and Development (NICHD) concluded that providing more intellectual stimulation for children is one way to improve America's child care.[19]

To take an online self-test on this chapter's contents, go to the Companion Website at *http://www.prenhall.com/ morrison*, select Chapter 2, then choose the Self-Test module.

* *Early literacy learning.* Brain research has created interest in the importance of early literacy development. There is a growing awareness of the critical role literacy plays in school and life success. Consequently, there are now more programs designed specifically to help young children get ready for learning to read. This emphasis on early literacy and learning to read will be evident in chapters throughout this book.

* *New curriculum initiatives.* In addition to early literacy, three other new curriculum initiatives involve wellness/healthy living, character/moral education, and mathematics. While early mathematics is not new, it is receiving new national attention. These topics are important because of the growing incidence of children's illnesses such as obesity and asthma, because society wants to rear more responsible and civil children, and because business and industry want employees who are mathematically literate.

Changes in society constantly cause changes in the field of early childhood education. One of your major challenges as an early childhood professional is to keep current in terms of new changes and directions in your field. In this way you will be able to judge what is best for young children and implement the best practices that will enable young children to succeed in school and life.

ACTIVITIES FOR PROFESSIONAL DEVELOPMENT

In this chapter, we have discussed the importance of keeping up to date with trends and issues in your profession. We have discussed how issues of early childhood education are constantly changing, what is taught, and how it is taught. Therefore, as an early childhood professional, you will constantly want to keep yourself up-to-date so that you can be on the cutting edge of your profession and provide the children in your program with the best education possible. Refer again to the "Professional Development Goal" at the beginning of this chapter, to the "Professional Development Checklist" on pages 20 and 21, how the six kindergarten teachers at Seneca Elementary School keep current in the profession on page 51, and how Joann DesLauriers, 2000 Disney's American Teacher Award Honoree, keeps current on page 44. Reviewing this information will provide helpful insights as you complete these exercises.

To view the online newspapers, go to the Companion Website at *http://www.prenhall. com/morrison*, select Chapter 2, then choose the Linking to Learning module.

1. Reading daily newspapers is one way to keep up-to-date in a changing society and in a changing educational environment. For two weeks, scan online the following newspapers:

New York Times
Washington Post
Los Angeles Times
Chicago Tribune

As you review, make predictions about how you believe early childhood education will change over the next five years.

2. Interview early childhood professionals and ask them what problems they face with the children in their programs as a result of divorce, abuse, and other types of stress in children's lives. Make a list of how they help children and families deal with these problems.

3. Interview early childhood professionals and ask them these questions:

   a. How have they kept up with changes in early childhood?

   b. To what changes have they had the hardest time adjusting?

   c. What changes do they like the most? the least?

   d. What advice do they have for future educators about how to keep up with change?

4. Contact agencies that provide services to single parents, teenage parents, and families in need. How do these services influence early childhood education programs in your local community?

5. Over several weeks or a month, collect articles from newspapers and magazines relating to infants, toddlers, and preschoolers and categorize them by topic (child abuse, nutrition, child development, etc.). What topics were given the most coverage? Why? What topics or trends are emerging in early education, according to this media coverage?

6. Over the next three or four months, keep a journal about changes you notice in the field of early childhood. Include these topics:

   a. What changes intrigue you the most?

   b. Not all changes are for the better. Make a list of changes that you think have a negative effect on children (e.g., rising poverty).

   c. Document the things you are doing personally and professionally to respond to changes in society and education.

For additional chapter resources and activities, visit the Companion Website at *http://www.prenhall.com/morrison*, select Chapter 2, then choose the Professional Development, Resources, or Linking to Learning modules.

FOCUS QUESTIONS

1. Why is it important to know about the ideas, contributions, and learning theories of great educators?

2. What are the basic beliefs of the individuals who have had the greatest influence on early childhood education?

3. How do the beliefs and practices of great educators influence early childhood education?

4. What is learning and how do theories of learning influence the teaching and practice of early childhood education?

chapter 3

History and Theories

FOUNDATIONS FOR TEACHING AND LEARNING

To review the chapter focus questions online, go to the Companion Website at *http://www.prenhall.com/morrison* and select Chapter 3.

 PROFESSIONAL DEVELOPMENT GOALS

HISTORICAL KNOWLEDGE

I am familiar with my profession's history, and I use my knowledge of the past to inform my practice.

THEORIES OF EARLY CHILDHOOD EDUCATION

I understand the principles of each major theory of educating young children. The approach I use is consistent with my beliefs about how children learn.

WHY IS THE HISTORY OF EARLY CHILDHOOD EDUCATION IMPORTANT?

To check your understanding of this chapter with the online Study Guide, go to the Companion Website at *http://www.prenhall.com/ morrison*, select Chapter 3, then choose the Study Guide module.

There is a history of just about everything. A history of teaching, a history of schools, and a history of early childhood education. While we don't need to know the history of dolls in order to buy a doll, if you are a doll collector, knowing the history of dolls is essential. The same applies to you as an early childhood educator.

When we know the beliefs, ideas, and accomplishments of people who have devoted their lives to young children, we realize that many of today's early childhood programs are built on enduring beliefs about how children learn, grow, and develop. There are at least three reasons why it is important to know about ideas and theories that have and are influencing the field of early childhood education.

Rebirth of Ideas

Good ideas and practices persist over time and tend to be reintroduced in educational thought and practices in ten- to twenty-year cycles. For example, many practices popular in the past—such as the teaching of reading through phonics, multiage grouping, and teacher-initiated instruction—are now popular once again in the first decade of the twenty-first century. I hope you will always be as amazed as I am about the way early childhood always seems to recycle enduring ideas and practices.

Build the Dream—Again

Many ideas of famous educators are still dreams because of our inability to translate dreams into reality. Nonetheless, the dreams of educating all children to their full potential are worthy ones, and we can and should use them as a base to build meaningful teaching careers and lives for children and their families. We have an obligation to make the bright visions others have had for children our own visions for them as well. After all, if we don't have bright visions for children, who will?

Implement Current Practice

Ideas expressed by early educators will help you better understand how to implement current teaching strategies, whatever they might be. For instance, Rousseau, Froebel, and Montessori all believed children should be taught with dignity and respect. Dignity and respect for all children are essential foundations of all good teaching and quality programs.

WHY ARE THEORIES OF LEARNING IMPORTANT?

When you try to explain plant growth to children or others you talk about soil, and sun, and water, and the need for fertilizer. Perhaps you even use the word *photosynthesis* as part of your theory of plant growth. How do children grow? How do children learn? I'm sure you have ideas and explanations based on your experiences to help answer these questions. We also have the theories of others to help us explain these questions. But what about child growth and learning?

Learning is the acquisition of knowledge, behaviors, skills, and attitudes. Learning is also an involved process, and many different educators have developed theories to explain how and why learning occurs in children. As a result of experiences, children change in their behavior, knowledge, skills, and attitude. So, we can also consider learning to be changes that occur in behavior over a period of time. Children who enter kindergarten in September are not the same children who exit kindergarten in May.

Theories are used to explain how children grow, develop, and learn. Learning theories are an important part of your professional practice for several reasons.

Thinking about Learning

Theories help us think about how children learn and enable us to make decisions about how to best support their development and learning. Thinking about learning and understanding how children learn makes it easier for you and others to plan and teach. In addition, thinking about learning and thinking about teaching are part of your reflective practice. Reflective practice involves deliberate and careful consideration about the children you teach, the theories on which you base your teaching, how you teach, what children learn, and how you will teach in the future. In a word, the reflective teacher is a thoughtful teacher. Reflective practice involves the three steps shown in Figure 3.1.

Communication

Theories enable you to explain to others, especially parents, how the complex process of learning occurs and what you and they can expect of children. Communicating with clarity and understanding to parents and others about how children learn is one of the most important jobs for an early childhood professional. To do this, you need to know the theories that explain how children develop and learn.

Evaluate Learning

Theories also enable you to evaluate children's learning in a number of ways. For example, theories set benchmarks so we can measure learning and cognitive growth. Also, theories describe behaviors and identify what children are able to do at certain ages. We can use this information to evaluate learning and plan for teaching. Evaluation of children's learning is another important job for a professional. We will discuss assessment of learning in Chapter 5.

⌒ FIGURE 3.1 **Pathways to Successful Teaching: Thinking, Planning, and Deciding**

Teaching involves many processes. Here are things that effective teachers do to teach well and help their students learn. Review these questions. What are the knowledge and skills you will want to work on most during your teacher preparation program?

STEP 1—THINKING BEFORE TEACHING

- What will I teach (content and standards)?
- How will I teach?
- What resources will I need?
- What background knowledge do my students have?

STEP 2—THINKING DURING TEACHING

- Have I used students' prior knowledge to gain their interest and give them a focus?
- Am I presenting the lesson well?
- Am I constantly evaluating my students?
- Am I responding to the immediate needs of my students?
- Am I introducing new concepts and information?
- Am I motivating and challenging my students to pursue their own learning and investigation of the topic/subject/theme?
- Am I reviewing and debriefing with my students?
- Am I summarizing information for my students?

STEP 3—THINKING AFTER TEACHING

- Have I been self-reflective and thoughtful about my teaching?
- How did I assess the success of my students?
- How will I report students' achievements to parents?
- How will I provide feedback to my students?
- What will I do differently the next time I teach a similar lesson?

Provide Guidance

Theories help us understand how, why, where, and when learning occurs. As a result, they can guide you in developing programs for children that support and enhance their learning. For example, as we will see shortly, what Piaget believed about how children learn directly influences classroom arrangement and what is taught and how it is taught. Developing programs and curriculum is an important part of professional practice. Thus, the history of early childhood and theories about how children learn enable you to fulfill essential dimensions of your professional role. Table 3–1 summarizes the contributions of famous educators to the early childhood field. Those educators are profiled in the following section.

TABLE 3–1

CONTRIBUTIONS OF FAMOUS PEOPLE TO EARLY CHILDHOOD EDUCATION

INDIVIDUAL AND DATES	MAJOR CONTRIBUTION	INFLUENCE ON MODERN THEORISTS
Martin Luther (1483–1546)	· Translated the Bible from Latin to vernacular language, allowing people to be educated in their own language. · Advocated establishing schools to teach children how to read.	· Universal education. · Public support of education. · Teaching of reading to all children.
John A. Comenius (1592–1670)	· Wrote *Orbis Pictus,* the first picture book for children. · Thought early experiences formed what a child would be like. · Said education should occur through the senses.	· Early learning helps determine school and life success. · Sensory experiences support and promote learning.
John Locke (1632–1704)	· Said children are born as blank tablets. · Believed children's experiences determine who they are.	· Learning should begin early. · Children learn what they are taught—teachers literally make children. · It is possible to rear children to think and act as society wants them to.
Jean-Jacques Rousseau (1712–1778)	· Advocated natural approaches to child rearing. · Felt that children's natures unfold as a result of maturation according to an innate timetable.	· Natural approaches to education work best (e.g., family grouping, authentic testing, and environmental literacy).
Johann H. Pestalozzi (1746–1827)	· Advocated that education should follow the course of nature. · Believed all education is based on sensory impressions. · Promoted the idea that mother could best teach children.	· Family-centered approaches to early childhood education. · Home schooling. · Education through the senses.
Robert Owen (1771–1858)	· Held that environment determines children's beliefs, behaviors, and achievements. · Believed society can shape children's character. · Taught that education can help build a new society.	· Importance of infant programs. · Education can counteract children's poor environment. · Early childhood education can reform society.
Friedrich Froebel (1782–1852)	· Believed children develop through "unfolding." · Compared children to growing plants. · Founded the kindergarten—"Garden of Children." · Developed gifts and occupation to help young children learn.	· Teacher's role is similar to a gardener. · Children should have specific materials to learn concepts and skills. · Learning occurs through play.

FAMOUS PERSONS AND THEIR INFLUENCE ON EARLY CHILDHOOD EDUCATION

Throughout history many people have contributed to our understanding of what children are like and how to best teach them. The following accounts will help you understand the history of early childhood and theories about how to best teach children.

Martin Luther

Martin Luther (1483–1546) emphasized the necessity of establishing schools to teach children to read. Luther replaced the authority of the Catholic Church with the authority of the Bible. Luther believed that individuals were free to work out their own salvation through the Scriptures. This meant that people had to learn to read the Bible in their native tongue.

 For links to many of Martin Luther's writings online, go to the Companion Website at *http://www.prenhall.com/morrison*, select Chapter 3, then choose the Linking to Learning module.

Luther translated the Bible into German, marking the real beginning of teaching and learning in people's native language. In these ways, the Protestant Reformation encouraged and supported popular universal education and the importance of learning to read.

Today, literacy for all is a national priority. First Lady Laura Bush says that, "if our children are not able to read, they are not able to lead."[1] So, as you can see, ensuring that all children can read and be taught in their native language as Luther suggested are issues we are still dealing with today.

John Amos Comenius

John Amos Comenius (1592–1670) spent his life teaching school and writing textbooks. Two of his famous books are *The Great Didactic* and the *Orbis Pictus* ("The World in Pictures"), considered the first picture book for children.

 For more information about how John Amos Comenius contributed to the "invention of childhood," go to the Companion Website at *http://www.prenhall.com/morrison*, select Chapter 3, then choose the Linking to Learning module.

Comenius believed education should begin in the early years because "a young plant can be planted, transplanted, pruned, and bent this way or that. When it has become a tree these processes are impossible."[2] Today, new brain research reminds us again that learning should begin early and that many "windows of opportunity" for learning occur early in life.

Comenius also thought that sensory education forms the basis for all learning and that insofar as possible, everything should be taught through the senses. This approach to education was endorsed by Montessori and forms the basis for much of early childhood practice to this day.

John Locke

John Locke (1632–1704) is best known for his theory of the mind as a blank tablet, or "white paper." By this, Locke meant that environment and experience literally form the mind. According to Locke, development comes from the stimulation

For links to important works by John Locke, go to the Companion Website at *http://www.prenhall.com/morrison*, select Chapter 3, then choose the Linking to Learning module.

children receive from parents and caregivers and through experiences in their environment.

The implications of this belief are clearly reflected in modern educational practice. The notion of the importance of environmental influences is particularly evident in programs that encourage and promote early education as a means of helping children get a good foundation for learning early in life. These programs assume that differences in learning, achievement, and behavior are attributable to environmental factors such as home and family conditions, socioeconomic background, and early education and experiences. The current move toward universal schooling for three- and four-year-olds is based on the premise that getting children's education right from the beginning can help overcome negative effects of poverty and neglect and can help erase differences in children's achievement due to difference in socioeconomic levels.

Jean-Jacques Rousseau

Jean-Jacques Rousseau (1712–1778) is best remembered for his book *Émile*, the opening lines of which set the tone for his education and political views: "God makes all things good; man meddles with them and they become evil."[3] Because of this belief, Rousseau advocated the "natural" education of young children, encouraging growth without undue interference or restrictions.

For more information about Jean-Jacques Rousseau, go to the Companion Website at *http://www.prenhall.com/morrison*, select Chapter 3, then choose the Linking to Learning module.

Rousseau also believed in the idea of unfolding, in which the nature of children—who and what they will be—unfolds as a result of development according to their innate timetables. Such an approach is at the heart of developmentally appropriate practice, in which childhood educators match their educational practices to children's developmental levels and abilities. Every day you will make decisions about how to make sure what you teach and how you teach it is appropriate for each child.

Johann Heinrich Pestalozzi

Johann Heinrich Pestalozzi (1746–1827) was influenced by both Comenius and Rousseau. Pestalozzi believed all education is based on sensory impressions and that through the proper sensory experiences, children can achieve their natural potential. To achieve this goal, Pestalozzi developed "object lessons," manipulatives that encouraged activities such as counting, measuring, feeling, and touching. Pestalozzi also wrote two books— *How Gertrude Teaches Her Children* and *Book for Mothers*—to help parents teach their young children in the home. Today, enter any major bookstore (either online or in the shopping mall) and you will see shelves jammed with books on how to parent, how to teach young children, how to guide children's behavior, and many other topics. You will be able to help parents by providing them with books and/or suggestions for books to read that will help them be better parents.

For more information about Johann Heinrich Pestalozzi, go to the Companion Website at *http://www.prenhall.com/morrison*, select Chapter 3, then choose the Linking to Learning module.

Robert Owen

Robert Owen (1771–1858) believed children's environments contribute to their beliefs, behavior, and achievement just as we believe this today. He maintained that individuals and society can use environments to shape children's character. Owen was also a utopian, believing that by controlling the circumstances and consequent outcomes of child rearing, it was possible to build a new and perhaps more perfect society. Such a view of child rearing makes environmental conditions the dominant force in directing and determining human behavior.

To implement his beliefs, Owen opened an infant school in 1816 in New Lanark, Scotland, designed to provide care for about a hundred children, ages eighteen months to ten years, while their parents worked in the cotton mills he owned. This led to the opening of the first infant school in London in 1818.

Several things about Owen's efforts and accomplishments are noteworthy. First, his infant school preceded Froebel's kindergarten by about a quarter century. Second, Owen's ideas and practices influenced educators concerning the importance of early education and the relationship between educational and societal improvements, an idea much in vogue in current educational practice. In addition, early childhood professionals also seek to use education as a means of reforming society and as a way of making a better world for everyone.

Friedrich Wilhelm Froebel

Friedrich Wilhelm Froebel (1782–1852) is known as the "father of the kindergarten."

Froebel's concept of children and learning is based in part on the idea of unfolding, also held by Comenius and Pestalozzi. According to their view, the teacher's role is to observe children's natural unfolding and provide activities that enable them to learn what they are ready to learn when they are ready to learn it.

 For a bibliography and biography of Friedrich Wilhelm Froebel, go to the Companion Website at *http://www.prenhall. com/morrison*, select Chapter 3, then choose the Linking to Learning module.

Froebel compared the child to a seed that is planted, germinates, brings forth a new shoot, and grows from a young, tender plant to a mature, fruit-producing one. He likened the role of teacher to a gardener. Think for a moment how we still use the teacher as gardener metaphor to explain our role as teachers of young children. In Froebel's *kindergarten,* or "garden of children," children learn about themselves and their environment primarily through play. I will have much more to say about play in other chapters because the process of learning through play is as important today as it was in Froebel's time. The concepts of unfolding and learning through play are two of Froebel's greatest contributions to early childhood education.

Froebel also developed a systematic, planned curriculum for the education of young children based on "gifts," "occupations," songs, and educational games. Think of these as similar to the materials and toys we have today to promote children's learning. For example, we teach the alphabet and other concepts with songs, use blocks to teach size and shape, and colored rods to teach concepts of length and seriation.

Froebel believed, as early childhood professionals believe today, that play is a process through which children learn. Learning flows from play. These children are engaged in play that supports their growth and development. Froebel urged early childhood educators to support the idea that play is the cornerstone of children's learning.

Gifts were objects for children to handle and use in accordance with teachers' instructions so they could learn shape, size, color, and concepts involved in counting, measuring, contrasting, and comparison. Figure 3.2 describes Froebel's gifts. Think of some specific examples of how they relate to educational toys and materials today.

Occupations were materials designed for developing various skills through activities such as sewing with a sewing board, drawing pictures by following the dots, modeling with clay, cutting, stringing beads, weaving, drawing, pasting, and folding paper. All of these activities are part of early childhood programs today.

Froebel devoted his life to developing both a program for young children and a system of training for kindergarten teachers. Many of his ideas and activities form the basis for activities in preschools and kindergartens today.

Maria Montessori and the Montessori Theory

For more information about Maria Montessori and the Montessori method, go to the Companion Website at *http://www.prenhall.com/ morrison*, select Chapter 3, then choose the Linking to Learning module.

Maria Montessori (1870–1952) developed a system for educating young children that has greatly influenced early childhood education. The first woman in Italy to earn a medical degree, she became interested in educational solutions for problems such as deafness, paralysis, and mental retardation.

At that time she said, "I differed from my colleagues in that I instinctively felt that mental deficiency was more of an educational than medical problem."[4]

While preparing herself for educating children, Montessori was invited to organize schools for young children of families who occupied tenement houses in Rome. In the first school, named the *Casa dei*

The orginal five gifts were published by Froebel in his lifetime. The remaining gifts were used by Frobel in his kindergarten and published after his death.

Source: Winfried Müller, Johannes Frobel Parker, and Bruce Watson. Available at http://www. froebelweb.com/web7010.html Used by permission.

Solids

* **First Gift: Color**
  Six colored worsted balls, about an inch and a half in diameter.

* **Second Gift: Shape**
  Wooden ball, cylinder, and cube, one inch and a half in diameter.

* **Third Gift: Number**
  Eight one-inch cubes, forming a two-inch cube ($2 \times 2 \times 2$).

* **Fourth Gift: Extent**
  Eight brick-shaped blocks ($2 \times 1 \times 1/2$), forming a two-inch cube.

* **Fifth Gift: Symmetry**
  Twenty-seven one-inch cubes, three bisected and three quadrisected diagonally, forming a three-inch cube ($3 \times 3 \times 3$).

* **Sixth Gift: Proportion**
  Twenty-seven brick-shaped blocks, three bisected longitudinally and six bisected transversely, forming a three-inch cube.

Surfaces

* **Seventh Gift**
  * **Squares:** Derived from the faces of the second or third gift cubes; entire squares—one and a half inches square of one-inch square and half-squares, squares cut diagonally.
  * **Equilateral triangles:** Length of side one inch or one inch and a half; entire triangles, half triangles—the equilateral triangle is cut in the direction of the altitude, yielding right scalene triangles, acute angles of 60 degrees and 30 degrees and thirds of triangles, in which the equilateral triangle is cut from the center to the vertices, yielding obtuse isosceles triangles, angles 30 and 120 degrees.

Lines

* **Eighth Gift**
  * **Straight:** Splints of various lengths.

Rings

* **Ninth Gift**
  * **Circular:** Metal or paper rings of various sizes; whole circles, half circles, and quadrants.

Points

* **Tenth Gift**
  Beans, lentils, or other seeds, leaves, pebbles, pieces of cardboard or paper, etc.

Bambini, or Children's House, she tested her ideas and gained insights into children and teaching that led to the perfection of her system. Chapter 4 provides a full description of the Montessori method which is currently used in over three thousand early childhood programs.

John Dewey and Progressive Education Theory

John Dewey (1859–1952) did more than any other person to redirect the course of education in the United States, and his influence is continuous.

For more information about John Dewey, go to the Companion Website at *http://www. prenhall.com/morrison*, select Chapter 3, then choose the Linking to Learning module.

Dewey's theory of schooling, usually called *progressivism,* emphasizes children and their interests rather than subject matter. From this child-centered emphasis come the terms *child-centered curriculum* and *child-centered school,* two topics very much in the forefront of educational practice today. Dewey believed that education "is a process of living and not a preparation for future living"[5] and that daily life should be a source of activities through which children learn about life and the skills necessary for living.

In a classroom based on Dewey's ideas, children are actually involved in activities, making and using things, solving problems, and learning through social interactions. Dewey felt that an ideal way for children to express their interests was through daily life-skills activities such as cooking and through occupations such as carpentry.

Although Dewey believed the curriculum should be built on the interests of children, he also felt it was the teacher's responsibility to plan for and capitalize on opportunities to use these interests to teach traditional subject matter. This idea is the basis for the **integrated curriculum,** in which one subject area is used to teach another. For example, reading is taught in math and science, just as math and science are used to teach reading. Teachers who integrate subjects, use thematic units, and encourage problem-solving activities and critical thinking are philosophically indebted to Dewey.

John Dewey represents a dividing line between the educational past and the educational present and future. This would be a good time for you to review and reflect on Figure 3.3, a time line of the history of early childhood education.

Jean Piaget and Constructivist Learning Theory

Jean Piaget (1896–1980) studied in Paris and worked with Theodore Simon at the Alfred Binet laboratory, standardizing tests of reasoning for use with children. Piaget was interested in how humans learn and develop intellectually, beginning at birth and continuing across the life span. He devoted his life to conducting experiments, observing children (including his own), and developing and writing about his **cognitive theory** approach to learning.

1524	Martin Luther argued for public support of education for all children in his *Letter to the Mayors and Aldermen of All the Cities of Germany in Behalf of Christian Schools*.
1628	John Amos Comenius's *The Great Didactic* proclaimed the value of education for all children according to the laws of nature.
1762	Jean-Jacques Rousseau wrote *Émile*, explaining that education should take into account the child's natural growth and interests.
1801	Johann Pestalozzi wrote *How Gertrude Teaches Her Children,* emphasizing home education and learning by discovery.
1816	Robert Owen set up a nursery school in Great Britain at the New Lanark Cotton Mills, believing that early education could counteract bad influences of the home.
1817	Thomas Gallaudet founded the first residential school for the deaf in Hartford, Connecticut.
1836	William McGuffey began publishing the *Eclectic Reader* for elementary school children; his writing had a strong impact on moral and literary attitudes in the nineteenth century.
1837	Friedrich Froebel, known as the "father of the kindergarten," established the first kindergarten in Blankenburgh, Germany.
1837	Horace Mann began his job as secretary of the Massachusetts State Board of Education; he is often called the "father of the common schools" because of the role he played in helping set up the elementary school system in the United States.
1856	Mrs. Margaretha Schurz established the first kindergarten in the United States in Watertown, Wisconsin; the school was founded for children of German immigrants, and the program was conducted in German.
1860	Elizabeth Peabody opened a private kindergarten in Boston, Massachusetts, for English-speaking children.
1871	First teacher-training program for teachers of kindergarten began in Oshkosh Normal School, Oshkosh, Wisconsin.
1871	The first public kindergarten in North America was started in Ontario, Canada.
1873	Susan Blow opened the first public school kindergarten in the United States in St. Louis, Missouri, as a cooperative effort with superintendent of schools, William Harris.
1876	A model kindergarten was shown at the Philadelphia Centennial Exposition.
1884	The American Association of Elementary, Kindergarten, and Nursery School Educators was founded to serve in a consulting capacity for other educators.
1892	The International Kindergarten Union (IKU) was founded.
1896	John Dewey started the Laboratory School at the University of Chicago, basing his program on child-centered learning with an emphasis on life experiences.
1907	Maria Montessori started her first preschool in Rome called Children's House; her now-famous teaching method was based on the theory that children learn best by themselves in a properly prepared environment.
1911	Margaret and Rachel McMillan founded an open-air nursery school in Great Britain in which the class met outdoors; emphasis was on healthy living.
1915	Eva McLin started the first U.S. Montessori nursery school in New York City.
1918	The first public nursery schools were started in Great Britain.
1919	Harriet Johnson started the Nursery School of the Bureau of Educational Experiments, later to become the Bank Street College of Education.
1921	Patty Smith Hill started a progressive, laboratory nursery school at Columbia Teachers College.
1921	A. S. Neill founded Summerhill, an experimental school based on the ideas of Rousseau and Dewey.
1922	Abigail Eliot, influenced by the open-air school in Great Britain and basing her program on personal hygiene and proper behavior, started the Ruggles Street Nursery School in Boston.
1924	*Childhood Education*, the first professional journal in early childhood education, was published by the IKU.

(Continued)

∽ **FIGURE 3.3** **Time Line of the History of Early Childhood Education**

1926	The National Committee on Nursery Schools was initiated by Patty Smith Hill at Columbia Teachers College; now called the National Association for the Education of Young Children, it provides guidance and consultant services for educators.	1968	The federal government established the Handicapped Children's Early Education Program to fund model preschool programs for children with disabilities.
1926	The National Association of Nursery Education (NANE) was founded.	1971	The Stride Rite Corporation in Boston was the first to start a corporate-supported child care program.
1930	The IKU changed its name to the Association for Childhood Education.	1972	The National Home Start Program was initiated for the purpose of involving parents in their children's education.
1935	First toy-lending library, Toy Loan, was founded in Los Angeles.	1975	Public Law 94-142, the Education for All Handicapped Children Act, was passed, mandating a free and appropriate education for all children with disabilities and extending many rights to parents of such children.
1943	Kaiser Child Care Centers opened in Portland, Oregon, to provide twenty-four-hour child care for children of mothers working in war-related industries.		
1946	Dr. Benjamin Spock wrote the *Common Sense Book of Baby and Child Care*.	1980	The first American lekotek (toy-lending library) opened its doors in Evanston, Illinois.
1950	Erik Erikson published his writings on the "eight ages or stages" of personality growth and development and identified "tasks" for each stage of development; the information, known as "Personality in the Making," formed the basis for the 1950 White House Conference on Children and Youth.	1982	The Mississippi legislature established mandatory statewide public kindergartens.
		1984	The High/Scope Educational Foundation released a study that documented the value of high-quality preschool programs for poor children. This study will be cited repeatedly in coming years by those favoring expansion of Head Start and other early-years programs.
1952	Jean Piaget's *The Origins of Intelligence in Children* was published in English translation.	1985	Head Start celebrated its twentieth anniversary with a Joint Resolution of the Senate and House "reaffirming congressional support."
1957	The Soviet Union launched *Sputnik*, sparking renewed interest in other educational systems and marking the beginning of the "rediscovery" of early childhood education.	1986	The U.S. Secretary of Education proclaimed the Year of the Elementary School, saying, "Let's do all we can this year to remind this nation that the time our children spend in elementary school is crucial to everything they will do for the rest of their lives."
1960	Katherine Whiteside Taylor founded the American Council of Parent Cooperatives for those interested in exchanging ideas in preschool education; it later became the Parent Cooperative Preschools International.	1986	Public Law 99-457, the Education of the Handicapped Act Amendments, established a national policy on early intervention that recognizes its benefits, provides assistance to states for building systems of service delivery, and recognizes the unique roles of families in the development of their children with disabilities.
1964	The Economic Opportunity Act of 1964 was passed, marking the beginning of the War on Poverty and the foundation for Head Start.		
1965	The Head Start program began with federal money allocated for preschool education; the early programs were known as child development centers.	1988	Even Start was established by the U.S. Department of Education as a parent education/literacy program.
1967	The Follow Through program was initiated to extend Head Start into the primary grades.		*(Continued)*

〰 **FIGURE 3.3   Time Line of the History of Early Childhood Education (*Continued*)**

1989	The United Nations Convention on the Rights of the Child was adopted by the UN General Assembly.		pregnant women and families with infants and toddlers.
1990	The United Nations Convention on the Rights of the Child went into effect following its signing by twenty nations.	1996	The Children's Defense Fund initiated the Stand for Children Campaign.
1990	Head Start celebrated its twenty-fifth anniversary.	1999	Florida became the first state in the nation to pass a statewide school voucher plan; the law gives children in academically failing public schools a chance to attend private, secular, and religious schools with public money.
1991	Education Alternatives, Inc., a for-profit firm, opened South Pointe Elementary School in Miami, Florida, the first public school in the nation to be run by a private company.	2000	Head Start celebrated its thirty-fifth anniversary.
1991	The Carnegie Foundation issued "Ready to Learn," a plan to ensure children's readiness for school.	2000	Goals 2000 celebrated ten years.
		2001	NAEYC celebrated its seventy-fifth anniversary.
1995	Head Start Reauthorization established a new program, Early Head Start, for low-income	2001	The Leave No Child Behind Education Act provides funding for early literacy and learning to read.

∽ **FIGURE 3.3   Time Line of the History of Early Childhood Education (Continued)**

PIAGET'S COGNITIVE DEVELOPMENT THEORY.   Piaget's theory explains how individuals think, understand, and learn. Piaget believed that intelligence is the cognitive, or mental, process by which children acquire knowledge. *Intelligence* is "to know" and involves the use of *mental operations* developed as a result of acting mentally and physically in and on the environment. Active involvement is basic to Piaget's theory that children develop intelligence through direct hands-on experiences with the physical world. These hands-on experiences provide the foundations for a "minds-on" ability to think and learn.

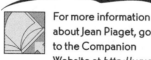

For more information about Jean Piaget, go to the Companion Website at *http://www. prenhall.com/morrison*, select Chapter 3, then choose the Linking to Learning module.

Piaget also thought intelligence has a biological basis. All organisms, including humans, adapt to their environments. For example, in the process of physical adaptation, individuals react and adjust to their environments. Piaget applied the concept of adaptation to the mental level, using it to explain how children change their thinking and grow cognitively as a result of encounters with parents, teachers, siblings, peers, and the environment.

CONSTRUCTIVISM AND COGNITIVE DEVELOPMENT.   Piaget's theory is a *constructivist* view of development. The **constructivist process** is defined in terms of the individual's organizing, structuring, and restructuring of experience—an ongoing lifelong process—in accordance with existing schemes of thought. In turn, these very schemes become modified and enriched in the course of interaction with the physical and social world.[6]

∽ **FIGURE 3.4 Basic Concepts of Constructivism**

Constructivist theory plays an important role in early childhood education. Think about how you can apply these principles to your teaching.

* Children construct their own knowledge through collaboration with others.

* Mental and physical activity is crucial for construction of knowledge. Knowledge is built step by step through active involvement—that is, through exploring objects in the environment and through problem solving and interacting with others.

* Children construct knowledge best through experiences that are of interest and meaningful to them.

* Cognitive development is a continuous process. It begins at birth and continues across the life span.

* Active learning is an important part of constructivism. Active learning means children are actively involved with a variety of manipulative materials in problem-solving activities.

Children, through activity and interaction with others, continuously organize, structure, and restructure experiences in relation to existing *schemes,* or mental images, of thought. As a result, children build their own intelligence. Review Figure 3.4 which lists key concepts of constructivism and consider how you can apply these ideas to your teaching.

COGNITIVE DEVELOPMENT AND ADAPTATION   According to Piaget, the adaptive process at the intellectual level operates much the same as at the physical level. The newborn's intelligence is expressed through reflexive motor actions such as sucking, grasping, head turning, and swallowing. Early in life, reflexive actions enable children to adapt to the environment and their intelligence develops.

For more information about constructivism, go to the Companion Website at *http://www.prenhall.com/morrison,* select Chapter 3, then choose the Linking to Learning module.

Through interaction with the environment, children organize sensations and experiences and grow mentally. Obviously, therefore, the quality of the environment and the nature of children's experiences play a major role in the development of intelligence. For example, José, with various and differing objects available to grasp and suck, and many opportunities for this behavior, will develop differentiated sucking organizations (and therefore an intelligence) quite different from that of Midori, who has nothing to suck but a pacifier. Consequently, one of your roles is to provide enriched environments for young children and work with parents to provide rich home learning environments.

Piaget believed that the opportunity to be physically and mentally involved in learning is necessary to mental development in the early years. What are some examples of how children's active involvement contributes to their learning?

LEARNING AS THE ADAPTATION OF MENTAL CONSTRUCTS. *Assimilation.* Piaget believed that adaptation is composed of two interrelated processes, assimilation and accommodation. *Assimilation* is the taking in of sensory data through experiences and impressions and incorporating them into existing knowledge. Through assimilation, children use old methods or experiences to understand and make sense of new information and experiences. In other words, children use their experiences and what they have learned from them to use as a basis for learning more. This is why quality learning experiences are so important. All experiences are not equal. Out of all the possible learning experiences you could provide, make sure the ones you select have the highest potential to promote learning.

Accommodation.   *Accommodation* is the process involved in changing old methods and adjusting to new situations. Robbie has several cats at home. When he sees a dog for the first time, he may call it a kitty. He has assimilated dog into his organization of kitty. However, Robbie must change (accommodate) his model of what constitutes "kittyness" to exclude dogs. He does this by starting to construct or build a scheme for dogs and thus what "dogness" represents.[7]

The processes of assimilation and accommodation, functioning together, constitute *adaptation.*

Equilibrium.   Equilibrium is another part of Piaget's theory of intelligence. Equilibrium is a balance between assimilation and accommodation. Diagrammed, the role of equilibrium in the constructivist process looks something like Figure 3.5.

Upon receiving new sensory and experiential data, children assimilate, or fit, these data into their already existing knowledge (scheme) of reality and the world. If the new data can be immediately assimilated, then equilibrium occurs. If unable to assimilate the data, children try to accommodate and change their

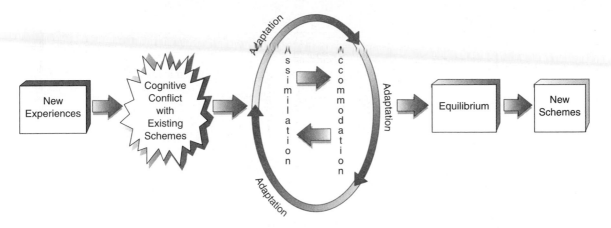

Intellectual functioning involves the mental changing of existing ideas, information, and knowledge to fit with new ideas and information as a result of experiences with people, places, and things.

FIGURE 3.5   The Constructivist Process

way of thinking, acting, and perceiving to account for the new data and restore the equilibrium to the intellectual system. It may well be that Robbie can neither assimilate nor accommodate the new data; if so, he rejects the data entirely.

Rejection of new information is common if experiences and ideas children are trying to assimilate and accommodate are too different from their past experiences and their level of knowledge and understanding. This partially accounts for Piaget's insistence that new experiences must have some connection or relationship to previous experiences. Child care and classroom experiences should build on previous life and school experiences.

Schemes.   Piaget used the term *scheme* to refer to units of knowledge that children develop through adaptation. Piaget believed that in the process of developing new schemes, physical activity is very important. Physical activity leads to mental stimulus, which in turn leads to mental activity—our hands-on minds-on concept. Thus, it is not possible to draw a clear line between physical activity and mental activity in infancy and early childhood. Teachers and parents should provide classrooms and homes that support active learning by enabling all children to explore and interact with people and objects in meaningful ways.

STAGES OF INTELLECTUAL DEVELOPMENT.   Figure 3.6 summarizes Piaget's developmental stages and provides examples of stage-related characteristics. As you review these now, keep in mind that Piaget contended developmental stages are the same for all children and that all children progress through each stage in the same order. The ages identified with each stage are only approximate and are not fixed. The sequence of growth through the developmental stages does *not* vary; the ages at which progression occurs *do* vary.

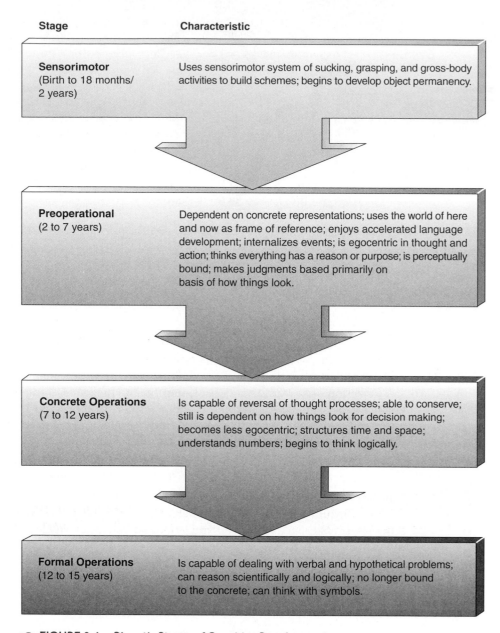

Stage	Characteristic
Sensorimotor (Birth to 18 months/ 2 years)	Uses sensorimotor system of sucking, grasping, and gross-body activities to build schemes; begins to develop object permanency.
Preoperational (2 to 7 years)	Dependent on concrete representations; uses the world of here and now as frame of reference; enjoys accelerated language development; internalizes events; is egocentric in thought and action; thinks everything has a reason or purpose; is perceptually bound; makes judgments based primarily on basis of how things look.
Concrete Operations (7 to 12 years)	Is capable of reversal of thought processes; able to conserve; still is dependent on how things look for decision making; becomes less egocentric; structures time and space; understands numbers; begins to think logically.
Formal Operations (12 to 15 years)	Is capable of dealing with verbal and hypothetical problems; can reason scientifically and logically; no longer bound to the concrete; can think with symbols.

☞ **FIGURE 3.6   Piaget's Stages of Cognitive Development**

For more information about child development, go to the Companion Website at *http://www.prenhall.com/morrison*, select any chapter, then choose Topic 2 of the ECE Supersite module.

Sensorimotor Stage. The sensorimotor stage is the first of Piaget's stages of cognitive development. When children use their primarily reflexive actions to develop intellectually, they are in the *sensorimotor stage*. During this period from birth to about two years, children use their senses and motor reflexes to build knowledge of the world. They use their eyes to see, mouths to suck, and hands to grasp. These reflexive actions help children construct a mental scheme of what is suckable and what is not (what can fit into the mouth and what cannot) and what sensations (warm and cold) occur by sucking. Children also use the grasping reflex in much the same way to build schemes of what can and cannot be grasped. Through these innate sensory and reflexive actions, they continue to develop an increasingly complex, unique, and individualized hierarchy of schemes about their world. What children are to become physically and intellectually is related to these sensorimotor functions and interactions. This is why it is important for professionals and others to provide quality experiences and environments for young children.

The following are characteristics of the sensorimotor period:

* Dependence on and use of innate reflexive actions which are the basic building blocks of intelligence
* Beginning development of object permanency, the understanding or awareness that objects exist even when they are not seen, heard, or touched
* Egocentricity, the mental and emotional condition in which children see themselves as the center of the world and believe that they cause many events
* Dependence on concrete representations (things) rather than symbols (words, pictures) for information
* By the end of the second year, less reliance on sensorimotor reflexive actions; beginning use of symbols for things that are not present

Preoperational Stage. The *preoperational stage,* the second stage of cognitive development, begins at two and ends at approximately seven years. Preoperational children are cognitively different from sensorimotor children in these ways:

* Rapidly accelerating language development
* Less dependence on sensorimotor actions
* Increased ability to internalize events and think by using symbols such as words to represent things

Preoperational children continue to be egocentric in many ways, expressing ideas and basing perceptions mainly on how they perceive or see things. Children learn to use symbols such as words or mental images to solve problems and think about things and people who are not present. How things look to preoperational children is the foundation for several other stage-related characteristics. First, when children look at an object that has multiple characteristics, such as a long, round, yellow pencil, they will "see" whichever of those qualities first catches their eye. Preoperational children's knowledge is based mainly on what they are able to see, simply because they do not yet have operational intelligence or the ability to think using mental images.

Second, the inability to perform operations makes it impossible for preoperational children to *conserve,* or understand that the quantity of an object does not change simply because some transformation occurs in its physical appearance. For example, show preoperational children two identical rows of checkers (see Figure 3.7). Ask whether each row has the same number of checkers. The children should answer affirmatively. Next, space out the checkers in one of the rows, and ask whether the two rows still have the same number of checkers. They may insist that more checkers are in one row "because it's longer." Children base their judgment on what they can see—namely, the spatial extension of one row beyond the other row. This example also illustrates that preoperational children are not

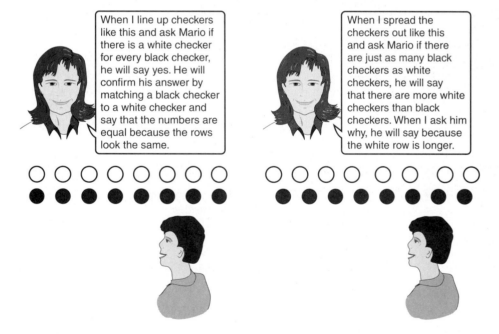

⚭ **FIGURE 3.7   Conservation in Preoperational Children**

Preoperational children's inability to perform operations makes it impossible for them to determine that the quantity of a group of objects does not change because some changes occur in how the objects look. Try this checker experiment with several children and see how they are thinking and making sense of their world based on how things look to them.

able to mentally reverse thoughts or actions, which in this case would require mentally putting the "longer" row back to its original length.

Preoperational children believe and act as though everything happens for a specific reason or purpose. This explains their constant and recurring questions about why things happen and how things work.

Preoperational children also believe everyone thinks as they think and acts as they do for the same reasons, and for this reason preoperational children have a hard time putting themselves in another's place. This helps explain why it is difficult for them to be sympathetic and empathetic.

Young children's egocentrism also helps explain why they tend to talk at each other rather than with each other. This dialogue between two children playing at a day care center illustrates one example of egocentrism:

Carmen:	My mommy's going to take me shopping.
Mia:	I'm going to dress this doll.
Carmen:	If I'm good, I'm going to get an ice cream cone.
Mia:	I'm going to put this dress on her.

The point is that egocentrism is a fact of cognitive development in the early childhood years. Developmentally appropriate practice means you will take this into account as you teach.

Concrete Operations Stage. **Concrete operations** is the third stage of operational or logical thought. Piaget defined an **operation** as an action that can be carried out in thought and in direct experiences and that is mentally and physically reversible. The concrete operations stage is often referred as the "hands-on" period of cognitive development because the ability to reason is based on tangible objects and real experiences.

Children in the *concrete operations stage,* from about age seven to about age twelve, can reverse mental operations. For example, operational children know that the amount of water in a container does not change when it is poured into a different shaped container. They can mentally reverse the operation.

You can encourage the development of mental processes during this stage through the use of concrete or real objects when talking about and explaining concepts. For example, instead of just giving the children a basket of beads to play with, ask them to sort the beads into a red group, a blue group, a yellow group, and a green group.

Concrete operational children begin to develop the ability to understand that change involving physical appearances does not necessarily change quality or quantity. They also begin to reverse thought processes, by going back over and "undoing" a mental action just accomplished.

The process of development from one cognitive stage to another is gradual and continual and occurs over a period of time as a result of maturation and experiences. No simple set of exercises will cause children to move up the developmental ladder. Rather, ongoing developmentally appropriate activities lead to conceptual understanding.

Formal Operations Stage.   The fourth stage of cognitive development and the second part of operational intelligence is **formal operations.** The *formal operations stage* begins at about twelve years of age and extends to about fifteen years. During this stage, children become capable of dealing with increasingly complex verbal and hypothetical problems and are less dependent on concrete objects. Children also develop the ability to reason scientifically and more logically.

Lev Vygotsky and Sociocultural Theory

For a bibliography of additional readings about Lev Vygotsky, go to the Companion Website at *http://www.prenhall.com/morrison,* select Chapter 3, then choose the Linking to Learning module.

Lev Vygotsky (1896–1934), a contemporary of Piaget, increasingly plays an influential role in how early childhood professionals teach.

Vygotsky's theory is a **sociocultural** theory because children's mental, language, and social development is supported and enhanced through social interactions with others. For Vygotsky, cognitive and social development is supported by social interactions, especially the interpersonal interactions among children, older peers, and adults. "Learning awakens a variety of developmental processes that are able to operate only when the child is interacting with people in his environment and in collaboration with his peers."[8]

For early childhood professionals, one of Vygotsky's most important concepts is that of the **zone of proximal development,** which he describes as

> that area of development into which a child can be led in the course of interaction with a more competent partner, either adult or peer. [It] is not some clear-cut space that exists independently of the process of joint activity itself. Rather, it is the difference between what the child can accomplish independ-

The zone of proximal development is the mental and social state of concept development and learning in which children are about to "go beyond" and achieve at higher levels with the assistance of more competent "others." In this way, learning and development are very social processes.

ently and what he or she can achieve in conjunction with another, more competent person. The zone is thus created in the course of social interaction.[9]

To summarize, the zone of proximal development (ZPD) represents the range of tasks that children cannot do independently but can do when helped by a more competent person—teacher, child, or other adult. Tasks below the ZPD, children can learn independently. Tasks, concepts, ideas, and information above the ZPD, children are not yet able to learn, even with help.

Vygotsky also believed communication or dialogue between teacher and child is very important and literally becomes a means for helping children *scaffold*, or develop new concepts and think their way to higher level concepts. **Scaffolding** is assistance of some kind that enables children to complete tasks they cannot complete independently. Figure 3.8 shows an example of a teacher providing instructional assistance of scaffolding with a child during a literacy lesson. When adults "assist" toddlers in learning to walk they are scaffolding from not being able to walk to being able to walk.

Many current instructional practices such as cooperative learning, joint problem solving, coaching, collaboration, mentoring, and other forms of assisted learning are based on Vygotsky's theory of development and learning.

Abraham Maslow and Self-Actualization Theory

Abraham Maslow (1890–1970) developed a theory of motivation called **self-actualization** based on the satisfaction of human needs. Maslow identified self-actualization, or self-fulfillment, as the highest human need but that children and adults don't achieve self-actualization until basic needs are satisfied. These basic needs include life essentials such as food, safety, and security; belongingness and love; achievement and prestige; and aesthetic needs. Everyone has these basic needs regardless of sexual orientation, race, gender, socioeconomic status, or age. Satisfaction of basic needs is essential for individuals to function well and to achieve all they are capable of achieving. We know that without air, water, or food, a child would die. We also know from basic brain research that water is essential for the proper functioning of the brain. Many teachers encourage their children to drink water as a means of ensuring that their brains have enough water to function well. The same applies to food. We know that when children are hungry they perform poorly in school. Children who begin school without eating breakfast don't achieve as well as they should and experience difficulty concentrating on their school activities. This explains why many early childhood programs provide children with breakfast, lunch, and snacks throughout the day.

Safety and security needs play an important role in children's lives. When children think that their teachers do not like them or are fearful of what their teachers say and how they treat them, they are deprived of a basic need. As a consequence, they do not do well in school and become fearful in their relationships with others. In addition, classrooms that have routines and predictableness provide children with a sense of safety and security.

For more information about Abraham Maslow's concept of self-actualization, go to the Companion Website at *http://www.prenhall.com/morrison*, select Chapter 3, then choose the Linking to Learning module.

10. Would any of you like to ask…

9. Hmm. I'm not sure I understand. Can you tell us exactly what happened?

8. I'll bet you mixed the ingredients together. Am I right?

7. How did you bake the cake?

6. What kind of cake was it?

5. Yes I see that you were behind your house patio, and it was a beautiful sunny day. What were you all doing?

4. Where were you when this was taken?

3. Who is that in the picture?

2. Can you tell us what is happening here?

1. Can you tell us a story about your photo?

FIGURE 3.8   The Scaffolding Process: Scaffolding Children's Language Development

Assistance in the zone of proximal development (ZPD) is called *scaffolding* and is a major component of teaching. Through scaffolding, the teacher guides and supports children's language learning by building on what they are already able to do, moving them to a higher level of language use. Take a few minutes to write a scaffolding script based on a favorite children's book.

Source: Text from *Implementing the Prekindergarten Curriculum Guidelines—Part I: Language Development.* Austin, TX: Texas Education Agency. Used with permission from the Texas Center for Reading and Language Development.

Children need to be loved and feel that they "belong" within their home and school in order to thrive and develop. All children have affectional needs that teachers can satisfy through smiles, hugs, eye contact, and nearness. For example, in my work with three- and four-year-old children, many want to sit close to me and want me to put my arms around them. They seek love and look to me and their teachers to satisfy this basic need.

Recognition and approval are self-esteem needs that relate to success and accomplishment. Children who are independent and responsible, and who achieve well have high self-esteem. Today, many educators are concerned about how to enhance children's self-esteem. A key way to achieve this goal is through increasing achievement.

Children like and appreciate beauty. They like to be in classrooms and homes that are physically attractive and pleasant. As an early childhood professional, you can satisfy aesthetic needs by being well-dressed and providing a classroom that is pleasant to be in by including plants and flowers, art, and music.

When children have these basic needs met they become self-actualized. They have a sense of satisfaction, are enthusiastic, and are eager to learn. They want to engage in activities that will lead to higher levels of learning. Figure 3.9 outlines

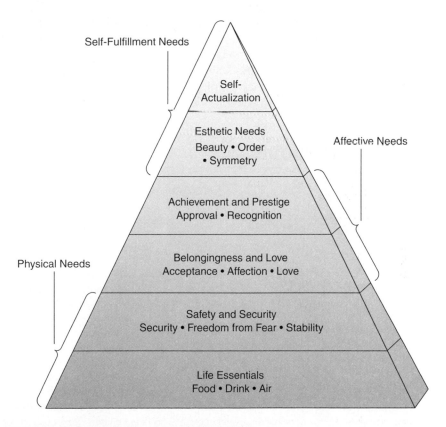

☞ **FIGURE 3.9   Maslow's Hierarchy of Human Needs**

Source: Maslow's hierarchy of human needs data from Motivation and Personality, 3rd ed. by Abraham H. Maslow. Revised by Robert Frager et al. Copyright © 1954, 1987 by Harper & Row, Publishers, Inc. Copyright © 1970 by Abraham H. Maslow. Reprinted by permission of Addison-Wesley Educational Publishers, Inc.

Maslow's Hierarchy of Needs. As you review these basic needs, think about how you can help children meet each of them.

Erik Erikson and Psychosocial Theory

Erik H. Erikson (1902–1994) developed his theory of **psychosocial development,** based on the premise that cognitive and social development occur hand in hand and cannot be separated. According to Erikson, children's personalities and social skills grow and develop within the context of society and in response to society's demands, expectations, values, and social institutions such as families, schools, and child care programs. Adults, especially parents and teachers, are key parts of these environments and therefore play a powerful role in helping or hindering children in their personality and cognitive development. For example, school-age children must deal with demands to learn new skills or risk a sense of incompetence, or a crisis of "industry"—the ability to do, be involved, be competent, and achieve—versus "inferiority"—marked by failure and feelings of incompetence. Many of the cases of school violence in the news today are caused in part by children who feel inferior and unappreciated and who lack the social skills for getting along with their classmates. Table 3–2 outlines the stages of psychosocial development according to Erikson, while the "Video Viewpoint" discusses emotional IQ.

Video Viewpoint

EMOTIONAL IQ

Researchers are now saying that the verbal intelligence of young children is not the only indicator of future success. Determining the emotional intelligence of people—including their reactions when they are angry, their ability to read others' nonverbal cues, and their self-control—may better identify individuals who can adapt to societal pressures and the demands of the workplace. Parents and early childhood professionals can play a role in helping children develop healthy emotional attitudes.

REFLECTIVE DISCUSSION QUESTIONS

Write down several examples of emotional intelligence. Give some examples of your personal emotional intelligence and how you manifest such emotions. How would you explain emotional intelligence to a parent? Why is impulse control so important in children's lives?

REFLECTIVE DECISION MAKING

How can you as an early childhood professional teach students about a healthy emotional intelligence? Give some examples of how you can role-play to demonstrate such emotions. What social skills can you help students learn to increase their emotional intelligence? What can you do to help children develop impulse control? Why is impulse control so important for success in life? What are some consequences of not being able to delay gratification and not being able to exercise impulse control? As an early childhood professional, how can you help children control their anger? Make a list of children's books and other materials that you could use to help children "read other children's emotions." What are some things that you can do to be your students' emotional tutor?

TABLE 3–2

ERIKSON'S STAGES OF PSYCHOSOCIAL DEVELOPMENT IN EARLY CHILDHOOD

Developmental Challenge	Approximate Ages	Characteristics	Role of Early Childhood Educators	Positive Outcome for Child
Basic trust vs. mistrust	Birth to 18 months or 2 years	Infants learn either to trust or mistrust that others will care for their basic needs, including nourishment, sucking, warmth, cleanliness, and physical contact.	Meet children's needs with consistency and continuity.	Views the world as safe and dependable
Autonomy vs. shame	18 months to 3 years	Toddlers learn to be self-sufficient or to doubt their abilities such as toileting, feeding, walking, and talking.	Encourage children to do what they are capable of doing; avoid shaming any behavior.	Learns independence and competence
Initiative vs. guilt	3 to 5 years (to beginning of school)	Children are learning and want to undertake many adult-like activities, sometimes overstepping the limits set by parents and thus feeling guilty.	Encourage children to engage in many activities; provide environment in which children can explore; promote language development.	Able to undertake a task, be active and involved
Industry vs. inferiority	Elementary	Children actively and busily learn to be competent and productive or feel inferior and unable to do things well.	Help children win recognition by producing things; recognition results from achievement and success.	Feelings of self-worth and industry

Howard Gardner and Multiple Intelligence Theory

Howard Gardner (b. 1943) has played an important role in helping educators re-think the concept of intelligence. Rather than relying on a single definition of intelligence, Gardner's philosophy of **multiple intelligences** suggests that people can be "smart" in many ways.

Gardner has identified nine intelligences: visual spatial, verbal/linguistic, mathematical/logical, bodily/kinesthetic, musical/rythmic, intrapersonal, interpersonal,

According to Gardner's theory of multiple intelligences, children demonstrate many types of intelligences. How would you apply his theory in the early childhood environment?

For more information about Howard Gardner's ideas, go to the Companion Website at *http://www.prenhall.com/morrison*, select any chapter, then choose Topic 3 of the ECE Supersite module.

naturalistic, and existentialist. Gardner's view of intelligence and its multiple components has and will undoubtedly continue to influence educational thought and practice. Review Figure 3.10 to learn more about these nine intelligences and their implications for teaching and learning.

E. D. Hirsch and Cultural Literacy Theory

E. D. Hirsch, Jr. (b. 1928), professor of English at the University of Virginia, is the contemporary articulator and proponent of cultural literacy. Hirsch outlined his essentialist position in his manifesto, *Cultural Literacy: What Every American Needs to Know.* According to Hirsch, **cultural literacy** is a knowledge of the facts and ideas that make up the "common core" of knowledge that forms the basis of American civilization and culture. In other words, everyone should be culturally literate and children should be schooled in the names, dates, places, and events that are significant to our nation's past and present. The "Professionalism in Practice" on page 86 shares an example of children building their cultural literacy.

Hirsch believes the lack of cultural literacy curriculum contributes to children's general failure and poor school performance. He maintains, for example, that one reason children don't read with comprehension and understanding is because they have a limited cultural background—what Hirsch calls "cultural currency"—necessary to understand what they read.

Hirsch is representative of a group who, since the 1980s, has led a revival in basic education. Many school districts and individual schools teach a core knowledge curriculum.

Visual/Spatial	Children who learn best visually and who organize things spatially. They like to see what you are talking about in order to understand. They enjoy charts, graphs, maps, tables, illustrations, art, puzzles, costumes—anything eye catching.
Verbal/Linguistic	Children who demonstrate strength in the language arts: speaking, writing, reading, listening. These students have always been successful in traditional classrooms because their intelligence lends itself to traditional teaching.
Mathematical/Logical	Children who display an aptitude for numbers, reasoning and problem solving. This is the other half of children who typically do well in traditional classrooms where teaching is logically sequenced and students are asked to conform.
Bodily/Kinesthetic	Children who experience learning best through activity: games, movement, hands-on tasks, building. These children were often labeled "overly active" in traditional classrooms where they were told to sit and be still!
Musical/Rhythmic	Children who learn well through songs, patterns, rhythms, instruments, and musical expression. It is easy to overlook children with this intelligence in traditional education.
Intrapersonal	Children who are especially in touch with their own feelings, values, and ideas. They may tend to be more reserved, but they are actually quite intuitive about what they learn and how it relates to themselves.
Interpersonal	Children who are noticeably people oriented and outgoing, and do their learning cooperatively in groups or with a partner. These children may have typically been identified as "talkative" or "too concerned about being social" in a traditional setting.
Naturalist	Children who love the outdoors, animals, and field trips. More than this, though, these students love to pick up on subtle differences in meaning. The traditional classroom has not been accommodating to these children.
Existentialist	Children who learn in the context of where humankind stands in the "big picture" of existence. They ask "Why are we here?" and "What is our role in the world?" This intelligence is seen in the discipline of philosophy.

∽ **FIGURE 3.10   Gardner's Nine Intelligences**

Howard Gardner has identified these nine intelligences. They help teachers understand how children learn differently and how to teach children according to their varying intelligences.

Source: Reprinted with permission from Walter McKenzie, Multiple Intelligences Overview.

Professionalism in Practice

AN "EDUCATIONAL HISTORY" LESSON

Laura Bilbro-Berry
North Carolina Teacher of the Year 2001

When I think about the history of the teaching profession and how I have integrated it into my teaching, I remember an occasion when I shared with my students the delightful picture book, *My Great Aunt Arizona,* by Gloria Houston. The book's main character is a teacher who inspired children in the days of the one-room schoolhouse. The illustrations by Susan Condie Lamb that accompany the text clearly depict daily classroom life in the past.

While reading the story to my second grade students, I turned the page to a description and illustration of an actual one-room class. When I read that the teacher taught children from multiple grade levels at the same time, my students were amazed. One child said, "You mean the teacher taught every grade all the time. Boy! I bet she was tired." I agreed that teacher, indeed, would have had a hard time teaching the younger and older children simultaneously.

Another child commented on the illustration of the classroom with its orderly rows of benches: "Where are the computers and shelves of math toys and books?" I explained that computers were not yet invented and that the manipulatives we use to learn were unheard of in those days. I also explained that books were very precious because they were so expensive and scarce. A classroom would not have anywhere near the books we have in our present-day classroom. The same child exclaimed, "Well, I sure am glad that I don't have to go to a school like that! How do they learn *anything* without computers?"

All of my students agreed that our classroom today was much better than that of the past. During this discussion, one child raised his hand and wanted to know what "that black box" in the middle of the room was. I explained to him that it was a wood stove that was used to heat the classroom, and that the teacher was responsible for making sure the stove had enough wood or coal to keep the room warm. I also shared that the teacher had to make sure the room was swept up and clean every day. The child who commented couldn't believe that the teacher had to be responsible for all those things. He asked, "Where was the custodian to do all that?" I had to explain that in a one-room schoolhouse there was only the teacher and the students—no computer, no math toys, and no custodian.

I was very pleased that the children were spontaneously asking the "right" questions. Not only were they

listening and discussing an outstanding piece of literature, but also they were learning about the history of education. We were definitely enjoying a "teachable moment." I continued reading the story and sharing the illustrations. After a few pages, one student raised his hand and asked, "How come all the children are white?"

What great timing! Here was another chance for me to share about the history of schooling in the United States. I explained to my students that at the time when the story was to have taken place, African American children normally didn't go to school. If they did, they went to a separate school. My students were truly shocked. They wanted to know *why* the African American students couldn't go to the same school as white kids. As tactfully as I could, I explained that in the past some people felt that African Americans and white people should not be together anywhere.

One wonderfully outspoken student put her hands on her hips and said, "Well, that's just about the stupidest thing I've ever heard of!" The old adage "out of the mouths of babes . . ." immediately came to mind. I stopped at this point and shared with the children how much things have changed since the time in which this story was framed. I used this aspect of the story to encourage some Internet research about segregation and integration that afternoon. The group also created a Venn diagram comparing schools of the present day to schools of the past.

I certainly never imagined the direction this simple story session would take my class and me when I was preparing my lesson plan for that day. I can honestly say that this was one of the finest discussions I've ever experienced in all my years of teaching. The *knowledge* gained for both the class *and* the teacher were well worth the detour.

Laura Bilbro-Berry is a second grade teacher at John C. Tayloe Elementary, Washington, North Carolina.

 To review the Professional Development Checklist and complete a Professionalism in Practice activity, visit the Companion Website at *http://www.prenhall.com/ morrison,* select Chapter 3, then choose the Professional Development module.

Many people have influenced and changed the course of early childhood education. That process continues today. Part of your role as an early childhood professional is to stay up to date and to be open to ideas and practices.

FROM LUTHER TO HIRSCH: BASIC CONCEPTS ESSENTIAL TO GOOD EDUCATIONAL PRACTICES

As They Relate to Children

For more information about how young children learn, go to the Companion Website at *http://www.prenhall.com/morrison*, select any chapter, then choose Topic 3 of the ECE Supersite module.

* Everyone needs to learn how to read and write.
* Children learn best when they use all their senses.
* All children are capable of being educated.
* All children should be educated to the fullest extent of their abilities.
* Education should begin early in life. Today especially there is an increased emphasis on beginning education at birth.
* Children should be appropriately taught what they are ready to learn when they are ready to learn it and should be prepared for the next stage of learning.
* Learning activities should be interesting and meaningful.
* Social interactions with teachers and peers are a necessary part of development and learning.
* All children have many ways of knowing, learning, and relating to the world (see the "Program in Action" on page 88).

As They Relate to Teachers

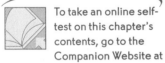

To take an online self-test on this chapter's contents, go to the Companion Website at *http://www.prenhall.com/morrison*, select Chapter 3, then choose the Self-Test module.

* Teachers should love and respect all children, have high expectations for them, and teach them to their highest capacities.
* Teachers should be dedicated to the teaching profession.
* Good teaching is based on a theory, a philosophy, goals, and objectives.
* Children's learning is enhanced through the use of concrete materials.
* Teaching should move from the concrete to the abstract.
* Observation is a key way to determine children's needs.
* Teaching should be a planned, systematic process.
* Teaching should be centered on children rather than adults or subjects.
* Teaching should be based on children's interests.
* Teachers should collaborate with children as a means of promoting development.
* Teachers should plan so they incorporate all types of intelligence in their planning and activities.

Program in Action

You don't have to be in early childhood education very long to hear a teacher say, "That boy is just sooooo active." Indeed, this statement often has a "well, what can you do" tone to it. At New City School, an independent school in St. Louis with students three years old through sixth grade, both the tone and the words are different even though we certainly have lots of active boys. Our statement, "That's a very bodily-kinesthetic" reflects our focus on Howard Gardner's multiple intelligences. We develop curriculum and look at children (and adults) from the belief that there are at least nine intelligences; bodily-kinesthetic, spatial, logical-mathematical, musical, linguistic, naturalistic, intrapersonal and interpersonal and existentialist. We believe children (and adults!) have strengths in all of these areas. We work to support children's growth in using their strengths and in understanding their particular strengths and those of others.

When New City teachers and administrators started working with Howard Gardner's multiple intelligences model about ten years ago, we quickly agreed that our preschool program had the fewest changes to make in order to reflect the multiple intelligences. Indeed, preschool programs in general with their use of centers and choice time have traditionally given children many opportunities to explore and create. Puzzle areas and art centers offer spatial choices; pretending provides many interpersonal options; games and manipulatives offer logical-mathematical, spatial, and interpersonal choices. The list is long.

How then has our program changed? Two changes come quickly to mind. First, we now have a framework with which to plan centers and assessment. Our preschool teachers use the multiple intelligences framework in planning centers and activities, checking themselves to make sure that children have opportunities to use and develop their various intelligences. Remember that b-k kid we talked about in the beginning? Rather than thinking about "containing him" with rules and time-outs, New City teachers plan centers making sure that there are bodily-kinesthetic activities available during choice time, not just at recess. Do we suddenly have an instant gym connected to our classroom? Definitely not! But, teachers now use adjacent halls and even classroom space for activities such as hopscotch, scooter boards, basketball, jump ropes and the like. Once children do activities, teachers provide parents and colleagues with as-

sessment information using the multiple intelligence framework. Parents receive information about their children through multiple page progress reports and portfolio nights; here again, the multiple intelligences focus is used in showing the children's work and sharing their progress. So, the parents of that child with strong bodily-kinesthetic intelligence learn that their child often chooses b-k related activities and that teachers use that bodily-kinesthetic strength in helping the child learn other things. Thus that child might practice counting while jumping rope or shooting baskets or learn letters by throwing bean bags at alphabet squares.

Secondly, we put a strong emphasis on the personal intelligences, intrapersonal, knowing yourself, and interpersonal, knowing how to work and play with others. Believing strongly that these talents can be developed just as a musical or linguistic talent, New City teachers have developed activities and assessment techniques to support growth in the personal intelligences. In our 4/5s classrooms, for example, teachers regularly schedule "Buddy Days" during choice time. On a Buddy Day, children are paired up by the teachers and must then work together to choose activities for the morning. Teachers model, problem solve, comfort, and support children as they learn to express their interests and accept the interests of their partners. Over the school year, these children learn to listen, negotiate, delay gratification, and solve problems with a variety of peers. Parents recognize the importance we place on the personal when they read our progress reports, where the first page is devoted entirely to the personal intelligences with assessment topics ranging from teamwork and appreciation for diversity to motivation and problem solving.

The multiple intelligences framework has allowed us to further develop an early childhood program where all of the intelligences of the children are appreciated.

Contributed by Barbara James Thompson, New City School, St. Louis, Missouri.

 To complete a Program in Action activity, visit the Companion Website at *http://www.prenhall.com/morrison*, select Chapter 3, then choose the Programs in Action module.

As They Relate to Parents

* The family is the most important institution in children's education and development. The family lays the foundation for all future education and learning.
* Parents are their children's primary educators; they are their children's first teachers. However, parents need help, education, and support to achieve this goal.
* Parents must guide and direct young children's learning.
* Parents should be involved in every educational program their children are involved in.
* Everyone should have knowledge of and training for child rearing.
* Parents and other family members are collaborators in children's learning.
* Parents must encourage and support their children's many interests and their unique ways of learning (see the "Technology Tie-In").

Technology Tie-In

FROM MOZART TO MONTESSORI: TEACHING THE FINE ARTS TO CHILDREN

Since the beginning of the recorded history of early childhood education, music and the arts have had an important place in the education of young children. Educators have supported children's involvement in music and the arts in three ways: appreciation, performance, and creation. You and I may not agree on the kind of music and art we like, but one thing is certain: We all like music and the arts of some kind, and they all affect us in some way. The same is true for children. I have not met a child who does not like to sing, dance, paint, and create.

Aristotle believed that art and drama were good for people because through them they were able to work out their emotions vicariously and as a result be calmer and better persons. Maria Montessori believed that children should be involved in learning about art and artists. Art appreciation is part of the Montessori curriculum and many Montessori classrooms have paintings by famous artists on display. We have read in this chapter about the high value Abraham Maslow places on creativity and the importance of creating aesthetically pleasing classrooms for young children. Some early childhood programs pro-

vide keyboard lessons and experiences for all children based on the link some research shows between learning music and high academic achievement. You can involve your children in music and the arts in many ways as appreciators, performers, and creators. All early childhood programs should involve all children in the arts. The following software suggestions are just one avenue you can use to encourage and support your children's fine arts skills.

Curious George Paint & Print Studio (Ages 4–9), Sunburst Technology

Draw & Paint Plus (Ages 4–9), Forest Technologies

JumpStart Music (Ages 5–8), Knowledge Adventure

Kid Work Deluxe (Ages 4–9), Knowledge Adventure

 To locate the resources on the Internet and to complete a technology activity, go to the Companion Website at
http://www.prenhall.com/morrison, select Chapter 3, then choose the Technology Tie-In module.

Throughout history all great educators have had a vision about what is best for young children and their families. Great educators are passionate about what they believe about children and how to best teach them what they need to know to be productive and involved citizens. The same is true today. Many educators, professional organizations, and politicians are passionately advocating for what they think are worthy goals and the best practices to achieve these goals. The Children's Defense Fund, a child advocacy organization, and President Bush both advocate that "No child should be left behind." But how to do this is at the heart of many educational debates today. As a practicing professional you will be involved in these debates. You will be asked to identify ideas and theories that will help all children be successful in school and life. Knowing the history of your profession and the theories that guide approaches to education will help you in this critical part of your professional practice. See Table 3–3 for a summary of these theories.

TABLE 3–3
LEARNING THEORIES THAT INFLUENCE EARLY CHILDHOOD EDUCATION

INDIVIDUAL AND DATES	MAJOR CONTRIBUTIONS	INFLUENCES ON MODERN EDUCATION
Maria Montessori (1870–1952)	· The Montessori Method for educating young children. · Learning materials to meet the needs of young children. · Sensory-based materials that are self-correcting. · Prepared environments are essential for learning. · Respect for children is the foundation of teaching.	· Large number of public and private Montessori schools that emphasize her approach, methods, and materials. · Renewed emphasis on preparing environment to support and promote children's learning. · Teacher training programs to train Montessori teachers.
John Dewey (1859–1952)	· Progressive education movement. · Children's interests form the basis of the curriculum. · Educate children for today—not tomorrow.	· Child-centered education. · Curriculum based on children's interests. · Discovery learning.
Jean Piaget (1896–1980)	· Theory of cognitive development based on ages and stages. · Children are "little scientists" and literally develop their own intelligence. · Mental and physical activities are important for cognitive development.	· Constructivist approaches to early childhood education. · Matching education to children's stages of cognitive development. · Active involvement of children in learning activities. · Project approach to learning.

(Continued)

Individual and Dates	Major Contributions	Influences on Modern Education
Lev Vygotsky (1896–1934)	· Sociocultural theory, which emphasizes importance of interpersonal relationships in social and cognitive development. · Concept of zone of proximal development—children can learn more with the help of a more competent person. · Communication between teachers and children can act as a means of scaffolding to higher levels of learning.	· Use of scaffolding techniques to help children learn. · Use of cooperative learning and other forms of social learning.
Abraham Maslow (1890–1970)	· Theory of self-actualization based on needs motivation. · Human development is a process of meeting basic needs throughout life. · Humanistic psychology.	· Importance of meeting basic needs before cognitive learning can occur. · Teachers develop programs to meet children's basic needs. · Growth of the self-esteem movement. · Emphasis on providing safety, security, love, and affection for all children.
Erik Erikson (1902–1994)	· Theory of psychosocial development—cognitive development occurs in conjunction with social development. · Life is a series of eight stages with each stage representing a critical period in social development. · How parents and teachers interact with and care for children helps determine their emotional and cognitive development.	· Play supports children's social and cognitive development. · The emotional plays as great a role as the cognitive in development. · All children need predictable, consistent, love, care, and education.
Howard Gardner (b. 1943)	· Theory of multiple intelligences. · Intelligence consists of nine abilities. · Intelligence is not a single broad ability, rather a set of abilities.	· Teachers develop programs and curricula to match children's particular intelligences. · Teacher individualizes curricula and approaches to children's intelligences. · More awareness and attention to multiple ways in which children learn and think.
E. D. Hirsch (b. 1928)	· Cultural literacy approach to education. · All children must have "a common cultural core" in order to be successful in school. · Cultural literacy curriculum.	· Increased emphasis on the "basics" and basic education. · Use of a core curriculum that emphasizes basic knowledge. · Emphasis on teacher-directed activities.

ACTIVITIES FOR PROFESSIONAL DEVELOPMENT

In this chapter we have stressed the importance of how the history of early childhood and theories of learning are foundational to your professional practice. Refer again to the "Professional Development Goals" at the beginning of the chapter, to the "Professional Development Checklist" on pages 20 and 21, and the educational history lesson of Laura Bilbro-Berry on page 86. After you have reviewed these, complete the following activities.

1. From John Dewey to the present, early childhood professionals have used children's interests as a basis for developing learning activities. In addition to being a good source of learning experiences, interests can also provide opportunities to develop skills and teach important information.

   a. Talk with some young children about what they like to do, their favorite activities, favorite television programs, and so on. Select several of these "interests" and plan three learning experiences you can use to teach skills related to literacy, math, and science.

   b. Do you think it is possible to base your entire curriculum and teaching activities on children's interests? Why? Why not?

2. Professionals are able to state and describe the theory or theories that form the basis for their philosophy and teaching practices. They are also able to explain their chosen theory to others. Very often professionals choose an *eclectic approach,* one in which they take the best ideas from several theories and combine them into their own. Identify and describe the major points of the theory or theories that guide your teaching.

3. Throughout the history of education, great educators have been concerned with what they believed was best for children; how best to teach them; and what it is worthwhile for children to know and be able to do.

   a. Based on the ideas and practices proposed by the persons discussed in this chapter, identify the teaching practices with which you most agree. State the learning outcomes you think are appropriate for all children.

   b. Review the curriculum goals and standards for the pre-K–3 grades in your local school district. Can you find examples to support that what educators identify as important knowledge and skills are substantiated by beliefs of great educators?

4. Think for a minute what would happen if you gave six-month-old Emily some blocks. What would she try to do with them? More than likely she would put them in her mouth. She wants to eat the blocks. On the other hand, if you gave blocks to Emily's three-year-old sister Madeline, she would try to stack them. Both Emily and Madeline want to be actively involved with things and people as active learners. This active involvement comes naturally for them. Observe children in a number of early childhood settings and identify five ways they learn through active learning.

5. You have just been assigned to write a brief historical summary of the major ideas of the educational pioneers you read about in this chapter. You are limited to fifty words for each person and are to write as though you were the person. For example:

> Locke: "At birth the mind is a blank slate and experiences are important for making impressions on the mind. I believe learning occurs best through the senses. A proper education begins early in life and hands-on experiences are an important part of education."

For additional chapter resources and activities, visit the Companion Website at *http://www.prenhall.com/morrison*, select Chapter 3, then choose the Professional Development, Resources, or Linking to Learning modules.

FOCUS QUESTIONS

1. Why are models of early childhood education important?
2. What are the basic features of early childhood education models, and how are they alike and different?
3. What decisions do you need to make to select a particular early childhood program as a basis for your practice?
4. How can you apply developmentally appropriate practice to your practice of early childhood education?

chapter 4

Implementing Early Childhood Programs

APPLYING THEORIES TO PRACTICE

To review the chapter focus questions online, go to the Companion Website at *http://www.prenhall.com/ morrison* and select Chapter 4.

PROFESSIONAL DEVELOPMENT GOAL

DELIVERING EDUCATION AND CHILD CARE

I am familiar with a variety of models and approaches for delivering education and child care, and I use this knowledge to deliver education and child care in a safe, healthy learning environment.

WHAT ARE PROGRAMS OF EARLY CHILDHOOD EDUCATION?

When we talk about programs for young children, we mean the philosophy that guides teaching and learning, the theories that underlie what is taught and how children learn, and the curricula that guide the activities and experiences provided for children. Some professionals adopt a well-recognized program such as Montessori as the basis for their own school or classroom. Others use an eclectic approach in which they integrate the best from a number of programs into their own unique approach to educating young children. High-quality early childhood professionals think seriously about what they want their children to learn and be able to do and how best to achieve these goals. They make decisions based on their knowledge and understanding of various models and how the basic features of these models agree with their philosophies of teaching and learning. Today, state and local standards identify what pre-k–3 children will learn. Many programs incorporate these standards into their curriculum. Regardless of what model you or others select to use as a basis for your program, you and they have to be accountable for your children learning state and local standards.

The Growing Demand for Quality Early Childhood Programs

As of spring 2001, 7,700 early childhood programs serving a half-million children were accredited by the National Association for the Education of Young Children (NAEYC).[1] These programs are only a fraction of the total number of early childhood programs in the United States. Think for a minute about what goes on in these and other programs from day to day. For some children, teachers and staff have developed well-thought-out and articulated programs that provide for their growth and development across all the developmental domains—cognitive, linguistic, emotional, social, and physical. In other programs, children are not so fortunate. Their days are filled with aimless activities that fail to meet their academic and developmental needs. At this time, when the United States is once again discovering the importance of the early years, the public wants early childhood professionals to provide the following:

To check your understanding of this chapter with the online Study Guide, go to the Companion Website at *http://www.prenhall.com/ morrison*, select Chapter 4, then choose the Study Guide module.

* Programs that will help ensure children's early school success and that will help them succeed in school and life. The public believes that too many children are being left out and left behind.

* The inclusion of early literacy and reading readiness activities in programs and curricula that will enable children to read on grade level in grades one, two, and three.

* Programs that will help children develop the social and behavioral skills necessary to help them lead civilized and nonviolent lives. In the wake of September 11, 2001 and daily news headlines about shooting and assaults by younger and younger children, the public wants early childhood pro-

grams to assume an ever growing responsibility for helping get children off to a nonviolent start in life.

As a result, there is a growing and critical need for programs that meet these demands. As you read about and reflect on the programs in this chapter, think about their strengths and weaknesses and the ways each tries to best meet the needs of children and families. Pause for a minute and review Table 4–1, which outlines the models of early childhood education discussed in this chapter.

Child Care

Child care is a comprehensive service to children and families that supplements the care and education children receive from their families. Comprehensive child, and academic care includes custodial care such as supervision, food, shelter, and other physical necessities as well as activities and experiences to support children's social, emotional, and academic development.

For more information about child care, go to the Companion Website at *http://www. prenhall.com/morrison*, select Chapter 4, then choose the Linking to Learning module.

Child care is also educational. It provides for the children's cognitive development and helps engage them in the process of learning that begins at birth. Quality child care does not ignore the educational needs of young children but incorporates learning activities as part of the curriculum. Furthermore, child care staff work with parents to help them learn how to support children's learning in the home. A comprehensive view of child care considers the child to be a whole person; therefore, the major purpose of child care is to facilitate optimum development of the whole child and support efforts to achieve this goal.

Why Is Child Care Popular?

Child care is popular for a number of reasons. First, recent demographic changes have created a high demand for care outside the home. There are more dual-income families and more working single parents than ever before. For example, nearly 62 percent of mothers with children under age three are employed, and it is not uncommon for mothers to return to work as early as six weeks after giving birth.

Second, child care is an important part of many politicians' solutions to the nation's economic and social problems. Child care is one means of implementing public policy and addressing political and social issues. For example, providing child care for the children of parents participating in work-training programs is part of government efforts to get people off welfare and help them join the workforce.

As demand for child care increases, you and your profession must participate in advocating for and creating quality child care programs that meet the needs of children and families. In the "Professionalism in Practice" feature on page 99, Jackye Brown, Executive Director of Atlanta's Children's Shelter, discusses her commitment to helping homeless children and their families.

TABLE 4-1

MODELS OF EARLY CHILDHOOD EDUCATION: SIMILARITIES AND DIFFERENCES

PROGRAM	MAIN FEATURES	THEORETICAL BASIS
High/Scope	· Plan-do-review teaching—learning cycle · Emergent curriculum—curriculum is not established in advance · Children help determine curriculum · Key experiences guide the curriculum in promoting children's active learning	· Piagetian · Constructivist · Dewey
Reggio Emilia	· Emergent curriculum—curriculum is not established in advance · Curriculum based on children's interests and experiences · Project-oriented curriculum · Thousand Languages of Children—symbolic representation of work and learning · Active learning · *Atelierista* (teacher trained in the arts) · *Atelier* (art/design studio)	· Piagetian · Constructivist · Vygotskian · Dewey
Head Start	· Curriculum and program outcomes determined by performance standards · Broad spectrum of comprehensive services, including health, administrative support, and parent involvement · Parents play a key role in program operation · No national curriculum—curriculum developed at the local level	· Whole child · Maturationist · Intervention approach to addressing child and societal problems
Child Care	· Comprehensive services · Program quality determined by each program · Each program has its own curriculum	· Whole child · Maturationist
Montessori	· Prepared environment supports, invites, and enables learning · Children educate themselves—self-directed learning · Sensory materials invite and promote learning · Set curriculum regarding what children should learn—Montessorians try to stay as close to Montessori's ideas as possible · Multi-age grouping · Students learn by manipulative materials and working with others · Learning takes place through the senses	· Respect for children · Educating the whole child · Active learning · The absorbent mind

Programs for young children are alike in some ways and different in some ways. You can use this table to help you understand program similarities and differences and to help you make decisions about what program or features of various programs you will use in your teaching of young children.

Professionalism in Practice

MAKING HOMELESS CHILDREN FEEL AT HOME

Jackye Brown,
Executive Director, Atlanta Children's Shelter, Atlanta, Georgia

The Atlanta Children's Shelter is a private, nonprofit program accredited by NAEYC that provides a safe, caring, developmentally appropriate environment for homeless children during the day. My beliefs are grounded in my twelve years of working with children and their families. My most basic belief is that all children can learn. This core belief guides all that I do. Believing in children's ability to learn is essential, especially when you provide services for homeless children.

The children we teach and care for are from unstable situations. They don't have a home to go to every day, so our program is their home while they are here. Our environment must foster the social, emotional, physical, cognitive, and language skills that are so vital for all children, but especially for homeless children. It is critical for us to help homeless children cope with their negative experiences so they can gain a positive outlook on life, have positive experiences, and develop to their fullest potential. We really care about our children, and this commitment to caring is important because of the trauma that our children and families have undergone.

When people ask me why our program is so successful, I always respond that is because we are uncompromising about certain basic core values, including quality, advocacy, and parent and community collaboration.

No program can or should sacrifice quality for young children. One way we address the quality issue is through NAEYC accreditation. Another is through seeing how we can better use all our space so that we can provide enriched environments for young children.

We place a high value on advocacy. We want the community to know about homeless children, their needs, and the things people can do to help. Advocacy is part of the basic job description of all early childhood professionals.

Part of our ongoing strategic plan is to develop ways that we can partner and collaborate with parents and the community. Our work with parents is as important as our work with children. Parents want to see their children do well in school and life. We serve a unique population. The parents are going through a traumatic time. They are homeless and many are battered women who are fleeing a violent situation. Some people think you can just work with children, but that is only half of the equation. You have to work with parents, too. Providing services to the family unit is the heart of early childhood practice.

We must collaborate with the community because we want to increase the number of programs like ours in order to serve more homeless families and children. We need to seek partnerships. All early childhood programs, regardless of the clientele they serve, must have community partnerships to be successful.

I make a special effort to work with and nurture new teachers. It is quite an adjustment for new teachers to acclimate to our population. We need teachers who can be consistent in their approach and who won't blame parents. They have to understand parents' situations. For many, child care for their children is not a high priority at this time in their lives. They are dealing with a whole lot of other things. To put it in terms of Maslow's hierarchy of needs, basic needs come first.

I am committed to seeing homeless children grow and develop. When I am having a down day, I go to the infant room and feed a baby or read a book to a toddler and I'm fine. Helping children and families is all the reward anyone needs in life.

 To review the Professional Development Checklist and complete a Professionalism in Practice activity, visit the Companion Website at *http://www.prenhall.com/morrison*, select Chapter 4, then choose the Professional Development module.

TYPES OF CHILD CARE PROGRAMS

Child care is offered in many places, by many persons and agencies that provide a variety of care and services. The options for child care are almost endless. However, regardless of the kinds of child care provided, the three issues of quality, affordability, and accessibility always are part of the child care landscape. Table 4–2 outlines the types of child care, their purposes, and their functions. Review the eight kinds of child care and compare their similarities and differences. Reflect on why there are so many different kinds of programs. Do you think parents in the United States would be best served by only one kind of child care program?

For a table showing the Leading Child Care Management Organizations in the United States, visit the Companion Website at *http://www.prenhall.com/ morrison*, select Chapter 4, then choose the Resources module.

The "Program in Action: Bridges Family Child Care" on pages 102 and 103 will help you envision how good family day care is much more than baby-sitting. As you read, consider if you would want your child placed in this program.

What Constitutes Quality Education and Care?

Although there is much debate about the quality of child care and what it involves, we can nonetheless identify the main characteristics of quality programs. The dimensions and indicators of quality child care are outlined in Table 4–3. Of the seven dimensions of quality listed, which do you think are the most important? Which of these do you think would be easiest or most difficult to advocate for?

Family day care is the preferred method of child care. Parents like a program for their children that approximates a homelike setting. What are some characteristics of a homelike setting you can incorporate into your classroom?

TABLE 4–2
TYPES OF CHILD CARE PROGRAMS

Type of Child Care	Purpose and Function
Family and relative care	Children are cared for by grandparents, aunts, uncles, or other relatives. Child care by family members provides children with the continuity and stability parents desire for their children.
Family care/Family day care	Child care is provided in a child's own family, or in a familylike setting. An individual caregiver provides care and education for a small group of children in his or her home.
Intergenerational care	Intergenerational child care programs integrate children and the elderly into an early childhood and adult care facility. The programs blend the best of two worlds: children and the elderly both receive care and attention in a nurturing environment.
Center child care	Center child care is conducted in specially designed and constructed centers, churches, YMCAs and YWCAs, and other such facilities.
Employer-sponsored child care	The most rapidly growing segment of the workforce is married women with children under the age of one. To meet the needs of working parents, employers are providing affordable, accessible, and quality child care.
Proprietary child care	Some child care centers are being run by corporations, businesses, or individual proprietors for the purpose of making a profit. Many of these programs emphasize their educational component and appeal to middle-class families who can pay for the promised services. Providing care for the nation's children is big business.
Child care for children with medical needs	When children get sick, parents must find someone who will take care of them or they must stay home. More and more programs are providing care for children with medical needs, such as care when they have illnesses (both contagious and noncontagious), broken bones, and other health problems that keep them from attending other regular child care programs.
Before- and after-school care	In many respects, public schools are logical places for before- and after-school care. They have the administrative organization, facilities, and staff to provide such care. Many taxpayers and professionals believe that schools should not sit empty in the afternoons, evenings, holidays, and summers.

These eight types of child care programs are all popular with parents. However, many parents prefer family and relative care and like to have their children cared for in a homelike setting. For a lot of parents, however, this type of care is not available.

Program in Action

BRIDGES FAMILY CHILD CARE

Welcome to the Bridges Community! Bridges is family child care. We work to model the child care experience after our natural human experience on earth. In a time when biological families now live great distances apart, we must develop relationships that we can depend on similar to the way that families have historically depended on each other. Modeling our program after the natural human experience influences our every decision in the design of our program, such as the number of children, the quality of food, the mix of ages, and the influence of the physical child care environment. With this as our "prime directive," we have incorporated what we know as early childhood educators to create a program that encourages exploration, challenges learning, emphasizes social and emotional development, offers wholesome and nutritious food, and provides quiet, restful spaces in a homelike, ecologically sensitive environment.

Bridges Child Care is committed to families by offering ongoing communication of the child's development and family concerns; sliding-scale fees that encourage accessibility, regardless of income; and networking with others for support services such as agencies that offer parent training, social support, and special needs support. Currently one-fourth of the children enrolled are children whose parents became pregnant as teenagers. We encourage parents in their parenting skills and share with them information on what has worked successfully for other families. We also try to keep current on community support services that they may be eligible to receive.

RATIOS

Our child:adult ratios reflect our biological capabilities. We have eight children and two staff present, a similar ratio to our natural order of procreating. We believe that the low child:adult ratio is the single greatest factor in providing high-quality care. In a group setting it can be challenging to complete a learning opportunity with a child when other children may have the need for guidance at the same time. With the use of volunteers we are able to enhance our program further to offer one-on-one interactions.

ACTIVITIES

By providing an environment with a range of self-directed options, children are able to determine what skills they would like to develop and work on. Opportunities such as a "help yourself project/art table" encourage creativity, as well as develop fine motor skills. Our cozy book area is stocked with pillows for quiet small group or even alone time for book exploration. An indoor cotton yoga swing (that doesn't hurt when a child gets bumped by it and is too thick to strangle anyone) provides large motor development and is in constant use! A permanently set up drum and percussion circle encourages regular sessions in music and rhythm and is located near the dramatic play area for children to merge music, dance, and drama. We sing routinely, borrowing tunes from other songs and singing about what we are doing or the qualities of a child. We have a table for puzzles and games that has limited choices through regular equipment rotation. One area is reserved specifically for rotating themes such as setting up a hospital scene, store, post office, and such. This area is most often set up as a response to the children's interests or experiences. We also go on field trips, four to five times per week. Each morning at breakfast we share our ideas about what we could do. After the discussion of ideas we vote to determine where we'll head out for that day. We talk about street safety, and we take many opportunities to learn about the earth, animals, business, and politics, as well as doing many large-motor activities.

SELF-CARE

As the children grow they are encouraged to wash, dress, and toilet independently. The children at Bridges are encouraged to "help themselves" more and more as their skills develop. Self-care is a process: through repetitive and consistent reminders children become responsible for themselves. Self-care is evolutionary: what is an accomplishment for one child becomes an expectation for another as their skills develop.

FOOD AND NUTRITION

In an effort to ensure that the children are receiving the best nutrients and are safe from additives, hormones, and pesticides, we make a great effort to serve mostly organic, almost exclusively vegetarian and non-processed food. We are able to do this mostly because we have made it a priority, looking again at our natural experience on earth, this time in regards to food. We routinely involve the children in cooking, composting, and gardening.

SOCIAL-EMOTIONAL DEVELOPMENT

At Bridges we feel that the one "job" of children in their early years is to learn how to live in the world with others. While each child differs in skill level of communication, each child is treated with great respect by the adults and is expected to treat others with respect. The conflict we deal with is a healthy part of development and is embraced at Bridges.

INCLUSIVITY

Our program primarily serves children two to five years old. However, we make exceptions based on individual needs. Bridges alumni include children who are blind, autistic, have had cerebral palsy, and have had other physical differences. Currently we have a child with Down's syndrome who has been with us for five years, as well as a child who was born to a mother using crack.

THE ENVIRONMENT

Bridges Child Care is located in a ninety-plus-year-old home. We have built a "school" addition using natural, nontoxic materials and recycled materials, which was designed by architects who specialize in environmentally friendly building designs and built in a communal setting. The children's "program" for those years evolved around exploring the work that had been done after child care hours, observing some of the process during construction, and "helping" when it was appropriate. We set up some small activities, such as mixing clay and straw, so they could get a sense of the process. We also talked about what other animals use to make homes and made bird nests from straw and clay. We made pumpkin pies from our gardens' harvest as "thank you" gifts for some of the folks who had helped. We now have separate spaces for learning and playing, eating, and resting. Having ample space in a well-designed child care facility is like having an extra staff person because the room works for us, in a supportive and functional way!

FAIR COMPENSATION

Bridges Family Child Care is committed to paying a living wage to the employees, which includes health care for full-time staff and paid continuing education, holidays, vacation, and personal days for all the staff. We are also asking the community to help us reach our goal in attaining the sufficient resources so that every staff member may be paid not just a living wage but a professional wage.

RESOURCES

We are continually evolving and developing our program to improve our service as well as enhance the resources. However, we feel that until public policy acknowledges that the cost of child care is a part of the cost of the greater societal infrastructure and contributes to our booming economy, the stability of child care will continue to be challenged. In Wisconsin we have nearly an equal amount of licensed child care facilities open each year as we have close. Can you imagine if we operated our public school systems this way?

Visit Bridges Family Child Care on the web.

Contributed by Vic McMurray, Bridges Family Child Care director, Madison, Wisconsin.

 To visit Bridges Family Child Care on the web and complete a Program in Action activity, go to the Companion Website at *http://www.prenhall.com/morrison,* **select Chapter 4, then choose the Programs in Action module.**

TABLE 4–3
DIMENSIONS AND INDICATORS OF QUALITY CHILD CARE

DIMENSION	INDICATOR
Meets children's developmental needs	Good care and education provides for children's needs and interests at each developmental stage. For example, infants need good physical care as well as continual love and affection and sensory stimulation.
Appropriate and safe environments	At all age levels, a safe and pleasant physical setting is important. Toddlers need safe surroundings and opportunities to explore. They need caregivers who support and encourage active involvement.
Appropriate caregiver: adult ratio	NAEYC guidelines for the ratio of caregivers to children are 1:3 or 1:4 for infants, 1:3 or 1:4 for toddlers, and 1:8 to 1:10 for preschoolers, depending on group size.
Developmentally appropriate programs	A program's curriculum should specify activities for children of all ages that caregivers can use to stimulate infants, provide for the growing independence of toddlers, and address the readiness and literacy needs of four- and five-year-olds. All programs should include education to meet the social, emotional, and cognitive needs of all children.
Family education and support	Parents and other family members should know as much as possible about the program their children are enrolled in, their children's growth and development, and the curriculum program of activities.
Staff education and development	All professionals should be involved in an ongoing program of training and development. The CDA program discussed in Chapter 1 is a good beginning for staff members to become competent and maintain necessary skills.
Program accreditation	Criteria for accreditation include interactions among staff, children, and parents; administration, staff qualifications, and staffing patterns; physical environment; health and safety; nutrition and food services; and program evaluation.

Very often you hear the term "high-quality care and education." What this means, in order for it to be true, is that a program demonstrates all seven of these characteristics.

The Effects of Care and Education on Children

High-quality early care and education have influences that last over a lifetime. Children who attend high-quality programs:

* had higher cognitive test scores than other children from toddler years to age twenty-one;
* had higher academic achievement in both reading and math from the primary grades through young adulthood;

* completed more years of education and were more likely to attend a four-year college;[2]
* had above-average scores on school readiness tests and are better able to express and understand language;[3]
* scored better in receptive language ability (i.e., understanding of language);[4]
* had better language skills than children in low-quality child care;[5]
* scored better in math ability than children in low-quality care; and[6]
* were better in math in all ages, from the preschool years through second grade.

Quality child care not only provides services to children and families, but it also increases children's opportunities for success in school and life. As an early childhood professional you can play a major role in helping ensure that all child care is high quality as you educate others about and advocate for children and families.

HIGH/SCOPE: A CONSTRUCTIVIST APPROACH

The **High/Scope** Educational Approach is based on Piaget's cognitive development theory. The curriculum is geared to the child's current stage of development and promotes the constructive processes of learning and broadens the child's emerging intellectual and social skills.[8]

High/Scope has three fundamental principles:

For more information about High/Scope, go to the Companion Website at *http://www. prenhall.com/morrison*, select Chapter 4, then choose the Linking to Learning module.

* Active participation of children in choosing, organizing, and evaluating learning activities, which are undertaken with careful teacher observation and guidance in a learning environment replete with a rich variety of materials located in various classroom learning centers.
* Regular daily planning by the teaching staff in accord with a developmentally based curriculum model and careful child observations.
* Developmentally sequenced goals and materials for children based on the High/Scope "key experiences."[9]

Basic Principles and Goals of the High/Scope Approach

The High/Scope program strives to

develop in children a broad range of skills, including the problem solving, interpersonal, and communication skills that are essential for successful living in a rapidly changing society. The curriculum encourages student initiative by providing children with materials, equipment, and time to pursue activities they choose. At the same time, it provides teachers with a framework for guiding children's independent activities toward sequenced learning goals.

The teacher plays a key role in instructional activities by selecting appropriate, developmentally sequenced material and by encouraging children to adopt an active problem-solving approach to learning. . . . This teacher-student interaction—teachers helping students achieve developmentally sequenced goals while also encouraging them to set many of their own goals—uniquely distinguishes the High/Scope curriculum from direct-instruction and child-centered curricula.[10]

The High/Scope approach influences the arrangement of the classroom, the manner in which teachers interact with children, and the methods employed to assess children. Review Figure 4.1 now to see how active learning forms the hub of the "wheel of learning" and is supported by the key elements of the curriculum.

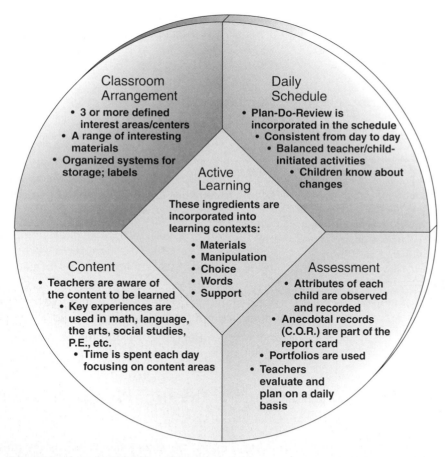

FIGURE 4.1   High/Scope Curriculum Wheel

This curriculum wheel illustrates how active learning is the case of the High/Scope program. Emphasis on active learning is one of the hallmarks of a constructivist approach to educating young children.

Source: Used with permission of David P. Weikart, president, High/Scope Educational Research Foundation, 600 N. River St., Ypsilanti, MI 48198-2898.

The Five Elements of the High/Scope Approach

Professionals who use the High/Scope curriculum are fully committed to providing settings in which children actively learn and construct their own knowledge. Teachers create the context for learning by implementing and supporting five essential elements: active learning, classroom arrangement, the daily schedule, assessment, and the curriculum (content).

For more information about the High/Scope curriculum model, go to the Companion Website at *http://www. prenhall.com/morrison*, select any chapter, then choose Topic 4 of the ECE Supersite model.

ACTIVE LEARNING.   Teachers support children's active learning by providing a variety of materials, making plans and reviewing activities with children, interacting with and carefully observing individual children, and leading small- and large-group active learning activities.

CLASSROOM ARRANGEMENT.   The classroom contains five or more interest centers that encourage choice. The classroom organization of materials and equipment supports the daily routine. Children know where to find materials and what materials they can use. This encourages development of self-direction and independence.

The teacher selects the centers and activities to use in the classroom based on several considerations:

* Interests of the children (e.g., preschool children are interested in blocks, housekeeping, and art)
* Opportunities for facilitating active involvement in seriation (e.g., big, bigger, biggest), numbers (e.g., counting), time relations (e.g., before-after), classification (e.g., likenesses and differences), spatial relations (e.g., over-under), and language development

Children can learn mathematics skills through activities that involve the manipulation of concrete objects, like blocks. What other active learning experiences can you use to help children discover principles of mathematics?

＊ Opportunities for reinforcing needed skills and concepts and functional (real-life) use of these skills and concepts

Classroom arrangement is an essential part of professional practice in order to appropriately implement a program's philosophy. This is true for Montessori, for High/Scope, and for every other program you may be involved with.

DAILY SCHEDULE.   The schedule considers developmental levels of children, incorporates a sixty- to seventy-minute plan-do-review process, provides for content areas, is as consistent throughout the day as possible, and contains a minimum number of transitions.

ASSESSMENT.   Teachers keep notes about significant behaviors, changes, statements, and things that help them better understand a child's way of thinking and learning. Teachers use two mechanisms to help them collect data: the key experiences note form and a portfolio. In addition, teachers use the Child Observation Record (COR) to identify and record children's progress in key behavioral and content areas.

CURRICULUM.   The High/Scope curriculum comes from two sources: children's interests and the key experiences, which are lists of observable learning behaviors (see Figure 4.2 for a partial list of key experiences in language and literacy). Basing a curriculum in part on children's interests is very constructivist and implements the philosophies of Dewey and Piaget.

A Daily Routine That Supports Active Learning

The High/Scope curriculum's daily routine is made up of a plan-do-review sequence that gives children opportunities to express intentions about their activities while keeping the teacher intimately involved in the whole process. The following five processes support the daily routine and contribute to its successful functioning.

PLANNING TIME.   Planning time gives children a structured, consistent chance to express their ideas to adults and to see themselves as individuals who can act on decisions.

The teacher talks with children about the plans they have made before the children carry them out. This helps children clarify their ideas and think about how to proceed. Talking with children about their plans provides an opportunity for the teacher to encourage and respond to each child's ideas, to suggest ways to strengthen the plans so they will be successful, and to understand and gauge each child's level of development and thinking style. Children and teachers benefit from these conversations and reflections. Children feel reinforced and ready to start their work, while teachers have ideas of what opportunities for extension might arise, what difficulties children might have, and where problem solving may be needed.

KEY EXPERIENCES.   Teachers continually encourage and support children's interests and involvement in activities, which occur within an organized environment and a consistent routine. Teachers plan from key experiences that may broaden and

☜ FIGURE 4.2   Key
Experiences in Language and
Literacy for a High/Scope K–3
Curriculum

These key experiences are
representative of the many that
are available for teachers to
choose from when identifying
learning activities for children.
In many ways, key experiences
are similar to standards that
state what children should
know and do.

Speaking and Listening

Speaking their own language or dialect

Asking and answering questions

Stating facts and observations in their own words

Using language to solve problems

Participating in singing, storytelling, poetic, and dramatic activities

Recalling thoughts and observations in a purposeful context

Acquiring, strengthening, and extending speaking and listening skills

    Discussing to clarify observations or to better follow direction

    Discussing to expand speaking and listening vocabulary

    Discussing to strengthen critical thinking and problem-solving
       activities

Reading

Experiencing varied genres of children's literature

Reading own compositions

Reading and listening to others read in a purposeful context

Using audio or video recordings in reading experiences

Acquiring, strengthening, and extending specific reading skills

    Auditory discrimination

    Letter recognition

    Decoding—phonetic analysis (letter/sound associations, factors
       affecting sounds, syllabication), structural analysis (forms,
       prefixes, suffixes)

    Vocabulary development

Expanding comprehension and fluency skills

    Activating prior knowledge

    Determining purpose, considering context, making predictions

    Developing strategies for interpreting narrative and expository text

    Reading varied genres of children's literature

strengthen children's emerging abilities. Children generate many of these experiences on their own; others require teacher guidance. Many key experiences are natural extensions of children's projects and interests. Refer again to Figure 4.2 to review a partial list of key experiences that support learning in the areas of language and literacy.

WORK TIME.   This part of the plan-do-review sequence is generally the longest time period in the daily routine. The teacher's role during work time is to observe children to see how they gather information, interact with peers, and solve problems. When appropriate, teachers enter into the children's activities to encourage, extend, and set up problem-solving situations.

CLEANUP TIME.   During cleanup time, children return materials and equipment to their labeled places and store their incomplete projects, restoring order to the classroom. All children's materials in the classroom are within reach and on open shelves. Clear labeling enables children to return all work materials to their appropriate places.

RECALL TIME.   Recall time, the final phase of the plan-do-review sequence, is the time when children represent their work time experience in a variety of developmentally appropriate ways. They might recall the names of the children they involved in their plan, draw a picture of the building they made, or describe the problems they encountered. Recall strategies also include drawing pictures, making models, physically demonstrating how a plan was carried out, or verbally recalling the events of work time. The teacher supports children's linking of the actual work to their original plan.

This review permits children to reflect on what they did and how it was done. It brings closure to children's planning and work time activities. Putting their ideas and experiences into words also facilitates children's language development. Most important, it enables children to represent to others their mental schemes.

Advantages

To review the High/Scope program, visit the Companion Website at *http://www. prenhall.com/morrison*, select Chapter 4, then choose the Linking to Learning module.

Implementing the High/Scope approach produces several advantages. It offers you and others a method for implementing a constructivist-based program that has its roots in Piagetian cognitive theory. Second, it is widely popular and has been extensively researched and tested. Third, there is a rather extensive network of training and support provided by the High/Scope Foundation. You can learn more about High/Scope through its website. Reviewing the website will help you decide if High/Scope is a program you would consider implementing in your classroom.

THE MONTESSORI METHOD

The **Montessori approach** is attractive to parents and teachers for a number of reasons. First, Montessori education has always been identified as a quality program for young children. Second, parents who observe a good Montessori program like what they see: orderliness, independent children, self-directed learning, a calm environment, and children at the center of the learning process. Third, some public schools include Montessori in their magnet programs, giving parents choices in the kind of program their children will have at their school. It is also used as a means of desegregation.

Over the past decade, the implementation of Montessori education has increased tremendously in both private and public school early childhood programs. Maria Montessori would probably smilingly approve of the contemporary use of her method once again to help change the nature and character of early childhood education.

The Role of the Montessori Teacher

The Montessori teacher demonstrates certain behaviors to implement the principles of this child-centered approach. The teacher's six essential roles in a Montessori program are shown in Figure 4.3. Review these six roles now and consider how you can apply them to your practice regardless of what kind of program you implement. Which of these six do you think is the most essential? Why?

Montessori contended, "It is necessary for the teacher to *guide* the child without letting him feel her presence too much, so that she may be always ready to supply the desired help, but may never be the obstacle between the child and his experience."[11] The teacher as guide is a pillar of Montessori practice. Being a guide, however, depends on how well the teacher follows the six roles in Figure 4.3.

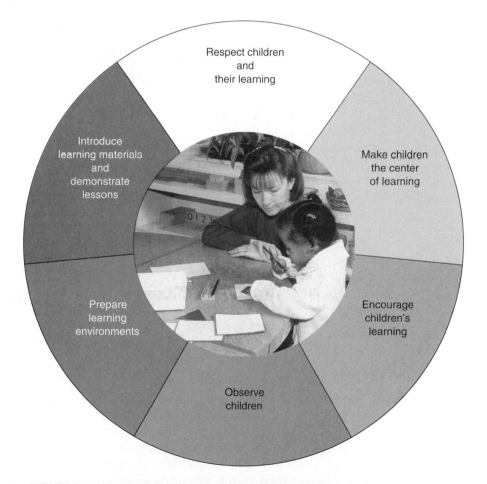

⌒ **FIGURE 4.3   Teacher's Role in a Montessori Classroom**

While these roles are especially prescribed for Montessori teachers, they are applicable to all teachers. You can use these essential roles to help you become a good teacher regardless of the type of program or curriculum you have in your classroom.

The Montessori Method in Action

In a prepared environment, certain materials and activities provide for three basic areas of child involvement: *practical life* or motor education, *sensory materials* for training the senses, and *academic materials* for teaching writing, reading, and mathematics. All these activities are taught according to prescribed procedures.

Practical Life

The prepared environment emphasizes basic, everyday motor activities, such as walking from place to place in an orderly manner, carrying objects such as trays and chairs, greeting a visitor, learning self-care skills, and doing other practical activities. For example, the "dressing frames" are designed to perfect the motor skills involved in buttoning, zipping, lacing, buckling, and tying. The philosophy for activities such as these is to make children independent of the adult and develop concentration. Water-based activities play a large role in Montessori methods, and children are taught to scrub, wash, and pour as a means of developing coordination. Figure 4.4 shows a pouring activity. Practical life exercises also include polishing mirrors, shoes, and plant leaves; sweeping the floor; dusting furniture; and peeling vegetables.

Montessorians believe that as children become absorbed in an activity, they gradually lengthen their span of concentration. As they follow a regular sequence of actions, they learn to pay attention to details. Montessori educators also believe that concentration and involvement through the senses enable learning to take place. Teacher verbal instructions are minimal; the emphasis in the instruction process is on *showing how*—modeling and practice.

Practical life activities are taught through four different types of exercises. *Care of the person* involves activities such as using the dressing frames, polishing shoes, and washing hands. *Care of the environment* includes dusting, polishing a table, and raking leaves. *Social relations* include lessons in grace and courtesy. The fourth type of exercise involves *analysis and control of movement* and includes locomotor activities such as walking and balancing.

Sensory Materials

For many early childhood educators the core of the Montessori program is the specialized set of learning materials that help children learn and which support Montessori's ideas about how to best facilitate children's learning. Many of these materials are designed to train and use the senses to support learning. Figure 4.5 shows basic Montessori sensory materials. As you review these materials, think about their purposes and how they act as facilitators of children's learning. Sensory materials include brightly colored rods and cubes and sandpaper letters. One purpose of these sensory materials is to train children's senses to focus on some obvious, particular quality. For example, with red rods, the

Materials: Tray, rice, two small pitchers (one empty, the other containing rice).

Presentation: The child must be shown how to lift the empty pitcher with the left hand and with the right, raise the pitcher containing rice slightly higher. Grasping the handle, lifting, and tilting are practiced. The spout of the full pitcher must be moved to about the center of the empty pitcher before the pouring begins. Set down both pitchers; then change the full one to the right side, to repeat the exercise.

When rice is spilled, the child will set the pitchers down, beside the top of the tray, and pick the grains up, one at a time, with thumb and forefinger.

Purpose: Control of movement.

Point of Interest: Watching the rice.

Control of Error: Hearing the rice drop on the tray.

Age: 2½ years.

Exercise: A container with a smaller diameter, requiring better control of movement. Control the amount of rice for the smaller container.

Note: Set up a similar exercise, using colored popcorn instead of rice.

Rice or
Popcorn

⌒ **FIGURE 4.4   Pouring**

quality of length; with pink tower cubes, size; and with bells, musical pitch. Montessori felt that children need help discriminating among the many stimuli they receive. Accordingly, the sensory materials help make children more aware of the capacity of their bodies to receive, interpret, and make use of stimuli. In this sense, the Montessori sensory materials are labeled *didactic,* designed to instruct and help children learn.

Second, the sensory materials help sharpen children's powers of observation and visual discrimination. These skills serve as a basis for general beginning

MATERIALS FOR WRITING AND READING	MATERIALS FOR MATHEMATICS
✳ *Ten geometric forms and colored pencils*. These introduce children to the coordination necessary for writing. After selecting a geometric inset, children trace it on paper and fill in the outline with a colored pencil of their choosing.	✳ *Number rods*. A set of red and blue rods varying in length from ten centimeters to one meter, representing the quantities one through ten. With the teacher's help, children are introduced to counting.
✳ *Sandpaper letters*. Each letter of the alphabet is outlined in sandpaper on a card, with vowels in blue and consonants in red. Children see the shape, feel the shape, and hear the sound of the letter, which the teacher repeats when introducing it.	✳ *Sandpaper numerals*. Each number from one to nine is outlined in sandpaper on a card. Children see, touch, and hear the numbers as the teacher or they say them. They eventually match number rods and sandpaper numerals. Children also have the opportunity to discover mathematical facts by using these numerals.
✳ *Movable alphabet, with individual letters*. Children learn to put together familiar words.	✳ *Golden beads*. A concrete material for the decimal system. The single bead represents one unit. A bar made up of ten units in a row represents a ten, ten of the ten bars form a square representing one hundred, and ten hundred squares form the cube representing one thousand.
✳ *Command cards*. These are a set of red cards with a single action word printed on each card. Children read the word on the card and do what the word tells them to do (e.g., run, jump).	

FIGURE 4.5   Montessori Sensory Materials

Montessori sensory materials are popular, attractive, and they support children's cognitive development. Authentic Montessori materials are very well made and are durable. Montessori believed children deserved quality learning materials.

reading readiness. Readiness for learning is highly emphasized in early childhood programs.

Third, the sensory materials increase children's ability to think, a process that depends on the ability to distinguish, classify, and organize. Children constantly face decisions about sensory materials: Which block comes next, which color matches the other, which shape goes where? These are not decisions the teacher makes, nor are they decisions children arrive at by guessing; rather, they are decisions made by the intellectual process of observation and selection based on knowledge gathered through the senses.

Finally, the sensory activities are not ends in themselves. Their purpose is to prepare children for the onset of the sensitive periods for writing and reading. In this sense, all activities are preliminary steps in the writing-reading process.

Materials for training and developing the senses have these characteristics:

* *Control of error.* Materials are designed so children, through observation, can see whether or not they have made a mistake while completing an activity. For example, if a child does not use the blocks of the pink tower in their proper order while building the tower, she does not achieve a tower effect.
* *Isolation of a single quality.* Materials are designed so that other variables are held constant except for the isolated quality or qualities. Therefore, all blocks of the pink tower are pink because size, not color, is the isolated quality.
* *Active involvement.* Materials encourage active involvement rather than the more passive process of looking. Montessori materials are "hands-on" in the truest sense of hands-on active learning.
* *Attractiveness.* Materials are attractive, with colors and proportions that appeal to children. In this sense, they help satisfy asthetic needs for beauty and attractiveness.

Academic Materials for Writing, Reading, and Mathematics

The third type of Montessori materials is academic, designed specifically to promote writing, reading, and mathematics. Exercises using these materials are presented in a sequence that supports writing as a basis for learning to read. Reading, therefore, emerges from writing. Both processes, however, are introduced so gradually that children are never aware they are learning to write and read until one day they realize they are writing and reading. Describing this phenomenon, Montessori said that children "burst spontaneously" into writing and reading. She anticipated contemporary practices such as the contemporary whole-language approach in integrating writing and reading and in maintaining that through writing children learn to read.

Montessori believed many children were ready for writing at four years of age. Consequently, children who enter a Montessori program at age three have done most of the sensory exercises by the time they are four. It is not uncommon to see four- and five-year-olds in a Montessori classroom writing and reading. In fact, children's success with early academic skills and abilities serves as a magnet to attract public and parental attention.

Additional Features

Other features of the Montessori system are *mixed-age grouping* and *self-pacing*. A Montessori classroom always contains children of different ages, usually from two and a half to six years. This strategy is becoming more popular in many early childhood classrooms. Advantages of mixed-age groups are that children learn from one another and help each other, a wide range of materials is available for all ages of children, and older children become role models and collaborators for younger children. Contemporary instructional practices of student mentoring, scaffolding, and cooperative learning all have their roots in and are supported by multi-age grouping.

In a Montessori classroom, children are free to learn at their own rates and levels of achievement. They decide which activities to participate in and work at their own pace. Through observation, the teacher determines when children have perfected one exercise and are ready to move to a higher level or different exercise. If a child is not able to correctly complete an activity, the teacher gives him additional help and instruction. Table 4–4 shows the instructional practices used in a Montessori program and how they apply to teacher roles and the curriculum. Review these practices now and think how they are similar to or different from instructional practices you have observed in other early childhood programs.

TABLE 4–4
MONTESSORI INSTRUCTIONAL PRACTICES

Integrated curriculum	Montessori provides an integrated curriculum in which children are actively involved in manipulating concrete materials across the curriculum—writing, reading, science, math, geography, and the arts. The Montessori curriculum is integrated by age and developmental level.
Active learning	In Montessori classrooms, children are actively involved in their own learning. Manipulative materials provide for active and concrete learning.
Individualized instruction	Curriculum and activities should be individualized for children. Individualization occurs through children's interactions with the materials as they proceed at their own rates of mastery.
Independence	The Montessori environment emphasizes respect for children and promotes success, both of which encourage children to be independent.
Appropriate assessment	Observation is the primary means of assessing children's progress, achievement, and behavior in a Montessori classroom. Well-trained Montessori teachers are skilled observers of children and adept at translating their observation into appropriate ways for guiding, directing, facilitating, and channeling children's learning.
Developmentally appropriate practice	What is specified in developmentally appropriate practice is included in Montessori practice. It is more likely that quality Montessori practitioners understand, as Maria Montessori did, that children are much more capable than some early childhood practitioners think.

These instructional practices, combined with the roles of the teacher (Figure 4.3) and the sensory materials (Figure 4.5), serve as the essential core of Montessori programs.

Montessori and Contemporary Practices

The Montessori approach has had a tremendous influence on approaches to early education. Many instructional practices used in contemporary early childhood programs have their basis in Montessori materials and practices. The Montessori method has many features to recommend it as a high-quality early childhood program and this accounts for its ongoing popularity. As you observe in early childhood programs, search for examples of Montessori influences.

 REGGIO EMILIA

Reggio Emilia, a city in northern Italy, is widely known for its approach to educating young children. Founded by Loris Malaguzzi (1920–1994), Reggio Emilia sponsors programs for children from three months to six years of age.

Basic Principles of the Reggio Emilia Approach

Certain essential beliefs and practices underlie the **Reggio Emilia** approach. These basic features are what defines the Reggio approach, makes it a constructivist program, and defines it as a model that attracts worldwide attention. The Reggio approach has been adapted and implemented in a number of U.S. early childhood programs.

Beliefs about Children and How They Learn

RELATIONSHIPS.   Education focuses on each child and is conducted in relation with the family, other children, the teachers, the environment of the school, the community, and the wider society. Each school is viewed as a system in which all these interconnected relationships are essential for educating children. In other words, as Vygotsky believed, children learn through social interactions and, as Montessori maintained, the environment supports and is important for learning.

For more information about the Reggio Emilia approach, go to the Companion Website at *http://www.prehall.com/morrison*, select Chapter 4, then choose the Linking to Learning module.

Teachers are always aware, however, that children learn a great deal in exchanges with their peers, especially when they interact in small groups. Such small groups of two, three, four, or five children provide possibilities for paying attention, hearing, and listening to each other, developing curiosity and interest, asking questions, and responding.

TIME.   Reggio Emilia teachers believe that time is not set by a clock and that learning continuity should not be interrupted by the calendar. Children's own sense of time and their personal rhythm are considered in planning and carrying out activities and projects. The full-day schedule provides sufficient time for being together among peers in an environment that is conducive to getting things done with satisfaction.

Teachers get to know the personal rhythms and learning styles of each child. This intensive getting to know children is possible in part because children stay with the same teachers and the same peer group for three-year cycles (infancy to three years and three years to six years).

For more information about the Reggio Emilia curriculum model, go to the Companion Website at *http://www.prehall.com/ morrison*, select any chapter, then choose Topic 4 of the ECE Supersite module.

ADULTS' ROLES.   Adults play a powerful role in children's lives. Children's well-being is connected with the well-being of parents and teachers. The well-being of all is supported by recognizing and supporting basic rights. Children have a right to high-quality care and education that supports the development of their potentials. This right is honored by adults and communities who provide these educational necessities. Parents have a right to be involved in the life of the school. As one parent remarked, "I'm not a visitor at school; this is my school!" Teachers have the right to grow professionally through collaboration with other teachers and parents.

The Teacher.   Teachers observe and listen closely to children to know how to plan or proceed with their work. They ask questions and discover children's ideas, hypotheses, and theories. They collaboratively discuss what they have observed and recorded, and they make flexible plans and preparations. Teachers then enter into dialogues with the children and offer them opportunities for discovering, revisiting, and reflecting on experiences. In this sense, teachers support learning as an ongoing process. Teachers are partners and collaborators with children in a continual process of research and learning.

The Atelierista.   An *atelierista* is a teacher trained in the visual arts, who works closely with other teachers and children in every preprimary school and makes visits to the infant-toddler centers. The atelierista helps children use materials to create projects that reflect their involvement in and efforts to solve problems.

Parents.   Parents are an essential component of Reggio, and they are included in the advisory committee that runs each school. Parents' participation is expected and supported and takes many forms: day-to-day interaction, work in the schools, discussion of educational and psychological issues, special events, excursions, and celebrations.

THE ENVIRONMENT.   The infant-toddler centers and school programs are the most visible aspect of the work done by teachers and parents in Reggio Emilia. They convey many messages, of which the most immediate is that they are environments where adults have thought about the quality and the instructive power of space.

The Physical Space.   The layout of physical space, in addition to welcoming whoever enters, fosters encounters, communication, and relationships. The arrangement of structures, objects, and activities encourages children's choices, supports problem solving, and promotes discoveries in the process of learning.

Reggio centers and schools are beautiful. There is attention to detail everywhere: in the color of the walls, the shape of the furniture, the arrangement of objects on shelves and tables. Light from the windows and doors shines through transparent collages and weavings made by children. Healthy, green plants are everywhere.

The environment is highly personal and full of children's own work. Everywhere there are paintings, drawings, paper sculptures, wire constructions, transparent collages coloring the light, and mobiles moving gently overhead. Such things turn up even in unexpected spaces like stairways and bathrooms.

The Atelier. The *atelier* is a special workshop or studio, set aside and used by all the children and teachers in the school. It contains a great variety of tools and resource materials, along with records of past projects and experiences.

In the view of Reggio educators, the children's use of many media is not art or a separate part of the curriculum but an inseparable, integral part of the whole cognitive/symbolic expression involved in the learning process.

Program Practices. Cooperation is the powerful mode of working that makes possible the achievement of the goals Reggio educators set for themselves. Teachers work in pairs in each classroom. They see themselves as researchers gathering information about their work with children by means of continual documentation. The strong collegial relationships that are maintained with teachers and staff enable them to engage in collaborative discussion and interpretation of both teachers' and children's work.

Documentation. Transcriptions of children's remarks and discussions, photographs of their activity, and representations of their thinking and learning using many media are carefully arranged by the *atelierista* and other teachers. These document children's work and the process of learning. This documentation has five functions:

1. To make parents aware of children's experiences and maintain their involvement
2. To allow teachers to understand children and to evaluate their own work, thus promoting professional growth
3. To facilitate communication and exchange of ideas among educators
4. To make children aware that their effort is valued
5. To create an archive that traces the history of the school and the pleasure of learning by children and their teachers

Curriculum and Practices. The curriculum is not established in advance. In this sense, Reggio is a process approach, not a set curriculum to be implemented. Teachers express general goals and make hypotheses about what direction activities and projects might take. After observing children in action, teachers compare, discuss, and interpret together their observations and make choices that they share with the children about what to offer and how to sustain the children in their exploration and learning. In fact, the curriculum emerges in the process of each activity or project and is flexibly adjusted accordingly through this continuous dialogue among teachers and with children.

Projects provide the backbone of the children's and teachers' learning experiences. These projects are based on the conviction that learning by doing is of great importance and that to discuss in groups and to revisit ideas and experiences is the premier way of gaining understanding and learning.

Ideas for projects originate in the experiences of children and teachers as they construct knowledge together. Projects can last from a few days to several months. They may start from a chance event, an idea or a problem posed by one or more children, or an experience initiated directly by teachers.

CONSIDERATIONS.   Keep a number of things in mind as you consider the Reggio Emilia approach and how it might relate to your work as an early childhood educator. First, its theoretical base rests within constructivism and shares ideas compatible with those of Piaget, Vygotsky, Dewey, Gardner, and Diamond (reflect on Table 4–1 again) and the concept or process of learning by doing. Second, there is no set curriculum. Rather, the curriculum emerges or springs from children's interests and experiences. This approach is, for many, difficult to implement and does not ensure that children will learn basic academic skills valued by contemporary American society. Third, the Reggio Emilia approach is suited to a particular culture and society. How this approach works, flourishes, and meets the educational needs of children in an Italian village may not necessarily be appropriate for meeting the needs of contemporary American children. The Italian view of education is that it is the responsibility of the state, and the state provides high levels of financial support. While education is a state function in the United States, traditionally local community control of education is a powerful and sacrosanct part of American education. Figure 4.6 offers an overview of programs inspired by Reggio Emilia in two U.S. classrooms.

PLEASANT LAKE ELEMENTARY SCHOOL, KINDERGARTEN CLASS
Pleasant Lake, Indiana

✳ The kindergarten class at Pleasant Lake Elementary serves thirty-eight children between the ages of five and seven. The curriculum is based on the interests of the children; the teacher's role in the process is to scaffold each child's learning, while documenting the accomplishments of the children.

The curriculum is based on asking questions that provoke thought and encourage individuality among the children. Group work and student-initiated projects propel the class forward. While students are encouraged to participate in projects, it is not necessary to be a part of every project. Field trips to various neighboring places enhance the use of the environment in education.

Parental involvement is highly encouraged. Involvement from parents is one of the major influences of Reggio Emilia within the Pleasant Lake Elementary class. The parent, like the environment, plays a key role in the education of the children.

✳ "Children served in this Reggio Emilia-inspired classroom now have the opportunity to experience learning without limits," says Debra Heck, the first teacher at Pleasant Lake Elementary to incorporate the Reggio curriculum. She carefully documents the children's progress and development throughout the year.

(Continued)

∽ FIGURE 4.6   Programs Inspired by Reggio Emilia

* Ms. Heck advises future Reggio Emilia candidates that Reggio Emilia is a way of thinking about learning, and not a method to be copied. It is a philosophy to learn from and build upon. One should start by reflecting on one's own practice and implementation, followed by reading various practices of Reggio Emilia and documenting the learning in one's classroom to analyze what is seen. A strong relationship must be built upon what is taught and what is seen, concluding with the implementation of the changes necessary to improve the learning environment.

*Information based upon and provided by the teachings of Debra Heck at Pleasant Lake Elementary. Ms. Heck holds a master's degree in early education with early childhood emphasis.

For more information on the Pleasant Lake Elementary School, visit the Companion Website at *http://www.prenhall.com/ morrison* select Chapter 4, then choose the Linking to Learning module.

CHILDREN FIRST
Durham, North Carolina

* A nonprofit NAEYC accredited child care program, Children First, run by parents and four staff members, educates ten children. The children range from ages two to five, with two teachers available at all times of the day. The philosophy of the program maintains "children as strong, capable, infinitely valuable and profound individuals."

    The curriculum can be summarized in four main aspects: family-centered, child-centered, developmentally appropriate, and Reggio-inspired. Educators offer guidance without taking the initiative away from the child. The environment is established to give children a choice of various activities. Field trips also aid in connecting the children with nature and the larger community.

    Children First works closely with parents to establish a strong parent-teacher cooperative: parents not only serve on the board of directors, but also they are highly encouraged to participate in the classroom.

* This genuine commitment to building a community among children, families, and teachers makes Children First a dedicated Reggio-inspired program. Children First also takes a nontraditional approach to discipline. To create a "safe school," teachers use gentle, respectful techniques to guide behavior. Moreover, children have a strong voice in constructing the rules they live by as a community.

* "Perhaps the most important thing Reggio has taught us to do here," says Donna King, teacher and administrator at Children First, "is to build a program, from day to day and year to year, that is built around and belongs to the people—children, parents, and teachers— who inhabit it." Mrs. King advises educators interested in the Reggio curriculum to remember that all children are competent and have a right to be both active in constructing the community and fulfilled by it. Also, educators must place absolute value on the quality of life—on beauty, joy, passion, nature, discovery, imagination, creativity—as opposed to focusing effort on "building the future," as so many American educators say.

*Information based upon the *Children First Parent Handbook.* Children First is a nonprofit organization housed in a private residence. Donna King is a teacher, administrator, and one of the founders of Children First.

☞ **FIGURE 4.6   Programs Inspired by Reggio Emilia** *(Continued)*

HEAD START

For more information about Head Start, go to the Companion Website at *http://www. prenhall.com/morrison*, select Chapter 4, then choose the Linking to Learning module.

Head Start is a federally funded early childhood program. Head Start began in 1965 and has grown in size and effectiveness. The purpose of Head Start is to give children from low-income families a "head start" for learning and to promote success in school and life.

Table 4–5, Head Start at a Glance, shows the extent to which Head Start influences the lives of children nationwide. The "Program in Action: New Horizons" on pages 124 and 125 portrays Head Start in action.

TABLE 4–5
HEAD START AT A GLANCE

CHILDREN	**857,664**
5-year-olds	5%
4-year-olds	56%
3-year-olds	33%
under 3	6%
RACIAL/ETHNIC COMPOSITION	
American Indian	3.3%
Hispanic	28.7%
Black	34.5%
White	30.4%
Asian	2.0%
Hawaiian/Pacific Islander	1.0%
NUMBER OF GRANTEES	**1,525**
Number of Classrooms	46,225
Number of Centers	18,200
Teachers	180,400
Volunteers	1,252,000
AVERAGE COST PER CHILD	**$5,951**
TOTAL CHILDREN SERVED TO DATE	**17,714,000**
ANNUAL BUDGET	**$6,199,812,000**

These facts and figures demonstrate the extent to which Head Start serves children and families and how influential it is in the early childhood arena. Head Start will continue to grow and the federal government will also continue to use Head Start as a means of reforming early childhood practice.

Source: Head Start 2000 Stastical Fact Sheet. Online souce available at http://www2.acf.dhhs.gov/programs

Head Start provides medical, dental, mental health, and nutrition services to preschool children. How does providing health services help achieve Head Start's goal of overall social competence for all children?

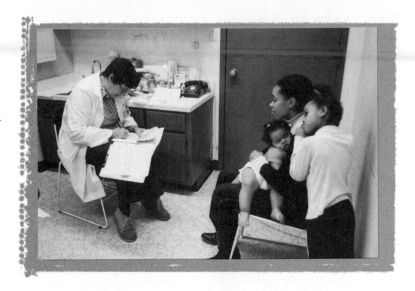

Basic Principles and Goals of Head Start

Head Start is based on the premise that all children have basic physical, social, emotional, and cognitive needs and that children of low-income families in particular can benefit from a comprehensive developmental program to meet these needs. The overall goal of Head Start is to bring about a greater degree of social and academic competence, enabling children to deal effectively with their environments and responsibilities in school and life.

Head Start's philosophy is that children can benefit most from a comprehensive, interdisciplinary program that fosters children's development. Furthermore, the entire family, as well as the community, must be involved. To achieve this mission, Head Start goals provide for:

* The improvement of children's health and physical abilities
* The encouragement of self-confidence, spontaneity, curiosity, and self-discipline, which will assist in the development of children's social and emotional health
* The enhancement of the children's mental processes and skills, with particular attention to conceptual and verbal skills
* The establishment of patterns and expectations of success for children, which will create a climate of confidence for their present and future learning efforts and overall development
* An increase in the ability of children and their families to relate to each other and to others in a loving and supporting manner
* The enhancement of the sense of dignity and self-worth within children and their families

Program in Action

NEW HORIZONS

Located in rural Macon County, North Carolina, just minutes away from the Great Smoky Mountains, is our New Horizons Center for Children and Families. The foundation for New Horizons is a Head Start program that expanded to encompass a parent/child center, subsidized day care, developmental day care, and Head Start Wraparound services. Wraparound services include services to families and a full range of physical and mental health. Built on a long-standing commitment to quality, our Macon Program for Progress (MPP) Head Start Centers are state licensed and fully accredited by the National Association for the Education of Young Children (NAEYC).

Head Start performance standards were revised effective January 1998, for the first time in more than twenty years. The new standards are based on three cornerstones: child development, community development, and staff development.

Implementing these standards has been a natural occurrence for us because the overall goal for MPP Head Start is *everyday excellence*. This goal is reflected in every aspect of our program, from curriculum development to collaboration with parents. Parents such as T. M. attest, "our Head Start program has many rewards for children and families."

> I live in a very rural community with no family here. When the child care center first opened, my daughter would not leave my sight. She had no idea how to play with other children. Now she looks forward to her school days more than anything.

Programs and facilities at New Horizons allow us to care for children ages six weeks to five years in four centers throughout Macon County. We are open year-round with child care available eleven and a half hours per day. We are fortunate to begin our services with a program funded by Head Start that allows services to families from pregnancy through age three, when a child would normally enter Head Start.

FOCUS ON INFANT CARE AND DEVELOPMENT

Getting to know, enjoy, and care for each child on an individual basis is at the heart of our curriculum for our 0–3 program. Caring for infants under the age of twelve months is more than bottles and diapers. Our teachers realize that they play an important role in the valuable learning experiences infants undergo in the first year of life.

Each infant has a primary caregiver. The selection of a primary caregiver is not necessarily by assignment. We find that personalities draw caregivers to infants.

We believe that the foundations of creativity develop in the early months of infant growth and are affected by the caregiver-child relationship. For example, it is crucial for babies to feel good about themselves and things they are learning. We are excited about the things our babies accomplish. We praise them for pulling up, crawling, waving, smiling, and any number of small accomplishments they make during the day. Babies thrive on the attention and look to the caregivers for their approval. They learn they can make things happen and are delighted that the teacher is excited about it, too!

The environmental considerations that we use to support individual development for infants are attachment, trust, mobility, senses, language, and health/safety.

* *Attachment* is a necessity for development and learning to occur. Comfortable chairs and floor

Program Management and Performance Standards

Head Start makes every effort to ensure that the management and governance of programs is effective and supports its performance standards.

All Head Start programs operate their programs and services according to these performance standards. The full set of current Head Start performance areas encourage one-to-one interaction with babies and encourage attachment. Small group size and low teacher:child ratios also help promote attachment as teachers interpret and meet the diverse needs of each infant.

* *Trust* is developed by the familiarity of the environment and by association with the same small group and with the same caregiver. A trusting relationship between child and caregiver is necessary for exploration and learning to occur. Additionally, predictable and consistent routines are used to nurture and create a feeling of security.

* *Mobility* is encouraged by allowing babies to play freely on the floor and protecting less mobile babies with soft barriers.

* *Senses* are stimulated with colorful and soft, safe toys. Care is taken to prepare the environment to avoid sensory overload.

* *Language development* is fostered by songs and rhythm, interesting objects, views outside, pictures, and experiences in which adults talk to infants. We recognize that before babies talk they do a lot of listening. We too listen to the sounds infants are hearing and observe their body language; we then talk to the infants about how they are reacting to the sounds and about what they may be thinking.

* *Health and safety awareness* by all staff members is habit. We respect infants' knowing what they need so we provide a safe environment for their natural development. Since we mainstream children with disabilities throughout the center, it is not unusual to have a baby with a heart monitor or other equipment. Differences in the needs of our children are embraced as a natural part of life.

SUPPORTING PARENTS AND PARENTING NEEDS

We recognize and encourage the fact that the parent is the best teacher in the child's life. Relationships are more intense with parents of infants than with older children. A deeper level of trust is involved, and teachers have a more intimate relationship with babies than they do with older children. It is imperative that we communicate in a collaborative manner with parents rather than take the role of the expert. Feeding schedules, for example, are completed and updated by the parent or guardian stating foods to be given along with preferred times and amounts. A daily feeding record is kept for each child along with times of diaper changes. Notations of a child's activities for the day are also recorded. The collaboration with parents comes with a commitment on our part to create and maintain effective communication and good relationships with parents.

Contributed by Betty De Pina, parent/child coordinator, and Sharon Franklin, lead teacher, 0–3 classrooms, New Horizons Center for Children and Families, Macon County, North Carolina.

 To complete a Program in Action activity, visit the Companion Website at *http://www.prenhall.com/morrison*, select Chapter 4, then choose the Programs in Action module.

 To locate the *Federal Register*, visit the Companion Website at *http://www.prenhall.com/morrison*, select Chapter 4, then choose the Linking to Learning module.

standards appears in the November 5, 1996, issue of the *Federal Register*. Although the Head Start Bureau provides guidance on implementing the performance standards, local agencies are responsible for designing programs to best meet the needs of children and their families.

Head Start Services

Head Start offers the following program services: education and development, parent involvement, health services (including nutrition and mental health), staff development, and administration.

CHILD EDUCATION AND DEVELOPMENT.   Performance standards for education and development for all children include providing children with a learning environment and the varied experiences that will help them develop socially, intellectually, physically, and emotionally in a manner appropriate to their age and state of development toward the overall goal of social competence.

Performance standards guide local agencies in developing their own programs that are unique and responsive to the children, families, and communities they serve. Thus, there is really no "national" Head Start curriculum.

SERVICES TO CHILDREN WITH DISABILITIES.   At least 10 percent of Head Start enrollment must consist of children with disabilities. Nationally, 13.4 percent of all children enrolled in Head Start have a disability. (In Chapter 10 you will find more information on educating children with disabilities.)

PARENT INVOLVEMENT/FAMILY PARTNERSHIPS.   From the outset, Head Start has been dedicated to the philosophy that to improve children's lives, corresponding changes must be made in parents' lives as well. Head Start provides a program that recognizes parents as (1) responsible guardians of their children's well-being, (2) prime educators of their children, and (3) contributors to the Head Start program and to their communities.

Head Start endeavors to cooperate and collaborate with families and communities by

* involving parents in educational activities of the program to enhance their role as the principal influence on their children's education and development;
* assisting parents to increase their knowledge, understanding, skills, and experience in child growth and development; and
* identifying and reinforcing experiences that occur in the home that parents can use as educational activities for their children.[12]

As shown in the following "Technology Tie-In," there are many ways to involve parents. In this technological age the Internet is one way to electronically connect parents, children, and programs.

HEALTH SERVICES.   Head Start assumes an active role in children's health. Children's current health status is monitored and reported to parents, and corrective and preventive procedures are undertaken with their cooperation.

Head Start also seeks to direct children and parents to existing mental health delivery systems such as community health centers. It does not intend to duplicate existing services, but to help parents become aware of and use available services.

Technology Tie-In

OPEN DOORS WITH THE INTERNET

Many early childhood programs proclaim that they have an open-door policy. For many parents, this invitation is seldom used. Now, however, the door is always technologically open.

When Jeff Bergau watches his two-year-old son taking a nap with his toy duck, he says, "It brings tears to my eyes because he's so sweet when he sleeps."

Even when he's at work, Bergau, vice president of Slack Barshinger Inc., a Chicago-based marketing firm, enjoys watching not only his child napping, but the normal routine of his son's day. How is Bergau able to keep in such close contact when he works a mile away from his toddler's child care center, Honey Tree, Inc., a preschool and infant program?

The answer is through the Internet.

Honey Tree provides parents with real-time images, but no audio, via the computer from 7 A.M. to 7 P.M. five days a week, the hours the early learning center is open.

"It was a huge selling point for us when we were trying to find a place for our son last April," said Bergau, whose wife Amy is a marketing consultant. "I go into my office, log on, and watch our son from my laptop, an Apple iBook, in color, on a 12-by-14-inch screen. It makes me feel he's part of my day every day. I often find him doing something extremely cute, and then I call my wife to make sure she logs on. And she does the same for me."

WatchMeGrow is the program that enables Jeff and his wife to constantly monitor the growth and development of their son while he is in child care. "Kiddiecam" services enable parents to monitor and respond to their children's care and education from a close-up and personal perspective, not just from a few parent notes or exchanged words at day's end.

Parents receive a password that allows them to go online and observe their child. Parents have two choices of viewing with WatchMeGrow. PictureOnTheWeb gives parents a large, high-quality still image of their children's classroom that is updated by clicking the refresh button and runs on a standard telephone line. ViewOnTheWeb offers parents a high-quality, streaming image that automatically refreshes every few seconds and offers a high-speed Internet connection.

What are your opinions regarding an Internet open-door policy via such programs as WatchMeGrow? Would WatchMeGrow or similar programs be one of the deciding factors in your selection of a child care program? Would you want parents to have Internet access to your classroom?

To learn more about the WatchMeGrow site and complete this Technology Tie-In activity, visit the Companion Website at *http://www.prenhall.com/morrison*, select Chapter 4, then choose the Technology Tie-In module.

NUTRITION. Head Start programs teach children how to care for their health, including the importance of eating proper foods and good dental health.

A basic premise of Head Start is that children must be properly fed to have the strength and energy to learn. This philosophy calls for teaching children good nutrition habits that will carry over for the rest of their lives and be passed on to their children. In addition, parents are given basic nutrition education so they, in turn, can promote good nutrition in their families.

Head Start programs design and implement a nutrition program that meets the nutritional needs and feeding requirements of each child, including those with

Promoting good nutrition for children and their families is an important part of the Head Start curriculum and helps establish lifelong attitudes toward healthy living.

special dietary needs and children with disabilities. Also, the nutrition program serves a variety of foods that involve cultural and ethnic preferences and broaden the children's food experiences.[13]

Providing Head Start Services

Head Start services are provided to children and families through a comprehensive child development program in any of three Head Start-approved program options. These three options are *center-based, home-based,* and a *combination* of center-based and home-based visits. Locally designed program options, developed by the local program to specifically meet the needs of children and families, are also permitted. For example, one such local option might be Head Start in family day care homes. In fact, this is a very popular local option.

Early Head Start

To take an online self-test on this chapter's contents, go to the Companion Website at *http://www.prenhall.com/ morrison*, select Chapter 4, then choose the Self-Test module.

Early Head Start (EHS) is a federally funded, community-based program for low-income families with infants and toddlers and pregnant women. Its mission is to promote healthy prenatal development for pregnant women, enhance the development of very young children, and promote healthy family functioning. Consequently, EHS enhances children's physical, social, emotional, and intellectual development; supports both parents in fulfilling their parental roles; and helps parents move toward economic independence. EHS programs offer core services, including high-quality early education (both in and out of the home) and family support services; home

Video Viewpoint

PARENTING: THE FIRST YEARS LAST FOREVER (EARLY HEAD START)

The federally funded Early Head Start program provides children younger than three in so-called at-risk families with the brain stimulation they need to grow and prosper and provides families with the support they need to raise healthy children.

REFLECTIVE DISCUSSION QUESTIONS

Why is it that some children seem smarter and learn faster than others? What difference do you think early intervention can make in a child's life? Why do you think

the government has continued to expand the Head Start program over the past four decades?

REFLECTIVE DECISION MAKING

Visit the Department of Health and Human Services website to learn more about Early Head Start. What are some of Early Head Start's goals and services? Are there any Head Start or Early Head Start programs in your area where you could visit or volunteer? Are there other resources in your community you could recommend to a parent in need?

visits; parent education; comprehensive health and mental health services, including services for women prior to, during, and after pregnancy; nutrition; and child care. EHS programs have the flexibility to respond to the unique strengths and needs of their own communities and of each child and family within that community. Consider the "Video Viewpoint: Parenting: The First Years Last Forever (Early Head Start)" which addresses the importance of parenting in child development and provides support for programs such as EHS.

Although all of the program models we have discussed in this chapter are unique, at the same time they all have certain similarities. All of them, regardless of their particular philosophical orientation, have as their primary goal the best possible education for all children. As an early childhood professional, you will want to decide which of these models and/or features of models you can embrace and incorporate into your own practice.

ACTIVITIES FOR PROFESSIONAL DEVELOPMENT

In this chapter we have examined model programs of early childhood education, their basic features, and the importance of providing the best possible education for all young children. Refer again to the "Professional Development Goal" at the beginning of the chapter, to the "Professional Development Checklist," on pages 20 and 21, and to the "Professionalism in Practice" by Jackye Brown on page 99. After you have reviewed these, complete the following activities.

1. When deciding about which of the models you would or would not implement, you must consider a lot of factors. Make a list of all the factors you would have to consider, such as materials needed, cost, community acceptance, and needed training.

2. As an early childhood professional, you will need to make decisions about what to teach and how to teach it. Choose one of the programs you read about in this chapter and explain how you would implement it in your classroom. Use the information from Activity 1 in your decision making. In your plans include a daily schedule and activities for children.

3. Make a chart with these headings:

   Program Features I Like   Features I Don't Like

   Complete your chart for each of the models we discussed in this chapter. Next, rank in order the models according to your first choice, second, third, and so forth.

4. Review your philosophy of education again. Now write a paragraph about how your philosophy does or does not align with the theory and assumptions of each program model we have discussed.

5. Review the learning theories we discussed in Chapter 3. Explain, with specific examples, how these theories have influenced the model programs.

For additional chapter resources and activities, visit the Companion Website at *http://www.prenhall.com/morrison*, select Chapter 4, then choose the Professional Development, Resources, or Linking to Learning modules.

FOCUS QUESTIONS

1. Why is it important for early childhood educators to know how to assess?
2. What are the purposes and uses of observation and assessment?
3. What are some ways you can assess children's development, learning, and behavior?
4. How can I ensure that my assessment and observation is developmentally appropriate and adheres to the ethics of the profession?

chapter 5

Observing and Assessing Young Children

GUIDING, TEACHING, AND LEARNING

To review the chapter focus questions online, go to the Companion Website at *http://www.prenhall.com/ morrison* and select Chapter 5.

 # PROFESSIONAL DEVELOPMENT GOAL

OBSERVATION AND ASSESSMENT

I pay attention to my students' actions and feelings. I evaluate students using appropriate and authentic measures. I use observation and assessment to guide my teaching.

Kindergarten teacher Tyron Jones wants to make sure Amanda knows the initial beginning sounds that he has taught the class during the last two weeks. First grade teacher Mindy McArthur wants to see how many words on the class word wall César knows. Third grade teacher José Gonzalez wants to know if his class can apply what they're learning to real-life situations. Decisions, decisions, decisions. All of these relate to how to assess learning and teaching.

Teachers' minutes, hours, and days are filled with assessment decisions. Questions abound: "What is Jeremy ready for now?" "What can I tell Maria's parents about her language development?" "The activity I used in the large-group time yesterday didn't seem to work well. What could I have done differently?" Appropriate assessment can help you find the answers to these and many other questions relating to how to teach and what is best for children in all areas of development.

To check your understanding of this chapter with the online Study Guide, go to the Companion Website at *http://www.prenhall.com/ morrison*, select Chapter 5, then choose the Study Guide module.

WHAT IS ASSESSMENT?

Much of children's lives are subject to and influenced by your assessment and the assessment of others. As an early childhood professional, assessment will influence your professional life and will be a vital tool of your professional practice. Assessment well done is one of your most important responsibilities, and it can enhance your teaching and children's learning.

For more information about the uses and abuses of assessment, go to the Companion Website at *http://www.prenhall. com/morrison*, select Chapter 5, then choose the Linking to Learning module to connect to the Pathways to School Improvements site.

Assessment is the process of collecting information about children's development, learning, health, behavior, academic progress, and need for special services in order to plan and implement curriculum and instruction. The terms *assessment* and *evaluation* are often used interchangeably. Review Figure 5.1 now which outlines the purposes of assessment. These purposes will help you understand how assessment relates to your many roles as a teacher.

You will use the following to help you assess your teaching and children's learning: observation, commercial and teacher-made tests and checklists, and student work samples and products. Assessment will provide you with constant feedback and information about your teaching and children's learning.

Why Is Assessment Important?

Assessment is important for early childhood professionals because of all the decisions they make about children when teaching and caring for them. The decisions facing our three teachers at the beginning of this chapter all involve how best to educate children. Like them, you will be called upon every day to make decisions

These are some of the reasons you will use assessment in your teaching. All of these purposes are important and if you use assessment procedures appropriately, you will help all children learn well.

PURPOSES OF ASSESSMENT AS IT RELATES TO:

Children

* Identify what children know

* Identify children's special needs

* Determine appropriate placement

* Select appropriate curricula to meet children's individual needs

* Refer children and, as appropriate, their families for additional services to programs and agencies

Families

* Communicate with parents to provide information about their children's progress and learning

* Relate school activities to home activities and experiences

Early Childhood Programs

* Make policy decisions regarding what is and is not appropriate for children

* Determine how well and to what extent programs and services children receive are beneficial and appropriate

Early Childhood Teachers

* Identify children's skills and abilities

* Make lesson and activity plans and set goals

* Create new classroom arrangements

* Select materials

* Make decisions about how to implement learning activities

* Report to parents and families about children's developmental status and achievement

* Monitor and improve the teaching-learning process

* Meet the individual needs of children

* Group for instruction

The Public

* Inform the public regarding children's achievement

* Provide information relating to students' schoolwide achievements

* Provide a basis for public policy (e.g., legislation, recommendations, and statements)

before you teach, during your teaching, and after your teaching. Whereas some of them will seem small and inconsequential, others will be "high stakes," influencing the life course of children. All your assessment decisions taken as a whole will direct and alter children's learning outcomes.

What Is Authentic Assessment?

For more information about authentic assessment, go to the Companion Website at *http://www.prenhall.com/ morrison*, select Chapter 5, then choose the Linking to Learning module.

Authentic assessment is the evaluation of children's actual learning and the instructional activities in which they are involved. The alternative would involve evaluating children using goals and objectives that were not part of their instructional program. Figure 5.2 outlines characteristics of authentic assessment. As you examine these characteristics, think about how you will apply them to your professional practice.

⌐ **FIGURE 5.2**
Characteristics of Authentic Assessment

Implementing authentic assessment strategies will help ensure that the information you gather will be useful and appropriate for all children. One of your assessment goals should be to try and ensure that your assessment is as authentic as possible.

Authentic Assessment:

* assesses children and their actual work. Some means for achieving this goal are: work samples, portfolios, performances, projects, journals, experiments, and teacher observations.

* is ongoing over the entire school year.

* is curriculum-embedded; that is, children are assessed on what they are actually learning and doing.

* is a cooperative process. Assessment involves many persons— children, teachers, parents, and other professionals. The goal here is to make assessment child-centered.

* employs a number of different ways to determine children's achievement and what they know and are able to do.

* takes into account children's cultural, language, and other specific needs.

* assesses the whole child rather than a narrow set of skills.

* is part of the learning process. For example, one third grader, as part of a project on the community, visited the recycling center. She made a presentation to the class in which she used the overhead projector to illustrate her major points, displayed a poster board with pictures she had taken of the center, and presented several graphs to show which products were recycled most. In this way, she was able to demonstrate a broader range of knowledge and skills she learned.

Methods of Assessment

As noted in the first item in Figure 5.2, authentic assessment includes a variety of ways to determine what children know and are able to do. One of your challenges will be to select and employ a number of different ways to evaluate children's progress in a variety of areas.

Using Portfolios to Assess

For more information about assessment of young children, go to the Companion Website at *http://www.prenhall.com/morrison*, select any chapter, then choose Topic 7 of the ECE Supersite module.

Today many teachers use **portfolios**—a purposeful compilation of children's work samples, products, and teacher observations collected over time—as a basis for assessing children's efforts, progress, and achievement. Before compiling students' portfolios, you will need to make decisions about the criteria you will use to decide what to put in the portfolios. Remember, a portfolio is not a dump truck. You don't include everything in it. Some criteria for what to include are:

* How will students participate in decisions about what to include?
* Do the materials show student progress over time?
* Do the materials demonstrate student learning of program and district standards and goals?
* Can you use the materials and products to adequately and easily communicate with parents about children's learning?
* Do the materials include examples to positively support students' efforts and progress?

Student products include written work, artwork, audiotapes, pictures, models, and other materials that attest to what children know and are able to do. Some teachers let children put their best work in their portfolios; others decide with children what will be included; still others decide for themselves what to include. Portfolios are very useful, especially during parents-teacher conferences. Such a portfolio includes your notes about achievement, teacher- and child-made checklists, artwork samples, photographs, journals, and other documentation.

Some teachers use technology to develop digital portfolios. These can stand alone or supplement the traditional portfolio. Digital portfolios include books and journals that children keep on computers and then illustrate with digital cameras.

An important point to remember, and one often overlooked, is that portfolios are only one dimension of your assessment of children's behavior and achievement. In the "Professionalism in Practice: Evaluating the Learning Process" on page 138 teacher Linda Sholar discusses how she uses portfolios to assess her kindergarten students' development.

Checklists

Checklists are excellent and powerful tools for observing and gathering information about a wide range of student abilities in all settings. Checklists can be

Professionalism in Practice

EVALUATING THE LEARNING PROCESS

Linda Sholar

Sangre Ridge Elementary School, Stillwater, Oklahoma

I have used student portfolios to evaluate my kindergarten students for fifteen years. Over time, however, I have redefined their purpose and identified several criteria to make more effective use of portfolios. I believe that the value of student portfolios is to provide a record of each student's process of learning and therefore collect student work based on the following criteria:

- Portfolio entries reflect a student's cognitive, social, emotional, and physical development.
- They provide a visual record of a student's process of learning over time.
- They encourage input from students, teachers, and parents.

My students and I together select the work samples. Each portfolio also includes a parent questionnaire, parent responses to conferences, individual assessment profiles, and anecdotal records. Because the volume of materials that can accumulate in a portfolio can become overwhelming, I use a table of contents in the format of a checklist stapled inside the folder, which makes it easy to examine the contents and determine at a glance what data I have to make wise instructional decisions and what information I still need.

The success of student portfolios as an evaluation tool depends on the appropriate assessment of individual students and on accurate, conscientious documentation of student growth.

APPROPRIATE ASSESSMENT

Appropriate assessment is the process of observing, recording, and documenting the work children do and how they do it. In my classroom, assessments are ongoing and occur as children perform daily classroom routines and participate in group time, share time, center time, and recess. I note which activities the children choose, how long they work on specific activities, and their process for completing activities. I observe students' learning styles, interest levels, skill levels, coping techniques, strategies for decision making and problem solving, and interactions with other children. Observations, however, have little value unless they are accurately documented.

ACCURATE DOCUMENTATION

To manage documentation more accurately and efficiently, I have developed or adapted a variety of forms to make systematic assessments. Throughout the year, I use these assessment tools to systematically record information on individual children in each area of their development. I use a symbol to date the occurrence of behaviors and describe and document skill proficiency as appropriate. Emphasis is on what each child can do, and each child's progress is compared with his or her prior work. As I review these individual assessments, I am able to quickly detect areas of growth.

a regular part of your teaching and can be used on a wide variety of topics and subjects. Some checklists can be developmental; others can help you assess behaviors, traits, skills, and abilities. In addition, the same checklists used over a period of time enable you to evaluate progress and achievement. Figure 5.3 is a checklist for assessing children's emergent literacy skills and can be used as a template or model to make other checklists. Review Figure 5.3 now and think about how you could modify it to assess children's technology use and skills. Some things for you to keep in mind when making and using checklists are:

Symbol System

+ = Progress is noted

√ = Needs more time and/or experience

* = See comments

In addition to the individual student profiles, I have also developed several class evaluation forms that allow me flexibility in recording observations quickly yet accurately. These forms are especially useful in planning group and/or individual instruction, and they provide additional documentation that supports the individual assessment records. For example, I make anecdotal records (on Post-It notes) of unanticipated events or behaviors, a child's social interactions, and problem-solving strategies. I transfer these Post-Its to a class grid so I can determine at a glance which children I have observed. The anecdotal records, along with the individual assessment profiles, become a part of each student's portfolio to be used for instructional planning and communicating with parents.

Throughout the year samples of students' work are dated and included in the portfolios. Quarterly work samples that I select include some that illustrate abilities with cutting activities, writing numbers (each child decides how far he or she can write), writing letters of the alphabet, and writing any words or stories a child can write independently (using either invented or conventional spelling). The children select samples of artwork and creative writing (e.g., journal entries, letters, or drawings they have done for parents).

USE OF INFORMATION

I use the information from student portfolios to plan classroom instruction for individuals and groups, to identify children who may need special help, and to confer with parents and colleagues. During conferences, I share with parents the student's assessment profile for the different areas of development, and together we examine samples of the child's work that support the assessment. Even though progress is visually obvious, I can also point out less obvious progress as we view the samples. I give conference response forms to parents and ask for comments or suggestions for additional portfolio entries. Using the portfolio, I am satisfied that I have gleaned an accurate assessment of and appreciation for each child's total development.

 To review the Professional Development Checklist and complete a Professionalism in Practice activity, visit the Companion Website at *http://www.prenhall.com/morrison*, select Chapter 5, then choose the Professional Development module.

* Each checklist should contain the qualities, skills, behaviors, and other information you want to observe. In other words, tailor-make each checklist to a specific situation.
* Make sure you are observing and recording accurately.
* File all checklists in students' folders for future reference and use.
* Use checklists as a basis for conferencing with children and parents.
* Use the information from checklists to plan for small-group and individual instruction.

NAME:	DATE:		AGE:	GRADE:
	Always	Sometimes	Never	Comments
Can see well—pictures, signs, and words				
Can hear well—can hear spoken words, attends to spoken language				
PRINT CONCEPTS				
Recognizes left-to-right sequencing				
Recognizes top, down directionality				
Asks what print says				
Connects meaning between two objects, pictures				
Models reading out loud				
Models adult silent reading (newspapers, books, etc.)				
Recognizes that print has different meanings (informational, entertainment, etc.)				
COMPREHENSION BEHAVIORS				
Follows oral directions				
Draws correct pictures from oral directions				
Recognizes story sequence in pictures				
Interprets pictures				
Sees links in story ideas				
Links personal experiences with text (story, title)				
Logically reasons story plot/conclusions				
Sees patterns in similar stories				
WRITING BEHAVIORS				
Makes meaningful scribbles (attempts to make letter-like shapes)				
Draws recursive scribbles (rows of letter-like writing)				
Makes strings of "letters"				
Uses one or more consonants to represent words				
Makes efforts to spell own words—inventive spellings				

FIGURE 5.3   **Emergent Literacy Behaviors Checklist**

Use this checklist as a guide to make your own checklists on any topic or subject area.

Screening Procedures

In your work with young children, have you ever wondered about the abilities of some children? Screening can help you find the answer. Screening is the process of identifying the particular physical, social, linguistic, and cognitive needs of children in order to provide appropriate programs and services.

Screening procedures give you and others a broad picture of what children know and are able to do, as well as their physical and emotional status. As gross indicators of children's abilities, screening procedures provide much useful information for decisions about placement for initial instruction, referral to other agencies, and additional testing that may be necessary to pinpoint a learning or health problem. Many school districts conduct a comprehensive screening assessment program in the spring for children who will enter kindergarten in the fall. Screening can include the following:

* Gathering information from parents about their children's health, learning patterns, learning achievements, personal habits, and special problems.
* Conducting a health screening, including a physical examination, health history, and a blood sample for analysis. (Keep in mind in Chapter 2 we identified lead poisoning as a major childhood disease.)
* Conducting vision, hearing, and speech screening.
* Collecting and analyzing data from former programs and teachers, such as preschools and child care programs.
* Using commercial screening instruments to help make decisions regarding children's placement in programs and need for special services.

Schools and early childhood programs frequently conduct comprehensive screening programs for all children for one or two days. Data for each child is evaluated by a team of professionals who make instructional placement recommendations and, when appropriate, advise additional testing and make referrals to other agencies for assistance.

Screening Instruments

Several screening instruments provide information for grouping and planning instructional strategies. Most can be administered by people who do not have specialized training in test administration. Parent volunteers often help administer screening instruments, some of which can be administered in about thirty minutes.

BRIGANCE® K and 1 Screen.   BRIGANCE® K and 1 screen is an evaluation for use in kindergarten and grade one. Skills assessed include: color recognition, vocabulary, counting, visual discrimination, gross motor skills, and the ability to follow directions.

DIAL-3.   The DIAL-3 (Developmental Indicators for the Assessment of Learning) is a norm-referenced instrument designed for screening large numbers of

Many school districts conduct a comprehensive screening for children entering kindergarten, which may include vision, hearing, and speech tests.

prekindergarten children. It requires approximately twenty-five to thirty minutes to administer and involves individual assessment in the following developmental areas: cognitive/basic concepts, language, motor, self-help, and social-emotional. The screening team consists of a coordinator, an operator for each of the skills areas screened, and aides or volunteers to register parents and children.

These and other similar assessments are classified as *formal assessments* because they have set guidelines and procedures for administration. Informal screening is what you and other professionals do when you gather information to make decisions such as small-group placement, instructional level, and so forth.

USING OBSERVATION TO ASSESS

Observation is one of the most widely used methods of assessment. Table 5–1 provides information and guidelines for using observation and other informal methods of assessment. They are labeled as *informal* because they do not entail standard guidelines for administration and use. Authentic assessment relies heavily on informal procedures. Study closely the eleven kinds of informal assessments in Table 5–1. You will use all of these in your work with young children.

Professionals recognize that children are more than what is measured by any particular standardized test. Observation is an "authentic" means of learning about children—what they know and are able to do, especially as it occurs in more naturalistic settings such as classrooms, child care centers, playgrounds, and homes. **Observation** is the intentional, systematic act of looking at the behavior of a child or children in a particular setting, program, or situation. Observation is sometimes referred to as "kid-watching" and is an excellent way to find out about children's behaviors and learning.

TABLE 5–1

INFORMAL METHODS FOR ASSESSMENT AND EVALUATION

Method	Purpose	Guidelines
Observation Kid watching—looking at children in a systematic way.	Enables teachers to identify children's behaviors, document performance, and make decisions.	Plan for observation and be clear about the purposes of the observation.
Authentic Is performance-based and is based on real-life activities.	Helps determine if children are applying what they have learned to real-life situations (e.g., applying math skills such as making change).	Make sure that what is assessed relates to real-life events, that the learner is involved in doing something, and that instruction has been provided prior to assessment.
Anecdotal Record Brief narrative account of an event or behavior.	Provides insight into a particular reason for behavior and provides a basis for planning a teaching strategy.	Record only what is observed or heard; should deal with the facts and should include the setting (e.g., where the behavior occurs) and what was said and done.
Running Record Focuses on a sequence of events that occurs over time.	Helps obtain a more detailed insight into behavior over a period of time.	Maintain objectivity and try to include as much detail as possible.
Event Sampling Focuses on a particular behavior during a particular event (e.g., behavior at lunch time, behavior on the playground, behavior in a reading group).	Helps identify behaviors during a particular event over time.	Identify a target behavior to be observed during particular times (e.g., bullying during transition activities).
Time Sampling Record particular events or behaviors at specific time intervals (e.g., five minutes, ten minutes).	Helps identify when a particular child demonstrates a particular behavior. Helps answer the question, "Does the child do something all the time or just at certain times and events?"	Observe only during the time period specified.
Rating Scale Contains a list for a set of behaviors.	Enables teachers to record data when they are observed.	Select the type of rating scale that is appropriate for what is rated. Make sure that key descriptors and the rating scale are appropriate for what is being observed.

(Continued)

143

TABLE 5–1
INFORMAL METHODS FOR ASSESSMENT AND EVALUATION *(Continued)*

METHOD	PURPOSE	GUIDELINES
Checklist A list of behaviors identifying what children can and cannot do.	Enables teachers to easily observe and check off what children know and are able to do.	Make sure that the checklist includes behaviors for the program and for learning (e.g., counts from 1 to 10, hops on one foot).
Work Sample Collections of children's work that demonstrate what they know and are able to do.	Provides a concrete example of learning; can show growth and achievement over time.	Make sure that work samples demonstrate what children know and are able to do. Let children help select what items they want to use as examples of their learning.
Portfolio Collections of children's work samples.	Provides documentation of a child's achievement in specific areas over time. Can include test scores, written work samples, videotapes, etc.	A portfolio is not a dumpster but a thoughtful collection of materials that documents learning over time.
Interview Engages children in discussion through questions.	Children can be asked to explain behaviors, work samples, or particular answers.	Ask questions at all levels of Bloom's taxonomy to gain insight into children's learning at all levels.

Informal methods of assessment are a powerful way for you to gather ongoing information about your children's learning and behavior. A good guideline is to assess all children as needed and to have new assessment data on every child every two to three weeks.

Purposes of Observation

Observation is designed to gather information on which to base decisions, make recommendations, develop curriculum, plan activities and learning strategies, and assess children's growth, development, and learning. For example, when professionals and parents sometimes look at children, they do not really "see" or concern themselves with what the children are doing or why. However, the significance and importance of critical behaviors go undetected if observation is done casually and is limited to "unsystematic looking." In order for you to make your observation count, review the purposes of observation as outlined in Figure 5.4. In the "Professionalism in Practice: Making a Difference," on pages 150 and 151, second grade teacher Lu Ann Harger shares her perspective on assessment and evaluation.

Intentional observation is a useful, informative, and powerful means for informing and guiding teaching and for helping ensure that all children learn. The advantages of gathering data through observation are shown in Figure 5.5. Review these six advantages now.

* *Determine the cognitive, linguistic, social, emotional, and physical development of children.* Using a developmental checklist is one way professionals can systematically observe and chart the development of children. Figure 5.3 shows a checklist for emergent literacy.

* *Identify children's interests and learning styles.* Today, teachers are very interested in developing learning activities, materials, and classroom centers based on children's interests, preferences, and learning styles.

* *Plan.* The professional practice of teaching requires planning on a daily, ongoing basis. Observation provides useful, authentic, and solid information that enables teachers to intentionally plan for activities rather than make decisions with little or no information.

* *Meet the needs of individual children.* Meeting the needs of individual children is an important part of teaching and learning. For example, a child may be advanced cognitively but overly aggressive and lacking the social skills necessary to play cooperatively and interact with others. Through observation, a teacher can gather information to develop a plan for helping him learn how to play with others.

* *Determine progress.* Systematic observation, over time, provides a rich, valuable, and informative source of information about how individuals and groups of children are progressing in their learning and behavior.

* *Provide information to parents.* Professionals report to and conference with parents on an ongoing basis. Observational information adds to other information they have, such as test results and child work samples, and provides a fuller and more complete picture of individual children.

* *Provide self-insight.* Observational information can help professionals learn more about themselves and what to do to help children.

⌐◦ **FIGURE 5.4   Purposes of Observation**

Observation is one of the most frequently used methods for finding out more about children. Systematic observation each day will enable you to meet children's learning needs and be a more effective teacher.

Observing is an excellent way to find out about a child's behavior and how well he is learning. What do you think this teacher can learn about this child from watching him complete the puzzle?

FIGURE 5.5   Advantages of Gathering Data Through Observation

The advantages of gathering information on children through observation are many and varied. Observation, well done, is probably the most effective means of assessment available to you.

* Enables professionals to collect information about children that they might not otherwise gather through other sources. A great deal of the consequences, causes, and reactions to children's behavior can be assessed only through observation. Observation enables you to gather data that cannot be assessed by formal, standardized tests, questioning, and parent and child interviews.

* Is ideally suited to learning more about children in play settings. Observation affords you the opportunity to note a child's social behavior in a play group and discern how cooperatively he or she interacts with peers. Observing a child at play gives professionals a wealth of information about developmental levels, social skills, and what the child is or is not learning in play settings.

* Allows you to learn a lot about children's pro-social behavior and peer interactions. It can help you plan for appropriate and inclusive activities to promote the social growth of young children. Additionally, your observations can serve as the basis for developing multicultural activities to benefit all children.

* Provides a basis for the assessment of what children are developmentally able to do. Many learning skills are developed sequentially, such as the refinement of large-motor skills before small-motor skills. Through observation, professionals can determine whether children's abilities are within a normal range of growth and development.

* Is useful to assess children's performance over time. Documentation of daily, weekly, and monthly observations of children's behaviors and learning provides a database for the cumulative evaluation of each child's achievement and development.

* Helps you provide concrete information for use in reporting to and conferencing with parents. Increasingly, reports to parents about children involve professionals' observations and children's work samples so parents and educators can collaborate to determine how to help children develop cognitively, socially, emotionally, and physically.

FIGURE 5.6   Effective Ways to Record Observational Data

Use these methods to help you quickly and easily gather and manage observational data. The important point is to make sure you record data while observing. Telling yourself you will remember seldom works!

* Wear an apron (a carpenter's apron works very well) with pockets to carry pens, note cards, and Post-It notes.

* Use Post-It notes to record observations. These can be easily added to students' notebooks, folders, etc.

* Use the literacy checklist shown in Figure 5.3, checklists you make yourself, and checklists found in other books.

* Use tape recorders, videotapes, and digital cameras to gather information. A problem with using a tape recorder is you have to transcribe your notes. Video recorders are probably best reserved for group observations. On the other hand, digital cameras are an excellent means of gathering and storing data.

Steps for Conducting Observations

Before we discuss the steps of observation in detail, look at Figure 5.6. It advises you on four effective ways to record your observational data. The four steps involved in the process of systematic, purposeful observation are listed in Figure 5.7. Review them now in preparation for our discussion of each of them.

STEP 1: PLAN FOR OBSERVATION.   Planning is an important part of the observation process. Everything you do regarding observation should be planned in advance of the observation. A good guide to follow in planning for observation is to ask the questions *who, what, where, when,* and *how.*

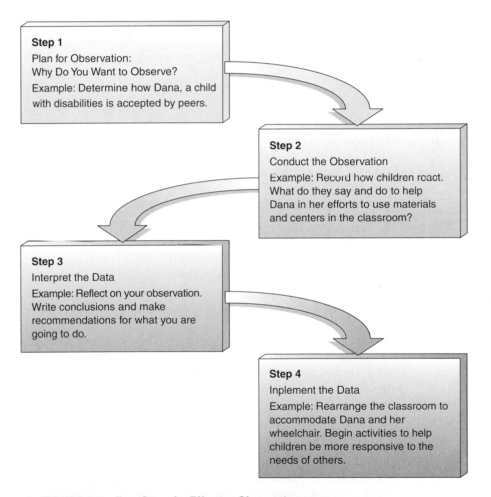

Step 1

Plan for Observation:
Why Do You Want to Observe?
Example: Determine how Dana, a child with disabilities is accepted by peers.

Step 2

Conduct the Observation
Example: Record how children react. What do they say and do to help Dana in her efforts to use materials and centers in the classroom?

Step 3

Interpret the Data
Example: Reflect on your observation. Write conclusions and make recommendations for what you are going to do.

Step 4

Inplement the Data
Example: Rearrange the classroom to accommodate Dana and her wheelchair. Begin activities to help children be more responsive to the needs of others.

☞ **FIGURE 5.7   Four Steps for Effective Observation**

Following these four steps will enable you to confidently and effectively use observation on a daily basis in your classroom.

Observing children at play enables teachers to learn about their developmental levels, social skills, and peer interactions. How might teachers use this information to plan future play-based activities?

Setting goals for observation is a crucial part of the planning process. Goals allow you to reflect on why you want to observe and thus direct your efforts to what you will observe. Stating a goal focuses your attention on the purpose of your observation. For example, suppose you want to determine the effectiveness of your efforts in providing an inclusive classroom or program, and in fully including an exceptional child into the classroom. Your goals might read like this:

Goal 1: To determine what modifications might be necessary in the classroom to facilitate access to all parts of the classroom for Dana in her wheelchair.

Goal 2: To assess the development of pro-social behavioral characteristics that other children display to Dana while interacting in the classroom. Goal setting sharpens your observation and makes it more effective.

STEP 2: CONDUCT THE OBSERVATION.   While conducting your observation, it is imperative that you be objective, specific, and as thorough as possible. For example, during your observation of Dana and her peers, you notice that there is not enough room for Dana to manipulate her wheelchair past the easel and shelf where the crayons are kept. None of her peers noticed that Dana could not reach the crayons and so did not help her get them. Dana had to ask one of the children to get the crayons for her. Now you have information that will enable you to take action.

STEP 3: INTERPRET THE DATA.   All observations can and should result in some kind of interpretation. Interpretation serves several important functions. First, it puts your observations into perspective—that is, in relation to what you already know and do not know about events and the behaviors of your children. Second, interpretation helps you make sense of what you have observed and enables you to use your professional knowledge to interpret what you have seen. Third, interpretation has the potential to make you learn to anticipate representative behavior indicative of normal growth and development under given conditions, and to recognize what might not be representative of appropriate growth, development, and learning for each child. Fourth, interpretation forms the foundation for the implementation, necessary adaptations, or modifications in a program or curriculum. In your observation, you can note that Dana's only exceptionality is that she is physically disabled. Her growth in other areas is normal, and she displays excellent social skills in that she is accepted by others, knows when to ask for help, and is able to ask for help. When Dana asks for help, she receives it.

Step 4: Implement the Data. The implementation phase means that you commit to do something with the results or the "findings" of your observation. For example, although Dana's behavior in your observation was appropriate, many of the children can benefit from activities designed to help them recognize and respond to the needs of others. In addition, the physical environment of the classroom requires some modification in the rearrangement of movable furniture to make it more accessible for Dana. Implementation means you report to and conference with parents or others as necessary and appropriate. Implementation—that is, doing something with the results of your observations—is the most important part of the observation process. The following "Program in Action" describes how the Daviess County Schools implemented a new curriculum based on recent research. As you read this

Program in Action

Graduation 2010: A Brain Research Initiative

Graduation 2010, a program of the Daviess County (Kentucky) Public Schools, is a curriculum designed to expand the learning capacity for children by taking into consideration those experiences that recent brain research indicates enhance brain development and learning. This program builds on the increase in learning that occurs when children are taught piano, foreign language, art, dance, and critical thinking at an early age. The eight program components of Graduation 2010 are the arts, music, foreign language, reading, critical thinking, health/emotional health, family involvement, and community involvement.

Kindergarten students who entered school in 1997 will graduate in the year 2010 having had thirteen years of an enhanced curriculum based on these experiences. All elementary students participate in the program, but the class of 2010 will be the first to have begun in kindergarten.

Every kindergarten student is learning to play the piano and being exposed to intense music instruction. The research is clear on the direct correlation between learning music and high academic achievement. Every

student is learning a foreign language, which develops new pathways in the brain. Every student will master the basic skill of reading before exiting the primary grades. All kindergarten students will experience dance, theater, and the visual arts. Every child will learn critical thinking skills, and nurses are available at every school to assist with health issues. Also, all students are learning to play chess through a teacher-developed curriculum. Family and community involvement is an important part of Graduation 2010, and all schools hold Back to School Picnics to stimulate family involvement.

Graduation 2010 is a program of the Daviess County Public Schools, Owensboro, Kentucky. For more information, contact Marilyn Mills, Graduation 2010 Coordinator, at mmills@dcps.org.

To complete a Program in Action activity, visit the Companion Website at _http://www. prenhall.com/morrison_, select Chapter 5, then choose the Programs in Action module.

Professionalism in Practice

MAKING A DIFFERENCE

Lu Ann Harger, Second Grade Teacher, Hinkle Creek Elementary, Noblesville, Indiana

USA Today All STAR Teacher Team — 2001

There are many ways to make a difference in a child's life. As a teacher, each year you are given the enormous honor of spending eight hours a day creating within a child a burning desire for learning. You have the opportunity to introduce your children to the wonders of numbers, letters, and words, to the history of their nation. You have the ability to create the "what if" and the "tell me more" in minds each day. But where to start this daunting task is difficult to say.

All things have a beginning, and nothing equals a sound beginning. Each year as the school year is ready to begin, I call all my students to introduce myself and our classroom, Camp Can Do, and put their minds at ease. Fear of the unknown is a great deterrent to success, and this phone call goes a long way in calming that fear. I ask them to bring a thinking cap along to help on tough assignments and, of course, I keep mine handy all year too!

As they begin the first week of school, activities are planned to get to know each other and to evaluate levels of learning. Students play the M&M game by choosing a handful and speaking about themselves according to the colors. Each child gets a chance to say the alphabet, show me crayons to match color words, read a set of selected grade level word lists, and read a passage aloud to me. As a class we sit in community circle and use cards to stimulate discussions. That way I can check for verbal expression, use of vocabulary words, life experiences, and comfort levels. Students also fill out a reading inventory on their likes and dislikes, play math games to show computation skills, and copy some basic words to evaluate their fine motor skills.

Now that I am on the right track evaluating my students, I work on my other team members, my parents. At the beginning of each school year at Parent Night, parents are asked to provide information about their child. Sure, I have permanent records to look over but mom and dad are the experts. They share fears and acts of bravery, favorites, past school experiences, and spe-

cial traits of their children. With their help I will gain a better understanding of their child, and they will understand how much I value their input. During the meeting I explain how our classroom, or Camp Can Do, is run and what we do each day. I also explain the importance of their role as communicator, coach, and study partner. In the end, I read *Leo the Late Bloomer* and reiterate that my plan this year is for everyone to make it, just like Leo. Now I have the complete package: parent input, student files, and my classroom evaluations. This is a sound beginning. Using this information, I can set up learning profiles for all my students that will be used throughout the year.

As the year's curriculum begins to unfold, I gather new information. In math, I pretest before each chapter to see what students know and do not know. Then throughout the lessons I group students according to their needs. Students work in many different groups by the year's end as their mastery of math skills is checked. Students are able to work on weak areas like time and money, but expand areas in which they are strong, like addition computation. In spelling, lists are modified according to learning levels. Everyone gets an opportunity to try the bonus words and earn a chance for spelling prizes. In reading and language arts, students work in small and large groups. They begin to take home simple readers or chapter books to become members of the Campfire Readers. Students work on partner reading books, enjoy the Scholastic Reader computer program books and add up pages read, and use trade books for readers during the year as well. Weekly reading conferences are held between students and myself to check on comprehension.

The use of various assessment tools provides me with a wide range of knowledge about each student. Some assessments can be as easy to use as a book discussion to determine my students' comprehension or a game to show knowledge gained. Assessments can also take the form of a Venn diagram for comparison or a poster giving facts about the animal students researched. Ongoing assessments, such as writing portfolios, can provide a big picture of skill growth by storing information in a time line fashion. Other assessments may be standardized, such as a math or reading test. No matter what type of assessment I might use, I think it is critical that my students be aware beforehand how they will be assessed and afterward take part in a discussion of the assessment tool. When I give a test of any kind, my students have a chance to talk over the items they missed. When using a less formal assessment such as a rubric, I give these out in advance. This gives students an idea of my expectations and a way to determine what they would like to accomplish.

No matter how you choose to assess your students, the most important thing to remember is that the assessment is only as good as the teacher using it. To keep the information meaningful, I look at the assessments I use with each unit I teach. Is there an area that I forgot to include? Are my students missing a question on a test in large numbers? Did this assessment give me the information I needed to know about my students' learning? What do the students think of the assessment? Is the information easy for me to understand? Is it easy to share with my students and my parents? Good assessments gather meaningful information that enhances children's learning. If my assessments are doing that, great! If not, I need to make a change so they are.

All of this information would mean nothing to the students or me if they were not engaged in their learning. Seven years ago, two colleagues and I investigated the idea of integrated instruction. Taking all our textbooks, we rebuilt our second grade curriculum from the ground up using our social studies standards as the base. The result was a full year of learning that was connected and meaningful. Students could learn about community workers and be reading a story for language arts on the same topic that week. The math lesson would also use community helpers as a base for the skill taught that week. The effort to make this possible was enormous and continues today as the plan is refined each year, but the results are worth it. Learning has become an "I get it" experience for my students. They see that our story for the week is about money and so are the math lessons. They understand that we are working on the skill of compound words because they are in our story for the week. Suddenly learning has an order and pattern that make their gathering of knowledge so much more genuine and long term. This connection of learning also brings strengths and weaknesses together that help improve both. This is real, lifelong learning!

Creating an environment where learning occurs is a huge key to successful students. We use these lifelong guidelines: Be truthful. Be trustworthy. Do your personal best. Appreciate others. Be an active listener. By expecting everyone in our classroom, including myself, to follow these guidelines, we create a place that is consistent, caring, and safe. Students know what to expect from day to day. By taking the time to listen to a story from home, provide a worry box to stuff concerns in, use mistakes as learning opportunities or help ease a fear, I am modeling these expectations. I am creating a place where my students feel comfortable, can take risks, and will grow as learners. From my most able student to my least, I hear them saying: I can do this, I will try.

Can this make a difference? We sure think so in room 12, or Camp Can Do as we like to call it. Never underestimate the potential of a child. If they shoot for the moon and miss, they will still wind up in the stars.

 To review the Professional Development Checklist and complete a Professionalism in Practice activity, visit the Companion Website at *http://www.prenhall.com/morrison*, select Chapter 5, then choose the Professional Development module.

feature think about how you could apply observation and other assessment strategies to evaluate children's learning.

A sample observation form you can use is shown in Figure 5.8. This form can be a useful tool for gathering observational data and it will prove helpful when planning for teaching and conferencing with parents. You can also check other resources to develop more specific observation guides you could use as checklists to track developmental behaviors with individual children.

REPORTING TO AND COMMUNICATING WITH PARENTS

Part of your responsibility as a professional is to report to parents about the growth, development, and achievement of their children. Some of your colleagues may view reporting to parents as a bother and wish they didn't have to do it. Nonetheless, reporting to and communicating with parents is one of your most important jobs. The following guidelines will help you meet this important responsibility of reporting your assessment information to parents:

For practice in observing and interpreting observation data, visit the Companion Website at *http://www.prenhall.com/ morrison*, select Chapter 5, then choose Observing Will in the Resources module.

*   *Be honest and realistic with parents.* Too often, teachers do not want to hurt parents' feelings. They want to sugarcoat what they are reporting. However, parents need your honest assessments about what their children know, are able to do, and will be able to do. With this honest assessment you can solicit their help in helping their children.
*   *Communicate to parents so they can understand.* What you communicate to parents must make sense to them. Parents must understand what you are saying. Reporting to parents often has to be a combination of written (in their language) and oral communication.
*   *Provide parents with ideas and information that will help them help their children learn.* Remember that you and parents are partners in helping children be successful in school and life.

For more information about assessment issues that relate to young children, go to the Companion Website at *http://www.prenhall.com/ morrison*, select Chapter 5, then choose the Linking to Learning module to connect to the National Education Goals Panel site.

Systematic observation of children represents a powerful way for you to learn about and guide and direct children's learning and behavior. If you learn to use it well, you and your children will benefit.

WHAT ARE THE ISSUES IN THE ASSESSMENT OF YOUNG CHILDREN?

As with almost everything that has been and will be discussed in this book, issues surround essential questions about what is good practice, what is inappropriate practice, and what is best for children and families. Assessment is no different. Let's examine some of the issues of assessment in early childhood.

☞ **FIGURE 5.8   Sample Observation Form**

Teacher's Name: _____

Date: _____

Time: _____

Location: _____

Classroom or Setting: _____

Purpose of Observing: _____

Prediction or Expectations of Findings: _____

Significant Events during Observation:

Reflective Analysis of Significant Event: (this reflection should include what you have learned):

List at least three ways you can use or apply what you observed to your future teaching:

Assessment and Accountability

To take an online self-test on this chapter's contents, go to the Companion Website at *http://www.prenhall.com/ morrison*, select Chapter 5, then choose the Self-Test module.

There is a tremendous emphasis on the use of standardized tests to measure achievement for comparing children, programs, school districts, and countries. This emphasis will continue for a number of reasons. First, the public, including politicians and legislatures, sees assessment as a means of making schools and teachers accountable for teaching the nation's children. Second, assessment is seen as playing a critical role in the reform of education. As long as there is a public desire to improve teaching and achievement, we will continue to see an emphasis on assessment for accountability purposes.

High-Stakes Testing

High-stakes testing occurs when standardized tests are used to make important, and often life-influencing, decisions about children. Standardized tests have specific and standardized content, administration, and scoring procedures and norms for interpreting scores. High-stakes outcomes include decisions about whether to

Report your assessment findings accurately and honestly to the parents of your students. How might such communication build trust?

admit children into programs (e.g., kindergarten) and whether to retain or promote children. Generally, the early childhood profession is opposed to high-stakes testing for children through grade three. However, as part of the accountability movement, many politicians and school administrators view high-stakes testing as a means of ensuring that children learn and that promotions are based on achievement. Many school critics maintain that in the pre-K and primary grades there is too much social promotion—that is, passing children from grade to grade merely to enable students to keep pace with their age peers.

At-Home Testing

Parents always like to know how their children are doing and what they are capable of doing. Evaluation and assessment of children outside the classroom has always been a reality. Many parents pay considerable amounts of money to know more about their children. The "Technology Tie-In: How Smart Is My Child?" illustrates how technology is influencing the testing of young children. As you read the "Technology Tie-In," think about some issues involved in this growing phenonomen. Also, think about your role in helping parents help their children reach their full potentials.

Today there is a great deal of emphasis on accountability. Teachers are asked to be accountable to parents, legislators, and the public. Providing for and conducting developmentally appropriate assessment of young children and their programs is one of the best ways that you can be accountable for what you do. Conducting appropriate assessment enables you to be accountable not only to parents and the public, but also to young children. You have accepted a sacred trust and have dedicated your life to helping children learn and develop. Effective assessment practices will help you achieve this goal.

Technology Tie-In

HOW SMART IS MY CHILD?

Without a doubt, education is big business, and the business of testing young children at school is one of the biggest businesses. Now, the business of testing young children has entered the home. Many parents want to know not only how smart their child is, but also what they can do to help their children learn and do better in school. William Bennett's new for-profit online school for kindergarten through high school markets a series of diagnostic tests for every major subject in every grade. Parents administer the tests and then have them scored online for a cost of from $50 to $100. Other for-profit companies that offer tests for children include LeapFrog and Smartkids. Smartkids sells a battery of CD-ROM tests for preschool to sixth grade for $24.95 each. The company also offers a list of products that will help children learn.

Visit these websites and determine whether or not you would recommend them to the parents of the children in your program.

 To complete this Technology Tie-In activity and others like it, visit the Companion Website at *http://www. prenhall.com/morrison*, select Chapter 5, then choose the Technology Tie-In module.

ACTIVITIES FOR PROFESSIONAL DEVELOPMENT

In this chapter, we have stressed the importance of appropriate assessment and observation as a basis for making decisions about what to teach children and how to teach them. We have also emphasized the importance of developing and implementing observation and assessment strategies in developmentally appropriate ways. Refer again to the "Professional Development Goal" at the beginning of the Chapter, to the "Professional Development Checklist" on page 20 and 21, to the "Professionalism in Practice" by Linda Sholar on pages 138 and 139, and the "Professionalism in Practice" by Lu Ann Harger on pages 150 and 151. After you have reviewed these, complete the following exercises.

1. Create an observation guide similar to Figure 5.8. Observe in an early childhood classroom and determine how effective you are at observing some aspect of children's development and learning.

2. Observe a particular child during play or another activity. Before your observation, make sure you follow the steps presented in this chapter. Use the information you gathered to plan a learning activity for the child. As you plan, determine what information you need that you didn't gather through observation. When you observe again, what will you do differently?

3. Interview several kindergarten and primary teachers and ask them to share with you their ideas and guidelines for assessing with portfolios. How can you apply this information to your teaching?

4. Review the contents of several children's portfolios. How are they similar and different? What do the contents tell you about the children? What would you include that wasn't included? What would you delete?

5. Frequently articles in newspapers and magazines address assessment and testing. Over a two-week period, review these sources and determine what assessment and evaluation issues are "in the news." Put these materials in your portfolio or teaching file.

6. Visit pre-K–3 programs in several different school districts. Make a list of the various ways they assess and of the instruments and procedures they use. Compare them with the ones identified in this chapter. How and for what purposes are the tests used? What conclusions can you draw from the information you gathered?

For additional chapter resources and activities, visit the Companion Website at *http://www.prenhall.com/morrison,* select Chapter 5, then choose the Professional Development, Resources, or Linking to Learning modules.

FOCUS QUESTIONS

1. How is brain research influencing the care and education of infants and toddlers?

2. What are the cognitive, language, and social milestones of infant and toddler development?

3. How can I use knowledge of infant and toddler development to guide my developmentally appropriate practice?

4. How can I provide quality programs for infants and toddlers?

chapter 6

Infants and Toddlers

FOUNDATIONAL YEARS FOR LEARNING

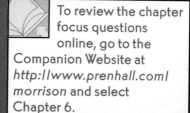

To review the chapter focus questions online, go to the Companion Website at *http://www.prenhall.com/morrison* and select Chapter 6.

 ## PROFESSIONAL DEVELOPMENT GOAL

DEVELOPMENTALLY APPROPRIATE PRACTICE

I understand children's developmental stages and growth from birth through age eight, and use this knowledge to implement developmentally appropriate practice. I do all I can to advance the physical, intellectual, social, and emotional development of the children in my care to their fullest potential.

*I*nterest in infant and toddler care and education is at an all-time high; it will continue at this level well into the future. The growing demand for quality infant and toddler programs stems primarily from the reasons discussed in Chapter 2. The popularity of early care and education is also attributable to a changing view of the very young and the discovery that infants are remarkably competent individuals. Let's examine the ways that infants' and toddlers' early experiences shape their future development.

PAINTING PORTRAITS OF CHILDREN

One of the purposes of this book is to help you understand what children are like. To help achieve this goal I have included a special feature titled "A Portrait of . . ." At the beginning of Chapters 6, 7, 8, and 9, you will have the opportunity to view a word portrait of the children under discussion. These portraits will provide you with an "up-close" look at infants, toddlers, preschoolers, kindergartners, and primary grade children. As you review each of these, use them to paint your own portraits of children. Begin this "paint your own portrait" process now by reviewing Figures 6.1 and 6.2 "that give characteristics" of infants and toddlers.

WHAT ARE INFANTS AND TODDLERS LIKE?

Think for a minute about your experiences with infants. What characteristics stand out most in your mind? I know that infants never cease to amaze me! Infants are capable of so many accomplishments. They are great imitators. Make a face at an infant and she will make a face back. Stick your tongue out at an infant and she will stick out her tongue at you. Talk to infants and they will "talk" back to you! One of the great delights and challenges of working with infants is that you will constantly discover the wonderful things infants can do.

To check your understanding of this chapter with the online Study Guide, go to the Companion Website at *http://www.prenhall.com/ morrison*, select Chapter 6, then choose the Study Guide module.

Have you ever tried to keep up with a toddler? Everyone who tries ends up exhausted at the end of the day! A typical response is, "They are into everything!" The infant and toddler years between birth and age three are full of developmental milestones and significant events. **Infancy,** life's first year, includes the first breath, the first smile, first thoughts, first words, and first steps. Significant developments continue during **toddlerhood,** the period between one and three years. Two of the most outstanding developmental milestones of these years are walking and rapid language development. Mobility and language are the cornerstones of autonomy that enable toddlers to become independent. These unique developmental events are significant for children as well as those who care for and teach them. How you and other early childhood professionals and parents respond to infants'

FIGURE 6.1   A Portrait of Infants

0–6-Month-Olds:

* use reflexive motor actions such as sucking and grasping.
* sit with support (4 months).
* mimic adults' facial expressions and gestures. True social interactions (reciprocity) begin to develop.
* move their body in response to human voice.
* when awake and alert, scan the environment.
* can discriminate among sweet, bitter, and salty.
* are active in their own development.
* have memory capabilities from birth.
* produce truly social smiles in response to people they know.

6–12-Month-Olds:

* have color vision.
* have visual acuity of 20/100 (can see clearly at 100 feet what an adult with normal vision sees clearly at 20 feet).
* sit without support (8 months).
* begin walking (12 months).
* have increased deliberation and purposefulness in response to adults.
* can say "Da-Da" and "ma-ma" (7–9 months).
* are active in their own development.
* continue improvement in memory abilities.
* develope emotional reaction of surprise.
* begin to react negatively to strangers (stranger distress).
* form specific infant-caregiver attachments.
* speak their first words.

These descriptions of behaviors and abilities paint a picture of some commonly and frequently observed characteristics of infants. As you observe and care for infants use this descriptive portrait to add other word descriptions. Keep in mind that all children are different and unique and that ages of development are approximate, especially in infancy.

first accomplishments and toddlers' quests for autonomy helps determine how they will develop and master life events.

As you work with infants, toddlers, and other children, constantly keep in mind that "normal" growth and development milestones are based on averages. "Average" is the middle ground of development (for example, Table 6–1 gives average heights and weights for infants and toddlers). You must also consider the

Toddlers:

* use first words—usually refer to people (mama) and objects (ball).

* have a vocabulary of about 50 words by 18 months.

* start to use two-word sentences.

* use one object for another—a paper cup is a telephone. This is representational thought.

* love to engage in pretend play.

* want to do things for themselves. They display increased independence from parents and caregivers.

* love to interact with others, especially other children. They become more aware of self and others.

* play a very active role in the parent/teacher/child relationship and interactions.

* show an awareness to social demands—understand certain things are forbidden.

These characteristics of toddlers only begin to paint the sketchiest portrait of who they are and what they can do. Although with infants we can see the differences in individual development, it is with toddlers that we really begin to observe the powerful influences heredity and environments exert. We can really see differences in how toddlers look, in how and what they learn, and how they interact with others. Also, during the toddler years parents and caregivers have to use skills that will enhance and maximize cognitive, language, and social development. For example, support and limit setting provide a framework or context in which toddlers can confidently develop in all areas. In addition, toddlerhood is a good time for using scaffolding procedures (appropriate guidance, advice, hints, questioning, etc.) to help toddlers learn new tasks. Toddlers are fun to observe and interact with. As you do, add to this portrait and paint your own real-life picture of what toddlers are like.

FIGURE 6.2   **A Portrait of Toddlers**

whole child and take into account cultural and family background, including nutritional and health history, to determine what is normal for individual children. Futhermore, when children are provided with good nutrition, health care, and a warm, loving emotional environment, development tends toward what is "normal" for each child. We begin now our look at young children with a discussion of the importance of the brain in ongoing growth and development.

YOUNG BRAINS: A PRIMER

Brain and child development research has created a great deal of interest in the first three years of life. Let's review some interesting facts about infant and toddler brain development and consider the implications they have for how you practice as a professional. Also review Figure 6.3, which shows the regions of the brain and their functional processes.

TABLE 6–1

AVERAGE HEIGHT AND WEIGHT OF INFANTS AND TODDLERS

| AGE | MALES | | FEMALES | |
---	HEIGHT (INCHES)	WEIGHT (POUNDS)	HEIGHT (INCHES)	WEIGHT (POUNDS)
Birth	19.9	7.2	19.6	7.1
3 months	24.1	13.2	23.4	11.9
6 months	26.7	17.3	25.9	15.9
9 months	28.5	20.2	27.7	18.9
1 year	30.0	22.4	29.3	21.0
1½ years	32.4	25.3	31.9	23.9
2 years	34.5	27.8	34.1	26.2
2½ years	36.3	30.1	35.9	28.5
3 years	38.0	32.4	37.6	30.7

Source: Based on data from Ross Products Division, Abbott Laboratories. "Physical Growth NCHS Percentiles Chart" (1999).

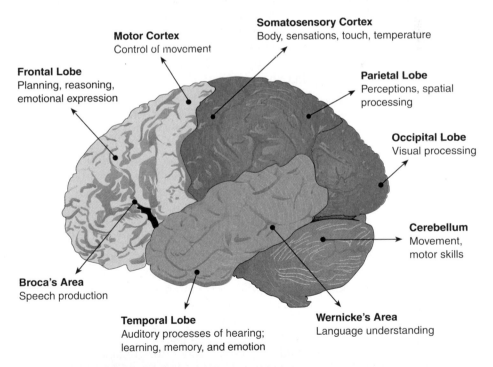

FIGURE 6.3   Brain Regions

Over the last decade, scientists and educators have spent considerable time and energy exploring the links between brain development and functions and classroom learning. Brain research provides many implications for how to develop enriched classrooms for children and for how to engage them in activities that will help them learn and develop to their optimal levels. Most important, brain research had made educators aware of the importance of providing young children stimulating activities early in life.

For more information about brain development, go to the Companion Website at *http://www.prenhall.com/morrison*, select Chapter 6, then choose the Linking to Learning module to connect to the I Am Your Child site.

The brain is a fascinating and complex organ. Anatomically, the young brain is like the adult brain, except it is smaller. The average adult brain weighs approximately 3 lb. At birth, the infant's brain weighs 14 oz.; at six months, 1.31 lb.; and at three years, 2.4 lb. So you can see that during the first two years of life the brain undergoes tremendous physical growth. The brain finishes developing at age ten, when it reaches its full adult size.

At birth, the brain has 100 billion neurons, or nerve cells, all it will ever have! It is important for parents and other caregivers to play with, respond to, interact with, and talk to young children because this is the way brain connections develop and learning takes place. As brain connections are used repeatedly, they become permanent. On the other hand, brain connections that are not used or used only a little may wither away. This withering away is known as **neural shearing** or **pruning.** This helps explain why children who are reared in language-rich environments do well in school, while children who are not reared in such environments may be at risk for academic failure.

Go to the Companion Website at *http://www.prenhall.com/morrison*, select Chapter 6, then choose the Linking to Learning module.

Also by the time of birth, these billions of neurons have formed over 50 trillion connections, or synapses, through a process called **synaptogenesis,** the proliferation of neural connections; this process will continue to occur until the age of ten. The experiences that children have help form these neural connections. Experiences count. If children don't have the experiences they need to form neural connections, they may be at risk for poor developmental and behavioral outcomes.

Children also need the right experiences at the right times. For example, the critical period for language development is the first year of life. It is during this time that the auditory pathways for language learning are formed. Beginning at birth, an infant can distinguish the sounds of all the languages of the world. But at about six months, through the process of neuron pruning or shearing, infants lose the ability to distinguish the sounds of languages they have not heard. By twelve months, their auditory maps are pretty well in place.[1] It is literally a case of use it or lose it.

Having the right experiences at the right time also relates to critical periods, developmental "windows of opportunity" or sensitive periods (discussed in Chapter 3) during which it is easier to learn something than it is at another time. (See Table 6–4, which shows the progress of vocabulary development in the early years.) This is another example of how experiences influence development. An infant whose mother or other caregiver talks to her is more likely to have a larger vocabulary than an infant whose mother doesn't talk to her.

For more information about the importance of the first three years of life, go to the Companion Website at *http://www.prenhall.com/morrison*, select Chapter 6, then choose the Linking to Learning module to connect to the Zero to Three site.

Figure 6.4 outlines some conclusions we can draw from our discussion about the brain. And, speaking of the brain, music is an excellent way to stimulate babies' brains. Refer to the "Technology Tie-In: Using Technology with Infants and Toddlers" on page 166 for some suggestions for how to do this.

FIGURE 6.4 Implications of Brain Research for Early Childhood Practice

* Babies are born to learn. They are remarkable learning instruments. Their brains make them so.

* Children's brain development and their ability to learn throughout life rely on the interplay between nature (genetic inheritance, controlled by 80,000 genes) and nurture (the experiences they have and the environments in which they are raised).

* What happens to children early in life has a long-lasting influence on how they develop and learn.

* Critical periods influence learning positively and negatively.

* The human brain is quite "plastic." It has the ability to change in response to different kinds of experiences and environments.

* Prevention and early intervention are more beneficial than later remediation.

* The brain undergoes physiological changes in response to experiences.

* An enriched environment influences brain development. (Figure 6.7 shows the characteristics of an enriched environment.)

NATURE, NURTURE, AND DEVELOPMENT

Does nature (genetics) or nurture (environment) play a larger role in development? This question is the center of a never-ending debate. At this time there is no one right and true answer because the answer depends on many things. On the one hand, many traits are fully determined by heredity. For example, your eye color is a product of your heredity. Physical height is also largely influenced by heredity, as are temperament and shyness. Certainly height can be influenced by nutrition, growth hormones, and other environmental interventions. But by and large, an individual's height is genetically determined.

On the other hand, nurturing and the environment in which children grow and develop play an important role in development. For example, environmental factors that play a major role in early development include nutrition, quality of the environment, stimulation of the brain, affectionate and positive relationships with parents, and opportunities to learn. Think for a moment about other kinds of environmental influences such as family, environment, school, and friends that affect development. The "Professionalism in Practice: Different Teaching Styles in an Infant/Toddler Program" by Martha Pratt on pages 168 and 169 will provide you with further insight into the powerful influences of caregiver relationships on infant and toddler development.

A decade or two ago, we believed that nature and nurture were competing entities and that one of these was dominant over the other. Today we understand that they are not competing entities; both are necessary for normal development,

Technology Tie-In

USING TECHNOLOGY WITH INFANTS AND TODDLERS

Technology includes more than computers. Other forms of technology that you can use with infants and toddlers are: compact discs, digital cameras, tape recorders, video cameras, and video recorders.

I'm sure you have heard the expression that a picture is worth a thousand words. Try using a digital camera (Polaroid and disposable cameras work well too) to take pictures of your children and use them to personalize their areas, to document learning, to build individual scrapbooks, etc. With digital cameras you can have an electronic record of your children's growth, development, and accomplishments. In addition you can e-mail pictures with notations to your parents. At Bright Horizons Family Solutions, Martha Pratt and her colleagues use a regular camera to document infants' milestone achievements such as rolling over. The pictures of an infant learning to roll over and finally achieving that milestone are put on a poster board and displayed in the hallway and/or on the room bulletin board. A short paragraph explains what is happening in the pictures and emphasizes the importance of the milestone.

Martha also uses a video camera to document significant learning. For example, she videotapes toddlers learning the words to songs. She then shows these videos to parents during conferences and stresses the importance of singing and rhyming.

If a picture is worth a thousand words, then a song is worth as much or more. Infants and toddlers love music. Music is literally a child's first language, as they cry, coo, and laugh. If you have ever rocked or sung to infants, you know how emotionally involved they become. Music elicits an emotional response that is beneficial to our brains and our general well-being. There is no better way to begin your involvement of music with children than with Mozart. Why Mozart? Because research suggests that listening to classical music promotes positive emotional responses, soothes and relieves stress, and focuses the mind. You can play music for children and involve them in making music as you and they sing, dance, clap, etc. Here are some suggestions for classical music you can play with and for children.

- ✳ *Beethoven for Babies: Brain Training for Little Ones*
- ✳ *The Mozart Effect: Music for Children, Vols. 1–3*
- ✳ *Bach for Babies: Fun and Games for Budding Brains*

 To complete this Technology Tie-In activity and others like it, visit the Companion Website at *http://www.prenhall.com/morrison*, select Chapter 6, then choose the Technology Tie-In module.

Video Viewpoint

BUILDING BRAINS: THE SOONER, THE BETTER

 Powerful research evidence exists that shows that the period from birth to age three is critical to a child's healthy growth and development and to later success in school and life.

REFLECTIVE DISCUSSION QUESTIONS

Some policy makers are realizing that if they spend money on early intervention in a child's first few years of life, while their brains are most changeable, the government will save money down the line on special education, foster care, and prisons. What are some of the other costs to society when children do not receive the care they need when they are young?

REFLECTIVE DECISION MAKING

What kind of interventions would most benefit the families in your neighborhood or school district? If you were to write a letter to your congressional representative suggesting that your state enact early intervention legislation and programming, what would you recommend?

Nature
- Genes
- Inherited Traits
  - Eye color
- Temperament
- Developmental Processes
  - Language
    Development
  - Physical
    Development
  - Cognitive
    Development
- Critical Periods for
  Development
  - Windows of
    Opportunity
  - Sensitive Periods

Nurture
- Environmental Influence
  - Health
  - Nutrition
  - Schooling
    Education
  - Social Relationships
  - Cultural
    Expectations
  - Socioeconomic
    Status
  - Family
    Relationships

∽ **FIGURE 6.5   Nature and Nurture: Dimensions of Development**

"All of this evidence—and a great deal more that is beyond the scope of this report [*Rethinking the Brain*]—leads to a single conclusion: how humans develop and learn depends critically and continually on both nature (an individual's genetic endowment) and nurture (the surroundings, care, stimulation, and teaching that are provided or withheld). The roles of nature and nurture in determining intelligence cannot be weighted quantitatively, genetic and environmental factors have a more dynamic, qualitative interplay that cannot be reduced to a simple equation. And both are crucial. New knowledge about brain function has ended the 'nature *or* nurture' debate once and for all."

Source: R. Shore, Rethinking the Brain: New Insights into Early Development. (*New York: Families and Work Institute, 1997*).

and it is the interaction between the two that makes us individuals (see Figure 6.5). Consider the questions posed in the "Video Viewpoint: Building Brains."

MOTOR DEVELOPMENT

Motor skills play an important part in all of life. Even more so, motor development is essential for infants and toddlers because it contributes to their intellectual and skill development. Table 6–2 lists infant and toddler motor milestones. Human motor development is governed by certain basic principles, as shown in Figure 6.6.

Professionalism in Practice

DIFFERENT TEACHING STYLES IN AN INFANT/TODDLER PROGRAM

Martha W. Pratt

Bright Horizons Family Solutions, Pacific Gas & Electric

The sum total of my twenty-five years of working with young children has repeatedly confirmed for me a fundamental fact stated elegantly by Jeree Pawl:

"How you are is as important as what you do." *

Early childhood professionals who are willing and able to practice from this premise in combination with an ongoing education in child development, health, and safety will make quality education available to all the infants and toddlers in their care. These infants and toddlers will be given unique chances to discover, understand, and make contributions to their own knowledge, which will help compose their lifetimes.

Ten "core concepts of development" are cited in a report from the National Academy of Science and Institute of Medicine of the National Research Council. Each of the ten concepts is of critical importance, but the essence of my core beliefs about infant and toddler education are expressed in concept #5:

Human relationships, and the effects of relationships on relationships, are the building blocks of healthy development. From the moment of conception to the finality of death, intimate and caring relationships are the fundamental mediators of successful human adaptation. Those that are created in the earliest years are believed to differ from later relationships in that they are formative and constitute a basic structure within which all meaningful development unfolds. [†]

In an infant/toddler classroom, the relationships are

✳ between the child and the caregiver,

✳ among the caregivers, and

✳ between caregivers and children's families.

Let me offer an example.

IN THE INFANT/TODDLER ROOM

Amy, a toddler teacher, was on her lunch hour. From just outside her classroom of two-year-olds, she saw Gloria give Kristen a healthy push. Kristen was pushed backward and knocked Lisa down, and Lisa began to cry. The loud and sudden cry startled two infants playing on the floor nearby, who also started to cry. Gloria moved toward Kristen again with the look of a challenger. Amy called Gloria's name sharply from the doorway and redirected the child's attention to a book lying on the floor. Josie, the teacher on the floor, was engaged with the children who were clustered about her. She had seen what happened and had not shown a notable reaction.

There was an angry exchange of eye contact and body language between the two teachers. The look from Amy to Josie clearly said, "Josie, why don't you just stop them from doing that?" Josie's response, conveyed, "Amy, I don't need your help."

An emotional clash like this can take place between staff members in any infant/toddler classroom. Sometimes the clash is not as simple as a look between two people. Discord between teachers is stressful and distracting for teachers, which in turn directly affects the emotional environment surrounding the children. In an infant or toddler classroom, a hostile exchange between caregiving adults that goes unacknowledged can quickly undermine the positive educational experience of those infants and toddlers.

In the now-troubled environment of Josie's and Amy's room, the carefully chosen developmentally appropriate materials, the soft colors of the walls and carpet, and the solid grounding in developmental theory these teachers studied so hard to acquire all become momentarily irrelevant.

Teacher/caregivers in group care can provide children with a range of stimulation and experience that promotes their development. But the range of stimulation and experience that takes place in a negatively charged environment can provide a similar range of undesirable effects for toddlers. We know these children to be involved in the critical learning task of how to BE in the world. They learn this through their own imitation and repetition of how all the people around them are.

What happened between Amy and Josie? The following day, talking together with a trusted supervisor, they realized the real problem was their own impatience with each other. The pushing, bumping, and protesting toddlers were typical twos practicing new, partly learned social skills. Each teacher had her own reaction but each desired the same end. This was yet another teaching/learning incident, of which their days were filled, sometimes to overflowing. They returned to work with a new level of understanding and trust in one another.

DIFFERENT WAYS OF BEING ARE ESSENTIAL

Different but caring teacher responses to a situation stem from many sources. There is always a difference in personal style among highly qualified individuals. Levels of knowledge, skill, and experience also vary. Teachers need to share their thoughts and plans with each other on a regular basis. If we hope to build trusting relationships among our children, we must have trusting relationships among ourselves.

Let me discuss differences in style. Style is the expression of a thought or feeling in a characteristic way. It is a manner of doing a task or using a tone of voice. It is a way of behaving with certain attitudes and actions, often developed as far back as our own childhood, or a way of performing learned from a classroom teacher or mentor. Within classroom relationships, there must always be room for differences in teaching style.

Style reflects culture, language, background, values, beliefs, traditions, and experiences. Varying practices that derive from differences in style are not only acceptable infant and toddler care, they are indispensable to quality education.

Early in my career I did not know that teachers could work together to accomplish a unity of goals. It was easy and satisfying to feel as if the responsibility was mine alone. Today I know that teachers bring richly different styles to teaching. A thorough knowledge of child development together with a variety of styles is what strengthens human relationships. The quality of the relationships is deeply entwined in the caregiving, teaching, and learning process. The best studies make clear that human relationships and the effects of relationships on relationships are the building blocks of healthy development. In my opinion, infant and toddler teachers who can make this a focal point of daily practice and overall philosophy are in the best position to succeed in creating and maintaining quality education for young children.

---

*J. H. Pawl, How You Are Is as Important as What You Do . . . in Making a Positive Difference for Infants, Toddlers and Their Families (Washington, DC: Zero To Three: National Center for Infants, Toddlers and Families, 1998).

†J. P. Shonkoff, From Neurons to Neighborhoods: The Science of Early Childhood Development (Washington, DC: The National Academy of Science, National Research Council, and Institute of Medicine, 2000).

 To review the Professional Development Checklist and complete a Professionalism in Practice activity, visit the Companion Website at http://www.prenhall.com/morrison, select Chapter 6, then choose the Professional Development module.

TABLE 6–2
INFANT AND TODDLER MOTOR MILESTONES

These age ranges indicate that children vary in the age at which they achieve major motor milestones. The important thing to observe is children's achievement of them.

BEHAVIOR	AGE RANGE OF ACCOMPLISHMENT
Lifts head	Birth
Arm and legs move equally	Birth
Smiles responsively	2 Months
Smiles spontaneously	3 Months
Rolls over	6 Months
Reaches for objects	6 Months
Sits without support	7 Months
Pulls self to stand	10 Months

Source: William K. Frankenburg, Josiah Dodde, et al. *Denver II Training Manual,* 1992. Denver Developmental Materials; PO Box 6919 Denver, CO 80206-0919. Used by permission.

☞ **FIGURE 6.6 Basic Principles of Motor Development**

Think for a minute of all of the life events and activities that depend on motor skills. Virtually everything! Now think about the role motor development plays in infant and toddler development. What will you do to ensure that your infants and toddlers develop good motor skills?

✳ Motor development is sequential.

✳ Maturation of the motor system proceeds from gross (large) to fine (small) behaviors. For example, as part of her learning to reach, Maria sweeps toward an object with her whole arm. Over the course of a month, however, as a result of development and experiences, Maria's gross reaching gives way to specific reaching, and she grasps for particular objects.

✳ Motor development is from cephalo to caudal—from head to foot (tail). This process is known as *cephalocaudal development.* At birth, Maria's head is the most developed part of her body; she holds her head erect before she sits, and her being able to sit precedes her walking.

✳ Motor development proceeds from the proximal (midline, or central part of the body) to the distal (extremities), known as *proximodistal development.* Maria is able to control her arm movements before she can control her finger movements.

Motor development plays a major role in cognitive and social development. For example, learning to walk enables young children to explore their environment, which in turn contributes to cognitive development. Can you think of other examples?

Motor development also plays a major role in social and behavioral expectations. For example, toilet training (also called toilet learning or toilet mastery) is a milestone of the toddler period. Many parents want to accomplish toilet training as quickly and efficiently as possible, but frustrations arise when they start too early and expect too much of children. Toilet training is largely a matter of physical readiness, and most child-rearing experts recommend waiting until children are two years old before beginning the training process.

INTELLECTUAL DEVELOPMENT

Reflect on the discussion of cognitive development in Chapter 4, and think about how a child's first schemes are sensorimotor. Piaget said that infants construct (as opposed to absorb) schemes using reflexive sensorimotor actions.

For more information about infant and toddler development, go to the Companion Website at *http://prenhall.com/ morrison*, select any chapter, then choose Topic 2 of the ECE Supersite module.

Infants begin life with only reflexive motor actions that they use to satisfy biological needs. Consider sucking, for example, an innate sensorimotor scheme. Kathy turns her head to the source of nourishment, closes her lips around the nipple, sucks, and swallows. As a result of experiences and maturation, Kathy adapts or changes this basic sensorimotor scheme of sucking to include both anticipatory sucking movements and nonnutritive sucking, such as sucking a pacifier or blanket.

Children construct new schemes through the processes of assimilation and accommodation. Piaget believed that children are active constructors of intelligence through assimilation (taking in new experiences) and accommodation (changing existing schemes to fit new information), which results in equilibrium.

Stages of Sensorimotor Intelligence

Sensorimotor cognitive development consists of six stages (shown in Table 6–3 and described in the following subsections). Let's follow Christina through her six stages of cognitive development.

STAGE 1: BIRTH TO ONE MONTH.   During this stage, Christina sucks and grasps everything. She is literally ruled by reflexive actions. Reflexive responses to objects are undifferentiated, and Christina responds the same way to everything. Sensorimotor schemes help her learn new ways of interacting with the world. New ways of interacting promote Christina's cognitive development.

Grasping is a primary infant sensorimotor scheme. At birth, Christina's grasping reflex consists of closing her fingers around an object placed in her hand. As Christina matures in response to experiences, her grasping scheme is combined with a delightful activity of grasping and releasing everything she can get her hands on!

STAGE 2: ONE TO FOUR MONTHS.   Sensorimotor behaviors not previously present in Christina's repertoire of behavior begin to appear: habitual thumb sucking (indicates hand-mouth coordination), tracking moving objects with the eyes, and moving the head toward sounds (indicates the beginning of the recognition of causality). Christina starts to direct her own behavior rather than being totally dependent on reflexive actions.

Primary circular reactions begin. A **circular response** occurs when Christina's actions cause her to react or when another person prompts her to try to repeat the original action. The circular reaction is similar to a stimulus-response, cause-and-effect relationship.

STAGE 3: FOUR TO EIGHT MONTHS.   Christina manipulates objects, demonstrating coordination between vision and tactile senses. She also reproduces events with the purpose of sustaining and repeating acts. The intellectual milestone of this stage is the beginning of **object permanence,** the concept that things that are out of sight continue to exist.

Secondary circular reactions begin during this stage. This process is characterized by Christina repeating an action with the purpose of getting the same response from an object or person. Christina will repeatedly shake a rattle to repeat the sound. Repetitiveness is characteristic of all circular reactions. Secondary here means that the reaction comes from a source other than the infant. Christina interacts with people and objects to make interesting sights, sounds, and events happen and last. Given an object, Christina will use all available schemes, such as mouthing, hitting, and banging; if one of these schemes produces an interesting result, she continues to use the scheme to elicit the same response. Imitation becomes increasingly intentional as a means of prolonging interest.

STAGE 4: EIGHT TO TWELVE MONTHS.   During this stage, characterized by coordination of secondary schemes, Christina uses means to attain ends. She moves objects out of the way (means) to get another object (end). She begins to search for

TABLE 6-3

STAGES OF SENSORIMOTOR DEVELOPMENT DURING INFANCY AND TODDLERHOOD

STAGE	AGE	COGNITIVE DEVELOPMENT AND BEHAVIOR
I. Reflexive action	Birth to 1 month	1. Infant engages in the reflexive actions of sucking, grasping, crying, rooting, and swallowing. 2. Reflexes are modified and become more efficient as a result of experiences, e.g., infant learns how much sucking is required to result in nourishment. 3. Reflexive schemes become adaptive to the environment. 4. Little or no tolerance for frustration or delayed gratification.
II. Primary circular reactions	1 to 4 months	1. Acquired adaptations are formed. 2. Reflexive actions are gradually replaced by voluntary actions. 3. Beginning of understanding of causality, evidenced when infant tries to repeat action that prompted response from caregiver. 4. Circular reactions result in modification of existing schemes.
III. Secondary circular reactions	4 to 8 months	1. Infants increase responses to people and objects. 2. Intentional activities increase. Infant's ability to initiate activities. 3. Beginning of object permanency.
IV. Coordination of secondary schemes	8 to 12 months	1. Increased deliberation and purposefulness in responding to people and objects. 2. First clear signs of developing intelligence. 3. Continued development of object permanency. 4. Actively searches for hidden objects. 5. Comprehends meanings of simple words.
V. Experimentation (tertiary circular reactions)	12 to 18 months	1. Active experimentation begins, as evidenced through trial and error. 2. Toddler spends much time "experimenting" with objects to see what happens. Toddler is literally "a little scientist." Insatiable curiosity. 3. Toddler differentiates self from objects. 4. Realizes that "out of sight" is not "out of reach." 5. Can find hidden objects in first location hidden. 6. Beginning of understanding of space, time, and causality of spatial and temporal relationships.
VI. Representational intelligence (intention of means)	18 to 24 months	1. Mental combinations evidenced by thinking before doing. Development of cause-effect relationships. 2. Representational intelligence begins. That is, the toddler is able to mentally represent objects. 3. Engages in imitative behavior, which is increasingly symbolic. 4. Beginnings of sense of time. 5. Aware of object permanence regardless of the number of invisible placements. 6. Searches for an object in several places. 7. Egocentric in thought and behavior.

hidden objects, although not always in the places they were hidden, indicating a growing understanding of object permanence.

STAGE 5: TWELVE TO EIGHTEEN MONTHS. This stage, the climax of the sensorimotor period, marks the beginning of truly intelligent behavior. Stage 5 is the stage of experimentation. Christina experiments with objects to solve problems, and her experimentation is characteristic of intelligence that involves tertiary circular reactions, in which she repeats actions and modifies behaviors over and over to see what will happen.

Christina and other toddlers are avid explorers, determined to touch, taste, and feel all they can. Novelty is interesting for its own sake, and Christina experiments in many different ways with a given object. For example, she will use any available item—a wood hammer, a block, a rhythm band instrument—to pound the pegs in a pound-a-peg toy.

STAGE 6: EIGHTEEN MONTHS TO TWO YEARS. This is the stage of symbolic representation, which occurs when Christina can visualize events internally and maintain mental images of objects not present. Representational thought enables Christina to solve problems in a sensorimotor way through experimentation and trial and error and predict cause-and-effect relationships more accurately. She also develops the ability to remember, which allows her to try out actions she sees others do. During this stage, Christina can "think" using mental images and memories, which enables her to engage in pretend activities. Christina's representational thought does not necessarily match the real world and its representations, which accounts for her ability to have other objects stand for almost anything: a wooden block is a car; a rag doll is a baby. This type of play, known as symbolic play, becomes more elaborate and complex in the preoperational period.

Providing an enriched environment is a powerful way to promote infants' and toddlers' overall development. Figure 6.7 identifies some of the essential elements of an enriched environment for young children.

∽ **FIGURE 6.7**
Characteristics of Enriched Environments for Young Children

Research studies repeatedly show that children who are reared, cared for, and taught in environments that are enriched are healther, happier, and more achievement oriented. How would you apply these characteristics to your program?

* Includes a wide variety of materials to support all areas of development—physical, social, emotional, and linguistic

* Enables children to be actively involved

* Provides for children's basic emotional needs—safety, security, love, and emotional support

* Encourages social interactions with other children and adults

* Provides for children's physical, nutritional, and health needs

* Provides activities based on children's interests and abilities

* Enables children to learn the basic language and cognitive skills necessary for future school success

Language development begins at birth. Infants and toddlers need to be surrounded by a rich linguistic environment that enables them to develop the literacy skills necessary for successful learning.

LANGUAGE DEVELOPMENT

Language development begins at birth. The first cry, the first coo, the first "da-da" and "ma-ma," the first words are auditory proof that children are participating in the process of language development. How does the infant go from the first cry to the first word a year later? How does the toddler develop from saying one word to several hundred words a year later? How does language development begin? What forces and processes prompt children to participate in this uniquely human endeavor? Let us examine some of the explanations.

Language Acquisition

Heredity plays a role in language development in a number of ways. First, humans have the respiratory system and vocal cords that make rapid and efficient vocal communication possible. Second, the human brain makes language possible. The left hemisphere is the center for speech and phonetic analysis and the brain's main language center, it does not have the exclusive responsibility for language. The right hemisphere plays a role in our understanding of speech intonations, which enables us to distinguish between declarative, imperative, and interrogative sentences. Without these processing systems, language as we know it would be impossible.

Theories of Language Development

Eric Lenneberg has studied innate language acquisition in considerable detail in many different kinds of children, including deaf children. According to Lenneberg, the capacities for speech production and related aspects of language acquisition develop according to built-in biological schedules. They appear when the time is ripe and not until then, when a state of what he calls "resonance" exists. The child literally becomes sensitive for language.

The idea of a sensitive period of language development makes a great deal of sense and had a particular fascination for Maria Montessori, who believed there were two such sensitive periods. The first begins at birth and lasts until about three years. During this time, children unconsciously absorb language from the environment. The second period begins at three years and lasts until about eight years. During this time, children are active participants in their language development and learn how to use their power of communication. Milestones of language development are listed in Table 6–4.

ENVIRONMENTAL FACTORS. While the ability to acquire language has a biological basis, the content of the language syntax, grammar, and vocabulary is acquired from

TABLE 6–4
LANGUAGE DEVELOPMENT IN INFANTS AND TODDLERS

MONTHS OF AGE	LANGUAGE
Birth	Crying
1½	Social smile
3	Cooing (long pure vowel sound)
5	"Ah-goo" (the transition between cooing and early babbling)
5	Razzing (child places tongue between lips and produces a "raspberry")
6½	Babbling (repetition of consonant sounds)
8	"Dada/Mama" (inappropriate)
10	"Dada/Mama" (appropriate)
11	One word
12	Two words
14	Three words
15	Four–six words
15	Immature jargoning (sounds like gibberish; does not include any true word)
18	Seven–twenty words
18	Mature jargoning
21	Two-word combinations
24	Fifty words
24	Two-word sentences
24	Pronouns (*I, me, you;* used inappropriately)

Source: A. J. Capute and P. J. Accardo, "Linguistic and Auditory Milestones During the First Two Years of Life," *Clinical Pediatrics* 17 (11) (November 1978): 848. Used by permission.

the environment, which includes parents and other people as models for language. Development depends on talk between children and adults, and between children and children. Optimal language development ultimately depends on interactions with the best possible language models. The biological process may be the same for all children, but the content of their language will differ according to environmental factors.

The Sequence of Language Development

Children develop language in predictable sequences.

FIRST WORDS.   The first words of children are just that, first words. Children talk about people: dada, papa, mama, mommie, and baby (referring to themselves); animals: dog, cat, kitty; vehicles: car, truck, boat, train; toys: ball, block, book, doll; food: juice, milk, cookie, bread, drink; body parts: eye, nose, mouth, ear; clothing and household articles: hat, shoe, spoon, clock; greeting terms: hi, bye, night-night; and a few words for actions: up, no more, off.

HOLOPHRASIC SPEECH.   Children are remarkable communicators without words. When children have attentive parents and teachers, they develop into skilled communicators, using gestures, facial expressions, sound intonations, pointing, and reaching to make their desires known and get what they want. Pointing at an object and saying, "uh-uh-uh" is the same as saying, "I want the rattle" or "Help me get the rattle." As a responsive caregiver you can respond by saying, "Do you want the rattle? I'll get it for you. Here it is!" One of the attributes of an attentive caregiver is the ability to read children's signs and signals, anticipating their desires even though no words are spoken.

The ability to communicate progresses from "sign language" and sounds to the use of single words. Toddlers are skilled at using single words to name objects, to let others know what they want, and to express emotions. One word, in essence, does the work of a whole sentence. These single-word sentences are called **holophrases.**

The one-word sentences children use are primarily referential (used primarily to label objects, such as "doll"), or expressive (communicating personal desires or levels of social interaction, such as "bye-bye" and "kiss"). The extent to which children use these two functions of language depends in large measure on the teacher and parent. For example, children's early language use reflects their mother's verbal style. This makes sense and the lesson is this: how parents speak to their children influences how their children speak.

SYMBOLIC REPRESENTATION.   Two significant developmental events occur at about the age of two. First is the development of **symbolic representation.** Representation occurs when something else stands for a mental image. For example, a word is used to represent something else not present. A toy may stand for a tricycle, a baby doll may represent a real person. Words become signifiers of things such as, ball, block, and blanket.

The use of mental symbols also enables the child to participate in two processes that are characteristic of the early years: symbolic play and the beginning of the use of words and sentences to express meanings and make references.

VOCABULARY DEVELOPMENT.   The second significant achievement that occurs at about two is the development of a fifty-word vocabulary and the use of two-word sentences. This vocabulary development and the ability to combine words mark the beginning of rapid language development. Vocabulary development plays a very powerful and significant role in school achievement and success. Research repeatedly demonstrates that children who come to school with a broad use and knowledge of words achieve better than their peers who do not have an expanded vocabulary. Adults are the major source of children's vocabularies.

TELEGRAPHIC SPEECH.   You have undoubtedly heard a toddler say something like "Go out" in response to a suggestion such as "Let's go outside." Perhaps you've said, "Is your juice all gone?" and the toddler responded, "All gone." These two-word sentences are called **telegraphic speech.** They are the same kind of sentences you would use if you wrote a telegram. The sentences are primarily made up of nouns and verbs. Generally, they do not have prepositions, articles, conjunctions, and auxiliary verbs.

MOTHERESE OR PARENTESE.   Many recent research studies have demonstrated that mothers and other caregivers talk to infants and toddlers differently than adults talk to each other. This distinctive way of adapting everyday speech to young children is called *motherese,*[2] or *parentese.* Characteristics of motherese are listed in Figure 6.8.

⌒ **FIGURE 6.8**
Characteristics of Motherese

Do all of these characteristics of motherese seem familiar to you? In working with parents of infants, what would you do to encourage them to use motherese with their children?

* The sentences are short, averaging just over four words per sentence with babies. As children become older, the length of sentences mothers use also becomes longer. Mothers' conversations with their children are short and sweet.

* The sentences are highly intelligible. When talking to their children, mothers tend not to slur or mumble their words. This may be because mothers speak slower to their children than they do to adults in normal conversation.

* The sentences are "unswervingly well formed"; that is, they are grammatical sentences.

* The sentences are mainly imperatives and questions, such as "Give Mommie the ball" and "Do you want more juice?" Since mothers can't exchange a great deal of information with their children, their utterances are such that they direct their children's actions.

* Mothers use sentences in which referents ("here," "that," "there") are used to stand for objects or people: "Here's your bottle." "That's your baby doll." "There's your doggie."

* Mothers expand or provide an adult version of their children's communication. When a child points at a baby doll on a chair, the mother may respond by saying, "Yes, the baby doll is on the chair."

* Mothers' sentences involve repetitions. "The ball, bring Mommie the ball. Yes, go get the ball. The ball, go get the ball."

NEGATIVES. If you took a vote on toddlers' favorite word, "no" would win hands down. When children begin to use negatives, they simply add "no" to the beginning of a word or sentence ("no milk"). As their "no" sentences become longer, they still put "no" first ("no put coat on"). Later, they place negatives appropriately between subject and verb ("I no want juice").

To complete a Program in Action activity, visit the Companion Website at *http://www.prenhall.com/ morrison*, select Chapter 6, then choose the Programs in Action module.

By the end of the preschool years, children have developed and mastered most language patterns. The basis for language development is the early years, and no amount of later remedial training can make up for development that should have occurred during this sensitive period for language learning.

Figure 6.9 provides guidelines that will help you promote children's language development to make sure your children get off to the best language start possible. The "Program in Action" on page 181 illustrates how one school district is ensuring that all babies get off to a great start with language.

DEVELOPMENTALLY APPROPRIATE INFANT AND TODDLER PROGRAMS

For more information about developmentally appropriate practice, go to the Companion Website at *http://www.prenhall. com/morrison*, select any chapter, then choose Topic 4 of the ECE Supersite module.

Most of the topics we discuss in this book have implications for infant and toddler education. First is the topic of developmental appropriateness. All early childhood professionals who provide care for infants and toddlers—indeed, for all children—must understand and recognize this important concept, which provides a solid foundation for any program. The NAEYC defines *developmentally appropriate* as having three dimensions:

* What is known about child development and learning knowledge of age-related human characteristics that permits general predictions within an age range about what activities, materials, interactions, or experiences will be safe, healthy, interesting, achievable, and also challenging for children.
* What is known about the strengths, interests, and needs of each individual child in the group to be able to adapt for and be responsive to inevitable individual variation.
* Knowledge of the social and cultural contexts in which children live to ensure that learning experiences are meaningful, relevant, and respectful for the participating children and their families.[3]

Based on these dimensions, professionals must provide different programs of activities for infants and toddlers. To do so, early childhood professionals must get parents and other professionals to recognize that infants, as a group, are different from toddlers and need programs, curricula, and environments specifically designed for them. This designing programs and practices specifically for different age groups is at the heart of developmentally appropriate practice. The early childhood education

* Treat children as partners in the communication process. Many infant behaviors, such as smiling, cooing, and vocalizing, serve to initiate conversation, and professionals can be responsive to these through conversations.

* Conversations are the building blocks of language development. Attentive and caring adults are infants' and toddlers' best stimulators of cognitive and language development.

* Talk to infants in a soothing, pleasant voice, with frequent eye contact, even though they do not "talk" to you. Most mothers and professionals talk to their young children differently from the way they talk to adults. They adapt their speech so they can communicate in a distinctive way called *motherese* or *parentese*. Mothers' language interactions with their toddlers are much the same as with infants. When conversing with toddlers who are just learning language, it is a good idea to simplify verbalization—not by using "baby talk," such as "di-di" for diaper or "ba-ba" for bottle, but rather by speaking in an easily understandable way. For example, instead of saying, "We are going to take a walk around the block so you must put your coat on," you would instead say, "Let's get coats on."

* Use children's names when interacting with them, to personalize the conversation and build self-identity.

* Use a variety of means to stimulate and promote language development, including reading stories, singing songs, listening to records, and giving children many opportunities to verbally interact with adults and other children.

* Encourage children to converse and share information with other children and adults.

* Help children learn to converse in various settings by taking them to different places so they can use their language with a variety of people. This approach also gives children ideas and events for using language.

* Have children use language in different ways. Children need to know how to use language to ask questions, explain feelings and emotions, tell what they have done, and describe things.

* Give children experiences in the language of directions and commands. Many children fail in school settings not because they do not know language, but because they have little or no experience in how language is used for giving and following directions. It is also important for children to understand that language can be used as a means to an end—a way of attaining a desired goal.

* Converse with children about what they are doing and how they are doing it. Children learn language through feedback—asking and answering questions and commending about activities—which shows children that you are paying attention to them and what they are doing.

* Talk to children in the full range of adult language, including past and future tenses.

⌒ **FIGURE 6.9 Promoting Language Development**

Supporting children's language development is one of the most important things you can do. Language development is vital for successful school accomplishments and social interactions.

Program in Action

BABY STEPS: FOCUS ON FAMILIES
Bakersfield City, California School District

Bakersfield City School District takes early childhood education to a new level through The Family Connection: A Commitment to Literacy, a program that includes visits to parents of newborns in the hospital and classes for new dads. If the district doesn't reach new parents in the hospital, it'll find them in the shopping mall.

This early connection among parents, children, and school is part of the district's goal to have children academically as well as physically, emotionally, and mentally prepared to enter kindergarten, says Jan Hensley, the district's director of child and family development.

"Children from birth to age seven are like little sponges," Hensley says. "They can absorb so much of what they need to succeed in school. The first day of kindergarten should not be their first school experience."

Over the last two years, the department has created family literacy projects under the Family Connection umbrella, including traditional preschool classes and two other programs, Baby Steps and Kid-City: Land of Literacy.

The Baby Steps program provides new parents with emotional support, a network of community-based resources, essential developmental information, and parenting classes. Parents of newborns are greeted at the county hospital with a "Welcome to Parenthood Kit," which includes the hospital visit and a kit equipped with a book, brochures, information linking families to available services, and a Mozart tape.

Family services aides have visited more than 4,000 new parents and their babies in the first two years of this project. Now that the project is countrywide, the prediction for 2001–2002 is to reach more than 11,000

babies and their families throughout the seven hospitals in the country. Parents are given guidance and support to establish a solid ground for cognitive skills and literacy for newborns. This project provides the framework to prepare parents for their job as their children's first and most influential teacher and helps to ensure that children in Kern County will be academically, socially, and emotionally prepared for kindergarten.

Kid-City: Land of Literacy is located in a shopping mall. It's set up like a preschool room with nine different centers. The centers focus on social, emotional, cognitive, and gross and fine motor development. "It's designed for people who don't qualify for free preschool but might not be able to afford private preschool," Hensley says.

Parents and children can spend time together, exploring the centers and working on projects at Kid-City from 9 A.M. to 4 P.M. weekdays.

Hensley says the board's commitment to increasing school readiness in kindergartners by embracing a family-based literacy program from birth is leading to greater success among the district's young students.

For more information, contact Superintendent Jean Fuller at (661) 631-4610 or by e-mail at *fuller@bcsd.k12.ca.us.* The district's website is at *http://www.bcsd.k12.ca.us.*

 To complete a Program in Action activity, visit the Companion Website at http://www.prenhall.com/morrison, select Chapter 6, then choose the Programs in Action module.

profession is leading the way in raising consciousness about the need to match what professionals do with children to children's development as individuals. We have a long way to go in this regard, but part of the resolution will come with ongoing training of professionals in child development and curriculum planning.

Finally, it is important to match professionals with children of different ages. Not everyone is emotionally or professionally suited to provide care for infants and toddlers. Both groups need adults who can respond to their particular needs and developmental characteristics. Infants need especially nurturing

⚭ A major part of your role as an early childhood professional is to provide a developmentally appropriate environment and activities for young children. This means that you must know infant/child development and individual children. You must also know how to apply that knowledge to a curriculum that will enable children to learn what they need to know for successful learning and living.

professionals; toddlers, on the other hand, need adults who can tolerate and allow for their emerging autonomy and independence.

MULTICULTURALLY APPROPRIATE PRACTICE

Children and families are not all the same. They do not all come from the same socioeconomic and cultural backgrounds, and they do not all rear their children the same way. Consequently, it is important for teachers and caregivers to get to know children and families and to be culturally sensitive in their care and education practices. Even so, it may be that because of background and culture parents and professionals may not always agree on a particular policy or practice. For example, many infant and toddler programs teach self-help skills early and encourage children to become independent as soon as possible. These practices may conflict with some parents' cultural beliefs and practices. When this happens, you ask yourself one of the ten questions as outlined in Figure 6.10 to help guide your practice and decision making. Also, consider the questions in the "Video Viewpoint: The First Three Years of Life."

CURRICULA FOR INFANTS AND TODDLERS

Curricula for infants and toddlers consist of all the activities and experiences they are involved in while under the direction of professionals. Consequently, early childhood professionals plan for all activities and involvement: feeding, washing, diapering/toileting, playing, learning and having stimulating interactions, outings, being involved with others, and having conversations. Professionals must plan the curriculum

∞ **FIGURE 6.10 Ten Questions to Guide Your Multicultural Practice with Infants and Toddlers**

Everyone who works with children must provide them with individually and culturally appropriate care and education. What are some things you can do now to prepare yourself for this important role?

Source: J. Gonzalez-Mena and N. P. Bhavnagri, (2000). "Diversity and Infant/Toddler Caregiving," Young Children, September 2000. (Washington, DC: National Education for the Association of Young Children), 33.

1. What is the cultural perspective of the family on this issue?

2. How do the family's child care practices relate to its cultural perspective?

3. What are the family's goals for the child, and how has the family culture influenced its goals?

4. In view of the goals, is the family's practice in the child's best interest?

5. Is there any sound research data indicating that the family's practice is doing actual harm?

6. Is the program's practice or policy universally applicable, or is it better suited to a particular culture?

7. Did the family choose the program because of its particular philosophy, even if it is based in a different culture from the family's own?

8. Have I attempted to fully understand the family's rationale for its practices, the complexity of the issues, and other factors that contribute to the practices?

9. Have I attempted to fully explain to the family my rationale for my practice and looked at the complexity of the issues and at how my own culture influences my rationale and perspective?

10. What are some creative resolutions that address both the parents' concerns and my own?

Video Viewpoint

THE FIRST THREE YEARS OF LIFE

The Carnegie Corporation released a study of how important the first three years of life are for stimulation and nurturing and what being deprived of experiences and opportunities in those years can mean for the future of our children and our nation.

REFLECTIVE DISCUSSION QUESTIONS

Why is this such an important issue for professionals? For parents? How does poverty negatively influence chil-dren's environments and prevent them from fully developing in the early years?

REFLECTIVE DECISION MAKING

What are some things you can do to improve the quality of children's environments in the first three years of life? How can parents improve the quality of home environments? What are some things educators and parents can do to provide infants and toddlers with appropriate attention and stimulation?

Program in Action

CHARLIE AND EMMA'S VERY, VERY GOOD DAY AT THE BRIGHT HORIZONS FAMILY CENTER

Imagine a warm, sunny, homey room—one part living room, one part playroom/laboratory for messy little scientists—and an adjacent, quiet, comfortable area for cribs and nursing moms. Small cozy spaces, pillows, a couch, places to be together with friends, places to be alone, places to use all your new motor skills, lots of good books, and abundant conversation. There are always laps, hugs, and smiles.

CHARLIE'S DAY

Twenty-two-month-old Charlie burst through the door, his dad trailing behind with eleven-month-old Emma in his arms. "Bunnies," he said excitedly to his teacher Alicia as he dumped his jacket in his cubby and climbed up next to her on the couch. They talked about his bunny sighting and waved Dad and Emma off. Alicia produced a book on bunnies, which he pored over while she greeted others.

Charlie's friends trickled in, and he and almost-preschooler Jerrod built and crashed walls with the brick blocks while waiting for breakfast. After a brief group get-together to welcome each other, sing, and talk about bunnies, new clothes, feeding the fish and the parakeet named Mr. Alejandro (don't ask), and other current events, Charlie's morning was spent experimenting with "chemistry and physics" with colored water and corks at the water table and a short visit to the infant room to spend time with Emma. He created a picture for Mom and moved around and over things, going in and out of the tent, "hiding" behind the couch, and spending forty-five minutes of wild abandon tearing about outdoors.

Of course, life has ups and downs—a bump on the knee, an unfortunate heated dispute with Jeremiah over a wagon that led to Charlie's temporary banishment from the path and redirection to the slide, enduring bossy five-year-old Ashley's proudly tying his shoe (Ashley already had the infallible air of the prom queen), and a short pout about not sitting next to Alicia at lunch. He almost remembered to go potty but was so busy, he didn't make it in time.

Lunch involved serious eating and silly discussions with Selena, who was teaching them some Spanish by speaking it to them, centering on, "Mi Madre takes me to." Charlie showed Nicholas how he could pour his own milk from the tiny pitcher into his cup. Then it was time for the one story and two poems they always read at nap, a successful trip to the potty, and nap. The nap recharged Charlie's batteries. Snack was ready for each child when he or she woke up, and then the group took a walk to find acorns and leaves for tomorrow's art. The rest of the afternoon was spent with Ashley and Nicholas playing with real pots, pans, and dishes. Best of all, Jerrod's 10-year-old brother read him a book on the couch after wrestling a bit with him. At 5:30 P.M. it was time to say good-bye and help Dad collect Emma.

EMMA'S DAY

What was the 352nd day of Emma's life like? After a weepy parting from Dad, she spent the day in "conversation"—great responsive language interactions. She explored the world with her mouth, nose, skin, and ears, and used her newfound skill of walking (actually, lurching about). She used the couch as a walking rail and a pull-me-up-space and had great delight using her whole body to explore the concepts of "over," "under," "around," "in," and "out" as she staggered and crawled around the room, over the footstool, under the table. She played peek-a-boo hiding in the big box. She splashed her fingers in the soapy tub of water with fourteen-month-old Keesha. She loved seeing her brother Charlie and survived his exuberant hug.

Between her three short naps, she ate lunch, lounged around with a bottle or two, and went for a buggy ride with Keesha, second favorite caregiver Tony, and two children from next door. She explored the damp grass and trees outside. Of course, Emma spent quite a bit of time being cared for by and endlessly "chatting" with her very special caregiver Kim, especially during the "prime times" of diapering and feeding. She was diapered three times with the requisite singing and tickle games and snuggled at least four or five times, reading picture books, rhyming, and having fascinating "conversations" as Kim talked about current events: the birds that they saw, the poop in her diaper, the water she drank, Charlie, and the zipper on her coat. She also watched closely as fourteen-month-old Nguyen and Tony did a fingerplay together.

Emma was busy. She "helped" Kim get the laundry out of the drier. Kim and Emma called Emma's mom to

184

congratulate her for her new promotion. Emma cried after hearing her mom, as did her mom at the wonderful gesture, but it was still worth it. Of course she fussed quite a bit and had a fit when Keesha's dad got too close. She cried a little bit when Kim left. She also burst into tears when Dad arrived, delighted beyond words to have him back. She held him close as he discussed her day with Tony.

The relaxed but full day of Charlie and Emma left them ready to go home with enough energy to handle the rush of reuniting with mom, sharing Charlie's picture, and spending some good time together before beginning it all over again the next day.

DECONSTRUCTING THE VERY, VERY GOOD DAY

Taking what we know about the development of children and the development of families, this was an extraordinarily good day for Charlie and Emma.

FAMILY.   Emma and Charlie are developing the foundations of a relationship that will last two lifetimes. They each spend forty-five hours a week at the center. They need time together, and they get it. The family is also a strong presence: from Charlie helping Dad with Emma to his picture for Mom and Emma's phone call.

RESPONSIVE INTERACTIONS WITH ABUNDANT LANGUAGE.   Charlie and Emma's days are filled with conversations with adults and other children. They aren't just talked to or at, questioned, or responded to. These are real give-and-takes, often initiated by a vocalization by the children. Their days are laced with books, poems, and singing.

UNDIVIDED ATTENTION.   There are a number of moments during the day when Charlie and Emma each have the undivided attention, the full human presence, of their primary caregiver—sometimes for chatting, sometimes for solace, and sometimes for helping them understand that group life has responsibilities. For that brief moment, the only thing in the world that matters is the interaction between the child and caregiver.

EXPLORATION.   Days are full of exploration inside and out, not only with toys but materials from real life and nature.

RELATIONSHIPS.   Emma and Charlie spend the day in a community, not just a room with children just like themselves. They have relationships with older and younger children and adults throughout the center. When the beloved primary caregivers Vicki or Kim are out, it is still a secure place for them to be.

TEACHING AND LEARNING.   Both Charlie and Emma learn from children and teach other children a thing or two.

EXPECTATIONS.   Charlie and Emma are respected as people and expected to behave appropriately. Charlie is learning social graces, and Emma is expected to fuss and cry as she navigates new waters.

PARENT PARTNERSHIP.   Charlie and Emma's mother and father are members of the family center community and are respected as the experts on their children. The care Emma and Charlie receive is based on a thorough mutual understanding between the family and the caregivers and on ongoing communication.

WHY A VERY, VERY GOOD DAY?

It wasn't a great day because it wasn't smooth and carefree. There were accidents and tears, teapot tempests, and the sweet sorrow of parting from loved ones. But it was a very, very good day for Charlie and Emma because everything really important that they needed happened. We don't know whether it was a great day for all the other children. But Alicia, Selena, Tony, Kim, and all the staff work hard to try to make it great for *each* child and *each* family *every* day. When it all comes together, ain't life grand?

By Jim Greenman, Senior Vice President of Bright Horizons Family Solutions. This company operates more than 350 family centers in the United States, England, and Ireland

 To complete a Program in Action activity, visit the Companion Website at *http://www.prenhall.com/morrison,* select Chapter 6, then choose the Programs in Action module.

To take an online self-test on this chapter's contents, go to the Companion Website at *http://www.prenhall.com/ morrison*, select Chapter 6, then choose the Self-Test module.

For additional Internet resources or to complete an online activity for this chapter, go to the Companion Website at *http://www.prenhall.com/ morrison*, select Chapter 6, then choose the Linking to Learning module.

so it is developmentally appropriate. Curriculum planning includes the following concepts:

* Self-help skills
* Ability to separate from parents
* Problem solving
* Autonomy and independence
* Assistance in meeting the developmental milestones associated with physical, cognitive, language, personality, and social development

Reflect upon the "Program in Action: Charlie and Emma's Very, Very Good Day at the Bright Horizons Family Center" on pages 184 and 185 and recall how learning occurred within the context of daily activities.

Infants and toddlers are interesting and remarkably competent individuals. The developmental and educational milestones of these years are the foundations of all that follow throughout life. All professionals must use their knowledge, understanding, energy, and talents to ensure that this foundation is the best it can be.

ACTIVITIES FOR PROFESSIONAL DEVELOPMENT

In this chapter we have stressed the developmental stages and growth of infants and toddlers and how to use this knowledge to implement developmentally appropriate practices in your classroom or program. Refer again to the "Professional Development Goal" at the beginning of the chapter, to the "Professional Development Checklist" on pages 20 and 21, and the "Professionalism in Practice" article on pages 168 and 169. After you have reviewed these, complete the following exercises.

1. You have been asked to speak to a group of parents about developmentally appropriate practice and how it applies to the education and development of infants and toddlers. Develop your presentation and list five specific suggestions you will make about key developmentally appropriate practices for infants and toddlers. Share your presentation with others or online in an early childhood discussion group.

2. Observe children between the ages of birth and eighteen months. Identify the six stages of sensorimotor intelligence by describing the behaviors you observed. Cite specific examples of secondary and tertiary reactions. For each of the six stages, develop two activities that would be cognitively and developmentally appropriate.

3. Visit at least two programs that provide care for infants and toddlers. Observe the curriculum to determine whether it is developmentally appropriate. Before you observe, develop an observational checklist based on guidelines provided in Chapter 5.

To view the NAEYC Developmentally Appropriate Practice in Early Childhood Programs Guidelines and the NAEYC Infant and Toddler Program Necessities, visit the Companion Website at *http://www.prenhall.com/ morrison*, select Chapter 6, then choose the Resources module.

What suggestions do you have for making the program more developmentally appropriate?

4. Developmentally appropriate practice must also be culturally appropriate. Visit centers that care for young children of different cultures to determine the role culture plays in how we care for and educate children. List the specific activities and materials that supported children's cultures. How would you enhance the cultural appropriateness of the program?

For additional chapter resources and activities, visit the Companion Website at *http://www.prenhall.com/morrison*, select Chapter 6, then choose the Professional Development, Resources, or Linking to Learning modules.

FOCUS QUESTIONS

1. What are the characteristics of preschoolers' physical, cognitive, and language growth and development?

2. How does play promote children's learning?

3. How are preschool programs changing and what issues do they face?

4. How can I apply developmentally appropriate practice to my teaching of preschoolers?

chapter 7

The Preschool Years

GETTING READY FOR SCHOOL

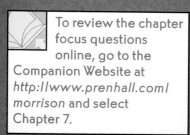
To review the chapter focus questions online, go to the Companion Website at *http://www.prenhall.com/ morrison* and select Chapter 7.

 # PROFESSIONAL DEVELOPMENT GOAL

DEVELOPMENTALLY APPROPRIATE PRACTICE

I understand children's developmental stages and growth from birth through age eight, and I use this knowledge to implement developmentally appropriate practice. I do all I can to advance the physical, intellectual, social, and emotional development of the children in my care to their fullest potential.

*T*he road to success in school and life begins long before kindergarten or first grade. The preschool years are assuming a more important place in the process of schooling, and many view the preschool years as the cornerstone for learning. As we begin our study of preschoolers, take a few minutes and review the portrait of preschoolers in Figure 7.1.

⌾ FIGURE 7.1   A Portrait of Preschoolers

Three-and Four-Year-Olds:

* are incessant askers of questions. "Why?'" "How come. . . .?" The preschool years could be called the "Age of a thousand questions" for all the questions preschoolers ask. Yet, this is how they learn about and make sense of themselves and their world.

* undergo a rapid increase in language development. Preschoolers have an average productive vocabulary (the number of words a child actually uses while speaking) of 4,000–6,000 words.

* use "scripts" for conversations and events—"We went to . . . we played . . . we came home."

* base their opinions and judgments on how things look to them, not necessarily how they really are.

* have a natural curiosity to explore.

* begin to explore adult roles—"I'm the mommy, you're the daddy." Social pretend play is a favorite way of learning.

* are greatly influenced by peers. Sibling relationships are important to preschoolers; they show clear playmate preferences and genuine friendships.

* are able and want to do things for themselves.

* can maintain organized behavior and can engage in activities that require several steps and concentration.

Preschoolers are fun to work with and teach. They are capable of remarkable achievements across all areas of cognitive, linguistic, and social development. In fact, they are one of my favorite groups to teach! One of the dramatic changes in early childhood education over the past decade is the inclusion of preschoolers in public school programs. Parents and teachers are discovering that preschoolers are capable of a great deal more cognitively and socially than they previously thought. What are some preschooler characteristics that you can add to this portrait?

WHAT IS PRESCHOOL?

Preschools are programs for three- to five-year-old children, before they enter kindergarten. Today it is common for many children to be in a school of some kind beginning as early as age two or three, and child care beginning at six weeks is commonplace for many children of working parents. Forty-one states currently invest in preschool education, in the form of public preschools or support for Head Start. Since 1997, New York has provided free early childhood education to every four-year-old whose parents want it. In Georgia, preschool programs are provided for all children. In 2001, the fifty states spent $2.1 billion on preschool care and education. Preschool education continues to grow, with greater numbers of four-year-olds entering preschools. Currently, about 725,000 three- to five-year-old children are in some kind of preschool program.

To check your understanding of this chapter with the online Study Guide, go to the Companion Website at *http://www.prenhall.com/ morrison*, select Chapter 7, then choose the Study Guide module.

Why Are Preschools Growing in Popularity?

A number of reasons help explain the current popularity of preschool programs. These reasons are shown in Figure 7.2. Review them now as a background for our discussion of the importance of preschool programs in young children's lives.

For more information about preschools, go to the Companion Website at *http://www. prenhall.com/morrison*, select Chapter 7, then choose the Linking to Learning module.

As preschool programs have grown in number and popularity over the last decade, they have also undergone significant changes in purposes. Previously, the predominant purposes of preschools were to help socialize children, enhance their social-emotional development, and get them ready for kindergarten or first grade. Today there is a decided move away from socialization as the primary function for enrolling children in preschool. Preschools are now promoted as places to accomplish the goals shown in Figure 7.3. These goals of the "new" preschool illustrate some of the dramatic changes that are transforming how preschool programs operate and teachers teach. Given the changing nature of the preschool, it is little wonder that the preschool years are playing a larger role in early childhood education.

WHAT ARE PRESCHOOLERS LIKE?

Today's preschoolers are not like the children of previous decades. Many have already attended one, two, or three years of child care. They have watched hundreds of hours of television. Many are technologically sophisticated. Many have experienced the trauma of family divorces or the psychological effects of abuse. Both collectively and individually, the experiential backgrounds of preschoolers are quite

⌐ FIGURE 7.2   Reasons for Popularity of Preschool Programs

From your reading and research, add to these reasons why preschool is popular. One thing is certain: preschool programs will become more numerous and will play a major role in children's development and learning.

* Many parents are frustrated and dissatisfied with efforts to find quality and affordable care for their children. They view public schools as the agency that can and should provide care and education for their children.

* With changing attitudes toward work and careers, more parents are in the workforce than ever before. Additionally, many parents believe it is possible to balance family and career. This in turn places a great demand on the early childhood profession to provide more programs and services, including programs for three- and four-year-olds.

* Parents, public policy planners, and researchers believe intervention programs designed to prevent such social problems as substance abuse and school dropout work best in the early years. Research supports the effectiveness of this early intervention approach. Quality early childhood programs help prevent and reduce behavioral and social problems.

* With growing concern on the part of corporations and businesses about the quality of the American workforce, business leaders see early education as one way of developing literate workers. Many preschool programs include work-related skills and behaviors in their curriculum. For example, learning how to be responsible and trustworthy are skills that are learned early in life. Likewise, being literate begins in the early years.

* Advocacy exists for publicly supported and financed preschools as a means of helping ensure that all children and their families, regardless of socioeconomic background, are not excluded from the known benefits of attending quality preschool programs.

* The new brain research helps make it clear that the foundation for learning is laid in the early years and that three- and four-year-old children are ready, willing, and able to learn.

For more information about preschoolers' development, go to the Companion Website at *http://www. prenhall.com/morrison,* select any chapter, then choose Topic 2 of the ECE Supersite module.

different from those of previous generations. These factors raise a number of imperatives for you and preschool teachers:

* Observe and assess children so that you know and understand what they know and are able to do.

* Conference and collaborate with parents in order to discover their children's unique experiences, abilities, and needs.

* Develop programs to meet the needs of today's children, not yesterday's children. As children change, so we must change our programs for them.

FIGURE 7.3   Goals of Preschool Education

Preschool goals are multifaceted and comprehensive. As you can see, preschools are envisioned as much more than only providing for children's social development, which historically has been their primary goal.

* Support and develop children's innate capacity for learning. The responsibility for "getting ready for school" has shifted from being primarily children's and parents' responsibilities to being a cooperative venture between child, family, home, schools, and communities. Review again the information on the importance of early learning for brain development discussed in Chapter 6. The same reasons for providing early education to infants and toddlers also apply to preschool children and their curriculum.

* Provide children the academic, social, and behavioral skills necessary for entry into kindergarten. Today a major focus is on developing preschool children's literacy and math skills.

* Use the public schools as a centralized agency to deliver services at an early age to all young children and their families.

* Deliver a full range of health, social, economic, and academic services to children and families. Family welfare is also a justification for operating preschools.

* Solve or find solutions for pressing social problems. The early years are viewed as a time when interventions are most likely to have long-term positive influences. Preschool programs are seen as ways of lowering the number of dropouts, improving children's health, and preventing serious social problems such as substance abuse and violence.

Physical and Motor Development

One noticeable difference between preschoolers and infants and toddlers is that preschoolers have lost most of their baby fat and taken on a leaner, lankier look. This "slimming down" and increasing motor coordination enables preschoolers to participate with more confidence in the locomotor activities so vitally necessary during this stage of growth and development. Both girls and boys continue to grow several inches per year throughout the preschool years. Table 7–1 shows the average height and weight for preschoolers. Compare these averages with the height and weight of preschoolers you know or work with.

Preschool children are learning to use and test their bodies. The preschool years are a time for learning what they can do individually and how they can do it. Locomotion plays a large role in motor and skill development and includes such activities as moving the body through space—walking, running, hopping, jumping, rolling, dancing, climbing, and leaping. Preschoolers use these activities to investigate and explore the relationships among themselves, space, and objects in space.

Preschoolers also like to participate in fine-motor activities such as drawing, coloring, painting, cutting, and pasting. Consequently, they need programs that

TABLE 7–1

AVERAGE HEIGHT AND WEIGHT OF PRESCHOOLERS

AGE	MALES		FEMALES	
	HEIGHT (INCHES)	WEIGHT (POUNDS)	HEIGHT (INCHES)	WEIGHT (POUNDS)
3 years	39	34.75	38.5	33.25
4 years	42	39.75	41.75	38.75
5 years	44	44.5	44	42.5

Source: Based on data from Baby Bag Online [*http://www.babybag.com*]. Reprinted by permission from Baby Bag, Inc.

provide action and play, supported by proper nutrition and healthy habits of plentiful rest and good hygiene. Good preschool programs provide for these unique physical needs of preschoolers and support their learning through active involvement.

Cognitive Development

Preschoolers are in the preoperational stage of intellectual development. As we discussed in Chapter 5, characteristics of the preoperational stage are (1) children grow in their ability to use symbols, including language; (2) children are not capable of operational thinking (an **operation** is a reversible mental action), which explains why Piaget named this stage preoperational; (3) children center on one thought or idea, often to the exclusion of other thoughts; (4) children are unable to conserve; and (5) children are egocentric.

Preoperational characteristics have particular implications for you and other early childhood professionals. You can promote children's learning during the preoperational stage of development by following the guidelines presented in Figure 7.4. As you review these six guidelines, start to plan for how you can apply them to your classroom.

Language Development

Children's language skills grow and develop rapidly during the preschool years. Vocabulary, the number of words children know, continues to grow. Sentence length also increases and children continue to master syntax and grammar.

During the preschool years, children's language development is diverse and comprehensive and constitutes a truly impressive range of learning. An even more impressive feature of this language acquisition is that children learn intuitively, without a great deal of instruction, the rules of language that apply to words and phrases they use. You can use many of the language practices recommended for

✳ *Furnish concrete materials to help children see and experience concepts and processes.* Children learn more from touching and experimenting with an actual object than they do from a picture, story, or video. If children are learning about apples, bring in a collection of apples for children to touch, feel, smell, taste, discuss, classify, manipulate, and explore. Collections also offer children an ideal way to learn the names for things, classify, count, and describe.

✳ *Use hands-on activities that give children opportunities for active involvement in their learning.* When you encourage children to manipulate and interact with the world around them, they begin to construct concepts about relationships, attributes, and processes. Through exploration, preoperational children begin to collect and organize data about the objects they manipulate. For example, when children engage in water play with funnels and cups, they learn about concepts such as measurement, volume, sink/float, bubbles and the prism, evaporation, and saturation.

✳ *Give children many and varied experiences.* Diverse activities and play environments lend themselves to teaching different skills, concepts, and processes. Children should spend time daily in both indoor and outdoor activities. Give consideration to the types of activities that facilitate large- and fine-motor, social, emotional, and cognitive development. For example, outdoor play activities and games such as tag, hopscotch, and jump rope enhance large-motor development; fine-motor activities include using scissors, stringing beads, coloring, and writing.

✳ *Model appropriate tasks and behaviors, as the preoperational child learns to a great extent through modeling.* Children should see adults reading and writing daily. It is also helpful for children to view brief demonstrations by peers or professionals on possible ways to use materials. For example, after children have spent a lot of time in free exploration with math manipulatives, teachers and others can show children patterning techniques and strategies they may want to experiment with in their own play.

✳ *Provide a print-rich environment to stimulate interest and development of language and literacy in a meaningful context.* The physical environment should display room labeling, class stories and dictations, children's writing, and charts of familiar songs and fingerplays. There should be a variety of literature for students to read, including books, magazines, and newspapers. Paper and writing utensils should be abundant to motivate children in all kinds of writing. Daily literacy activities should include opportunities for shared, guided, and independent reading and writing; singing songs and fingerplays; and creative dramatics. Children should be read to every day.

✳ *Allow children periods of uninterrupted time to engage in self-chosen tasks.* Children benefit more from large blocks of time provided for in-depth exploration in meaningful play than they do from frequent, brief ones. It takes time for children to become deeply involved in play, especially imaginative and fantasy play. Morning and afternoon schedules should each contain at least two such blocks of time.

⌒ **FIGURE 7.4   Guidelines for Promoting Preschoolers' Cognitive Development**

By following these practices, you can provide for the cognitive needs of all preschoolers. What would you need to do to implement these best practices?

Physical activities contribute to children's physical, social, emotional, linguistic, and cognitive development. It is essential that programs provide opportunities for children to engage in active play both in indoor and outdoor settings. What are some things that children can learn through participation in playground activities?

infants and toddlers to support preschoolers' language development. The "Professionlism in Practice: Fostering a Foundation for Learning," by Joyce Edwards of Baines Lower Elementary School in Louisiana, discusses how teachers must embrace opportunities that enable language and mathmatical development.

READY TO LEARN: READY FOR SCHOOL

School **readiness** is a major topic of debate in discussions of both preschool and kindergarten programs. The early childhood profession is reexamining "readiness," its many interpretations, and the various ways the concept is applied to educational practices.

For most parents, *readiness* means that their children have the knowledge and abilities necessary for success in preschool and for getting ready for kindergarten. Figure 7.5 shows what kindergarten teachers believe are important factors for kindergarten readiness. These are some of the things children should know and be able to do *before* coming to kindergarten. Thus they shape, influence, and inform the preschool curriculum and the activities of preschool teachers. Review these now and think about their implications for what you will teach preschoolers to know and do.

Discussions about readiness have changed the public's attitude about what it means. Responsibility for children's early learning and development is no longer placed solely on children and their parents but rather is seen as a shared responsibility among children, parents, families, early childhood professionals, communities, states, and the nation. The NAEYC has adopted the following position statement on school readiness:

Professionalism in Practice

FOSTERING A FOUNDATION FOR LEARNING

Joyce Edwards

Principal, Baines Lower Elementary School, St. Francisville, Louisiana

The day is full of opportunities to participate in language.

The Baines Lower Elementary School provides services for 425 students pre-K through first grade in one of the most impoverished parishes (school districts) in Louisiana. I believe teachers must embrace opportunities that enable children to grow, develop, and learn in an active, developmentally appropriate environment. In this kind of environment, the teacher is the facilitator of learning and children are free to make discoveries for themselves.

I believe academic development is important and is the foundation for learning. Readiness for learning is developed in the home and in preschool. A print-rich environment that fosters literacy and language development is essential. In our program, we stress early literacy through the use of a lot of books and shared reading experiences. We provide lots of opportunities for children to read and write throughout the day.

Mathematical development is important because math experiences help children make sense of their world. Also, math, like reading is a basic skill that children will need throughout their lives. Creative and dramatic expressions are also important for young children. They need opportunities to express themselves creatively. In addition, it is important for preschoolers to have the social-emotional development that will enable them to follow learning routines, play and work in small groups, and learn to take turns.

Our program is successful because we have knowledgeable and dedicated teachers. They are all certified in early childhood education and have a good understanding of how children learn. We do a lot of professional development and provide the training that will help teachers become even better teachers.

New teachers need to have an open attitude and embrace opportunities to grow. If they do this, they will succeed. New teachers need a mentor who will provide them with support and help. If new teachers are not assigned a mentor teacher by their administration, they should seek out a great teacher who will help them. All teachers must be willing to learn and improve. Self-improvement is part of what being a professional is all about. Teaching is hard work, but if teachers work hard they will be successful.

 To review the Professional Development Checklist and complete a Professionalism in Practice activity, visit the Companion Website at *http://www.prenhall.com/morrison*, select Chapter 7, then choose the Professional Development module.

The National Association for the Education of Young Children (NAEYC) believes that those who are committed to promoting universal school readiness must

1. address the inequities in early life experience so that all children have access to the opportunities which promote school success;
2. recognize and support individual differences among children; and
3. establish reasonable and appropriate expectations of children's capabilities upon school entry.[1]

☞ **FIGURE 7.5   What Kindergarten Teachers Believe Preschoolers Should Know When Entering Kindergarten**

In addition to being physically healthy, rested, and well-nourished these are some dimensions of readiness that kindergarten teachers say are important. You can use those dimensions as guidelines for what to include in your preschool program.

Source: *M. D. Welch, & B. White, Teacher and Parent Expectations for Kindergarten Readiness. ERIC Document Reproduction Service No. ED437225, May 1999. Used by permission of the author.*

* Can communicate needs, wants, and thoughts verbally
* Is enthusiastic and curious approaching new activities
* Takes turns and shares
* Has good problem-solving skills
* Is able to use pencils or paintbrushes
* Is not disruptive of the class
* Knows the English language
* Is sensitive to other children's feelings
* Sits still and pays attention
* Knows the letters of the alphabet
* Can follow directions
* Identifies primary colors and basic shapes

The "Video Viewpoint: Improving Intelligence in Children" considers the role of early childhood professionals in helping preschoolers achieve their full potential.

Important Readiness Skills

All children need important skills to be ready for learning and school. These skills and behaviors include language, independence, impulse control, interpersonal skills, experiential background, and physical and mental health. The following sections cover each of these topics and the information will help you incorporate them into your planning and teaching.

LANGUAGE.   Language is the most important readiness skill. Children need language skills for success in school and life. Important language skills include:

* **Receptive language,** such as listening to the teacher and following directions
* **Expressive language,** demonstrated in the ability to talk fluently and articulately with teacher and peers, the ability to express oneself in the language of the school, and the ability to communicate needs and ideas
* **Symbolic language,** knowing the names of people, places, and things, words for concepts, and adjectives and prepositions

In addition, children need language skills related to reading readiness. Two of the most important reading readiness skills are the ability to recognize and name the letters of the alphabet and to make the sounds of the letters. More preschool programs are including these important skills in their curricula.

Video Viewpoint

IMPROVING INTELLIGENCE IN CHILDREN

Scientists have discovered that if certain brain cells are not engaged by certain ages, the cells die off. They have also found some keys to helping children's brains to develop more fully.

REFLECTIVE DISCUSSION QUESTIONS

What are some consequences for society and for children of not providing them with the early stimulation they need to grow their brains? How does the phrase "use it or lose it" apply to children's neurological development? How early in life should parents begin to promote language development in their children?

REFLECTIVE DECISION MAKING

Make a list of things you can do to stimulate early language development. Interview a music educator about how exposing children to music stimulates logical thinking. What are some math games you can teach young children to promote higher level thinking skills?

INDEPENDENCE.   **Independence** means the ability to work alone on a task, take care of oneself, and initiate projects without always being told what to do. Independence also includes mastery of self-help skills, including dressing skills, health skills (toileting, hand washing, and brushing teeth), and eating skills (using utensils and napkins, serving oneself, and cleaning up). Independence is a highly regarded American ability. However, it is not a capacity that is valued by all cultures. This means you will have to work with children and their parents in culturally sensitive ways as you support children's growing independence. Review again the guidelines for culturally appropriate practice in Chapter 6.

IMPULSE CONTROL.   **Controlling impulses** includes working cooperatively with others; not hitting others or interfering with their work; developing an attention span that permits involvement in learning activities for a reasonable length of time; and being able to stay seated for a while. Children who are not able to control their impulses are frequently (and erroneously) labeled hyperactive (ADHD) or learning disabled (LD). These are also children who are *most* likely to *not* receive the individual attention they need and are therefore at risk for failure.

INTERPERSONAL SKILLS.   **Interpersonal skills** include getting along and working with both peers and adults. Parents frequently say the primary reason they want their children to attend preschool is "to learn how to get along with others." All preschool programs are experiences in group living, and children should have the opportunity to interact with others to become successful in a group setting. Interpersonal skills include cooperating with others, learning and using basic manners, and, most important, learning how to learn from and with others. Recall that Lev Vygotsky believed that learning is a social activity. Constructivist practice is based on the important premise of social learning, that is, that people help people learn. The following "Technology Tie-In: Using Technology to Promote Children's Social Development" explores ways in which technology can assist in children's social development.

EXPERIENTIAL BACKGROUND.   Experiential background is important to readiness because experiences are the building blocks of knowledge, the raw materials of cognitive development. Children must go places—the grocery store, library, zoo—and they must be involved in activities—creating things, painting, coloring,

Technology Tie-In

USING TECHNOLOGY TO PROMOTE CHILDREN'S SOCIAL DEVELOPMENT

Perhaps you have heard some critics claim that computers and other technology interfere with children's social development. Let's look at this argument and consider some things you can do to ensure that your use of technology with young children supports and enhances their social development.

Social development involves interacting with and getting along with other children, siblings, parents, and teachers. Social development also includes the development of self-esteem, the feelings children have about themselves. During the early childhood years, true peer relationships begin to emerge. Children's interactions and relationships with others enlarge their views of the world and of themselves. Early childhood is also a time when children are learning self-control and self-reliance. Adults expect children to develop self-regulation, control aggression, and function without constant supervision. How children meet these expectations has tremendous implications for the development of self-concept and self-esteem. Finally, during the early childhood years children are learning about adult roles thorough play and real-life activities. As children learn about adult activities, they learn about others and themselves.

You can use computers and other technology to help children develop positive peer relationships, grow in their abilities of self-regulation and self-control, explore adult roles, and develop positive self-esteem. Here are some things you can do to accomplish these goals.

✳ Have children work on projects together in pairs or small groups. Several children can work on computer and other projects at the same time.

Make sure that the computer has several chairs to encourage children to work together. Learning through technology is not inherently a solitary activity. You can find many ways to make it a cooperative and social learning experience.

✳ Provide children opportunities to talk about their technology projects. Part of social development includes learning to talk confidently, explain, and share information with others.

✳ Encourage children to explore adult roles related to technology, such as newscaster, weather forecaster, and photographer. Invite adults from the community to share with children how they use technology in their careers. Invite a television crew to show children how they broadcast from community locations.

✳ Read stories about technology and encourage children to talk about technology in their lives and the lives of their families.

As you explore other ways to promote children's social development through technology, remember that all dimensions of children's development are integrated. The cognitive, linguistic, social, emotional, and physical support and depend on each other, and technology can positively support all of these dimensions of development.

To complete this Technology Tie-In activity and others like it, visit the Companion Website at *http://www.prenhall.com/ morrison*, select Chapter 7, then choose the Technology Tie-In module.

experimenting, discovering. Children can build only on the background of information they bring to new experiences. Varied experiences, for example, are the context in which children learn words, and the number and kinds of words children know is a major predictor of the ability to learn to read and of their school success.

PHYSICAL AND MENTAL HEALTH.   Children must have good nutritional, mental, and physical health habits that will enable them to participate fully in and profit from any program. They must also have positive, nurturing environments and caring professionals to help them develop a self-image for achievement. Today, more attention than ever is paid to children's health and nutrition. Likewise, the curriculum at all levels includes activities for promoting wellness and healthy living.

Readiness and Culture

All children are always ready for some kind of learning. Children always need experiences that will promote learning and get them ready for the next step. As early childhood educators, we should constantly ask such questions as: What does this child know? What can I do to help this child move to the next level of understanding?

Readiness is a function of culture. Professionals have to be sensitive to the fact that different cultures have different values regarding the purpose of school, the process of schooling, children's roles in the schooling process, and the family's and culture's roles in promoting readiness. Professionals must learn about other cultures, talk with parents, and try to find a match between the process and activities of schooling and families' cultures. Providing culturally sensitive, supportive, and responsive education is the responsibility of all early childhood professionals. Review again the ten questions of culturally sensitive caregiving in Figure 6.9.

PRESCHOOL CURRICULUM, GOALS, AND STATE STANDARDS

The purposes of preschool are changing dramatically. More and more, preschools are seen as places that get children ready for kindergarten. What was traditionally taught in kindergarten is now taught in the preschool. The preschool curriculum is now stressing academic skills related to reading, writing, and math as well as social skills.

For more information about preschool curricula and teaching strategies, go to the Companion Website at *http://www.prenhall.com/morrison*, select any chapter, then choose Topic 6 of the ECE Supersite module.

Increasingly, the responsibility for setting the preschool curriculum is being taken over by state departments of education through **standards,** statements of what preschoolers should know and be able to do. For example, Figure 7.6 depicts part of the Texas Prekindergarten Guidelines for language. Other curriculum areas are mathematics, science, social studies, fine arts, health and safety, personal and social development, physical development, and technology applications. You can access the full text of the Texas Prekindergarten Guidelines through the Companion Website. One point is that preschool goals and learning standards are being set by state departments of education. A second point is that the preschool curriculum is becoming more academics-focused.

Listening Comprehension

* Listens with increasing attention
* Listens for different purposes (e.g., to learn what happened in a story, to receive instructions, to converse with an adult or peer)
* Understands and follows simple oral directions
* Enjoys listening to and responding to books
* Listens to and engages in several exchanges of conversations with others
* Listens to tapes and records, and shows understanding through gestures, actions, and/or language
* Listens purposefully to English-speaking teachers and peers to gather information and shows some understanding of the new language being spoken by others (ESL)

Speech Production and Speech Discrimination

* Perceives differences between similar-sounding words (e.g., "coat" and "goat," "three" and "free," [Spanish] "juego" and "fuego")
* Produces speech sounds with increasing ease and accuracy
* Experiments with new language sounds
* Experiments with and demonstrates growing understanding of the sounds and intonation of the English language (ESL)

Vocabulary

* Shows a steady increase in listening and speaking vocabulary
* Uses new vocabulary in everyday communication
* Refines and extends understanding of known words
* Attempts to communicate more than current vocabulary will allow, borrowing and extending words to create meaning
* Links new learning experiences and vocabulary to what is already known about a topic
* Increases listening vocabulary and begins to develop a vocabulary of object names and common phrases in English (ESL)

Verbal Expression

* Uses language for a variety of purposes (e.g., expressing needs and interests)
* Uses sentences of increasing length (three or more words) and grammatical complexity in everyday speech

(Continued)

∽ **FIGURE 7.6   Texas Prekindergarten Guidelines for Language and Literacy**

State standards that identify what children should know and be able to do are common for grades K–12. Standards now also are reforming and shaping preschool programs and curricula as these Texas standards demonstrate.

Source: *Texas Education Agency. (1999). Texas PreKindergarten Curriculum Guidelines. Available Online. Adapted from the Texas Prekindergarten Curriculum Guidelines.*

* Uses language to express common routines and familiar scripts

* Tells a simple personal narrative, focusing on favorite or most memorable parts

* Asks questions and makes comments related to the current topic of discussion

* Begins to engage in conversation and follows conversational rules (e.g., staying on topic and taking turns)

* Begins to retell the sequence of a story

* Engages in various forms of nonverbal communication with those who do not speak his/her home language (ESL)

* Uses single words and simple phrases to communicate meaning in social situations (ESL)

* Attempts to use new vocabulary and grammar in speech (ESL)

Phonological Awareness

* Becomes increasingly sensitive to the sounds of spoken words

* Begins to identify rhymes and rhyming sounds in familiar words, participates in rhyming games, and repeats rhyming songs and poems

* Begins to attend to the beginning sounds in familiar words by identifying that the pronunciations of several words all begin the same way (e.g., "dog," "dark," and "dusty," [Spanish] "casa," "coche," and "cuna")

* Begins to break words into syllables or claps along with each syllable in a phrase

* Begins to create and invent words by substituting one sound for another (e.g., bubblegum/gugglebum, [Spanish] calabaza/balacaza)

Print and Book Awareness

* Understands that reading and writing are ways to obtain information and knowledge, generate and communicate thoughts and ideas, and solve problems

* Understands that print carries a message by recognizing labels, signs, and other print forms in the environment

* Understands that letters are different from numbers

* Understands that illustrations carry meaning but cannot be read

* Understands that a book has a title and an author

* Begins to understand that print runs from left to right and top to bottom

* Begins to understand some basic print conventions (e.g., the concept that letters are grouped to form words and that words are separated by spaces)

* Begins to recognize the association between spoken and written words by following the print as it is read aloud

* Understands that different text forms are used for different functions (e.g., lists for shopping, recipes for cooking, newspapers for learning about current events, letters and messages for interpersonal communication)

☞ **FIGURE 7.6   Texas Prekindergarten Guidelines for Language and Literacy** *(Continued)*

Appropriate Preschool Goals

Whereas goals of individual preschools vary and are influenced by state standards, all programs should have certain essential goals. Most quality preschools, however, plan goals in these areas: social and interpersonal skills, self-help and intrapersonal skills, learning how to learn and developing a love for learning, academics, thinking skills, learning readiness, language and literacy, character education, music and the arts, wellness and healthy living, and independence. These goals and how to achieve them are outlined in detail in Table 7–2.

 PRESCHOOL PROGRAMS

Play has traditionally been the heart of preschool programs. It is and will continue to be important in preschool programs. Children's play results in learning. Therefore, play is a process through which children learn, and preschool programs should support learning through play. The "Program in Action: The Value of Play" on pages 206 and 207, explores classroom examples of how play can influence development.

TABLE 7–2
PRESCHOOL GOALS

GOAL	DIMENSIONS
Social and Interpersonal Skills	· Helping children learn how to get along with other children and adults and how to develop good relationships with teachers · Helping children learn to help others and develop caring attitudes
Self-Help and Intrapersonal Skills	· Modeling for children how to take care of their personal needs, such as dressing (tying, buttoning, zipping) and knowing what clothes to wear · Eating skills (using utensils, napkins, and a cup or glass; setting a table) · Health skills (how to wash and bathe, how to brush teeth) · Grooming skills (combing hair, cleaning nails)
Learning to Learn and Learning Readiness	· Promoting self-help skills to help children develop good self-image and high self-esteem · Helping children learn about themselves, their family, and their culture · Developing a sense of self-worth by providing experiences for success and competence · Teaching persistence, cooperation, self-control, and motivation · Facilitating readiness skills related to school success, such as following directions, learning to work alone, listening to the teacher, developing an attention span, learning to stay with a task until it is completed, staying in one's seat, and controlling impulses
Academics	· Teaching children to learn their names, addresses, and phone numbers · Facilitating children's learning of colors, sizes, shapes, and positions such as under, over, and around

(Continued)

TABLE 7–2
PRESCHOOL GOALS *(Continued)*

Goal	Dimensions
Academics *(cont.)*	· Facilitating children's learning of numbers and prewriting skills, shape identification, letter recognition, sounds, and rhyming · Providing for small-muscle development
Thinking Skills	· Providing environments and activities that enable children to develop the skills essential to constructing schemes in a Piagetian sense—classification, seriation, numeration, and knowledge of space and time concepts—which form the basis for logical-mathematical thinking · Giving children opportunities to respond to questions and situations that require them to synthesize, analyze, and evaluate
Language and Literacy	· Providing opportunities for interaction with adults and peers as a means of developing oral language skills · Helping children increase their vocabularies · Helping children learn to converse with other children and adults · Building proficiency in language · Developing literacy skills related to writing and reading · Learning the letters of the alphabet · Being familiar with a wide range of books
Character Education	· Having a positive mental attitude · Being persistence · Having respect for others · Being cooperative · Being honesty · Being trustworthy
Music and the Arts	· Using a variety of materials (e.g., crayons, paint, clay, markers) to create original work · Using different colors, surface textures, and shapes to create form and meaning · Using art as a form of self-expression · Participating in music activities · Singing a variety of simple songs · Responding to music of various tempos through movement
Wellness and Healthy Living	· Providing experiences that enable children to learn the role of good nutritional practices and habits in their overall development · Providing food preparation experiences · Introducing children to new foods, a balanced menu, and essential nutrients
Independence	· Helping students become independent by encouraging them to do things for themselves · Giving children reasonably free access to equipment and materials · Having children be responsible for passing out, collecting, and organizing materials

These represent essential goals for all preschool programs that you will want to implement in your professional role of educator of young children.

Program in Action

THE VALUE OF PLAY

Early childhood educators have long recognized the value of play for social, emotional, and physical development. Recently, however, play has attracted greater importance as a medium for literacy development. It is now recognized that literacy develops in meaningful, functional social settings rather than as a set of abstract skills taught in formal pencil-and-paper settings.

Literacy development involves a child's active engagement in cooperation and collaboration with peers; it builds on what the child already knows with the support and guidance of others. Play provides this setting. During observation of children at play, especially in free-choice, cooperative play periods, one can note the functional uses of literacy that children incorporate into their play themes. When the environment is appropriately prepared with literacy materials in play areas, children have been observed to engage in attempted and conceptual reading and writing in collaboration with other youngsters. In similar settings lacking literacy materials, the same literacy activities did not occur.

To demonstrate how play in an appropriate setting can nurture literacy development, consider the following classroom setting in which the teacher has designed a veterinarian's office to go along with a class study on animals focusing in particular on pets.

The dramatic play area is designed with a waiting room, including chairs; a table filled with magazines, books, and pamphlets about pet care; posters about pets; office hour notices; a "No Smoking" sign; and a sign advising visitors to "Check in with the nurse when arriving." On a nurse's desk are patient forms on clipboards, a telephone, an address and telephone book, appointment cards, and a calendar. The office contains patient folders, prescription pads, white coats, masks, gloves, a toy doctor's kit, and stuffed animals for patients.

Ms. Meyers, the teacher, guides students in using the various materials in the veterinarian's office during free-play time. For example, she reminds the children to read important information they find in the waiting area, to fill out forms about their pets' needs, to ask the nurse for appointment times, or to have the doctor write out appropriate treatments or prescriptions. In addition to giving directions, Ms. Meyers also models behaviors by participating in the play center with the children when first introducing materials.

This play setting provides a literacy-rich environment with books and writing materials; modeles reading and writing by the teacher that children can observe and emulate; provides the opportunity to practice literacy in a real-life situation that has meaning and function; and encourages children to interact socially by collaborating and performing meaningful reading and writing activities with peers. The following anecdotes relate the type of behavior Ms. Meyers observed in the play area.

For more information about early childhood play, go to the Companion Website at *http://www.prenhall.com/ morrison*, select Chapter 7, then choose Topic 5 of the ECE Supersite module.

The notion that children learn and develop through play began with Froebel. Since his time, most early childhood programs have incorporated play into their curricula.

Montessori viewed children's active involvement with materials and the prepared environment as the primary means by which they absorb knowledge and learn. John Dewey believed that children learn through play and that children should have opportunities to engage in play associated with everyday activities (e.g., the house center, post office, grocery store, doctor's office).

Jessica was waiting to see the doctor. She told her stuffed animal dog, Sam, not to worry, that the doctor would not hurt him. She asked Jenny, who was waiting with her stuffed animal cat, Muffin, what the kitten's problem was. The girls agonized over the ailments of their pets. After a while they stopped talking and Jessica picked up the book *Are You My Mother?* and pretended to read to her dog. Jessica showed Sam the pictures as she read.

Preston examined Christopher's teddy bear and wrote a report in the patient's folder. He read his scribble writing out loud and said, "This teddy bear's blood pressure is twenty-nine points. He should take sixty-two pills an hour until he is better and keep warm and go to bed." At the same time he read, he showed Christopher what he had written so he could understand what to do.

When selecting settings to promote literacy in play, choose those that are familiar to children and relate them to themes currently being studied. Suggestions for literacy materials and settings to add to the dramatic play areas include the following:

✳ A fast-food restaurant, ice cream store, or bakery suggests menus, order pads, a cash register, specials for the day, recipes, and lists of flavors or products.

✳ A supermarket or local grocery store can include labeled shelves and sections, food containers, pricing labels, cash registers, telephones, shopping receipts, checkbooks, coupons, and promotional flyers.

✳ A post office to serve for mailing children's letters needs paper, envelopes, address books, pens, pencils, stamps, cash registers, and labeled mailboxes. A mail carrier hat and bag are important for children who deliver the mail and need to identify and read names and addresses.

✳ A gas station and car repair shop, designed in the block area, might have toy cars and trucks, receipts for sales, road maps for help with directions to different destinations, automotive tools and auto repair manuals for fixing cars and trucks, posters that advertise automobile equipment, and empty cans of different products typically found in service stations.

Contributed by Lesley Mandel Morrow, professor and coordinator of early childhood programs, Rutgers University.

 To complete a Program in Action activity, visit the Companion Website at *http://www. prenhall.com/morrison*, select Chapter 7, then choose the Programs in Action module.

Piaget believed play promotes cognitive knowledge and is a means by which children construct knowledge of their world. He thought that through active involvement, children learn.

Vygotsky viewed the social interactions that occur through play essential to children's development. He believed that children learn through social interactions with others social skills such as cooperation and collaboration that promote and enhance their cognitive development.

Providing opportunities for children to choose among well-planned, varied learning activities enhances the probability that they will learn through play.

⊂◯ **FIGURE 7.7   What Children Learn through Play**

When properly planned and facilitated, play is an appropriate and powerful way for children to learn. Your professional roles in supporting children's play are outlined in Figure 7.8 on page 213.

⁕ Learn concepts
  ⁕ Physical concepts associated with the five senses—touching, tasting, smelling, seeing, and hearing
  ⁕ Logical-mathematical concepts associated with classification, seriation, numeration, space (over, under, etc.) and time (before, after, etc.)
⁕ Develop social skills
  ⁕ Sharing
  ⁕ Taking turns
  ⁕ Negotiating
  ⁕ Compromising
  ⁕ Leading
⁕ Develop physical skills
  ⁕ Using fine and large muscles
⁕ Develop and practice language and literacy skills
  ⁕ Phonological awareness—learning how sounds make up words and are used in words
  ⁕ Conversation skills (e.g., taking turns and responding appropriately)
⁕ Enhance self-esteem
  ⁕ Demonstrating accomplishments and abilities
  ⁕ Relating own accomplishments to those of peers
⁕ Master life situations and prepare for adult life and roles
  ⁕ Learning how to become independent
  ⁕ Thinking
  ⁕ Making decisions
  ⁕ Cooperating/collaborating with others

Figure 7.7 shows some of the things children learn through play. In addition, the "Professionalism in Practice: You Can't Fly by the Seat if Your Pants" by Deborah Austin on page 210 discusses how teachers can connect everything children do in their play to learning objectives.

Kinds of Play

Children engage in many kinds of play. Table 7–3 shows Mildred Parten's (children's play researcher, now deceased) stages and descriptions of children's social play.

Social play supports many important functions. First, it provides the means for children to interact with others and learn many social skills. Children learn how to

Puppets and plays provide many opportunities for children to learn and interact with others. Indeed, the props that professionals provide for children to play with contribute to all of children's learning, but in particular their literacy development. What literacy skills are these children learning?

TABLE 7–3
TYPES OF SOCIAL PLAY

TYPE OF PLAY	DESCRIPTION/PURPOSE
Unoccupied Play	The child does not play with anything or anyone; the child merely stands or sits, without doing anything observable.
Solitary Play	Although involved in play, the child plays alone, seemingly unaware of other children.
Onlooker Play	The child watches and observes the play of other children; the center of interest is others' play.
Parallel Play	The child plays alone but in ways similar to and with toys or other materials similar to those of other children.
Associative Play	Children interact with each other, perhaps by asking questions or sharing materials, but do not play together.
Cooperative Play	Children actively play together, often as a result of organization by the teacher.

Observing children's social play is a good way to sharpen your observation skills and to learn more about children's play and the learning that occurs through play. Develop an observational checklist based on ideas presented in Chapter 5. Social play follows the general sequence shown in this table. Observe to determine the ages at which children engage in each type of play.

Source: Mildred Parten, "Social Play Among Preschool Children," *Journal of Abnormal and Social Psychology 27* (1933): 243–269.

Professionalism in Practice

YOU CAN'T FLY BY THE SEAT OF YOUR PANTS
Deborah Austin
Principal, Early Childhood Learning Center, La Marque Independent School District, La Marque, Texas

At our Early Childhood Learning Center, which serves four- and five-year-old children in an inclusive setting, we believe, as did John Dewey, that children learn by doing and by getting involved with things. Children need a concrete approach to learning, and they need to manipulate everything. We always have to remember that children require a hands-on approach and that they learn best by touching and making physical connections to words, concepts, and things. We try to relate everything children do to the real world of people and things. This is what makes learning come alive in meaningful ways.

We believe that children learn through play and that play should have an academic focus. Teachers can connect everything children do in their play to learning objectives. For example, are children using words and sentences appropriately in their conversations with others? You can incorporate math into children's play while they are setting a table. You can ask how many are coming to lunch, how many knives, forks, and spoons they will need, and so forth. We work as a total faculty on developing learning through real-life applications. For example, in our center hallway, we have an attendance chart that shows the classrooms with perfect attendance. On the chart, a Christmas tree represents one day of perfect attendance, and a snowman represents five days of perfect attendance. Our preschoolers can tell which classroom has the most perfect attendances and which is second, third, and last. This fun activity involves second and third grade math level skills, but

because we do it in fun ways and apply it to everyday life, our preschoolers learn it.

It is important for teachers to help children make connections and relate them to learning. You can't just put a group of kids in a block corner and hope they learn what they need to learn. We follow the Texas Prekindergarten Guidelines, which specify what preschool children should know and be able to do, so we have to make sure that our children learn. While we emphasize academics, we also want children to become well rounded and this comes from a balance of academic and social development. When children leave our school, we want them to be able to say that they learned and that they were loved.

Teachers are the keys to assuring that children learn and are loved. I tell new teachers that they have to plan more than they ever thought they would have to plan to help children master desired learning outcomes. Teaching is an organized profession, and it takes organized teachers to practice the art of teaching. You can't fly by the seat of your pants and hope to be a good teacher.

 To review the Professional Development Checklist and complete a Professionalism in Practice activity, visit the Companion Website at *http://www.prenhall.com/morrison*, select Chapter 7, then choose the Professional Development module.

compromise ("OK, I'll be the baby first and you can be the mommy"), be flexible ("We'll do it your way first and then my way"), resolve conflicts, and continue the process of learning who they are. Second, social play provides a vehicle for practicing and developing literacy skills. Children have others with whom to practice language and from whom to learn. Third, play helps children learn impulse control; they realize they cannot always do whatever they want. And fourth, in giving a child other children with whom to interact, social play negates isolation and helps children learn how to have the social interactions so vital to successful living.

In addition to social play, other types of play and their benefits and purposes are shown in Table 7–4. Carefully study these kinds of play and plan for how you will include them in your program. Then consider how play increases children's interest in learning in the "Video Viewpoint: Wild about Learning" on page 213.

Early Childhood Professionals and Play

You and your colleagues are the key to promoting meaningful play, which promotes a basis for learning. How you prepare the environment for play and the attitudes you have toward it determine the quality of the children's learning. Your responsibilities for supporting a quality play curriculum are shown in Figure 7.8. After reviewing your responsibilities for play, think about what you need to do to prepare yourself to help ensure quality play experiences for all children.

Dramatic play promotes children's understanding of concepts and processes. Here, play allows children to explore their feelings and ideas about medical practitioners and medical settings.

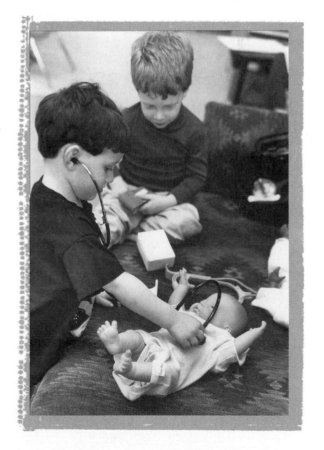

TABLE 7–4
OTHER TYPES OF PLAY

Type of Play	Purpose/Benefit
Cognitive Play	Froebel, Montessori, and Piaget recognized the value of cognitive play. They all saw children's active participation as a direct link to knowledge and development. From a Piagetian perspective, play is literally cognitive development.
Functional Play	Functional play occurs during the sensorimotor period and in response to muscular activities and the need to be active. Functional play is characterized by repetitions, manipulations, and self-imitation. Functional play allows children to practice and learn physical capabilities while exploring their immediate environments. Very young children are especially fond of repeating movements for the pleasure of it. They engage in sensory impressions for the joy of experiencing the functioning of their bodies. Repetition of language is also a part of functional play.
Symbolic Play	Piaget referred to symbolic play as "let's pretend" play. During this stage, children freely display their creative and physical abilities and social awareness in a number of ways—for example, by pretending to be something else, such as an animal. Symbolic play also occurs when children pretend that one object is another—that a building block is a car, for example—and may also entail pretending to be another person—a mommy, daddy, or caregiver.
Playing Games with Rules	This kind of play begins around age seven or eight and involves learning to play within rules and limits. Games with rules are common in middle childhood and adulthood as well.
Informal or Free Play	Informal play occurs when children play in an environment that contains materials and people with whom they can interact. Learning materials may be grouped in centers with similar equipment: a kitchen center, a dress-up center, a block center, a music and art center, a water or sand area, and a free play center, usually with items such as tricycles, wagons, and wooden slides for promoting large-muscle development. The atmosphere of a free play is informal, unstructured, and unpressured. Play and learning episodes are generally determined by the interests of the children. Outcomes of free play are socialization, emotional development, self-control, and concept development.
Sociodramatic (Pretend) Play	Dramatic play allows children to participate vicariously in a wide range of activities associated with family living, society, and their and others' cultural heritage. Dramatic play is generally of two kinds: *sociodramatic* and *fantasy*. Sociodramatic play usually involves everyday realistic activities and events, whereas fantasy play typically involves fairy tale and superhero play. In sociodramatic play, children have an opportunity to express themselves, assume different roles, and interact with their peers. Sociodramatic play acts as a nonsexist and multicultural arena in which all children are equal.
Outdoor Play	Children's play outside is just as important as inside play. Outdoor environments and activities promote large- and small-muscle development and body coordination as well as language development, social interaction, and creativity. The outdoor area is a learning environment and, as such, the playground should be designed according to learning objectives. Indoor learning can also occur outdoors. Easels, play dough, and dramatic play props can further enhance learning opportunities.
Rough-and-Tumble Play	All children, to a greater or lesser degree, engage in rough-and-tumble play. One theory of play says children play because they are biologically programmed to do so; that is, it is part of children's (and adults') genetic heritage to engage in play activities. Rough-and-tumble play activities enable children to learn how to lead and follow, develop physical skills, interact with others in different ways, and grow in their abilities to give and take.

Play occurs in many types and forms. Your understanding of each of these will enable you to implement a meaningful program of learning through play.

Video Viewpoint

WILD ABOUT LEARNING

The NAEYC Guidelines for Developmentally Appropriate Practice recommend that young children have ample amounts of time and proper environments in which to play, since children do a great deal of learning when they play.

REFLECTIVE DISCUSSION QUESTIONS

In what ways does play help a child's social, cognitive, emotional, and physical development? What is the role of structured play (team sport participation, music lessons, scouting, etc.) in relation to free play?

REFLECTIVE DECISION MAKING

Visit a preschool, day care center, or grade school and observe a group of children at play. What are they doing? What learning is taking place? How do the activities, the people they interact with, the objects around them, and the immediate environment affect their play? Based on your observations, what could you do as an early childhood professional to promote meaningful learning experiences through play?

✳ Plan to implement the curriculum through play. Integrate specific learning activities with play to achieve learning outcomes. Play activities should match children's developmental needs and be free of gender and cultural stereotypes. Professionals have to be clear about curriculum concepts and ideas they want children to learn through play.

✳ Provide time for learning through play. Include play in the schedule as a legitimate activity in its own right.

✳ Create environments that ensure children will learn through play. Create both indoor and outdoor environments that encourage play and support its role in learning.

✳ Organize the classroom or center environment so that cooperative learning is possible and active learning occurs.

✳ Provide materials and equipment that are appropriate to children's developmental levels and which support a nonsexist and multicultural curriculum.

✳ Educate assistants and parents about how to promote learning through play.

✳ Supervise play activities and participate in children's play. In these roles, help, show, and guide. Model when appropriate and refrain from interfering when appropriate.

✳ Observe children's play. Teachers can learn how children play and the learning outcomes of play to use in planning classroom activities.

✳ Question children about their play. Discuss what children did during play, and "debrief" children about what they have learned through play.

✳ Provide for safety in indoor and outdoor play.

∽ **FIGURE 7.8   How Professionals Support Children's Play**

Teachers are the key persons responsible for the quality of children's play. These are some of the ways you can create an environment that ensures children will have meaningful and joyful play experiences.

Although we want children to be involved in child-initiated and active learning, sometimes it is necessary to directly teach children certain concepts or skills. What concepts or skills is this teacher directly teaching these children?

THE PRESCHOOL DAILY SCHEDULE

What should the preschool day schedule be like? Although a daily schedule depends on many things—your philosophy, the needs of children, parents' beliefs, and state and local standards—the following descriptions illustrate what you can do on a typical preschool day.

This preschool schedule is for a whole-day program; many other program arrangements are possible. Some preschools operate half-day, morning-only programs five days a week; others operate both a morning and an afternoon session; others operate only two or three days a week. However, an important preschool trend is toward full-day, full-year programs.

OPENING ACTIVITIES.   As children enter, the teacher greets each individually. Daily personal greetings make the children feel important, build a positive attitude toward school, and provide an opportunity to practice language skills. Daily greetings also give the teacher a chance to check each child's health and emotional status.

Children usually do not arrive all at one time, so the first arrivals need something to do while others are arriving. Offering a free selection of activities or letting children self-select from a limited range of quiet activities (such as puzzles, pegboards, or markers to color with) are appropriate.

GROUP MEETING/PLANNING.   After all children arrive, they and the teacher plan together and talk about the day ahead. This is also the time for announcements, sharing, and group songs and for children to think about what they plan to learn during the day.

LEARNING CENTERS.   After the group time, children are free to go to one of various learning centers, organized and designed to teach concepts. Table 7–5 lists

TABLE 7–5
LEARNING CENTERS

CENTER	CONCEPTS	CENTER	CONCEPTS
Housekeeping	· Classification · Language skills · Sociodramatic play · Functions · Processes	Woodworking Art	· Following directions · Functioning · Planning · Whole/part · Color
Water/sand	· Texture · Volume · Quantity · Measure		· Size · Shape · Texture · Design
Blocks	· Size · Shape · Length · Seriation · Spatial relations	 Science	· Relationship · Identification of odors · Functions · Measure · Volume
Books/language	· Verbalization · Listening · Directions · How to use books · Colors · Size · Shapes · Names	 Manipulatives	· Texture · Size · Relationship · Classifications · Spatial relationships · Shape · Color · Size
Puzzles/perceptual development	· Size · Shape · Color · Whole/part · Figure/ground · Spatial relations		· Seriation

These are some of the learning centers you can use to make your preschool program meaningful for your children. Think of other kinds of centers you can create to help children learn the knowledge, skills, and concepts they will need for success in kindergarten.

types of learning centers and the concepts each is intended to teach. You should plan for the concepts and skills you want children to learn in each center. Also, every center should be a literacy center; that is, there should be materials for writing and reading in each center.

BATHROOM/HAND WASHING.   Before any activity in which food is handled, prepared, or eaten, children should wash and dry their hands. You should instruct children in proper hand-washing procedures.

SNACKS.   After center activities, a snack is usually served. It should be nutritionally sound and something the children can serve (and often prepare) themselves.

OUTDOOR ACTIVITY/PLAY/WALKING.   Outside play should be a time for learning new concepts and skills, not just a time to run around aimlessly. Children can practice climbing, jumping, swinging, throwing, and using body control. Teachers may incorporate walking trips and other events into outdoor play.

BATHROOM/TOILETING.   Bathroom/toileting times offer opportunities to teach health, self-help, and intrapersonal skills. Children should also be allowed to use the bathroom whenever necessary.

LUNCH.   Lunch should be a relaxing time, and the meal should be served family style, with professionals and children eating together. Children should set their own tables and decorate them with placemats and flowers they can make in the art center or as a special project. Children should be involved in cleaning up after meals and snacks.

RELAXATION.   After lunch, children should have a chance to relax, perhaps to the accompaniment of teacher-read stories, records, and music. This is an ideal time to teach children breathing exercises and relaxation techniques.

NAP TIME.   Children who want or need to should have a chance to rest or sleep. Quiet activities should be available for those who do not need to or cannot sleep on a particular day. In any event, nap time should not be forced on any child.

CENTERS OR SPECIAL PROJECTS.   Following nap time is a good time for center activities or special projects. Special projects can also be conducted in the morning, and some may be more appropriate then, such as cooking something for snack or lunch. Special projects might involve cooking, holiday activities, collecting things, work projects, art activities, and field trips.

GROUP TIME.   The day can end with a group meeting to review the day's activities. This meeting develops listening and attention skills, promotes oral communication, stresses that learning is important, and helps children evaluate their performance and behavior.

How you structure the day for your children will determine in part how and what they learn. You will want to develop your daily schedule with attention and care.

QUALITY PRESCHOOL PROGRAMS

Parents often wonder how to select a good preschool program. They will ask you for your suggestions and advice. You can use the guidelines shown in Table 7–6 to help parents and others arrive at an appropriate preschool decision. You can also use these guidelines to help ensure that you are providing a quality program.

TABLE 7–6

INDICATORS OF A GOOD QUALITY PRESCHOOL

QUALITY INDICATOR	QUALITY DESCRIPTION
Physical Accommodations	What are the physical accommodations like? Is the facility pleasant, light, clean, and airy? Is it a physical setting where you would want to spend time? (If not, children will not want to, either.) Are plenty of materials available for the children to use?
Children's Emotional States	Do the children seem happy and involved? Or passive? Is television used as a substitute for a good curriculum and quality professionals?
Types of Materials	What kinds of materials are available for play and learning? Is there variety and an abundance of materials? Are there materials (like puzzles) that help children learn concepts and think?
Balance of Activities	Is there a balance of activity and quiet play and of individual, small-group, and large-group activities? Child-directed and professional-directed activities? Indoor and outdoor play?
Health and Safety	Is the physical setting safe and healthy?
Philosophy and Goals	Does the school have a written philosophy and goals? Does the program philosophy agree with the parents' personal philosophy of how children should be reared and educated? Are the philosophy and goals appropriate for the children being served?
Literacy Development	Is there an emphasis on early literacy development? Do teachers read to children throughout the day? A general rule of thumb is that teachers should read to children at least twenty minutes a day. Are there books and other materials that support literacy development? Another rule of thumb is that preschool children should be familiar with 75 to 100 books by the time they enter kindergarten.
Written Curriculum	Is there a written curriculum designed to help children learn skills for literacy, math, and science? Does the curriculum provide for skills in self-help; readiness for learning; and cognitive, language, physical, and social-emotional development?
Daily Plans	Does the staff have written plans? Is there a smooth flow of activities, or do children wait for long periods "getting ready" for another activity? Lack of planning indicates lack of direction. Although a program whose staff does not plan is not necessarily a poor program, planning is one indicator of a good program.
Adult:Child Ratio	What is the adult:child ratio? How much time do teachers spend with children one-to-one or in small groups? Do teachers take time to give children individual attention? Do children have an opportunity to be independent and do things for themselves?
Staff Interaction	How does the staff relate to children? Are the relationships loving and caring?

(Continued)

TABLE 7–6

INDICATORS OF A GOOD QUALITY PRESCHOOL *(Continued)*

Quality Indicator	Quality Description
Guiding Behavior	How do staff members handle typical discipline problems, such as disputes between children? Are positive guidance techniques used? Are indirect guidance techniques used (e.g., through room arrangement, scheduling, and appropriate activity planning)? Is there a written discipline philosophy that agrees with the parents' philosophy?
Gender and Cultural Needs	Are staff personnel sensitive to the gender and cultural needs and backgrounds of children and families? Are the cultures of all children respected and supported?
Outdoor Activities	Are there opportunities for outdoor activities? Is there a variety of activities?
Mealtime	How is lunchtime handled? Are children allowed to talk while eating? Do staff members eat with the children? Is lunchtime a happy and learning time?
Staff Turnover	Is there a low turnover rate for teachers and staff? Programs that have high and constant turnovers of staff are not providing the continuity of care and education that children need.
Staff Education	What kind of education or training does the staff have? The staff should have training on how to develop the curriculum and teach young children.
Director Qualifications	Is the director well educated? The director should have at least a bachelor's degree in childhood education or child development. Can the director explain the program? Describing a typical day can be helpful. Is she or he actively involved in the program?
Staff-Adult Relationships	How does the staff treat adults, including parents? Does the program address the needs of children's families? Staff should provide for the needs of families as well as children.
Cost and Affordability	Is the program affordable? If a program is too expensive for the family budget, parents may be unhappy in the long run. Parents should inquire about scholarships, reduced fees, fees adjusted to income level, fees paid in monthly installments, and sibling discounts.
Parent Satisfaction	Are parents of children enrolled in the program satisfied? One of the best ways to learn about a program is to talk to other parents.
Hours and Services	Do the program's hours and services match parents' needs? Too often, parents have to patch together care and education to cover their work hours.
Emergency Care	What are the provisions for emergency care and treatment?
Ill Children	What procedures are there for taking care of ill children?

Share these quality program indicators with parents and your colleagues. Taken as a whole, they will enable you to provide quality programs and will enable parents to select quality programs for their children.

Successful Transitions to Kindergarten

A transition is a passage from one learning setting, grade, program, or experience to another. You can help ensure that the transitions preschool children make from home to preschool to kindergarten are happy and rewarding experiences.

You can help children make transitions easily and confidently in several ways, as shown in Figure 7.9. Remember that transitions can be traumatic experiences for children. When transitions are hurried, unplanned, and abrupt, they can cause social, emotional, and learning problems. On the other hand, quality transitions, based on Figure 7.9, can be learning experiences for children.

FIGURE 7.9 Helping Children Make Transitions

Successful transitions of any kind play a powerful role in children's cognitive and emotional well-being. Any transition should be well thought out and planned.

* Educate and prepare children ahead of time for any new situation. Children can practice routines they will encounter when they enter kindergarten.

* Alert parents to new and different standards, dress, behavior, and parent—teacher interactions.

* Give children an opportunity to meet their new teachers.

* Let parents know ahead of time what their children will need in the new program (e.g., lunch box, change of clothing).

* Provide parents of children with special needs and bilingual parents with additional help and support during the transition.

* Offer parents and children an opportunity to visit programs. Children will better understand the physical, curricular, and affective climates of the new programs if they visit in advance.

* Cooperate with the staff of any program the children will attend to work out a transition plan.

* Exchange class visits between preschool and kindergarten programs. Class visits are an excellent way to have preschool children learn about the classrooms they will attend as kindergartners. Having kindergarten children visit the preschool and tell the preschoolers about kindergarten provides for a sense of security and anticipation.

* Work with kindergarten teachers to make booklets about their program. These booklets can include photographs of children, letters from kindergarten children and preschoolers, and pictures of kindergarten activities. These books can be placed in the reading centers where preschool children can "read" about the programs they will attend.

* Hold a "kindergarten day" for preschoolers in which they attend kindergarten for a day. This program can include such things as riding the bus, having lunch, touring the school, and meeting teachers.

THE FUTURE OF PRESCHOOL EDUCATION

The further growth of public preschools for three- and four-year-old children is inevitable. This growth, to the point where all children are included, will take decades, but it will happen. Most likely, the public schools will focus more on programs for four-year-old children and then, over time, include three-year-olds. A logical outgrowth of this long-term trend will be for the public schools to provide services for even younger children and their families. One thing is certain: preschool as it was known a decade ago is not the same preschool of today. Ten years from now preschools will again be different from those of today. Your challenge is to develop the professional skills necessary to assume a leadership role in the development of quality, universal preschool programs for all children.

 To take an online self-test on this chapter's contents, go to the Companion Website at *http://www.prenhall.com/ morrison*, select Chapter 7, then choose the Self-Test module.

ACTIVITIES FOR PROFESSIONAL DEVELOPMENT

In this chapter we have stressed the importance of how to apply developmentally appropriate practice to teaching in the preschool years. Refer again to the "Professional Development Goal" at the beginning of the chapter, to the "Professional Development Checklist" on pages 20 and 21, and the "Professionalism in Practice" features on pages 197 and 210. After you have reviewed these, complete the following exercises.

1. Visit preschool programs in your area. Determine their philosophies and find out what goes on in a typical day.
   a. How do their philosophies compare to your philosophy?
   b. Make a list of activities and practices you thought were developmentally appropriate. Make another list of developmentally inappropriate practices. How would you change the practices to make them appropriate?
2. Based on material presented in this chapter, develop a set of guidelines for ensuring that preschool programs would be developmentally appropriate. Develop guidelines for the environment, curriculum, and teaching practices.
3. Observe children's play, and give examples of how children learn through play and what they learn.
4. Contact your state department of education and ask for the prekindergarten guidelines or standards. Compare these to the Texas Prekindergarten Guidelines. Begin to decide how you can integrate your understanding of developmentally appropriate practice with what state standards are requiring that children should know and be able to do.

For additional chapter resources and activities, visit the Companion Website at *http://www.prenhall.com/morrison*, select Chapter 7, then choose the Professional Development, Resources, or Linking to Learning modules.

FOCUS QUESTIONS

1. What is the history of the kindergarten and how has it changed from Froebel to the present?

2. What are appropriate goals, objectives, and curriculum for kindergarten programs?

3. How can I use knowledge of developmentally appropriate practice to help me teach kindergarten children?

chapter 8

Kindergarten Today

MEETING ACADEMIC AND DEVELOPMENTAL NEEDS

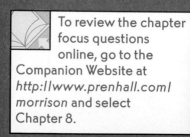

To review the chapter focus questions online, go to the Companion Website at *http://www.prenhall.com/ morrison* and select Chapter 8.

 ## PROFESSIONAL DEVELOPMENT GOAL

DEVELOPMENTALLY APPROPRIATE PRACTICE

I understand children's developmental stages and growth from birth through age eight, and I use this knowledge to implement developmentally appropriate practice. I do all I can to advance the physical, intellectual, social, and emotional development of the children in my care to their fullest potential.

THE HISTORY OF KINDERGARTEN EDUCATION

Froebel's educational concepts and kindergarten program were imported to the United States in the nineteenth century, virtually intact, by individuals who believed in his ideas and methods. The growth of the kindergarten movement in the United States was based on the vision and efforts of many people.

To check your understanding of this chapter with the online Study Guide, go to the Companion Website at *http://www.prenhall.com/ morrison*, select Chapter 8, then choose the Study Guide module.

Margarethe Schurz established the first kindergarten in the United States in 1856 at Watertown, Wisconsin. Schurz's program was conducted in German, as were many of the kindergarten programs of the time, since Froebel's ideas of education appealed especially to bilingual parents. Schurz influenced Elizabeth Peabody who opened her kindergarten in Boston in 1860. She is generally credited as kindergarten's main promoter in the United States.

Milton Bradley, the toy manufacturer, attended a lecture by Peabody and, as a result, began to manufacture Froebel's gifts and occupations. He also published Froebel's *Paradise of Childhood,* America's first book on kindergarten.

Susan E. Blow founded the first public kindergarten in St. Louis, Missouri, in 1873. Endorsement of the kindergarten program by the public school system did much to increase its popularity and spread the Froebelian influence within early childhood education.

Patty Smith Hill thought that while the kindergarten should remain faithful to Froebel's ideas, it should nevertheless be open to innovation and move into the twentieth century. More than anyone else, Hill is responsible for kindergarten as we know it today.

Hill's influence is evident in the format of many present-day preschools and kindergartens. Free, creative play, in which children use materials as they wish, was Hill's idea. She also introduced large blocks and centers where children could engage in housekeeping, sand and water play, and other activities.

Although kindergartens are rapidly evolving to meet the needs of society and families, we must nonetheless acknowledge the people and ideals on which the first kindergartens were based. Today, as in the past, the goals and curricula of the kindergarten are undergoing dramatic change in response to changing children and a changing society.

WHAT ARE KINDERGARTEN CHILDREN LIKE?

Kindergartners, children ages five and six, are confident, eager to be involved, and want to and can accept a great deal of responsibility. They like working on projects, experimenting, and interacting cooperatively with others. Their combination of a can-do attitude and their cooperation and responsibility make them a delight to teach.

Kindergarten children are in a period of rapid intellectual and language growth. They have a tremendous capacity to learn new words. This helps explain kindergarten children's love of big words and their ability to say and use them. This is nowhere more apparent than in their fondness for dinosaurs and words

Today, kindergarten is a universal part of schooling, enrolling children from different cultures and socioeconomic backgrounds and, subsequently, different life experiences. How can professionals help ensure that kindergarten experiences meet the unique needs of each child?

 For more information about kindergartners' development, go to the Companion Website at *http://www.prenhall.com/morrison*, select any chapter, then choose Topic 2 of the ECE Supersite module.

such as *brontosaurus*. Kindergarten children like and need to be involved in many language activities.

Additionally, kindergartners like to talk. Their desire to be verbal should be encouraged and supported with many opportunities to engage in various language activities such as singing, telling stories, being involved in drama, and reciting poetry.

From ages five to seven, children's average weight and height approximate each other. Review Table 8–1, which depicts these similarities. Figure 8.1 is a descriptive portrait of kindergarten children. Another way to get a snapshot "portrait" of kindergarten children is to examine what they know when they enter kindergarten.

Figure 8.2 provides you a snap shot of what children know when they enter kindergarten. Review it now to broaden your understanding of kindergarten children. As you read the information give on the figure ask yourself these questions: Why can't greater percentages of children accomplish the identified academic skills? What implication does this information have for my work with parents? Keep in mind that kindergarteners know more than what is described and many know a great deal less. For example, many immigrant children in border states, such as Texas and California, are illiterate in their native language.

WHO ATTENDS KINDERGARTEN?

Froebel's kindergarten was for children three to seven years of age. In the United States, kindergarten is for five- and six-year-old children before they enter first grade. Since the age at which children enter first grade varies, the ages at which they enter kindergarten also differ. Many parents and professionals support an older

TABLE 8–1
AVERAGE HEIGHT AND WEIGHT OF KINDERGARTNERS

| | MALES | | FEMALES | |
AGE	HEIGHT (INCHES)	WEIGHT (POUNDS)	HEIGHT (INCHES)	WEIGHT (POUNDS)
5 years	44	44.5	44	42.5
6 years	46.75	48.5	46	47.5
7 years	49	54.5	48	53.5
8 years	51	61.25	50.75	60.75

Remember that averages are just that—averages. Children are different because of their individual differences. Ongoing growth and development tend to accentuate these differences.

Source: Based on data from Baby Bag Online [*http://www.babybag.com/articles/htwt_av.htm*]. Reprinted with permission from Baby Bag, Inc.

∽ **FIGURE 8.1   A Portrait of Kindergartners**

Kindergartners:

* are confident—can follow directions and take responsibility for learning.

* want to work—be involved.

* are full of energy—like active, physical activities.

* can accept growing amounts of responsibility.

* are very sociable and friendly.

* have a growing vocabulary.

* like to talk—they are good and confident conversationalists.

* are inquisitive—have insatiable curiosity.

* have tremendous capacity for learning.

* can engage in activities for extended periods of time.

These words paint a picture of some of the common and frequently observed characteristics of kindergarten children. Use this descriptive portrait to add other words as you observe and work with kindergarten children. Keep in mind that all children are different and that generalizations are only that.

rather than a younger kindergarten entrance age because they think older children are more "ready" for kindergarten and will learn better. Whereas in the past children had to be five years of age prior to December 31 for kindergarten admission in many districts, today the trend is toward an older admission age. Many school districts require that children be five years old by September 1 of the school year.

∽ **FIGURE 8.2   What Do Kindergarten Children Know?**

What children know when they enter kindergarten helps determine their success in school and what and how they are taught. This figure shows a national picture of the knowledge, behaviors, and health status of children entering kindergarten.

Source: U.S. Department of Education, National Center for Education Statistics, Entering Kindergarten: A Portrait of American Children When They Begin School: Findings from the Condition of Education 2000, Nicholas Zill and Jerry West, NCES 2001-035 (Washington, DC: U.S. Government Printing Office, 2001).

Academic Skill/Behavior	% of Children
* Recognize lower- and uppercase letters by name	66%
* Know English print is read left to right—from the end of one line to the beginning of the next line; know where a story ends	61%
* Know beginning sounds of words	29%
* Know ending sounds of words	17%
* Count ten objects, identify numerals and shapes	94%
* Count twenty objects, judge relative length	58%
* Can read two-digit numerals, identify ordinal position (third flower in a row of four), and recognize the next number in a sequence	20%
Health Status	
* Excellent health	51%
* Very good health	83%
* Overweight	10%
Behavior Indicators	
* Consistently more active than peers	18%
* Difficulty paying attention	13%
* Difficulty articulating words	11%
* Exhibit positive approaches to learning—eager to learn, pay attention reasonably well, persist in completing tasks	75%

Universal Kindergarten

Just as support is growing for universal preschools, it should come as no surprise that there is wide public support for compulsory and tax-supported universal public kindergarten. In keeping with this national sentiment, most children attend kindergarten, though it is mandatory in only twelve states (Arkansas, Delaware, Florida, Oklahoma, South Carolina, Ohio, Kentucky, Maryland, New Mexico, Rhode Island, West Virginia, and Tennessee) and the District of Columbia. Because public school kindergarten is so widespread, it is now considered the first grade of school. It is important for you to know that kindergarten is considered a time for serious learning and accomplishment.

The public and public schools support and provide different kinds of kindergartens, all designed to meet the needs of children. Figure 8.3 shows some of these kindergarten programs and practices available for children today. In addition,

Kindergarten Programs

Although kindergarten programs come in many types, they all have some constant features. Increasingly, kindergarten is considered the real beginning of school. Accordingly, the purposes and curriculum are changing.

Program: *Developmental Kindergarten*

Purposes:

* Provide a prekindergarten experience for behaviorally and developmentally delayed children
* Help children succeed in school
* Give at-risk children an extra year to develop
* Help prevent school failure

Program: *Transitional Kindergarten*

Purposes:

* Give children two years of a kindergarten experience
* Provide children opportunity to progress at their own pace
* Prevent stigma of failure
* Give children the "gift of time" to develop, mature, and learn

Program: *Mixed-Age Kindergarten (See also Figure 8.4)*

Purposes:

* Provide for multi-age groups of children, age span of two or three years
* Support children's social development (they have more and less socially advanced peers with whom to interact)
* Enable older children to act as teachers, tutors, and mentors
* Support a wide range of academic abilities
* Support continuous progress of learning

Program: *Traditional Kindergarten*

Purposes:

* Provide for the developmental needs of all children
* Emphasize learning through play and active learning
* Focus on social and emotional development

Program: *Academic Focused Kindergarten**

Purposes:

* Provide for the developmental needs of all children
* Provide balance between play, active learning, and teacher initiated, guided, and intentional teaching
* Ensure that children learn the knowledge, skills, and behaviors necessary for success in first grade

* "Academic Focused" should not be interpreted to mean that children are sitting in straight rows working on worksheets under the stern direction of the teacher. Rather, there is an emphasis on learning academic skills—reading, science, and math—in developmentally appropriate ways.

Children are born to learn. Learning is not something children "get ready for," but is a continuous process. What factors do you think are critical to support children's readiness to learn?

multi-age grouping is also popular in kindergarten, offering many benefits for children and teachers. Review Figure 8.4 for ideas about how to meet the needs of kindergarten children through multi-age grouping.

In the "Professionalism in Practice: How Kindergarten Is Changing" on page 230, educator Addie Gaines discusses how kindergarten has evolved during her career.

KINDERGARTEN TODAY

Kindergarten practice has changed since Froebel's time. Kindergarten as it was known five years ago is not the same as kindergarten today. Kindergarten twenty years from now will be vastly different than it is today. Kindergarten is in a transitional stage from a program that focuses primarily on social and emotional development to one that emphasizes academics, especially early literacy, math and science, and activities that prepare children to think and problem solve. These changes represent a transformation of great magnitude and will have a lasting impact on kindergarten curriculum and teaching into the future. Several reasons account for this transformation, many of which we have already discussed in Chapter 2. Table 8–2 shows how kindergarten is changing and the reasons for these changes.

Regardless of the grade or age group they teach, all early childhood teachers have to make decisions regarding what curriculum and activities they will provide for their children. When making decisions about what kindergarten should be like, you can consider what NAEYC identifies as ten signs of a good kindergarten. These are shown in Figure 8.5.

For more information about kindergarten curricula and teaching, go to the Companion Website at *http://www.prenhall.com/morrison*, select any chapter, then choose Topic 6 of the ECE Supersite module.

Multi-age grouping provides another approach to meeting the individual and collective needs of children. In a mixed-age group there is a diversity of abilities, at least a two-year span in children's ages, and the same teacher.

✳ Provides materials and activities for a wider range of children's abilities.

✳ Creates a feeling of community and belonging that is supported as a result of children spending at least two years in the group.

✳ Supports social development by providing a broader range of children to associate with than in a same-age classroom. Children have more and less socially and academically advanced peers with whom to interact. In the mixed-age classroom, the teacher encourages and supports cross-age academic and social interactions. Older children act as teachers, tutors, and mentors. Younger children are able to model the academic and social skills of their older class members.

✳ Supports the scaffolding of learning.

✳ Provides for a continuous progression of learning.

Professionalism in Practice

HOW KINDERGARTEN IS CHANGING

Addie Gaines has taught kindergarten for eleven years and is currently elementary assistant principal at Seneca Elementary School in Seneca, Missouri. This is how she sees kindergarten changing:

"I think that not only is the focus more academic, but school districts, state education departments, and the federal government are putting more and more pressure to produce measurable results. This is usually in the form of demanding increased test scores at all levels. There is a sense of seriousness in regard to student learning even at the earliest levels. In Missouri there are state test requirements that schools must meet in order to have accreditation during the third cycle of the Missouri School Improvement Program (MSIP), which is beginning this year. Although the earliest state tests are given in third grade, these tests are intended to measure what the students have learned in all previous grades. Kindergarten, first and second grade teachers must teach the district curriculum, which is aligned to the MAP (Missouri Assessment Program) Test and designed to have the students prepared for the subject matter tests given at the assigned grade levels.

"The major challenge of teaching kindergarten is meeting the individual needs of the students while ensuring that the local and state standards are met. I still believe in starting where the child is and taking them towards the goals that have been set. Determining where that child is includes the knowledge base and skills they have, as well as their attention span and maturity. We have to remember that kids are still kids and to build upon their interests and strengths while keeping in mind their developmental levels and learning styles. With the diversity in students in any given class, it is a daunting task to provide what is best and needed to each one."

To review the Professional Development Checklist and complete a Professionalism in Practice activity, visit the Companion Website at *http://www.prenhall.com/morrison*, select Chapter 8, then choose the Professional Development module.

TABLE 8–2
HOW KINDERGARTEN IS CHANGING

CHANGE	REASONS FOR CHANGE
Longer School Day—Transition from half-day to full-day programs	• Changes in society. • Working parents. • Recognition that earlier is better. • Research that shows that a longer school day helps children academically.
Emphasis on Academics: • Literacy • Math • Science	• Standards that specify what children should know and be able to do. State standards now include the kindergarten year. • More children attending preschool who now know what was traditionally taught in kindergarten. • Early education and skill learning prevents grade failure and school dropout.
More Testing	• Accountability movement. • District testing that begins in third grade and earlier puts more emphasis on what kindergarten children should learn.
Enriched Curriculum with Emphasis on Literacy Designed to Have Children Ready to Read by Entry into First Grade	• Recognition that literacy and reading are pathways to success in school and life. • Learning to read is the new civil rights for children.

Kindergarten education is literally changing before our eyes! These are some of the ways it is changing and the reasons why. One of your roles as a professional is to keep up-to-date with changes in your field.

DEVELOPMENTALLY APPROPRIATE PRACTICE IN THE KINDERGARTEN

For more information about developmentally appropriate practice, go to the Companion Website at *http://www.prenhall. com/morrison*, select any chapter, then choose Topic 4 of the ECE Supersite module.

Developmentally appropriate practice involves teaching and learning that is in accordance with children's physical, cognitive, social, linguistic, individual, and cultural development. Professionals help children learn and develop in ways that are compatible with how old they are and who they are as individuals (e.g., their background of experiences and culture). Early childhood professionals who embody the qualities of good kindergarten teachers are those who teach in developmentally appropriate ways. Figure 8.6 depicts some of the implications of developmentally appropriate practice for kindergarten programs.

FIGURE 8.5   NAEYC's Ten Signs of a Good Kindergarten

These are good guidelines to help you in your kindergarten teaching. Think about how you would implement them and what you need to learn in order to do so.

Source: Copyright © 1996 by the National Association for the Education of Young Children. Early Years Are Learning Years Series. "Top Ten Signs of a Good Kindergarten Classroom," on NAEYC website at http://www.naeyc.org//resources/eyly/1996/12.htm.

1. Children are playing and working with materials or other children. They are not aimlessly wandering or forced to sit quietly for long periods of time.

2. Children have access to various activities throughout the day, such as block building, pretend play, picture books, paints and other art materials, and table toys such as LEGOs, pegboards, and puzzles. Children are not all doing the same things at the same time.

3. Teachers work with individual children, small groups, and the whole group at different times during the day. They do not spend time only with the entire group.

4. The classroom is decorated with children's original artwork, their own writing with invented spelling, and dictated stories.

5. Children learn numbers and the alphabet in the context of their everyday experiences. Exploring the natural world of plants and animals, cooking, taking attendance, and serving snacks are all meaningful activities to children.

6. Children work on projects and have long periods of time (at least one hour) to play and explore. Filling out worksheets should not be their primary activity.

7. Children have an opportunity to play outside every day that weather permits. This play is never sacrificed for more instructional time.

8. Teachers read books to children throughout the day, not just at story time.

9. Curriculum is adapted for those who are ahead as well as for those who need additional help. Because children differ in experience and background, they do not learn the same things at the same time in the same way.

10. Children and their parents look forward to school. Parents feel safe sending their child to kindergarten. Children are happy; they are not crying or regularly sick.

LITERACY AND KINDERGARTEN CHILDREN

Literacy education is an important and highly visible curriculum topic. Literacy is discussed in virtually all educational circles, and early childhood educators are talking about how to promote it. Literacy has replaced reading readiness as the main objective of many kindergarten and primary programs. Literacy means the ability to read, write, speak, and listen, with emphasis on reading and writing well. To be literate also means reading, writing, speaking, and listening within the context of one's cultural and social setting.

FIGURE 8.6
Developmentally Appropriate Practice in Kindergarten

Implementing developmentally appropriate practice is one of your professional responsibilities. Think about how you would use these guidelines in your classroom or program.

* Learning must be meaningful to children and related to what children know. Children find things meaningful when they are interesting to them and they can relate to them.

* All children do not learn in the same way, nor are they interested in learning the same thing as everyone else all the time. Thus, teachers must individualize their curriculum as much as possible. All quality educational approaches provide for it.

* Learning should be physically and mentally active; that is, children should be actively involved in learning activities by building, making, experimenting, investigating, and working collaboratively with their peers.

* Children should be involved in hands-on activities with concrete objects and manipulatives. Emphasis is on real-life activities as opposed to workbook and worksheet activities.

Literacy and early reading education is a hot topic in kindergarten for a number of reasons. First, the National Adult Literacy Survey estimates that over 50 million Americans are functionally illiterate at or below a fifth grade reading level. Second, when we compare the U.S. literacy rate with that of other countries, we do not fare well. Many industrialized countries have higher literacy rates than the United States.[1] Third, many high school graduates do not have the basic literacy skills required for today's high-tech jobs. Fourth, educators and social policy planners are seeking ways to teach all children to read at or above their particular grade level. Figure 8.7 outlines twelve essential components of research-based programs designed to promote reading.

What all of this means is that the goals for kindergarten learning are higher than they have ever been and they will continue to get higher.

Literacy and Reading

Today, early childhood professionals place a high priority on children's literacy and reading success. Literacy involves reading, writing, speaking, and listening. Professionals view literacy as a process that begins at birth (perhaps before) and continues to develop across the life span, through the school years.

The process of becoming literate is also viewed as a natural process; reading and writing are processes that children participate in naturally, long before they come to school. No doubt you have participated with or know of toddlers and preschoolers who are literate in many ways. They "read" all kinds of environmental print such as signs (McDonald's) and labels (Campbell's Soup) and menus and other symbols in their environments. Figure 8.8 lists typical accomplishments of kindergartners on the path to literacy, while Figure 8.9 defines common terms used in discussing literacy with parents and colleagues.

These twelve components will help you develop a strong beginning reading program for your children. Several of these components mention decoding strategies. **Decoding** is the process whereby children identify words through context or letter sound associations. Decoding is frequently used synonymously with phonics.

Source: Texas Reading Initiative, *Beginning Reading Instruction. Austin, TX: Texas Education Agency Publications Division.*

1. Children have opportunities to expand their use and appreciation of oral language.

2. Children have opportunities to expand their use and appreciation of printed language.

3. Children have opportunities to hear good stories and informational books read aloud daily.

4. Children have opportunities to understand and manipulate the building blocks of spoken language.

5. Children have opportunities to learn about and manipulate the building blocks of written language.

6. Children have opportunities to learn the relationship between the sounds of spoken language and the letter of written language.

7. Children have opportunities to learn decoding strategies.

8. Children have opportunities to write and relate their writing to spelling and reading.

9. Children have opportunities to practice accurate and fluent reading in decodable stories.

10. Children have opportunities to read and comprehend a wide assortment of books and other texts.

11. Children have opportunities to develop and comprehend new vocabulary through wide reading and direct vocabulary instruction.

12. Children have opportunities to learn and apply comprehension strategies as they reflect upon and think critically about what they read.

The nation has set a goal of having all children read and write at or above level by grade three. What are some activities and practices you can implement to will help ensure that all children achieve this national goal?

* Knows the parts of a book and their functions
* Begins to track print when listening to a familiar text being read or when rereading own writing
* "Reads" familiar text emergently (i.e., not necessarily verbatim from the print alone)
* Recognizes and can name all uppercase and lowercase letters
* Understands that the sequence of letters in a written word represents the sequence of sounds (phonemes) in a spoken word (alphabetic principle)
* Learns many, though not all, one-to-one letter-sound correspondences
* Recognizes some words by sight, including a few very common ones *(the, I, my, you, is, are)*
* Uses new vocabulary and grammatical constructions in own speech
* Makes appropriate switches from oral to written language styles
* Notices when simple sentences fail to make sense
* Connects information and events in texts to life and life experiences to texts
* Retells, reenacts, or dramatizes stories or parts of stories
* Listens attentively to books the teacher reads to class
* Can name some book titles and authors
* Demonstrates familiarity with a number of types or genres of text (e.g., storybooks, expository texts, poems, newspapers, and everyday print such as signs, notices, labels)
* Correctly answers questions about stories read aloud
* Makes predictions based on illustrations or portions of stories
* Demonstrates understanding that spoken words consist of phonemes
* Given spoken sets like "dan, dan, den," can identify the first two as the same and the third as different
* Given spoken sets like "dak, pat, zen," can identify the first two as sharing one identical sound
* Given spoken segments, can merge them into a meaningful target work
* Given a spoken word, can produce another word that rhymes with it
* Independently writes many uppercase and lowercase letters
* Uses phonemic awareness and letter knowledge to spell independently (invented or creative spelling)
* Writes (unconventionally) to express own meaning
* Builds a repertoire of some conventionally spelled words
* Shows awareness of distinction between "kid writing" and conventional orthography
* Writes own name (first and last) and the first names of some friends or classmates
* Can write most letters and some words when they are dictated

∽ **FIGURE 8.8   What Should Kindergarten Children Know?**

A question that all teachers face is "What should I teach?" This leads to a further question: "What should my children learn and know?" Sources for answering these important questions are state standards and information from research as outlined in this figure.

Source: Adapted with permission from M. S. Burns, P. Griffin, and C. E. Snow. Starting Out Right: A Guide to Promoting Children's Reading Success. *Copyright 1999 by National Academy of Sciences. Courtesy of the National Academy Press, Washington D. C.*

∽ **FIGURE 8.9**
Reading/Literacy Instructional Terminology

These are terms you will want to know and use. They are an important part of being able to "talk the talk" of your profession. You will use these terms in your work with parents, colleagues, and the community.

Alphabet knowledge The knowledge that letters have names and shapes and that letters can represent sounds in language.

Alphabetic principle Awareness that each speech sound or phoneme in a language has its own distinctive graphic representation and an understanding that letters go together in patterns to represent sounds.

Comprehension In reading, the basic understanding of the words and the content or meaning contained within printed material.

Decoding Identifying words through context and *phonics*.

Onset-rime The onset is any consonant(s) that precede the vowel, and the rime is the vowel plus any succeeding consonants. In pig, *p* is the onset and *ig* is the rime.

Orthographic awareness Familiarity with written symbols and an understanding of the relationships between these symbols and the sounds they represent.

Phoneme The smallest unit of speech that makes a difference to meaning.

Phonemic awareness The ability to deal explicitly and segmentally with sound units smaller than the syllable.

Phonics The learning of alphabetic principles of language and knowledge of letter-sound relationships. Children learn to associate letters with the phonemes (basic speech sounds) to help break the alphabetic code.

Phonological awareness The ability to manipulate language at the levels of syllables, rhymes, and individual speech sounds.

Print awareness The recognition of conventions and characteristics of a written language.

Developing Literacy and Reading in Young Children

Literacy and reading are certainly worthy national and educational goals, not only for young children but for everyone. However, how best to promote literacy has always been a controversial topic.

What do children need to know to become good and skillful readers? Research identifies the following:[2]

* Knowledge of letter names
* Speed at which children can name individual letters
* Phonemic awareness (letter-sound awareness)
* Experience with books and being read to.

One of the ways you can give children experiences with books is through "talking books." The "Technology Tie-In: Twelve Things you Can Do with Talking Books in a Computer Center" on pages 238 and 239 provides you with ways you can use talking books in your program.

Basal approaches and materials used for literacy and reading development often emphasize one particular method. One of the most popular methods is the **sight word approach** (also called *whole-word* or *look-say*) in which children are presented whole words *(cat, bat, sat)* and develop a "sight vocabulary" that enables them to begin reading and writing. Many early childhood teachers label objects in their classrooms (door, bookcase, etc.) as a means of teaching a sight vocabulary. Word walls are popular in kindergarten and primary classrooms. A word wall is a bulletin board or classroom display area on which high frequency and new words are displayed. The words are arranged alphabetically.

A second popular approach is based on **phonics instruction,** which stresses teaching letter-sound correspondence. By learning these connections, children are able to combine sounds into words (C-A-T). The proponents of phonics instruction argue that letter-sound correspondences enable children to make automatic connections between words and sounds and, as a result, to sound out words and read them on their own. From the 1950s up until the present time there has been much debate about which of these two approaches to literacy development is best. Today, there is a decided reemphasis on the use of phonics instruction. One reason for this emphasis is that the research evidence suggests that phonics instruction enables children to become proficient readers.[3]

Another method of literacy and reading development, the **language experience approach** (LEA)**,** follows the philosophy and suggestions inherent in progressive education philosophy. This approach to reading instruction is child centered, links oral and written language, and maintains that literacy education should be meaningful to children and should grow out of experiences that are interesting to them. LEA is based on the premise that what is thought can be said, what is said can be written, and what is written can be read. Children's experiences are a key element in such child-centered approaches. Many teachers transcribe children's dictated "experience" stories and use them as a basis for writing and for reading instruction.

Beginning about 1980, early childhood practitioners in the United States were influenced by literacy education approaches used in Australia and New Zealand. These influences gradually developed into what is known as the **whole language approach** to literacy development. Since whole language is a philosophy rather than a method, its definition often depends on who is using the term. This approach nonetheless advocates using all aspects of language—reading, writing, listening, and speaking—as the basis for developing literacy. Children learn about reading and writing by speaking and listening; they learn to read by writing, and they learn to write by reading. Basic philosophical premises of whole language include:

＊ It is child centered. Children, rather than teachers, are at the center of instruction and learning. Thus, children's experiences and interests serve as the context for topics and as a basis for their intrinsic motivation to read, write, and converse. In this way, literacy learning becomes meaningful and functional for children.

Technology Tie-In

TWELVE THINGS YOU CAN DO WITH TALKING BOOKS IN A COMPUTER CENTER

1. Listen to the story first.	Watch, listen to, interact with, think about, and talk about the story. Children should have the opportunity to enjoy the digital, multimedia features of the story and to take the stance of an appreciative audience member.
2. Read along with the story.	This form of digital choral reading is helpful for less confident students who can read and who have some automatic sight word recognition, but lack fluency and need support.
3. Echo read the story teacher reads and child repeats it).	This form of reading is especially helpful for children who need support with sight words and decoding.* (Decoding is the ability to pronounce a word; decoding is often called phonics.)
4. Read it first, then listen.	Students who need practice and a safe environment for taking risks in attempts to read aloud may benefit from attempting to read phrases first, then listening to the text read aloud on screen.
5. Partner read in digital Readers' Theater.	Invite a small group of children to gather at the computer center. Each child is involved in casting the experience by either being assigned or given a choice of a story character. As the text is presented on screen, students read the dialogue for their characters, serve as narrator, or read one line at a time.
6. Look for letters or words you know.	Young children who are just gaining the concept of letters may benefit from sitting down with a mentor and pointing out letters that they recognize.
7. Select words with same sounds.	Almost any CD-ROM story may be used as a springboard for a same-sound word search.
8. Select rhyming words.	When word patterns are studied in class during ongoing literacy instruction, children will wish to seek out similar rhyming patterns in words they encounter in CD-ROM talking books that use rhyme patterns.

∗ Social interaction is important and part of the process of becoming literate. Lev Vygotsky (see Chapter 3) stressed the social dimensions of learning. Through interaction with others, and with teachers, children are able to develop higher cognitive learning. This process of learning through social interaction is referred to as *socially constructed knowledge.*

∗ Spending time on the processes of reading and writing is more important than spending time on learning skills for getting ready to read. Consequently, from the moment they enter the learning setting, children are involved in literacy activities by being read to; "reading" books, pamphlets, magazines, etc.; scribbling; "writing" notes; and so forth.

9. Read along with a book copy.	Children may be invited to pay closer attention to the unique features of CD-ROM talking books when they are asked to compare the digital version with a book version of the story.
10. Tell how one screen fits with other screens.	A higher order thinking skill that is helpful for students' comprehension of print-based books involves the use of intratextual connections; that is, connections that children make across and within a story.
11. Tell how special effects fit the story.	One of the unique features of CD-ROM talking books is the use of multimedia special effects such as music, dynamic color tones (as when a sunny sky turns to a pastel sunset on a screen), sound effects, and cinematic animation.
12. Tell about similar stories.	Intertexual connections, recalling how events in one story are similar to other stories or to personal experience, are a central part of the type of comprehending in which good readers engage.[†]

*R. G. Heckelman. *A Neurological-Impress Method of Remedial-Reading Instruction,* Academic Therapy, 4 (1969): 277–282.

[†]C. C. Block. *"Comprehension: Crafting Understanding."* In L. B. Gambrell, L. M. Morrow, S. B. Neuman, & M. Pressley, eds., "Best Practices In Literacy Instruction" (New York: Guilford Press, 1999), 98–118.

Source: *Linda D. Labbo. "12 Things Young Children Can Do with a Talking Book in a Classroom Computer Center," The Reading Teacher, vol. 54, no. 7 (April 2000): 544.*

Technology and literacy development are uniquely suited to each other. Review these twelve ideas for how to use talking books in a computer center. What will you have to know and be able to do in order to use these suggestions in a kindergarten or primary grade classroom?

 To complete this Technology Tie-In activity and others like it, visit the Companion Website at *http://www.prenhall.com/ morrison*, select Chapter 8, then choose the Technology Tie-In module.

* Reading, writing, speaking, and listening are taught as an integrated whole, rather than in isolation of each other.
* Writing begins early. This means that children are writing from the time they enter the program.
* Children's written documents are used as reading materials.
* Themes or units of study are used as a means of promoting interests and content. Generally, themes are selected cooperatively by children and teachers and are used as a means of promoting ongoing intrinsic interest in literary processes.

Reading and written language acquisition is a continuum of development. Think of children as being on a continuous journey toward full literacy development! Regardless of what method you use to teach children how to read, the goal is that they should learn to read—and read on or above grade level—so they can do well in school and life.

Whole language dominated early childhood practice from about 1990 through 2000. However, growing numbers of critics of this approach, including parents and the public, maintain that because it is a philosophy rather than a specific approach, it does not teach children the skills necessary for good reading. Additionally, some teachers have difficulty explaining the whole language approach to parents, and some find it difficult to implement as well. Further, some research has indicated that whole language approaches do not result in the high levels of reading achievement claimed by supporters. As a result, proponents of phonics instruction are aggressively advocating a return to this approach as one that will best meet the needs of parents, children, and society.

A Balanced Approach

As with most things, a balanced approach is the best, and many early childhood advocates are encouraging literacy approaches that provide a balance between whole language methods and phonics instruction and that meet the specific needs of individual children. One thing is clear: systematic instruction that enables children to acquire skills they need to learn to read is very much in evidence in today's early childhood classrooms. It is likely that the debate over "the best approach" will continue. At the same time, efforts will increase to integrate the best of all approaches into a unified whole to make all children confident readers. The "Professionalism in Practice" on pages 242 and 243 explores the language arts curriculum used in one kindergarten classroom.

Supporting Children's Learning to Read

A primary goal of kindergarten education is for children to learn how to read. Teachers must instruct, support, and guide children in helping them learn what is necessary for them to be successful in school and life. Figure 8.10 lists some of the things you can do to motivate children's learning. Also, stop for a minute and reflect on what we said in Chapter 3 about Vygotsky's theory of scaffolding children's learning. Review the "Program in Action: An Idea for the Classroom from the Classroom" on pages 244 and 245.

SUPPORTING CHILDREN'S ATTITUDE TOWARD LEARNING

The experiences children have before they come to kindergarten often influence the success of their kindergarten years. Three areas are particularly important in influencing children's success in kindergarten: children's skills and prior

∽ **FIGURE 8.10**
Suggestions for Motivating Children to Read

Some of the best ways to motivate children to read are to read to them daily and to provide a literacy-rich environment for them. Implementing these guidelines will help ensure that your children have the foundation they need to begin reading.

Source: *From L. M. Morrow, Literacy Development in the Early Years: Helping Children Read and Write, 4th Ed, © 2001. Reprinted/ adapted by permission by Allyn & Bacon).*

- Include a variety of different types of books, such as picture books without words, fairy tales, nursery rhymes, picture storybooks, realistic literature, decodable and predictable books, information books, chapter books, biographies, big books, poetry, and joke and riddle books.

- Provide other types of print such as newspapers, magazines, and brochures.

- Introduce and discuss several books each week (may be theme-related, same authors, illustrators, types of books, etc.).

- Have multiple copies of popular books.

- Provide a record-keeping system for keeping track of books read (may include a picture-coding system to rate or evaluate the book).

- Showcase many books by placing them so the covers are visible, especially those that are new, shared in read-aloud sessions, or theme related.

- Organize books on shelves by category or type (may color code).

- Provide comfortable, inviting places to read (pillows, rugs, a sofa, large cardboard boxes, etc.).

- Encourage children to read to "friends" (include stuffed animals and dolls for "pretend" reading).

- Have an Author's Table with a variety of writing supplies to encourage children to write about books.

- Have a Listening Table for recorded stories and tapes.

Professionalism in Practice

PHILOSOPHY: KINDERGARTEN LANGUAGE ARTS CURRICULUM

The philosophy that guides the kindergarten language arts curriculum is based on the premise that teachers can cultivate and teach skills needed for reading and writing success.

Teachers recognize that children enter kindergarten with a wide range of language experiences, concepts, and skills. They employ large-group, small-group, and individual instruction to ensure that the weakest to strongest language learner will acquire appreciation of language, advance in skill development, and feel successful each day in the process.

We believe (and research supports) that young children learn best in a child-centered environment through an integrated curriculum that balances teacher-directed and child-initiated activities.

Kindergarten children's language development is enhanced through:

* Exposure to quality literature (nursery rhymes, poetry, classic tales)
* Frequent demonstrations of proficient reading and writing by the teacher and other adults
* Formal and informal practice (workbook, journal writing, retellings, dramatizations, songs, artwork, creative play)

A key priority is to prepare children with the prereading foundation skills directly related to successful reading achievement in grade one. Current research and practice point to four component concepts that, when mastered in kindergarten, ensure reading in first grade. They are:

1. Print Awareness
   * Knowledge that people read the text, not just look at the pictures
   * Awareness of how to read a book—right side up, starting with the first page and continuing to the end; the left page is read first; text is read from left to right
   * An understanding that words are units separated by spaces

2. Knowledge of the Alphabet
   * Being able to recognize and name all the letters (in and out of order)

3. Phonemic Awareness
   * Knowing that letters represent speech sounds that can be manipulated (added, deleted, transposed)

4. Sight Vocabulary
   * Ability to recognize a number of words (fifteen to eighteen) instantly (at sight)
   * Usually acquired through frequent story reading (with the child encouraged to follow along) and by attending to environmental print

For young children, the language arts (reading, writing, listening, and speaking) mutually reinforce one another. Growth in one leads to growth in the others—hence, the term *integrated language arts*.

school-related experiences; children's home lives; and preschool and kindergarten classroom characteristics. Research demonstrates the following in relation to these three areas:[4]

* Children who are socially adjusted do better in school. For example, kindergarten children whose parents initiate social opportunities for them are better adjusted socially and therefore can do better.
* Rejected children have difficulty with school tasks.

GUIDING PRINCIPLES OF OUR INTEGRATED LANGUAGE ARTS CURRICULUM

1. Oral language proficiency is related to growth in reading and writing. Therefore, children need frequent opportunities for verbal expression.
2. Children learn from the language they hear. Therefore, the richer the language environment, the richer the language learning.
3. Children imitate the language they hear and read and use it as part of their own. Therefore, teachers select high-quality, award-winning children's literature to read to children daily.
4. Writing opportunities have been proven to facilitate word analysis and word recognition in young children. Therefore, teachers engage children in journal writing and functional writing (writing for real purposes and real audiences), although they may not yet be able to read.

RATIONALE

Encouraging kindergarten children to write (after they know approximately ten to fifteen consonant sound-symbol associations) heightens phonemic awareness. Strong phonemic awareness results in greater receptivity to phonics instruction (formally taught in first grade).

Children are encouraged to write words the way they sound. This practice is frequently called "inventive," "developmental," or "transitional" spelling. Because strong phonemic awareness leads to receptivity to phonics instruction, early writing has become a kindergarten priority and is widely practiced. This writing "experimentation" is temporary and is followed by a gradual and predictable transition to conventional spelling.

The kindergarten language arts curriculum integrates reading, writing, listening, and speaking with age-appropriate activities that support children of varying experiences and abilities. The curriculum balances teacher-directed and child-initiated activities using the finest children's literature and research-supported practices such as providing early writing opportunities for pre-grade readers. Major emphasis is placed upon the teaching of print awareness, knowledge of the alphabet, phonemic awareness, and sight word acquisition. It is paramount that parents know and understand our goals for their children. Therefore, we consider parent communication a priority. We also realize the critical role that parent participation plays in the literacy acquisition of young children. Hence, we provide many opportunities for parents to join in this important endeavor of producing children who can use language skillfully and effectively.

Contributed by Phyllis Trachtenburg, Elementary Reading Specialist at Moorestown Township, NJ, Public Schools.

 To review the Professional Development Checklist and complete a Professionalism in Practice activity, visit the Companion Website at *http://www.prenhall.com/ morrison*, select Chapter 8, then choose the Professional Development module.

* Children with more preschool experiences have fewer adjustments to make in kindergarten.
* Children whose parents expect them to do well in kindergarten do better than children whose parents have low expectations for them. Children who have teachers with high expectations also do better in school.
* Developmentally appropriate classrooms and practices make it easier for children to learn.

Program in Action

LANGUAGE PROGRAM FOR KINDERGARTEN

The following is a description of a model for organizing and managing an early literacy program beginning in kindergarten. The model is based on practices of teachers identified by their supervisors as exemplary based on observation of their teaching.

8:30–9:00: As soon as the children entered Ms. Asbury's class, they began to engage in literacy activities. They located their name and photograph on the attendance chart and turned the picture face up to indicate their attendance. Children who were buying lunch signed their names under their choices on the lunch chart. The children then focused their attention on the daily jobs chart, on which Ms. Asbury changed the children's names every day after school. Those with morning jobs quickly got busy. Damien watered the plants while Angel fed the rabbit. Stephanie and Justin were the reporters whose job it was to write one or two sentences of daily news, such as what was going to happen during the school day.

The children who were not assigned morning jobs were given a choice of three activities in which they could engage: journal writing, independent or buddy reading, or solving the daily word problem.

9:00–9:40: During the whole-group morning meeting, math and language concepts were integrated in a discussion around the calendar and the weather. The children counted how many days had passed and how many days remained in January. They wrote the date in tallies and represented it in popsicle sticks grouped in tens and ones. Discussion about the calendar was rich with new words learned in the winter thematic unit. The two daily reporters read their news aloud.

Ms. Asbury then began to write a theme-related morning message containing news about an upcoming trip to the ice skating rink. She modeled conventions of print and good penmanship and punctuated her writing with explanations about how print works. Because she was working on punctuation with her students, she included a question and an exclamatory sentence in her message. This prompted discussion and explanation of the question mark and the exclamation point and their appropriate use.

Next, two children shared things brought from home with the class. In the biweekly newsletter, Ms. Asbury had explained to the parents that the children were learning about winter. She asked them to help the children choose something related to winter to bring to school and to write three clues about what they chose. The item and the clues were carried to school in a paper bag marked "secret" and "keep out." Each child removed the clues from their bag, being careful not to expose the item they brought. As they read aloud each clue, they called on a classmate to guess the secret item.

Ms. Asbury then read a theme-related piece of children's literature, *The Wild Toboggan Ride* (Reid & Fernandes, 1992), about the last toboggan ride of the day, which becomes a zany adventure for a little boy, his grandpa, and some surprised toboggan riders.

Next, Ms. Asbury used a directed listening and thinking activity format. She set a purpose for reading by asking the children to listen while she read in order to learn who rides on the toboggan and why the ride is "wild." While reading aloud, she encouraged the children to join in by reading the repeated words and phrases.

After the story, the class talked about who rode on the toboggan and how they became involved in the ride down the hill. As the characters in the story were mentioned, Ms. Asbury wrote what the children said about their role in the story onto sentence strips. She then asked the children to read the strips and put them in the order in which they happened. Then she introduced the words "first," "next," and "last" as a means to express sequence in a story.

9:40–11:15 Ms. Asbury began her Reading Workshop. She explained and modeled center activities for the children to participate in while she met with small groups for guided reading instruction. The following activities were available to the children during Reading Workshop:

READING ALONE OR BUDDY READING

Each child had a small basket containing books that were on the child's independent reading level. Books read during guided reading groups were placed in the basket along with self-selected texts from the classroom library. Because theme-related books were featured in the class library and in classroom activities, many children were reading books about winter.

WRITING CENTER

In the writing center, children wrote their responses to the shared book reading of *The Wild Toboggan Ride*.

LISTENING CENTER

In this center, the children listened on headsets to tape-recorded stories. Ms. Asbury had placed several theme-based books of assorted genres in this area. She also had made available two tape recorders for the students to record and listen to their own reading of favorite stories and poems.

WORD STUDY

A copy of the winter words list was kept in this area. Today, Ms. Asbury asked the children to choose a word from the list and, using letter tiles, see how many new words they could make from the letters of the selected word.

COMPUTER CENTER

Two computers were used throughout the day. This morning, two children were copying winter poems, which had been learned earlier that week.

SCIENCE CENTER

Ms. Asbury was planning to conduct an experiment with the class later in the day. The children would be timing how long it took different frozen items to melt. She wanted the children to think about, write, and explain their estimations before carrying out the experiment.

ART CENTER

Materials for making puppets were available to the children in this area. Ms. Asbury had chosen three winter stories with well-defined, sequenced plot episodes for use during shared reading. The children selected characters from the stories to make as puppets, which could be used in retellings of the stories.

9:50–11:15: While the children engaged in the self-directed activities, Ms. Asbury met with small groups of students for guided reading instruction. She had organized her class into five groups of four to five children who had similar reading behaviors, had control of like reading strategies, and who were reading on the same level. It was common for the children to move frequently from group to group based on Ms. Asbury's ongoing assessment of the children's progress. She met with each group three or four times a week for 20–30 minutes. After each group, she selected one child to focus on and assessed reading development by taking a running record and listening to a story retelling.

11:20–11:30: Cleanup, bathroom.

11:30–12:20: Lunch and recess followed Reading Workshop.

12:20–12:30: When the children returned from recess, Ms. Asbury read aloud from *Little Polar Bear, Take Me Home!* (deBeer, 1996).

12:30–1:15: This afternoon's instruction began with Writing Workshop. Ms. Asbury started the workshop with a 10-minute minilesson about the use of capital letters and punctuation. She noticed during her writing conferences with the students that they needed review about when to use capitals. Though most students were using periods and quotation marks regularly, she wanted them to use question marks and exclamation points consistently.

She had written a paragraph from *Little Polar Bear, Take Me Home!* onto an overhead transparency. She omitted capitals and punctuation from the paragraph. As a class, the children discussed where and why capitals and punctuation needed to be inserted as they edited the paragraph. The children were then dismissed to get their writing folder and worked for the remaining 35 minutes. Many chose to write books related to the winter theme.

1:15–2:00: After Writing Workshop, Ms. Asbury conducted the whole-group science lesson on melting.

2:00–2:45: The science lesson was followed by a 45-minute Math Workshop.

2:45–3:00: The day concluded with a 10-minute whole-class meeting in which two students' accomplishments were applauded: Paul and Linda had completed publishing their books that day and would share them with the class tomorrow. Ms. Asbury then gave last-minute reminders about homework and returning permission slips.

Source: From L. M. Morrow, Literacy Development in the Early Years: Helping Children Read and Write, 4th Ed, © 2001. Reprinted/ adapted by permission by Allyn & Bacon).

 To complete a Program in Action activity, visit the Companion Website at *http://www.prenhall.com/morrison,* select **Chapter 8, then choose the Programs in Action module.**

To take an online self-test on this chapter's contents, go to the Companion Website at *http://www.prenhall.com/ morrison,* select Chapter 8, then choose the Self-Test module.

* Books, videos, computer-based learning materials, and other materials designed for children in the home improve the chances that children will be successful in school.

Figure 8.11 provides additional research relating to kindergarten. There is a great deal of public and professional interest in kindergarten, and a growing body of research supports this interest and can help guide practices.

Many Maryland Kindergartners Are Not Ready for School

Maryland kindergarten teachers assessed the readiness of children for formal education. The results showed that 50.9 percent of the children were rated fully ready in physical development to enter kindergarten, 48.3 percent in social and personal development, 43.2 percent in the arts, 34.7 percent in language and literacy, 34.7 percent in mathematical thinking, 33.8 percent in social studies, and 20.5 percent in scientific thinking.*

How Do Kindergartners Perform over Time?

What are kindergarten children like? What do they really know? How do they learn? These are questions that intrigue researchers, teachers, and parents. One way to answer these questions is through longitudinal research in which researchers gather information on children over a period of time. The Early Childhood Longitudinal Study, Kindergarten Class of 1998–99 (ECLS-K), sponsored by the U.S. Department of Education, National Center for Education Statistics (NCES), began following a nationally representative sample of some 22,000 kindergartners. Data will be collected not only in the fall of kindergarten but also spring kindergarten, fall first grade, spring first grade, spring third grade and spring fifth grade. In the fall of kindergarten, data were collected from children, their parents and their teachers. Information from children was gathered during an individualized in-person assessment with the child in the child's school, parents were interviewed over the phone, and teachers were given self-administered questionnaires. These are some findings:[†]

1. As children enter kindergarten for the first time, they differ in their cognitive skills and knowledge. Children's reading, mathematics, and general knowledge are related to their age as they enter kindergarten, the level of their mother's education, their family type, the primary language spoken in the home, and their race/ethnicity.

2. In reading, mathematics and general knowledge, older kindergartners (born in 1992) outperform the younger kindergartners (born September through December 1993). The older kindergartners are more likely to score in the highest quartile of the distribution of scores than the younger kindergartners.

(Continued)

☞ **FIGURE 8.11   Research in the Kindergarten**

3. Children's performance in reading, mathematics, and general knowledge increases with their level of their mothers' education. Kindergartners whose mothers have more education are more likely to score in the highest quartile in reading, mathematics, and general knowledge than all other children.

4. Children's performance in reading, mathematics, and general knowledge differs by their family type: kindergartners from two-parent families are more likely to score in the highest quartile in reading, mathematics, and general knowledge than children from single-mother families.

Redshirting for Success?

The practice of redshirting children—that is, delaying their entry into kindergarten—is viewed by some parents as a way of giving children a social and academic advantage. But does redshirting really help?

Using a representative sample of Wisconsin school districts, researchers examined the school records of more than 8,000 students to depict patterns of school entry, promotion, subsequent special services, and student achievement. Results indicate that approximately 7 percent of the sample had delayed school entry, and those children were primarily boys with birth dates immediately before the entrance cutoff. They found that redshirts and retainees are more likely to receive special education services than their peers who enter and are promoted on time. The achievement of redshirts is comparable to their normally entered peers, whereas retainees perform at lower levels.

In addition, the researchers conclude at best, redshirts achieve on par with their grade-level peers, including summer birthday children who have entered on time (although they are not on top as some would suggest), whereas retainees fare less well.[‡]

Research plays an important role in early childhood practice. It guides decisions about how and what to teach children and how to best provide for their needs. However, you have to weigh the results of research against your experiences and against other research findings. For example, the research on redshirting seems to indicate that delayed entry into kindergarten does not have long-term benefits. Yet the data from the Early Childhood Longitudinal Study report that older kindergartners perform better than younger kindergartners. How do you account for these two apparent contradictory findings?

∽ **FIGURE 8.11   Research in the Kindergarten** *(Continued)*

Research about kindergarten is bursting out all over. This research is due in part to the popularity of kindergarten, kindergarten's new role as the first year of school, and the radical changes occurring in the kindergarten curriculum. This figure outlines some of the major research that is documenting how kindergarten teaching and learning are changing.

*Sources: *Olson, Lynn. "Most Md. Kindergartners Not School-Ready," Education Week on the Web. March 7, 2001. [Online: http:llwww.edWeek.comlewlewstory.Cfm?slug=25Md.h20].*

[†] U.S. Department of Education, National Center for Education Statistics, Early Childhood Longitudinal Study, Kindergarten Class of 1998–99 (ECLS-K). [Online: http:llnces.ed.govleclslkindergartenlotherpubs.htm].

[‡] M. Elizabeth Graue and James DiPerna, "Redshirting and Early Retention: Who Gets the 'Gift of Time' and What Are Its Outcomes?", American Educational Research Journal, vol. 37, no. 2 (Summer 2000): 509.

How successful children are in kindergarten depends on how well all who have a stake in children's education cooperate. More and more we realize that when early childhood teachers work with parents, children's achievement increases. If we are interested in providing good preschools, kindergartens, and primary schools, then we will include parents in planning and making decisions. From our discussion you now have many ideas about how kindergarten is changing and the direction it will evolve over the next decade.

ACTIVITIES FOR PROFESSIONAL DEVELOPMENT

In this chapter, we have stressed the importance of developmentally appropriate practice in kindergarten. Refer again to the "Professional Development Goal" at the beginning of this chapter, the "Professional Development Checklist" on pages 20 and 21, and the "Professionalism in Practice" account on pages 242 and 243. Now complete the exercises.

1. Do you think as a teacher you are oriented more toward a kindergarten program based on academics or social-emotional play? How would you explain your beliefs on this topic during an interview for a teaching job?

2. Do you support an earlier or later entrance age to kindergarten? Why? If your local legislator wanted specific reasons, what would you tell him or her? Ask other teachers their opinion on this topic and compare their viewpoints to yours.

3. Give examples from your observations of kindergarten programs to support one of these opinions:

   a. Society is expecting too much of kindergarten children.

   b. Many kindergartens are not teaching children enough.

   c. Current changes occurring in the kindergarten are necessary and appropriate.

4. How to conduct developmentally appropriate practices in the ever changing kindergarten is a major issue. Review Table 8–2, "How Kindergarten Is Changing." For each of the changes listed, make suggestions for how you could accommodate that change through developmentally appropriate practice in your classroom.

For additional chapter resources and activities, visit the Companion Website at *http://www.prenhall.com/morrison*, select Chapter 8, then choose the Professional Development, Resources, or Linking to Learning modules.

FOCUS QUESTIONS

1. What are the unique physical, cognitive, language, and psychosocial characteristics of primary children?

2. How is the curriculum of the primary grades changing?

3. How can I apply developmentally appropriate practice to my teaching in the primary grades?

chapter 9

The Primary Grades

PREPARATION FOR LIFELONG SUCCESS

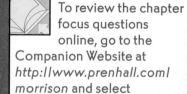

To review the chapter focus questions online, go to the Companion Website at *http:llwww.prenhall.coml morrison* and select Chapter 9.

PROFESSIONAL DEVELOPMENT GOAL

DEVELOPMENTALLY APPROPRIATE PRACTICE

I understand children's developmental stages and growth from birth through age eight, and I use this knowledge to implement developmentally appropriate practice. I do all I can to advance the physical, intellectual, social, and emotional development of the children in my care to their fullest potential.

With the renewed interest in the first five years, the years from six to eight are also getting their share of attention. All of the reasons for changes in preschool and kindergarten education apply to the primary grades as well. However, it is in the primary grades that, as the saying goes, the buck stops! The primary grades are where state and district tests are given to measure grade-level achievement and to evaluate how well students have learned and teachers have taught.

As a result, the primary curriculum is changing for these specific reasons: more and higher state standards; high-stakes testing; increased emphasis on academics related to reading, mathematics, and science; concerns about children's character; and new information about children's increasingly poor health status.

Primary Children: Growth and Development

All children share common developmental characteristics, yet they are unique and individual. Although the common characteristics of children guide our general practice of teaching, we still must always account for the individual needs of children. As background for our discussion of what primary age children are like, review Figure 9.1 which paints a portrait of children ages six to eight.

Physical Development

To check your understanding of this chapter with the online Study Guide, go to the Companion Website at *http://www.prenhall.com/morrison*, select Chapter 9, then choose the Study Guide module.

Two words describe the physical growth of primary age children: *slow* and *steady*. Children at this age experience continual growth, develop increasing control over their bodies, and explore the things they are able to do.

From ages five to eight, children's average weight and height approximate each other, as shown in Table 9–1. The weight of boys and girls tends to be the same until about age nine, when girls pull ahead of boys in both height and weight. Wide variations appear in both individual rates of growth and development and among the sizes of individual children. These differences in physical appearance result from genetic and cultural factors, nutritional intake and habits, health care, and experiential background.

Motor Development

Six-year-old children are in Erikson's initiative stage of psychosocial development; seven- and eight-year-old children are in the industry stage. Children are intuitively driven to initiate activities, and are learning to be competent and productive individuals. The primary years are thus a time to use and test developing motor skills. Their growing confidence and physical skills are reflected in games involving

⌒ FIGURE 9.1   Portrait of Primary (Ages 6–8) Children

Primary Children:

* have a growing capacity for systematic thinking.
* love to tell jokes and play jokes on others.
* have a growing capacity to think logically.
* make effective use of classification skills to organize information.
* have increased ability to control their attention.
* have increased memory skills—like to memorize facts.
* are able to benefit from didactic (direct) teaching by teachers and parents.
* like to work with peers and benefit from cooperative learning experiences.
* develop loyal friendships.
* have acquired the basic rules for thinking and reasoning.
* have a growing understanding of the role of parent and teacher authority.
* are eager to learn and are very helpful around the home and classroom.
* enjoy engaging in group sports, soccer and little league baseball, and individual sports such as karate and gymnastics. Their physical development makes them more capable of sport and game participation and their cognitive development enables them to make sense of rules.

The primary school years are a good time to observe the differences in children's development and how these differences are reflected in their behavior and learning. For many teachers, grades one to three are their favorite grades to teach because of children's industriousness and cooperation. However, keep in mind that with the current emphasis on standards and testing, the primary grades are more critical than ever for cognitive development and the learning of academic knowledge and skills. As with our other word portraits of children, add your descriptions to the above and create your own picture of children in the primary grades.

For more information about the development of children in the primary grades, go to the Companion Website at *http://www.prenhall. com/morrison*, select any chapter, then choose Topic 2 of the ECE Supersite module.

running, chasing, and kicking. A nearly universal characteristic of children in this period is their almost constant physical activity.

Differences between boys' and girls' motor skills during the primary years are minimal—their abilities are about equal. Teachers, therefore, should not use gender as a basis for limiting boys' or girls' involvement in activities. Children in the primary grades are also more proficient at school tasks that require fine motor skills, such as writing, making artwork, and using computers. In addition, primary children want to and are able to engage in real-life activities. They want the "real thing." In many ways this makes teaching them easier and more fun, since many activities have real-life applications.

TABLE 9–1
AVERAGE HEIGHT AND WEIGHT FOR PRIMARY CHILDREN

Conduct your own survey of the height and weight of primary age children. Compare your findings with this table. What conclusions can you draw?

	MALES		FEMALES	
AGE	HEIGHT (INCHES)	WEIGHT (POUNDS)	HEIGHT (INCHES)	WEIGHT (POUNDS)
6 years	46.75	48.5	46	47.5
7 years	49	54.5	48	53.5
8 years	51	61.25	50.75	60.75
9 years	53.25	69	53.25	69

Source: Based on data from Baby Bag Online [*http://www.babybag.com/articles/htwt_av.htm*]. Reprinted with permission from Baby Bag, Inc.

Today there is a greater emphasis on children's cognitive development and activities that promote reading, math, and science. What are some things you can do to help children be successful in these areas?

Cognitive Development

Children's cognitive development during the primary school years enables them to do things as first, second, and third graders that they could not do as preschoolers or kindergartners. A major difference between younger and primary age children is that the older children's thinking has become less egocentric and more logical.

Concrete operational thought is the cognitive milestone that enables children between ages seven and eleven to think and act as they do. Logical operations, although more sophisticated than in preoperational children, still require concrete objects and referents in the here and now. Abstract reasoning comes later, in the formal operations stage during adolescence.

Moral Development

For more information about Lawrence Kohlberg and the stages of moral development, go to the Companion Website at *http://www.prenhall.com/morrison*, select Chapter 9, then choose the Linking to Learning module.

Jean Piaget and Lawrence Kohlberg are the leading proponents of a developmental stage theory of children's moral growth. Table 9–2 outlines their stages of moral development during the primary years. Review these now and consider how you can apply the implications to your teaching. Remember that children's moral and character development are important topics, especially after recent tragic events such as the shooting at Columbine and the terrorist attacks of September 11, 2001.

You can learn more about Kohlberg's stages of moral development by accessing the Companion Website.

TABLE 9–2
MORAL DEVELOPMENT IN THE PRIMARY YEARS

THEORIST	MORAL STAGE AND CHARACTERISTICS	IMPLICATIONS FOR TEACHERS
Jean Piaget	1. Relations of Constraint: Grades 1–2 Concepts of right and wrong determined by judgments of adults—morality is based on judgments of adults. 2. Relations of Cooperation: Grades 3–6 Exchange of viewpoints with others helps determine what is good/bad and right/wrong.	• Provide children with many opportunities to make moral decisions and judgments. • Look for opportunities every day in every classroom for moral decisions. Responsibility comes from opportunities to be responsible. • Provide many examples of moral values and decisions. This can occur through stories.
Lawrence Kohlberg	1. Preconventional Level: Ages 4–10 Morality is a matter of good or bad based on a system of punishment and rewards as administered by adults in authority positions. • Stage 1—Punishment and obedience: Children operate within and respond to physical consequences of behavior. • Stage 2—Instrumental-relativist orientation: Children's actions are motivated by satisfaction of needs (you scratch my back, I'll scratch yours).	• Use children's out-of-classroom experiences as a basis for discussion involving moral values. • Provide children many opportunities to interact with children of different ages and cultures.

Knowing children's stages of moral development will help you guide them in this important area. In addition, today there is much emphasis on character education, which is closely aligned with moral education.

The Contemporary Primary School

As you have learned in Chapters 1–8, reform is sweeping across the educational landscape. Nowhere is this more evident than in the primary grades. Schooling in the primary years has become a serious enterprise for political, social, and economic reasons. Educators, parents, and politicians realize it is better to prevent illiteracy, school dropout, and many social problems in the early childhood years than wait until middle and senior high school, when changing students is more difficult and expensive. Also, the public is not happy about continuing reports of declining educational achievement. So, demands for higher achievement and more rigorous teaching and learning begin in first grade and continue in grades two and three.

The Integrated Curriculum

A lot of change has occurred in the primary grades since the 1990s, with more change on the way. Single-subject teaching and learning are out; integration of subject areas is in. Curriculum leaders want to help students relate what they learn in math to what they learn in science, and they want them to know that literacy is applied across the curriculum. One goal of contemporary curriculum reform is to help students make sense of what they learn in all areas of the curriculum and apply it to life.

Students sitting in single seats, in straight rows, solitarily doing their own work has been replaced by students learning together in small groups. The teacher's roles as facilitator, learning collaborator, and coach remain popular. However, intentional, systematic instruction is becoming more prevalent as teachers strive to teach children the skills they need for success. Letter grades and report cards are still widely used, although narrative reports (in which teachers describe and report on student achievement), checklists (which describe the competencies students have demonstrated), parent conferences, portfolios containing samples of children's work, and other tools for reporting achievement are used to supplement letter grades.

Figure 9.2 shows some of the critical features of an effective primary classroom designed to help children learn in today's demanding educational environment. How might these features influence how you would teach in grades one to three?

When you integrate across curriculum areas, how to evaluate and assess is sometimes an issue. The "Technology Tie-In: Using Electronic Portfolios" on page 257, provides one solution for cross-referencing and documenting learning.

Pro-social and Conflict Resolution Education

All early childhood professionals, parents, and politicians believe that efforts to reduce incidents of violence and uncivil behavior begin in the preschool and primary years. Consequently, they place emphasis on teaching children the fundamentals of peaceful living, kindness, helpfulness, and cooperation. You can follow the suggestions in Figure 9.3 to foster the development of pro-social skills in your classroom. Remember that a peaceful classroom and program begins with you and in your relationship with your children and colleagues.

∽ **FIGURE 9.2 Features of the Contemporary Primary Classroom**

Classrooms not only support children's learning, but they also help ensure that all children learn to their full capacities. Part of your role is to use these features to help you provide the best learning environment possible for all children.

* Literacy is emphasized across all content areas.

* A high priority is placed on learning to read, to read on grade level, and to read with comprehension and fluency.

* Thinking skills are taught and practiced.

* A sense of community prevails. Children learn from each other, and teachers and children respect each other.

* Teachers and administrators have high expectations for all children.

* Teachers believe that all children *will* learn.

* Families are in partnership with the school, children, and teachers.

* All activities are multiculturally sensitive.

* Assessment is authentic and ongoing.

* The majority of classroom time is spent on teaching, learning, and acquiring academic-related knowledge and skills.

Technology Tie-In

USING ELECTRONIC PORTFOLIOS

In Chapter 5, "Observing and Assessing Young Children," we discussed the use of portfolios to assess and evaluate children's work and achievement. Frequently, material that is placed in a portfolio consists of paper and pencil products, art projects, and other physical artifacts. These portfolios usually are file boxes, three-ring binders, and folders. Teaching in grades one through three offers an excellent opportunity to keep electronic portfolios. Like traditional portfolios, electronic portfolios are records of learning, growth, change, and achievement. They document what students know and are able to do. They paint a portrait of a student at a particular time and over time. They are like an archeological record of student accomplishment that can be easily updated and expanded. Electronic portfolios can consist of separate electronic artifacts such as videos, tape recordings, and digital pictures, or the portfolio could consist of one floppy disc or CD.

Some equipment you will need to get started on your electronic portfolios are a computer, digital camera, multimedia software (such as HyperStudio), and a scanner. If you are just getting started using technology in your classroom, you will probably want to start with a small group of students as you and they learn. You will find that electronic portfolios are great student motivators and are good ways to integrate learning. They certainly involve active learning.

 To complete this Technology Tie-In activity and others like it, visit the Companion Website at *http://www. prenhall.com/morrison*, select Chapter 9, then choose the Technology Tie-In module.

⌒ **FIGURE 9.3   Building a Peaceful Classroom**

Today, especially with the events of September 11, 2001, and following, teachers and parents are more interested than ever in how to promote intercultural harmony and peaceful living. Review these nine things you can do to promote pro-social skills in your students.

✳ Be a good role model for children. Demonstrate in your life and relationships with children and other adults the behaviors of cooperation and kindness that you want to encourage in children. Civil behavior begins with courtesy and manners. You can model these and help children do the same.

✳ Provide positive feedback and reinforcement when children perform pro-social behaviors. When rewarded for appropriate behavior, children tend to repeat the behavior. ("I like how you helped Tim get up when you accidentally ran into him. I'll bet that made him feel better.")

✳ Provide opportunities for children to help and show kindness to others. Cooperative programs between primary children and nursing and retirement homes are excellent opportunities to practice kind and helping behaviors.

✳ Conduct classroom routines and activities so they are as free of conflict as possible. Provide opportunities for children to work together and practice skills for cooperative living. Design learning centers and activities for children to share and work cooperatively.

✳ Provide practice in conflict resolution skills. Skills include taking turns, talking through problems, compromising, and apologizing. A word of caution regarding apologies: too often, an apology is a perfunctory response on the part of teachers and children. Rather than just saying the often-empty words "I'm sorry," it is far more meaningful to help one child understand how another is feeling. Encouraging empathic behavior in children is a key to developing pro-social behavior.

✳ Conduct classroom activities based on multicultural principles that are free from stereotyping and sexist behaviors.

✳ Read stories to children that exemplify pro-social behaviors, and provide such literature for them to read.

✳ Counsel and work with parents to encourage them to limit or eliminate altogether their children watching violence on television, attending R-rated movies, playing video games with violent content, and buying CDs with objectionable lyrics.

✳ Help children feel good about themselves, build strong self-images, and be competent individuals. Children who are happy, confident, and competent feel good about themselves and are more likely to behave positively toward others.

Character Education

For more information about character education curricula, go to the Companion Website at *http://www.prenhall. com/morrison*, select Chapter 9, then choose the Linking to Learning module.

For more information on Georgia's Quality Core Curriculum, go to the Companion Website at *http://www.prenhall. com/morrison*, select Chapter 9, then choose the Linking to Learning module.

Character education is closely aligned with pro-social and conflict resolution education. Character education is rapidly becoming a part of many early childhood programs. The three Rs have been expanded to six: reading, writing, arithmetic, reasoning, respect, and responsibility. Respect and responsibility are now part of the primary curriculum for a number of reasons. Although everyone believes children have to learn how to count, the public and educators also believe that schools have to teach children what counts. Character education is now a high priority for all early childhood educators. President George W. Bush has challenged the public to consider the importance of teaching children values and to create "communities of character" around them.[1] Character education activities designed to teach specific character traits are now commonplace in the curriculum of the primary grades.

Whereas educators may argue over what character traits to teach, there is no longer a debate over whether they should be taught. Some common characteristics are shown in Figure 9.4. After you review Figure 9.4, what other traits would you add to the list?

Many state departments of education have curriculum material concerning character education. Georgia, for example, has a list of core values, Quality Core Curriculum (QCC), that are taught in the Georgia public schools. You can access these through the Companion Website.

Children not only have to learn how to count, they need to know what counts. Helping children develop positive character traits is now a standard part of the curricula of many early childhood programs. What are some character traits that you believe should be taught to young children?

∽ **FIGURE 9.4** Teaching Children What Counts

Teaching children important character traits is now a top priority in many early childhood classrooms. Increasingly, parents and society are looking to early childhood programs, K-3, to instill in the nation's children character traits such as those shown here. What other character traits would you add to this list? Pick two of these character traits and develop a lesson plan for each one. How would you explain to others reasons for the growth of the character education movement?

There is universal agreement that children need to learn important character traits. The debate will continue to rage about what traits to teach. However, most parents agree that their children should learn:

✳ Responsibility	✳ Courage
✳ Cooperation	✳ Friendship
✳ Respect for others	✳ Optimism
✳ Compassion	✳ Honesty
✳ Self-discipline	✳ Perseverance
✳ Selflessness (Friendship)	✳ Future-mindedness
✳ Tolerance	✳ Purposefulness

Teaching Thinking

As stated previously, reasoning has been added as one of the six Rs of early childhood programs. Educators believe that if students can think, they can meaningfully engage in subject matter curriculum and the rigors and demands of the workplace and life. As a result, many teachers are including the teaching of thinking in their daily lesson plans.

Table 9–3 shows examples of questions you can use to promote thinking. They are based on Benjamin Bloom's hierarchy of questioning levels. A major teaching objective is to ask students questions from top to bottom of the hierarchy. For example, recall of knowledge is the lowest level of thinking and evaluation is the highest. In addition, instead of asking children to recall information, teachers ask them to think critically about information, solve problems, and reflect. Some thinking skills you can teach are shown in Figure 9.5. To promote thinking in your classroom follow these guidelines:

* Give children the freedom and security to be creative thinkers.
* Encourage children to search for other answers and alternative solutions rather than settling for one "right" answer.
* Create classroom cultures in which children have the time, opportunity, and materials with which to be creative.
* Integrate thinking into the total curriculum so that children learn to think during the entire school day.

In the "Professionalism in Practice: The Magic Teacher's Philosophy on Early Childhood Education" on pages 264 and 265, Jayné Anthony shares ideas for creating "magic" in the primary classroom.

TABLE 9–3
APPLYING BLOOM'S TAXONOMY TO EARLY CHILDHOOD CLASSROOMS

COMPETENCE	SKILLS DEMONSTRATED	SAMPLE QUESTIONS
Knowledge	· Observation and recall of information · Knowledge of dates, events, places · Knowledge of major ideas · Mastery of subject matter · *Question Cues:* List, define, tell, describe, identify, show, label, collect, examine, tabulate, quote, name, who, when, where, etc.	· How would you describe the size of an elephant? · Tell me three things that you can do with a soccer ball.
Comprehension	· Understand information · Grasp meaning · Translate knowledge into new context · Interpret facts, compare, contrast · Order, group, infer causes · Predict consequences · *Questions Cues:* Summarize, describe, interpret, contrast, predict, associate, distinguish, estimate, differentiate, discuss, extend	· How are sounds different (contrasting)? · What is the main idea or point of the book we just read together? Explain.
Application	· Use information · Use methods, concepts, theories in new situation · Solve problems using required skills or knowledge · *Question Cues:* Apply, demonstrate, calculate, compete, illustrate, show, solve, examine, modify, relate, change, classify, experiment, discover	· Construct two buildings in the math area, one tall building and one short building. · How would you organize your paintings to show your mother which one you painted first and which one you painted last?
Analysis	· Seeing patterns · Organization of parts · Recognition of hidden meanings · Identification of components · *Question Cues:* Analyze, separate, order, explain, connect, classify, arrange, divide, compare, select, explain, infer	· What are the parts of the clarinet? Why do you think the bottom of the clarinet is bell-shaped? · If you see your friend lying down on the playground, crying, what do you suppose happened that caused your friend to do that?
Synthesis	· Use old ideas to create new ones · Generalize from given facts · Relate knowledge from several areas · Predict, draw conclusions · *Question Cues:* Combine, integrate, modify, rearrange, substitute, plan, create, design, invent, what if?, compose, formulate, prepare, generalize, rewrite	· Can you create a new color by mixing paints? Predict what color the new color will be most like. · Imagine yourself as a Pilgrim boy or girl. How would your life be the same as it is now? How would your life be different than it is now?
Evaluation	· Compare and discriminate between ideas · Assess value of theories, presentation · Make choices based on reasoned argument · Verify value of evidence · Recognize subjectivity · *Question Cues:* Assess, decide, rank, grade, test, measure, recommend, convince, select, judge, explain, discriminate, support, conclude, compare, summarize	· Let's decide what the three most important rules of our classroom should be. · Which one of your paintings is your favorite? Why?

Source: Based on the Counseling Services of University of Victoria Website, http://www.coun.uvic.ca/learn/program/hndouts/ bloom.html. From Bloom, B. S. (Ed.), 1956. *Taxonomy of Educational Objectives: The Classification of Educational Goals, Handbook I. Cognitive Domain.* New York; Toronto: Longmans, Green.

Thinking is an important life and job-related skill. Employers say that the ability to think is one of the main characteristics they look for when hiring new employees. Learning to think begins in the early childhood years and early childhood is viewed as the time when commonly taught thinking skills such as these should be integrated into the curriculum. Part of your job as an early childhood educator, regardless of the age or grade of children you teach, is to make thinking part of your curriculum and children's daily routines.

Sources: P. Kneedler, "California Assesses Critical Thinking." in A. Costa (Ed.), Developing Minds: A Resource Book for Teaching Thinking *(Alexandria, VA: Association for Supervision and Curriculum Development, 1985), p. 277;* H. Taba, Teacher's Handbook for Elementary Social Studies *(Reading, MA: Addison-Wesley, 1967), pp. 92–109;* S. Willis, "You CAN Teach Thinking Skills." Instructor, February 1993.

* Analyzing—examining something methodically; identifying the parts of something and the relationships between those parts.
* Inferring—drawing a reasonable conclusion from known information.
* Comparing and contrasting—noting similarities and differences between two things or events.
* Predicting—forecasting what will happen next in a given situation, based on the circumstances.
* Hypothesizing—developing a reasonable explanation for events, based on an analysis of evidence.
* Critical thinking—the process of logically and systematically analyzing problems, data, and solutions to make rational decisions about what to do or believe. Skills involved in critical thinking include:
  * Identifying central issues or problems.
  * Comparing similarities and differences.
  * Determining which information is relevant.
  * Formulating appropriate questions.
  * Distinguishing among facts, opinion, and reasoning judgment.
  * Checking consistency.
  * Identifying unstated assumptions.
  * Recognizing stereotypes and clichés.
  * Recognizing bias, emotional factors, propaganda, and semantic slanting.
  * Recognizing different value systems and ideologies.
  * Evaluating the adequacy of data.
  * Predicting probable consequences.
* Reasoning deductively—applying general principles to specific cases.
* Reasoning inductively—deriving general principles from an analysis of individual cases. Thinking skills both in deductive and inductive reasoning include:
  * Enumerating, listing
  * Grouping
  * Labeling, categorizing
  * Identifying critical relationships
  * Making inferences
  * Predicting consequences, explaining unfamiliar phenomena, hypothesizing
  * Explaining and/or supporting the predictions and hypotheses
  * Verifying predictions
* Organizing—imposing logical order on something.
* Classifying—putting things into groups based on shared characteristics.
* Making decisions—examining alternatives and, for sound reasons, choosing one.
* Solving problems—analyzing a difficult situation and thinking creatively about how to resolve it.

School-to-Careers

Today, one of the emphases in all of education is to devise ways to help students apply what they learn in school to real life and real careers such efforts are known as school-to-work or school-to-career programs. Basic work-related skills are literacy skills: reading, writing, speaking, thinking and decision making, working cooperatively with others, career and other job-related skills such as making change and using technology.

For example, in the Western Dubuque (Iowa) Community Elementary Schools, one K–6 elementary school researched careers. Kindergartners made a video in which they described what skills they would need to do their jobs and what salaries they expected. They also made a computer slide show with pictures they had taken. These students actually learned how to program their own photos into the computer to be included in their reports. Then they typed the information on their picture pages, and these were printed as books. Each grade had a completed career book by the end of the year. For the past three years, counselors have developed Career Portfolios on each child to build a record of the activities completed. Third graders visited area businesses and then created newspaper ads based on the information they learned about them. These were published in the local paper and paid for by the businesses.[2] The Montrose school partnership in the "Program in Action: The Montrose School-to-Career Education Partnership" on pages 266 and 267 illustrates in more detail how school-to-career programs work.

Learning how to work with and get along well with others is considered an essential workplace skill. Attitudes toward working cooperatively with others are developed in the early years of schooling. How will you, an early childhood teacher, organize the classroom and other environments to support children's cooperative efforts and interactions?

Professionalism in Practice

THE MAGIC TEACHER'S PHILOSOPHY ON EARLY CHILDHOOD EDUCATION
Jayné Anthony, Walnut Hill Elementary
Disney's American Teacher Award Honoree 2001

A school psychologist has given me the nickname of the Magic Teacher. Although amusing, this name conjures up serious implications and responsibilities. I prefer to think of myself as a hardworking dreamweaver who occasionally needs the assistance of magic.

We are children only one time. It is a brief and fleeting period. As a teacher, I struggle to stay in touch with the wonder of childhood. I must stop talking, and remember to listen. I must be a sounding board, rather than the speaker. We are not preparing children to stay children. We are preparing little people to do great feats. What a complex process! This is why magic is needed.

Children must be empowered. To survive into the adult years ahead, children need all the knowledge and wisdom we can give them. They also need unconditional support. We must validate and clarify. Of course, we are patient, sensitive, and responsive. But more importantly, we must teach children to survive. We must provide the security and stability so that students can take chances and be risk takers. I cannot give them an invisible shield to protect them from danger, but I can arm them with knowledge to make appropriate decisions and a bag of tricks to help them win against adversity.

I want my students to persevere when confronted by the dragons of ignorance, the griffins of violence, and the goblins of fear. Children come to school with incredible potential. Whether they are under-experienced or over-privileged, we still have the task of teaching. This is where the magic begins. We move beyond evaluators and into the realm of magicians. We have the task of ascertaining which learning components are ready to ignite, where the gaps exist, and when to let go. As the learning process reaches this point, a magic teacher becomes the risk taker.

I guided my own child successfully to adulthood. I am willing to accept the charter to guide other young children along their journey. I believe in implementing developmentally appropriate practices. Children are truly individuals evolving on their own timeline. As teachers of children, we should be mindful that the curriculum guide or the basal text does not always determine a child's readiness.

This is not magic.

This is reality. Developmentally appropriate practices allow a child to do what comes naturally. When instruction is rooted in developmental theory, a solid foundation is constructed that will form the basis on which a life is built. By touching, seeing, hearing, and experiencing, children remember.

Magic occurs.

Have you ever seen a magic classroom? Please come in. It does not matter how old you are. We are all learners. We are all teachers. I'll teach you how to read. Will you teach me how to paint a rainbow? Can we write a story together? Shall we write a play or make a puppet show? One group of children creates their own big book. Shall we sit in our magic school bus and work on our own project?

Child-friendly environments are educationally sound and appropriate. Early childhood experiences must not be limited to cut-and-paste or cookie-cutter art projects! Choices allow growth and experimentation. Learning styles and varied modalities are addressed with ease. Children learn to be self-directed or team players. Self-esteem is enhanced. Good decisions are encouraged and risk taking is celebrated. Mistakes are allowed. This is not a punitive environment. The harsh realities of the world are looming nearby. This classroom is a haven. All students have success on varied levels. We are concerned with process, not just product. This is a "please touch–please do" classroom. As you observe, note that this is a classroom of courtesy and respect. We are supportive of each other. We champion our peers and celebrate each other's successes. This is a happy room and many adults come to enjoy the atmosphere. They find that they can learn here, too.

I love teaching. I love to teach children. The process of watching children create, develop, and grow is the most exciting thing I have ever experienced. I teach each child the way I taught my own child. I teach with the most serious of intent even when I am at my most playful. I am a part of each child I have taught. Each experience prepares us for the next. I will use any resource at my disposal to make a difference. If magic can help me be an effective teacher, so be it.

May I share with you how I cast a spell and turn thematic learning into a magical learning experience? I am still responsible for incorporating learner standards, curriculum components, and solid instruction. Teachers must create innovative ways to make learning meaningful. Let me give you a specific example of how I achieve this in my classroom.

Thanksgiving epitomizes the spirit of America. It goes beyond turkey and conjures up the spirit of family, freedom, and community. Celebrating this holiday has been a religious and historic tradition in my family. I began my quest to bring the true spirit of Thanksgiving to my students.

As I explored the concept of harvest with my students, one child expressed her dread of the upcoming Thanksgiving. "I hate Thanksgiving! It's boring! It's grown-ups, turkey, and television!" I accepted the challenge to prove the greater meaning of our national holiday. I began to consider ways to facilitate meaningful experiences involving children in a celebration of brotherhood. I went back in memory and sought those lessons that had made Thanksgiving special in my childhood.

The key was *active* participation. Why couldn't we churn butter, bake cornbread, prepare pies, and peel potatoes? Why couldn't children share a feast that we prepared as a team? Why couldn't we celebrate similarities and put aside differences? After all, we are a classroom community.

My work began in earnest. The goal was to provide sound cross curriculum instruction in a month long thematic study for twenty-two children. I had the task of matching learner standards and curriculum components with cooking and feast preparation in a classroom setting.

After reading a variety of books about Pilgrims and Native Americans, we wrote and performed a play about the first Thanksgiving. We created costumes, used Native American music, and retold the story through our own understandings. Although some were dressed as Pilgrims and others as Native Americans, we were one family. We discovered that, even today, we had Pilgrims in our school from other nations. A special moment came when a Native American student within our classroom was no longer ashamed to be an Apache.

Stereotypic images of Indians disappeared as we created story skins from brown grocery bags, learned a round dance to the tune of an Indian flute, and practiced weaving beside the classroom tipi. The children began to appreciate Native American culture and gained new insights from stories and legends. Crafting rattles, drums, vests, and necklaces from recycled materials, we danced to bridge past and present.

By the time we reached the stage for food preparation, the children were two hundred percent involved. We were ready to measure, mash, and churn. More important, we were a tightly knit community working on a common goal. Economic and cultural differences had disappeared. We were truly a family!

Urban children assume corn comes in cans, mashed potatoes come in boxes, and butter comes in sticks. Cautiously stripping shucks, junior cooks reveal kernels, cobs, and silks. Great pride comes from peeling slippery potatoes and mashing them with butter you've just churned. Who would have dreamed that splashing cream in a churn could make butter? Cooked carrots are delicious when you scrape them by hand. Fried apple pies surpass candy bars when you fold and pinch your own crust. Corn bread is tasty if you carefully measure and combine cornmeal with egg and milk. Along the way you discover the difference between a cup and a tablespoon. Firsthand knowledge is the most powerful. Children learn best by doing. This causes developmentally appropriate practice to go from the textbook to the classroom table.

We wrote letters, invited families, and completed feast preparation. Two and a half days of constant activity culminated in a delicious community meal. Curiously, parents said that they saw significant changes in their children during this month of learning and growing. The project had given children a new maturity, increased knowledge and self-assurance, and enhanced their sense of belonging. Their personal journals were filled with powerful observations and evidence of learning. We had all shared a common enrichment experience. Children learn best through active participation. I still do the feast every November, but, more importantly, I build community every day of every year.

Now that I have imparted a major trick from my magic bag, you can begin your apprenticeship and practice your craft. Look at each teachable moment and every element of instruction with new eyes. Teaching is hard work but, when done well, elevates instruction to magic. Keep in touch with your imagination. Remember that when you structure for your students' success, you create your own. I believe that it is our mission to create lifelong learners. Take the challenge!

 To review the Professional Development Checklist and complete a Professionalism in Practice activity, visit the Companion Website at *http://www.prenhall.com/ morrison,* **select Chapter 9, then choose the Professional Development module.**

Program in Action

THEORY

Third graders are eager to learn about the world of work, and they love field trips and classroom visitors. Teachers are eager to keep the curriculum fresh and relevant. Businesses are eager to support schools and to share their expertise and sites. Combine this energy and desire to build a dynamic relationship among elementary students, teachers, and local business—an education partnership with curriculum punch.

HISTORY

In 1996–1997 Montrose school district (Montrose, Colorado) prioritized development of a School-to-Career component for elementary education. To ensure community support and buy-in, the district's School-to-Career leadership formed a lively, mutually respectful partnership with the Montrose Chamber of Commerce.

PROCESS

The chamber's Education Committee linked with School-to-Career to expand the education partnership program. The Education Committee guides the entire program using district input and technical assistance from the School-to-Career coordinator. Third grade teachers are invited to participate and asked to identify what type of business or government entity would be the best match for their classroom. The committee recruits businesses based on the teachers' desires and the committee's knowledge of the community.

The committee pairs a business with one or two elementary classrooms, targeting third grade. The business partners agree to participate in a minimum of three classroom activities during the school year. They host at least one field trip, which includes a visit to the work site. The school district assumes financial responsibility for field trip costs.

The Education Committee facilitates two yearly meetings among principals, teachers, and business people. These meetings orient all participants, evaluate activities, and make program recommendations. However, the main agenda item is brainstorming, which nourishes ideas for classroom curriculum links and activities. Teachers and their business partners use the "Education Partnership Planning Guide," which formalizes activity plans for the school year.

Program emphasis for teachers is on meshing the in-place curriculum with the expertise and knowledge of their chosen partner. The emphasis for business is on bringing relevancy to the classroom by showcasing the skills, equipment, and occupations within its organizational structure. For students the emphasis is on understanding how what they are learning in school is useful and necessary in the world of work.

Teachers and business partners discover curriculum possibilities and implement them according to student ability. The bottom line, the main goal, is to expand students' knowledge and basic skills with immediate application in the classroom curriculum.

EXAMPLES

BANKING. Norwest Bank links money management to the math curriculum and sponsors an in-depth tour of the bank, including seeing lots of money and the safe. Norwest brings tellers, the CEO, the director of security, the maintenance supervisor, and loan officers to the classroom to share their workday responsibilities. Students count and sort money, learn basic budgeting, and write practice checks. One field trip was to a bank client, Reclamation Metals, where the students observed recycling in progress and began to understand the relationship banks have to community projects.

AEROSPACE INDUSTRY. Scaled Technology is a partner with a class that is participating in a project involving students collecting data for the Citizen Explore Satellite. Scaled Technology engineers talk about how satellites orbit and what the word *orbit* means. Students collect data using aerosol and ultraviolet meters. The business partner helps the students learn how the instruments work and how to collect and record data. Lessons about the scientific method are also part of what employees of the company will teach. The field trip is to the manufacturing plant where satellite parts are designed and built.

NEWSPAPERS. A journalist partners a class. She meets with students in groups of two or three, assisting with writing, editing, inspiring, and some classroom publishing. This partnership enhances language arts curriculum and the district's literacy efforts.

CITY GOVERNMENT. The City of Montrose partnership meshes perfectly with the social studies curriculum. In preparation for a tour of all departments at City Hall, the students discuss job opportunities at the city level. From information provided about each employee, the students choose a job and write about it. The first hour includes all departments housed at City Hall. Students meet the city manager, mayor, and department heads of Planning, Engineering, Legal, Information Technology, Human Resources, and so on. Once, the city planner explained his current assignment to study the population growth and find correct placement for a new elementary school. He provided the students with a colorful map containing all the pertinent demographic information and asked the students to formulate a recommendation to the school board on the new school site. Students leave City Hall eagerly anticipating the second field trip, which includes the City Shop, Animal Shelter, and Wastewater Treatment Plant. A third activity involves the students conducting a city council meeting by role-playing city council members and staff in the actual council chambers.

BUREAU OF LAND MANAGEMENT. Bureau of Land Management (BLM), like many public agencies, has a mission statement requiring interaction with communities. The BLM leads its classroom partners into the world of environmental issues by having the students study and do experiments about soil types. Erosion and land management practices are the topics of discussion when students visit a site that illustrates soil issues.

COUNTY GOVERNMENT. The district judge partners with a class by linking to the social studies and health curricula. He discusses the judicial functions of government with students and encourages them to lead a drug-free and crime-free life. The students tour the criminal justice center courtroom, jail, and police headquarters.

FIRE DEPARTMENT. The Fire Department partnership enhances the students' use of math, understanding of electricity, and health issues while also providing a service learning project. The students conducted a neighborhood survey of smoke detector use. The results were analyzed by finding the mean, median, and mode. The department provided batteries to the students to distribute to the elderly. The class also inventoried the school's use of electrical outlets and learned why overloaded circuits can start fires. As part of health study, the students learned about CPR, first aid, and the dangers of smoking. The students made fire hats and were in charge of an actual fire drill at the school. The trip to the fire station was almost anticlimactic after all this excitement!

NATURAL RESOURCES CONSERVATION SERVICE. A specialist with the NRCS visits the class throughout the year and brings fresh ideas to parts of the science curriculum that touch on natural resources. A study of the nutrient cycle, for instance, resulted in the students building worm bins in jars, then studying how worms help decompose almost anything. Field trips to habitat reclamation projects enliven the classroom activities.

CONCLUSION

In this elementary School-to-Career program, the Chamber of Commerce and school district discovered that a generous definition of the word *business* strengthens program diversity and community involvement. They actively recruit employers outside the normal school support loop. The data supports this and other strategies: participation in the first year included six schools and four businesses; participation in the second year involved sixteen classrooms and twelve businesses.

The elementary level School-to-Career program energizes and provides focus for the curriculum. It generates close school and community collaboration, increases mutual understanding about the daily challenges of education, and promotes program ownership. The Montrose Education Partnership firmly believes that curriculum-linked, reality-based experiences in the world of employment successfully launches students' dreams for a productive future.

Text contributed by Carol Parker, the Montrose School-to-Career Partnership.

 To visit the Colorado Department of Education's School-to-Career website and complete a Program in Action activity, visit the Companion Website at *http://www.prenhall.com/ morrison,* select Chapter 9, then choose the Program in Action module.

The New Literacy

Just as in preschool and kindergarten, today's primary classroom decidedly emphasizes literacy development and reading. In fact, this emphasis is apparent in all the elementary grades, pre-K to 6. Society and parents want children who can speak, write, and read well.

As discussed in Chapter 8, more states are adopting standards to promote children's literacy and reading development. Figure 9.6 shows the reading standards for grades one, two, and three in Florida. As you review the Reading Standards for Florida, think how you would achieve them in your classroom, because this is exactly what you will be expected to do.

The New Mathematics

For a complete list of reading supplements and links to learning on the Internet, go to the Companion Website at *http://www.prenhall.com/ morrison*, select Chapter 9, then choose the Professional Development module.

Mathematics is being reemphasized as an essential part of primary education. Just as reading is receiving a great deal of national attention, so too is mathematics. Figure 9.7 shows the California Standards for Mathematics in grades one, two, and three.

The term *new math* is not new. It has been around since the 1960s. What differentiates the "old" math from the "new"? Memorization and drill characterize the old or traditional math. The new math, sometimes referred to as the "new-new math," emphasizes hands-on activities, problem solving, group and team work, application and use of mathematical ideas and principles to real-life events, daily use of mathematics, and an understanding of and use of math understandings and competencies. The new math seeks to have students be math-smart and creative users of math in life and workplace settings. The ten standards of the National Council of Teachers of Mathematics identify these understandings and competencies as: number and operations, algebra, geometry, measurement, data analysis and probability, problem solving, reasoning and proof, communications, connections, and representation.

The following information and vignette from the National Council of Teachers of Mathematics will help you understand the standard of communication and how it can be applied to the primary grades.

An important step in communicating mathematical thinking to others is organizing and clarifying one's ideas. When students struggle to communicate ideas clearly, they develop a better understanding of their own thinking. Working in pairs or small groups enables students to hear different ways of thinking and refine the ways in which they explain their own ideas. Having students share the results of their small-group findings gives teachers opportunities to ask questions for clarification and to model mathematical language. Students in prekindergarten through grade two should be encouraged to listen attentively to each other, to question others' strategies and results, and to ask for clarification so that their mathematical learning advances.

GRADE 1

The first grade student:

* uses prior knowledge, illustrations, and text to make predictions.
* uses basic elements of phonetic analysis (for example, hears, segments, substitutes, and blends sounds in words).
* uses sound/symbol relationships as visual cues for decoding.
* uses beginning letters (onsets) and patterns (rhymes) as visual cues for decoding.
* uses structural cues to decode words (for example, word order, sentence boundaries).
* uses context clues to construct meaning (meaning cues; (for example, illustrations, knowledge of the story and topic).
* cross-checks visual, structural, and meaning cues to figure out unknown words.
* knows common words from within basic categories.
* uses knowledge of individual words in unknown compound words to predict their meaning.
* uses resources and references to build upon word meanings (for example, beginning dictionaries and available technology).
* uses knowledge of suffixes (including -er, -est, -ful) to determine meaning of words.
* develops vocabulary by listening to and discussing both familiar and conceptually challenging selections read aloud.
* uses a variety of strategies to comprehend text (for example, retelling stories in correct sequence, recalling details, rereading).
* knows the main idea or theme and supporting details of a story or informational piece.
* uses specific details and information from a text to answer literal questions.
* makes inferences based on text and prior knowledge (for example, regarding traits, feelings, actions of characters).
* identifies similarities and differences between two texts (for example, in topics, characters, problems).
* selects material to read for pleasure (for example, favorite books and stories).
* reads aloud familiar stories, poems, and passages.
* reads for information used in performing tasks (for example, directions, graphs, charts, signs, captions).
* uses background knowledge and supporting reasons from the text to determine whether a story or text is fact or fiction.
* uses simple reference material to obtain information (for example, table of contents, fiction and nonfiction books, picture dictionaries, audiovisual software).
* alphabetizes words according to the initial letter.
* uses alphabetical order to locate information.

(Continued)

FIGURE 9.6   **Reading Standards for Florida**

The second grade student:

* uses prior knowledge, illustrations, and text to make and confirm predictions.
* blends sound components into words.
* applies knowledge of beginning letters (onsets) and spelling patterns (rhymes) in single and multisyllable words as visual cues for decoding.
* uses a variety of structural cues (for example, word order, prefixes, suffixes, verb endings) to decode unfamiliar words.
* uses a variety of context cues to construct meaning (meaning cues: (for example, illustrations, diagrams, information in the story, titles and headings, sequence).
* cross-checks visual, structural, and meaning cues to figure out unknown words.
* identifies simple, multiple-meaning words.
* uses knowledge of contractions, base words, and compound words to determine meaning of words.
* uses knowledge of prefixes (including un-, re-, pre-, mis-) and suffixes (including -er, -est, -ful) to determine meaning of words.
* knows homophones, synonyms, and antonyms for a variety of words.
* develops vocabulary by reading independently and listening to and discussing both familiar and conceptually challenging selections.
* uses resources and references to build upon word meanings (for example, dictionaries, glossaries).
* uses a variety of strategies to comprehend text (for example, self-monitoring, predicting, retelling, discussing, restating ideas).
* summarizes information in texts (including but not limited to central idea, supporting details, connections between texts).
* uses specific ideas, details, and information from text to answer literal question.
* makes connections and inferences based on text and prior knowledge (for example, order of events, possible outcomes).
* understands similarities and differences across texts (for example, topics, characters, problems).
* selects materials to read for pleasure, as a group or independently.
* reads aloud with fluency and expression from developmentally appropriate material (including but not limited to reading phrases rather than word-by-word; attending to punctuation; interjecting a sense of feeling, anticipation, characterization).
* reads informational texts for specific purposes (including but not limited to performing a task, learning a new task, sequentially carrying out the steps of a procedure, locating information to answer a question).
* uses simple reference material (for example, table of contents, dictionary, index, glossary).
* alphabetizes words according to initial and second letter.
* uses parts of a book to locate information, including chapter titles, guide words, and indexes.
* generates questions about topics of personal interest.

(Continued)

⌒ **FIGURE 9.6 Reading Standards for Florida** *(Continued)*

The third grade student:

* uses text features to predict content and monitor comprehension (for example, uses table of contents, indexes, captions, illustrations, key words, preview text).

* uses knowledge of formats, ideas, plots, and elements from previous reading to generate questions and make predictions about content of text.

* uses decoding strategies to clarify pronunciation (for example, less common vowel patterns, homophones).

* uses context clues (for example, known words, phrases, structures) to infer the meaning of new and unfamiliar words, including synonyms, antonyms, and homophones.

* makes, confirms, and revises predictions.

* establishes a purpose for reading (for example, entertainment, skimming for facts, answering a specific question).

* uses a variety of strategies to determine meaning and increase vocabulary (for example, prefixes, suffixes, root words, less common vowel patterns, homophones, compound words, contractions).

* discusses meanings of words and develops vocabulary through meaningful real-world experiences.

* develops vocabulary by reading independently and using reference books.

* uses a variety of strategies to monitor reading in third grade or higher texts (for example, rereading, self-correcting, summarizing, checking other sources, class and group discussions, reading on, trying alternative pronunciations, asking questions).

* understands explicit and implicit ideas and information in third grade or higher texts (for example, main idea, implied message, relevant supporting details and facts, chronological order of events).

* identifies author's purpose in a simple text.

* recognizes when a text is intended primarily to persuade.

* knows personal preferences for fiction and nonfiction texts (for example, novels, stories, poems, biographies, journals, magazines, interviews).

* reads and organizes information (for example, in story maps, graphs, charts) for different purposes (for example, being informed, following directions, making a report, conducting interviews, taking a test, performing a task).

* knows the difference between a fact and an opinion.

* understands the use of comparison and contrast within a selection.

* uses a variety of reference materials to gather information, including multiple representations of information (for example, maps, charts, photos).

⌒ **FIGURE 9.6   Reading Standards for Florida** *(Continued)*

Source: *"Curriculum, Instruction & Assessment: Curriculum Support,"* Sunshine State Standards, *Florida Department of Education, 2000.* [*Online:* http://www.firn.edu/doe/menu/sss.htm].

GRADE 1

Number Sense

1.0 Students understand and use numbers up to 100
2.0 Students demonstrate the meaning of addition and subtraction and use these operations to solve problems
3.0 Students use estimation strategies in computation and problem solving that involve numbers that use the ones, tens, and hundreds places

Algebra Functions

1.0 Students use number sentences with operational symbols and expressions to solve problems

Measurement and Geometry

1.0 Students use direct comparison and nonstandard units to describe the measurement of objects
2.0 Students identify common geometric figures, classify them by common attributes, and describe their relative position or their location in space

Statistics, Data Analysis, and Probability

1.0 Students organize, represent, and compare data by category on simple graphs and charts
2.0 Students sort objects and create and describe patterns by numbers, shapes, sizes, rhythms, or colors

Mathematical Reasoning

1.0 Students make decisions about how to set up a problem
2.0 Students solve problems and justify their reasoning
3.0 Students note connections between one problem and another

GRADE 2

Number Sense

1.0 Students understand the relationship between numbers, quantities, and place value in whole numbers up to 1,000
2.0 Students estimate, calculate, and solve problems involving addition and subtraction of two- and three-digit numbers
3.0 Students model and solve simple problems involving multiplication and division
4.0 Students understand that fractions and decimals may refer to parts of a set and parts of a whole
5.0 Students model and solve problems by representing, adding, and subtracting amounts of money
6.0 Students use estimation strategies in computation and problem solving that involve numbers that use the ones, tens, hundreds, and thousands places

Algebra and Functions

1.0 Students model, represent, and interpret number relationships to create and solve problems involving addition and subtraction

(Continued)

FIGURE 9.7   California Standards for Math

Measurement and Geometry

1.0 Students understand that measurement is accomplished by identifying a unit of measure, iterating (repeating) that unit, and comparing it to the item to be measured
2.0 Students identify and describe the attributes of common figures in the plane and of common objects in space

Statistics, Data Analysis, and Probability

1.0 Students collect numerical data and record, organize, display, and interpret the data on bar graphs and others representations
2.0 Students demonstrate an understanding of patterns and how patterns grow and describe them in general ways

Mathematical Reasoning

1.0 Students make decisions about how to set up a problem
2.0 Students solve problems and justify their reasoning
3.0 Students note connections between one problem and another

GRADE 3

Number Sense

1.0 Students understand the place value of whole numbers
2.0 Students calculate and solve problems involving addition, subtraction, multiplication, and division
3.0 Students understand the relationship between whole numbers, simple fractions, and decimals

Algebra and Functions

1.0 Students select appropriate symbols, operations, and properties to represent, describe, simplify, and solve simple number relationships
2.0 Students represent simple functional relationships

Measurement and Geometry

1.0 Students choose and use appropriate units and measurement tools to quantify the properties of objects
2.0 Students describe and compare the attributes of plane and solid geometric figures and use their understanding to show relationships and solve problems

Statistics, Data Analysis, and Probability

1.0 Students conduct simple probability experiments by determining the number of possible outcomes and make simple predictions

Mathematical Reasoning

1.0 Students make decisions about how to approach problems
2.0 Students use strategies, skills, and concepts in finding solutions
3.0 Students move beyond a particular problem by generalizing to other situations

∞ **FIGURE 9.7   California Standards for Math** *(Continued)*

Source: Mathematics Content Standards for California Public Schools: K–12, copyright 1997, *California Department of Education*, P.O. Box 271, Sacramento, CA 95814. [*Online:* http://www.cde.ca.gov/standards/].

Adequate time and interesting mathematical problems and materials, including calculators and computer applications, encourage conversation and learning among young students, as demonstrated in the following episode, drawn from a classroom experience:

Rosalinda, usually a quiet child, was very excited to learn how to skip-count to 100 on the calculator. However, she was puzzled when counting to 100 by threes. "It always goes over 100!" she exclaimed. The teacher encouraged Rosalinda and her partner to investigate the phenomenon. Over several days, the students talked together about why the calculator did not display 100 when they counted by threes. They used the hundred board and counters along with their calculator and concluded that equal groups of twos could be made with 100 counters but not equal groups of threes. The investigation resulted in a chart that Rosalinda and her partner made to explain to the class what they had figured out and how the calculator had supported their conclusions.

Experiences such as this help students see themselves as problem posers and also see how tools such as calculators can be used to support their mathematical investigations.[3]

As you can see, the new math may be a whole lot different than what you were taught and how you were taught it. One of your professional challenges will be to creatively apply the standards of new math to your classroom.

End of Social Promotion

Not surprisingly, with the new directions in primary education, educators are taking a new look at grade failure and retention practices. Retention as a cure for poor achievement or nonachievement is popular, especially with many politicians, educators, and the public. Despite the use of retention as a panacea for poor achievement, a review of the research reveals that achievement-based promotion does not deal effectively with the problem of low achievement. Better and more helpful approaches to student achievement include the following strategies:

* Use promotion combined with individualized instruction.
* Promote to a transition class in which students receive help to master skills not previously achieved.
* Use after-school and summer programs to help students master skills.
* Provide children specific and individualized help in mastery of skills.
* Work with parents to teach them how to help their children work on mastery of skills.
* Identify children who may need help before they enter first grade so that developmental services are provided early.
* Use multi-age grouping as a means of providing for a broader range of children's abilities and to provide children the benefits that come from multi-age grouping.

⁎ Have a teacher teach the same group of children over a period of several years as a means of getting to know children and their families and, as a result, better provide for children's educational and developmental needs. This approach is also called **sustained instruction**, or **looping**. Looping allows teachers to spend two or more years with the same group of same-age children and is one alternative to failure and social promotion. In other words, a teacher engaged in looping begins teaching kindergarten children and then teaches the same group as first graders, and perhaps as second graders. Another teacher might do the same with second, third, and fourth graders. Other names for looping are student-teacher progress, multi-year instruction, and multi-year grouping. Advantages of looping are listed in Figure 9.8.

⁎ Use a nongraded classroom approach. The nongraded classroom as its name implies does not have a grade designation. The children in the classroom could be in any grade, for example, grades one, two, and three. In the nongraded classroom, individual differences are recognized and taken into account. One purpose of the nongraded classroom is to provide a seemless transition between grades. The state of Kentucky mandates that grades one through three be nongraded.

FIGURE 9.8   Advantages of Looping

Looping is a practice whose time has come, and it is catching on in schools throughout the country. Based on these advantages you may want to consider looping and advocate for its use.

Source: *Susan Black, "Together Again: The Practice of Looping Keeps Students with the Same Teachers."* American School Board Journal *(June 2000): 43.*

⁎ Looping enables teachers to develop a family atmosphere for teachers and children to develop long-term relationships.

⁎ Looping provides a sense of stability and security, especially for young children.

⁎ Looping provides freedom to expand and enrich the curriculum vertically and horizontally over a two-year period.

⁎ Teachers have the opportunity to monitor children's progress more closely over a two-year period before seeking child study team input. Also, teachers can really focus on learning, as one first grade teacher exclaims: "I love looping; I've had two years to help my children become readers—good readers—who love learning. Looping has made the difference."*

⁎ Teachers can gain weeks of instructional time at the beginning of the school year because they already know the children. They don't have to spend additional time assessing abilities and learning styles. Also, children know what is expected of them, so they are ready to go with learning.

⁎ Looping supports individualized instruction because teachers are more familiar with the strengths and weaknesses of each child.

⁎ Looping grants teachers an opportunity to stay fresh and grow professionally by changing their grade-level assignments every year.

More efforts are being made to provide family-like classroom environments for children. Mixed-age grouping and looping are two ways to achieve this goal. Do you think you would like to engage in looping? Why, or why not?

Advocates of nongraded classrooms offer the following advantages:

* Provide opportunities for individualized instruction
* Create an enhanced social atmosphere (older children help younger children, and there are more opportunities for role modeling)
* Result in reduced or few, if any, retentions
* Eliminate need for students to progress through a grade-level curriculum in a lock-step approach with age peers

Any effort to improve student achievement must emphasize helping children rather than using practices that threaten to detract from their self-image and make them solely responsible for their failure.

One thing is clear about the future of the primary grades: There will be more emphasis on academics, higher achievement, and helping students be successful. Figure 9.9 shows some of the things you can do to create conditions in your classroom to support children's learning.

The primary grades represent the heartland of early childhood education. In these grades, all of the readiness activities and early skill acquisition are applied

* Materials are in abundant supply for reading, writing, language development, and content area development (e.g., books about math, science, social studies, the arts).

* Learning centers reflect content areas.

* Literature of all genres supports content area learning centers, and materials provide for and emulate real work experiences (i.e., the waiting room, the restaurant).

* Materials and instruction provide for interdisciplinary integrated approaches.

* Program, learning, and environment are coordinated so that materials support and align with outcomes and standards.

* Teacher instruction (teacher-directed instruction and intentional teaching) and active student involvement are balanced.

* Centers support literacy. All centers have materials that support reading and writing.

* Children's products are displayed and valued.

* Technology supports and enriches basic skill and concept learning. Children use technology to make presentations, projects, and reports.

* Families, other adults, and the community are connected to classroom learning.

* Children are valued and respected. The classroom is a community of learners. Children learn to live and learn in peace and harmony.

* High expectations for all are an essential part of the classroom culture.

* Assessment is continuous and appropriate and is designed to support teaching and learning.

* Thinking is considered a basic skill and is integrated through all areas of the curriculum.

FIGURE 9.9   Conditions That Support Learning in Primary Classrooms

Classroom environment plays a powerful role in children's learning. How well you arrange the classroom and provide learning materials will determine how well your students learn.

and bear fruit. The primary grades are also the bridge from the early years to the intermediate and middle childhood years. These grades represent the end of early learning and the beginning of the years of testing and accountability. Just as what comes before the primary grades is important, what happens to children in the primary grades—how well they are taught and how well they learn—will determine to a large extent their school and life success.

ACTIVITIES FOR PROFESSIONAL DEVELOPMENT

In this chapter we have stressed the importance of how the primary grades are changing and how to apply developmentally appropriate practice to the teaching of young children. Refer again to the "Professional Development Goal" at the beginning of the chapter and to the "Professional Development Checklist" on pages 20 and 21, and also review the "Professionalism in Practice" by Jayné Anthony on pages 264 and 265. After you review these, complete the following exercises.

1. One of the goals of the federal government and many states is that all children should be able to read on grade level by grade three.
   a. Why do you think this has become such an important goal?
   b. Why do you think this goal was set for grade three rather than another grade?
   c. What are some things you can do to help children achieve this goal in developmentally appropriate ways?
2. Professionals are able to articulate their reasons for wanting to teach a particular grade.
   a. Explain in detail why you would or would not want to teach one of the primary grades.
   b. Based on your reasons, make revisions in your philosophy of teaching.
3. What do you think are the most important subjects of the primary grades? Why? How would you agree or disagree with those who think any subjects other than reading, writing, and arithmetic are a waste of time?
4. Inquire whether any schools in your area offer character education programs.
   a. Compile a list of character traits you believe are most important for teaching young children.
   b. Ask parents and community members what they believe are the most important traits.

For additional chapter resources and activities, visit the Companion Website at *http://www.prenhall.com/morrison,* select Chapter 9, then choose the Professional Development, Resources, or Linking to Learning modules.

chapter 10

FOCUS QUESTIONS

1. What is the basis for inclusion of children with disabilities in early childhood programs?

2. What is multicultural education and how can you infuse multicultural content in your programs and activities?

3. How can you meet the special needs of all children in developmentally appropriate ways?

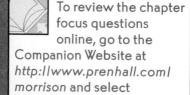

To review the chapter focus questions online, go to the Companion Website at *http://www.prenhall.com/ morrison* and select Chapter 10.

Educating Children with Diverse Backgrounds and Special Needs

ENSURING ALL CHILDREN LEARN

 ## PROFESSIONAL DEVELOPMENT GOAL

EDUCATING ALL STUDENTS

I understand that all children are individuals with unique strengths and challenges. I embrace these differences, work to fulfill special needs, and promote tolerance and inclusion in my classroom. I value and respect the dignity of all children.

Children with diverse backgrounds and special needs are in every program, school, and classroom in the United States. As an early childhood professional, you will teach students who have a variety of special needs. They may come from low-income families and various racial and ethnic groups; they may have exceptional abilities or disabilities. You and your colleagues will be challenged to provide for all students an education that is appropriate to their physical, intellectual, social, and emotional abilities and to help them achieve their best.

CHILDREN WITH DISABILITIES

To check your understanding of this chapter with the online Study Guide, go to the Companion Website at *http://www.prenhall.com/ morrison*, select Chapter 10, then choose the Study Guide module.

Children with special needs and their families should receive education and services that will help them succeed in school and life. You will be a key player in the process of ensuring that they receive such services. The federal government has passed many laws protecting and promoting the rights and needs of children with disabilities. One of the most important federal laws is the Individuals with Disabilities Education Act (IDEA).

As with many special areas, the field of children with special needs has a unique vocabulary and terminology. The glossary in Figure 10.1 will help you as we begin our discussion of IDEA and as you work with children and families.

The Individuals with Disabilities Education Act (IDEA)

The purpose of IDEA is to ensure that all disabled children have available to them "a free appropriate public education which emphasizes special education and related services designed to meet their unique needs, to assure that the rights of disabled children and their parents or guardians are protected, to assist States and localities to provide for the education of all children with disabilities, and to assess and assure the effectiveness of efforts to educate children with disabilities."[1]

For more information about answers to frequently asked questions about IDEA, go to the Companion Website at *http://www.prenhall.com/ morrison*, select Chapter 10, then choose the Linking to Learning module to connect to the IDEA Practices site.

IDEA defines **children with disabilities** as those children with mental retardation, hearing impairments (including deafness), speech or language impairments (including blindness), serious emotional disturbance, orthopedic impairments, autism, traumatic brain injury, other health impairments, or specific learning disabilities; and who, by reason thereof, need special education and related services.[2]

Table 10–1 lists the number of persons from age six to age twenty-one with disabilities in the various categories. About 10 to 12 percent of the nation's children have disabilities. What this means for you is that in your classroom of 20 to 25 students you will have at least two to three children with some kind of disability.

These are terms you will need to know in your teaching of children with disabilities.

Adaptive education: Modifying programs, environments, curricula, and activities to provide learning experiences that help all students achieve desired education goals.

Children with disabilities: Replaces former terms such as *handicapped.* To avoid labeling children, do not use the reversal of these words (e.g., *disabled children*).

Co-teaching: The process by which a regular classroom professional and a special educator or a person trained in exceptional student education team teach, in the same classroom, a group of regular and mainstreamed children.

Early intervention: Providing services to children and families as early in the child's life as possible to prevent or help with a special need or needs.

Exceptional student education: Replaces the term *special education;* refers to the education of children with special needs.

Full inclusion: The mainstreaming or inclusion of all children with disabilities into natural environments such as playgrounds, family day care centers, child care centers, preschool, kindergarten, and primary grades.

Individualized education plan (IEP): A written plan for a child stating what will be done, how it will be done, and when it will be done.

Integration: The education of children with disabilities along with typically developing children. This education can occur in mainstream, reverse mainstream, and full-inclusion programs.

Least restrictive environment (LRE): Children with disabilities are educated with children who have no disabilities. Special classes, separate schooling, or other removal of children with disabilities from the regular educational environment occurs only when the nature or severity of the disability is such that education in regular classes with the use of supplementary aids and services cannot be achieved satisfactorily.

Limited English proficiency (LEP): Describes children who have limited English skills.

Natural environment: Any environment in which it is natural for any child to be, such as home, child care center, preschool, kindergarten, and primary grades.

Reverse mainstreaming: The process by which typically developing children are placed in programs for children with disabilities. In reverse mainstreaming, children with disabilities are in the majority.

Typically developing children: Children who are developing according to and within the boundaries of normal growth and development.

TABLE 10–1

NUMBER OF STUDENTS AGES 6 THROUGH 21 SERVED UNDER IDEA IN THE 1998–99 SCHOOL YEAR

TYPE OF DISABILITY	NUMBERS SERVED
All Disabilities	5,541,166
Specific Learning Disabilities	2,817,148
Speech and Language Impairments	1,074,548
Mental Retardation	611,076
Emotional Disturbance	463,262
Multiple Disabilities	107,763
Hearing Impairments	70,883
Orthopedic Impairments	69,495
Other Health Impairments	220,831
Visual Impairments	26,132
Autism	53,576
Deaf-Blindness	1,609
Traumatic Brain Injury	12,933
Developmental Delay	11,910

Source: U.S. Department of Education, Office of Special Education Programs, Data Analysis System (DANS).

IDEA's SIX PRINCIPLES.   IDEA establishes six principles for professionals to follow as they provide educational and other services to children with special needs:

* Zero reject: a rule of educating all students and excluding none
* Nondiscriminatory evaluation: a rule of fair evaluation to determine whether a student has a disability and, if so, of what the student's education should consist
* Appropriate education: a rule of individualized education that benefits the student in making progress toward the national policy goals
* Least restrictive placement/environment: a rule that students with disabilities must, to the maximum extent appropriate for each one, be educated with students who do not have disabilities (their education being in the academic, extracurricular, and other school activities in which students without disabilities participate)
* Procedural due process: a rule that allows schools and parents to resolve their differences by mediation and, if not by that means, by having hearings before impartial hearing officers or judges
* Parental and student participation: a rule of shared decision making, in which educators, parents, and students collaborate in deciding what the student's education should entail[3]

All early childhood programs should address the individual needs of children with disabilities. How can you use the IEPs to ensure that those needs are being met?

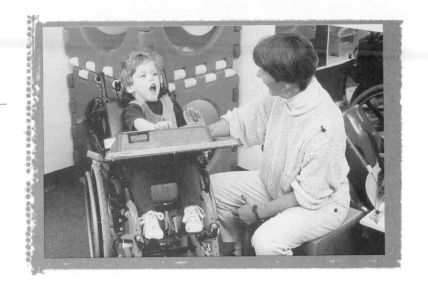

Figure 10.2 lists the disabilities covered under IDEA. Make yourself familiar with each of these and consider how you might meet the needs of children with these disabilities.

GUARANTEEING A FREE AND APPROPRIATE EDUCATION. IDEA mandates a free and appropriate education (FAPE) for all persons between the ages of three and twenty-one. In addition, IDEA provides federal money to state and local educational agencies to guarantee students a free appropriate public education.

State and local agencies, however, must agree to comply with the federal law or else they will not receive federal money. One of the facts of public education is that there is a lot of federal money for special services to children, such as the school lunch program, bilingual programs, and exceptional student education. Exceptional education and related services specified by IDEA are listed in Figure 10.3.

CREATING AN INDIVIDUALIZED EDUCATION PROGRAM. Exceptional student education laws mandate the creation of an **individualized education program (IEP),** which requires a plan for the individualization of each student's instruction. This requires creating learning objectives and basing students' learning plans on their specific needs, disabilities, and preferences, as well as on those of their parents. A collaborative team of regular and special educators creates these objectives. The IEP must specify what will be done for the child, how and when it will be done, and by whom, and this information must be in writing. In developing the IEP, a person trained in diagnosing disabling conditions, such as a school psychologist, must be part of the IEP team, which includes the parent and, when appropriate, the child. Figure 10.4 identifies the members of the IEP team as mandated by federal law. The IEP has

For more information about IEPs or for a guide to writing and developing IEPs, go to the Companion Website at *http://www.prenhall.com/ morrison*, select Chapter 10, then choose the Linking to Learning module.

As an early childhood educator, you will have children with special needs in your classroom. The following disabilities qualify children for special education services under IDEA:

1. *Autism:* A developmental disability significantly affecting verbal and nonverbal communication and social interaction, generally evident before age three, which adversely affects educational performance.

2. *Deafness:* A hearing impairment which is so severe that a child is impaired in processing linguistic information through hearing, with or without amplification, which adversely affects educational performance.

3. *Deaf-blindness:* Simultaneous hearing and visual impairment, the combination of which causes such severe communication and other developmental and educational problems that a child cannot be accommodated in special education programs solely for children with deafness or children with blindness.

4. *Hearing impairment:* A hearing impairment, whether permanent or fluctuating, which adversely affects a child's educational performance but which is not included under the definition of "deafness."

5. *Mental retardation:* Significantly sub-average general intellectual functioning existing concurrently with deficits in adaptive behavior and manifested during the developmental period, which adversely affects a child's educational performance.

6. *Multiple disabilities:* Simultaneous impairments (such as mental retardation/blindness, mental retardation/orthopedic impairment, etc.), the combination of which causes such severe educational problems that the child cannot be accommodated in a special education program solely for one of the impairments.

7. *Orthopedic impairment:* A severe orthopedic impairment which adversely affects a child's educational performance. The term includes impairments caused by a congenital anomaly (e.g., clubfoot, absence of some member, etc.).

8. *Other health impairment:* Having limited strength, vitality, or alertness, due to chronic or acute health problems such as a heart condition, tuberculosis, rheumatic fever, nephritis, asthma, sickle cell anemia, hemophilia, epilepsy, lead poisoning, leukemia, or diabetes, which adversely affects a child's educational performance. According to the Office of Special Education and Rehabilitative Services' clarification statement of September 16, 1991, eligible children with AIDS may also be classified under "other health impairment."

9. *Serious emotional disturbance:* A condition exhibiting one or more of the following characteristics over a long period of time and to a marked degree, which adversely affects educational performance: (A) an inability to learn that cannot be explained by intellectual, sensory, or health factors; (B) an inability to build or maintain satisfactory interpersonal relationships with peers and teachers; (C) inappropriate types of behavior or feelings under normal circumstances; (D) a general pervasive mood of unhappiness or depression; or (E) a tendency to develop physical symptoms or fears associated with personal or school problems. The term includes children who have schizophrenia. The term does not include children who are socially maladjusted, unless it is determined that they have a serious emotional disturbance.

(Continued)

FIGURE 10.2   Disabilities Covered under IDEA

10. *Specific learning disability:* A disorder in one or more of the basic psychological processes involved in understanding or in using language, spoken or written, which may manifest itself in an imperfect ability to listen, think, speak, read, write, spell, or do mathematical calculations. The term includes such conditions as perceptual disabilities, brain injury, minimum brain dysfunction, dyslexia, and developmental aphasia. The term does not include children who have learning problems which are primarily the result of visual, hearing, or motor disabilities, of mental retardation, of emotional disturbance, or of environmental cultural, or economic disadvantage.

11. *Speech or language impairment:* A communication disorder such as stuttering, impaired articulation, a language impairment, or a voice impairment, which adversely affects a child's educational performance.

12. *Traumatic brain injury:* An injury to the brain caused by an external physical force, resulting in total or partial functional disability or psychosocial maladjustment, or both, which adversely affects educational performance. The term does not include brain injuries that are congenital or degenerative, or brain injuries induced by birth trauma.

13. *Visual impairment, including blindness:* A visual impairment that, even with correction, adversely affects a child's educational performance. The term includes both children with partial sight and those with blindness.

⌦ **FIGURE 10.2   Disabilities Covered under IDEA** *(Continued)*

You can be reasonably assured that you will have children with some of these disabilities in your classroom. Plan now for generic ways you can meet their needs. You will outline specific ways on each child's IEP.

Source: *The Individuals with Disabilities Education Act Amendments of 1997 (IDEA '97 Final Regulations). 34 CFR Part 300. Assistance to States for the Education of Children with Disabilities. [Online:* http://www.ideapractices.org/lawsandregs.htm].

several purposes, which are described in Figure 10.5. Review these now before reviewing the completed IEP shown in Figure 10.6. In addition, IDEA provides funds for infants and toddlers to receive early intervention services, which are outlined in Figure 10.7.

INDIVIDUALIZED FAMILY SERVICE PLAN.   Infants, toddlers, and their families also have the right to an **individualized family service plan (IFSP),** which specifies what services they will receive. The IFSP is designed to help families reach the goals they have for themselves and their children. The IFSP provides for:

✳ Multidisciplinary assessment developed by a multidisciplinary team and the parents. Planned services must meet developmental needs and can include special education, speech and language pathology and audiology, occupational therapy, physical therapy, psychological services, parent and family training and counseling services, transition services, medical diagnostic services, and health services.

1. "Audiology" includes identification of children with hearing loss; determination of the range, nature, and degree of hearing loss; and creation and administration of programs for [treatment and] prevention of hearing loss.
2. "Counseling services" means services provided by qualified social workers, psychologists, guidance counselors, or other qualified personnel.
3. "Early identification and assessment of disabilities in children" means the implementation of a formal plan for identifying a disability as early as possible in a child's life.
4. "Medical services" means services provided by a licensed physician to determine a child's medically related disability that results in the child's need for special education and related services.
5. "Occupational therapy" includes improving, developing, or restoring functions impaired or lost through illness, injury, or deprivation.
6. "Parent counseling and training" means assisting parents in understanding the special needs of their child and providing parents with information about child development.
7. "Physical therapy" means services provided by a qualified physical therapist.
8. "Psychological services" includes administering psychological and educational tests, and other assessment procedures; interpreting assessment results; obtaining, integrating, and interpreting information about child behavior and conditions relating to learning; consulting with other staff members in planning school programs to meet the special needs of children as indicated by psychological tests, interviews, and behavioral evaluations; and planning and managing a program of psychological services, including psychological counseling for children and parents.
9. "Recreation" includes assessment of leisure function, therapeutic recreation services, recreation programs in schools and community agencies, and leisure education.
10. "Rehabilitative counseling services" means services that focus specifically on career development, employment preparation, achieving independence, and integration in the workplace and community of a student with a disability.
11. "School health services" means services provided by a qualified school nurse or other qualified person.
12. "Social work services in schools" includes preparing a social or developmental history on a child with a disability, group and individual counseling with the child and family, working with those problems in a child's living situation (home, school, and community) that affect the child's adjustment in school, and mobilizing school and community resources to enable the child to learn as effectively as possible in his or her educational program.
13. "Speech pathology" includes identification, diagnosis, and appraisal of specific speech or language impairments, provision of speech and language services, and counseling and guidance of parents, children, and teachers regarding speech and language impairments.
14. "Transportation" includes travel to and from school and between schools, travel in and around school buildings, and specialized equipment (such as special or adapted buses, lifts, and ramps), if required to provide special transportation for a child with a disability.
15. "Assistive technology and services" are devices and related services that restore lost capacities or improve capacities.

∽ **FIGURE 10.3   Services Provided by IDEA**

When providing services for children with disabilities, it is important for them to receive specific services that will help them learn. This is why IDEA identifies some, but not all, of the services that will help achieve this goal.

Source: The Individuals with Disabilities Education Act Amendments of 1997 (IDEA '97 Final Regulations). 34 CFR Part 300. Assistance to States for the Education of Children with Disabilities. [Online: http://www.ideapractices.org/lawsandregs.htm].

Certain individuals must be involved in writing a child's Individualized Education Program. An IEP team member may fill more than one of the team positions if properly qualified and designated. For example, the school system representative may also be the person who can interpret the child's evaluation results.

Source: *Office of Special Education and Rehabilitative Services (2000),* A Guide to the Individualized Education Program *(Washington, DC: U.S. Department of Education).* [*Online:* http://www.ed.gov/offices/OSERS/OSEP/Products/IEP_Guide/IEP_Guide.pdf].

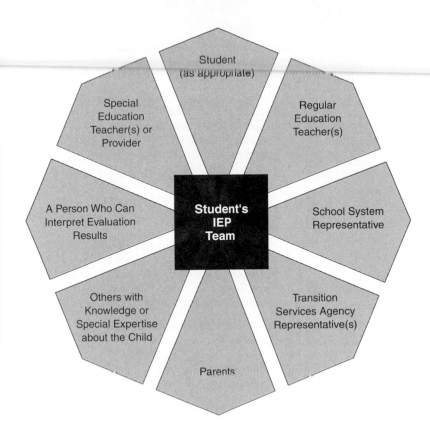

◌ FIGURE 10.5   The IEP: Purposes and Functions

The IEP is one of the most important educational documents in the education of children with disabilities. It literally constitutes a contract between the school system, the children, and parents.

* Protects children and parents by ensuring that planning will occur.

* Guarantees that children will have plans tailored to their individual strengths, weaknesses, and learning styles.

* Helps professionals and other instructional and administrative personnel focus their teaching and resources on children's specific needs, promoting the best use of everyone's time, efforts, and talents.

* Helps ensure that children with disabilities will receive a range of services from other agencies. The plan must not only include an educational component, but also specify how the child's total needs will be met.

* Helps clarify and refine decisions as to what is best for children, where they should be placed, and how they should be taught and helped.

* Ensures that children will not be categorized or labeled without discussion of their unique needs.

* Reviewed at least annually; encourages professionals to consider how and what children have learned, determine whether what was prescribed is effective, and prescribe new or modified strategies.

INDIVIDUALIZED EDUCATION PROGRAM

Student: _Amy North_   Age: _9_   Grade: _1_   Date: _Oct 17, 2001_

1. Unique Characteristics or Needs: Noncompliance
   Frequently noncompliant with teacher's instructions
   Present Levels of Performance
   Complies with about 50 percent of teacher's requests/commands
   Special Education, Related Services, and Modifications
   Implemented immediately, strong reinforcement for compliance with teacher's
      instructions (Example: "Sure I will" plan including precision requests and reinforcer
      menu for points earned for compliance, as described in *The Tough Kid Book* by Rhode,
      Jenson, and Reavis, 1992); within 3 weeks, training of parents by school psychologist
      to use precision requests and reinforcement at home.
   Objectives (including Procedures, Criteria, and Schedule)
   Within one month, will comply with teacher's requests/commands 90 percent of the
      time; compliance monitored weekly by teacher
   Annual Goals
   Will become compliant with teacher's requests/commands

2. Unique Characteristics or Needs: Reading
   2a. Very slow reading rate
   2b. Poor comprehension
   2c. Limited phonics skills
   2d. Limited sight-word vocabulary

1. Present Levels of Performance
   2a. Reads stories of approximately 100 words on first-grade reading level at
      approximately 40 words per min.
   2b. Seldom can recall factual information about stories immediately after reading them
   2c. Consistently confuses vowel sounds, often misidentifies consonants, and does not
      blend sounds
   2d. Has sight-word vocabulary of approximately 150 words

2. Special Education, Related Services, and Modifications
   2a-2c. Direct instruction 30 minutes daily in vowel discrimination, consonant
      identification, and sound blending; begin immediately, continue throughout
      school year
   2a & 2d. Sight-word drill 10 minutes daily in addition to phonics instruction and daily
      practice; 10 minutes practice in using phonics and sight-word skills in reading
      story at her level; begin immediately, continue for school year

3. Objectives (including Procedures, Criteria, and Schedule)
   2a. Within 3 months, will read stories at her level at 60 words per minute with 2 or fewer
      errors per story; within six months, 80 words with 2 or fewer errors, performance
      monitored daily by teacher or aide

(Continued)

⚭ FIGURE 10.6   Sample Excerpt from an IEP

2b. Within 3 months will answer oral and written comprehension questions requiring recall of information from stories she has just read with 90 percent accuracy (e.g., Who is in the story? What happened? Why?) and be able to predict probable outcomes with 80 percent accuracy; performance monitored daily by teacher or aide

2c. Within 3 months, will increase sight-word vocabulary to 200 words, within 6 months to 250 words, assessed by flashcard presentation

4. Annual Goals
2a-2c. Will read fluently and with comprehension at beginning-second-grade level

⌒ **FIGURE 10.6   Sample Excerpt from an IEP** *(Continued)*

The IEP plays an important role in ensuring that children receive an individualized education through a range of services that are appropriate for them. How would an IEP help teachers work collaboratively with other professionals to guarantee that children receive the services they need?

Source: D. P. Hallahan and J. M. Kauffman, Exceptional Learners: Introduction to Special Education, *8th ed. (Boston: Allyn & Bacon, 2000). Reprinted by permission.*

⌒ **FIGURE 10.7   Services That Can Be Provided to Infants and Toddlers with Special Needs**

Infants and toddlers also have special needs that can be met through these services. Meet with a special educator in your program or school district to determine specific examples of how these services are provided for young children.

* Assistive technology devices and services
* Audiology
* Family training, counseling, and home visits
* Health services
* Medical services for diagnosis or evaluation
* Nursing services
* Nutrition services
* Occupational therapy
* Physical therapy
* Psychological services
* Service coordination services
* Social work services
* Special instruction
* Speech-language pathology
* Transportation and related costs
* Vision services

  * A statement of the child's present levels of development; a statement of the family's strengths and needs in regard to enhancing the child's development; a statement of major expected outcomes for the child and family; the criteria, procedures, and timeliness for determining progress; the specific early intervention services necessary to meet the unique needs of the child and family; the projected dates for initiation of services; the name of the case manager; and transition procedures from the early intervention program into a preschool program.

Helping parents of children with disabilities is an important role of all early childhood professionals. Figure 10.8 outlines some of the things you and your program can do in this helping relationship. Chapter 12 will provide you a comprehensive program for involving and collaborating parents and families.

∽ **FIGURE 10.8   Strategies for Involving Parents of Children with Special Needs**

Parents and other family members of children with disabilities need your help and support in teaching and caring for their educational needs. These are some things you can do to ensure your involvement of parents goes well for everyone. Additional ideas for parent and family involvement are found in Chapter 12.

Source: Reaching All Families— Creating Family Friendly Schools, Office of Educational Research and Improvement, *U.S. Department of Education, 1996.*

ADMINISTRATORS CAN HELP TEACHERS AND PARENTS BY:

  * Establishing parent resource centers to help parents and teachers develop good working relationships.

  * Providing basic training to help parents understand special education and the role of the family in cooperative planning as well as offering workshops on topics requested by parents.

  * Making available up-to-date information and resources for parents and teachers.

  * Encouraging creation of early childhood and preschool screening programs and other community services that can be centered in the schools.

TEACHERS CAN:

  * Make it clear to parents that you accept them as advocates who have an intense desire to make life better for their children.

  * Provide parents with information about support groups, special services in the school and the community, and family-to-family groups.

  * Offer parents referrals to helpful groups.

  * Encourage parents to organize support systems, pairing families who can share experiences with each other during school activities.

  * Involve parents in specific projects centered on hobbies or special skills that parents can share with students in one or several classes.

  * Discuss a child's special talents with parents and use that positive approach as a bridge to discuss other issues.

Inclusive classrooms educate students with disabilities in the least restrictive educational environment. What would you say to a parent of a child without a disability who questions the idea of an inclusive classroom?

The "Programs in Action" on pages 294 and 295 offer a profile of inclusion at a Florida elementary school and a look at an early intervention program for infants and toddlers with disabilities and their families.

A CONTINUUM OF INCLUSIVE SERVICES.   A continuum of services means that a full range of services is available for children from the most restrictive to the least restrictive placements. This continuum implies a graduated range of services, with one level of services leading directly to the next. For example, a continuum of services for students with disabilities would define institutional placement as the most restrictive and a general education classroom as the least restrictive. There is considerable debate over whether providing such a continuum is an appropriate policy. Advocates of inclusion say that the approach works against developing truly inclusive programs in regular education classrooms.

Inclusive classrooms offer many benefits for children. They demonstrate increased acceptance and appreciation of diversity, develop better communication and social skills, show greater development in moral and ethical principles, create warm and caring friendships, and demonstrate increased self-esteem.

Program in Action

Alimacani Elementary School is a National Model Blue Ribbon school located in Jacksonville, Florida. The faculty, staff, and community have consistently worked together to live up to their vision that "Alimacani is a place where education is a treasure and children are inspired to reach for their dreams."

The school serves pre-K–5 students. It originally included self-contained classes for kindergarten children with varying exceptionalities. After several years of serving the youngsters using a traditional self-contained model and mainstreaming individually as appropriate, frustration ran high. Although the children with disabilities were occasional visitors to the kindergarten classes, they were never a part of the general classroom learning and social community. As our team of kindergarten teachers looked at this model of serving children, we brainstormed ideas of how to better meet the needs of individual students. After many difficult conversations, we agreed to focus on a model that would best serve the needs of all of our children. We decided to take the entire population of children with special needs and include them in regular kindergarten classes, matching children with teacher strengths.

As our vision for inclusion was first formed, we were anxious and unsure. We would have to teach with other teachers and give up ownership of children and space. All of our roles would change. We had read about the benefits of collaboration with our colleagues, but we knew that the reality of so intimate a bond would require trust, respect, a great deal of faith, and a strong sense of humor!

Despite our reservations and uncertainty, we were full of enthusiasm! Our expectations changed daily. Even our assignments changed, as we enrolled and identified a record number of kindergarten children with special needs. In partnership with parents of the children with disabilities and with parents of typically developing children, we stretched, bent, and broadened our ideas. In most cases, visitors could not identify the children with disabilities in our classrooms from their typically developing peers. They also could not always identify general education teachers from special educators. Eighteen children with a variety of special needs were included in three different kindergarten classes during that initial year, including children with Down syndrome, autism, mild physical and mental disabilities, attention deficit hyperactivity disorder, Asperger's syndrome, fetal alcohol syndrome, learning disabilities, and developmental delays.

To say that the first year was a success is an understatement. Without exception, we felt that we had done a better job of educating exceptional children than we had ever achieved in our self-contained model. We also learned that we did not have to sacrifice the many for the few. Our typically developing population of kindergartners thrived with the new responsibilities of helping their peers. As we came together to develop alternative methods of instruction for children with special needs, we found many of those same methods reaching our typically developing children. We were extremely proud of all of our kindergartners at the end of the year as they marched ahead into first grade.

Even with our own successes, we have come to believe that inclusion is not for everyone. We believe that there must continue to be an array of services to meet individual needs. We believe that we must learn to first look at the needs of our students, and then design programs and assign personnel to make learning successful.

Visit the inclusive classrooms of Dayle Timmons, Marie Rush, Kerry Rogers, and Lori Medlock on the web.

Text contributed by Dayle Timmons, Marie Rush, Kerry Rogers, and Lori Medlock of Alimacani Elementary School.

 To visit these inclusive classrooms and to complete a Program in Action activity, visit the Companion Website at *http://www. prenhall.com/morrison*, select Chapter 10, then choose the Programs in Action module.

Program in Action

BRIDGES FOR FAMILIES EARLY INTERVENTION PROGRAM

The Bridges for Families Early Intervention Program (Madison, Wisconsin) is a family-centered, community-based, birth to three years, early intervention program for infants and toddlers with disabilities and their families. The program is housed within the Waisman Center University Affiliated Program, University of Wisconsin-Madison.

The program operates from the philosophy that:

* Parents and professionals are full partners in the planning, coordination, and implementation of early intervention services.
* The overall purpose of early intervention is to support families and enhance their abilities to meet the needs of their children with special needs.
* Services in Madison need to be a collaborative effort among agencies providing early intervention services.
* An early intervention program needs to be flexible, have an array of services and parent involvement options, and continually adapt to the changing needs of families and the community.

The program is community based and offers services to approximately 250 families a year in a variety of natural environments, including, but not limited to, family homes, family day care homes/centers, child care centers, early childhood programs, and other community sites where children and their families spend their days. Bridges has eighteen staff members, some who work part time to accommodate individual preferences and family situations. Primary program staff include early childhood special education teachers, physical therapists, occupational therapists, speech and language pathologists, and social workers. At least two staff members have children with special needs, offering unique perspectives to families served by the program and insights to improve staff practices. Others such as grandparents, early childhood teachers, and child care providers are brought into the team for individual children as needed.

Parents, program staff, and other community providers work together to develop Individualized Family Service Plans (IFSPs) for each child and family. These plans summarize the goals for each child and state the types, frequency, and duration of services to be provided to each child and family and the locations where they will be provided. The plans are based on the child's developmental needs and family concerns, priorities, and resources. Service coordinators then help identify and link families with community supports and resources.

On a typical day, a teacher or therapist will make three to five different home or community visits to work directly with a child in his or her family home or child care setting. Once or twice a week, staff conduct evaluations or meet with families to develop IFSPs. Time is built into the week for team meetings focused on program development and growth, case-based problem-solving discussions, routine staff meetings, and staff supervision and support. Commitment to this time has contributed to team functioning, program outcomes, and staff morale.

Parents are actively involved in many aspects of the program. They participate on advisory boards, serve as family mentors for university students, speak at local and statewide early intervention training activities, speak at university courses, and participate in local and statewide parent leadership and support sessions.

Visit the Bridges for Families Early Intervention Program on the web.

Text contributed by Linda Tuchman, program director.

 To visit the Bridges for Families Early Intervention Program and complete a Program in Action activity, visit the Companion Website at _http://www.prenhall.com/ morrison_, select Chapter 10, then choose the Programs in Action module.

Children with Attention Deficit Hyperactivity Disorder (ADHD)

Students with **attention deficit hyperactivity disorder (ADHD)** generally display cognitive delays and have difficulties in three specific areas: attention, impulse control, and hyperactivity. To be classified as having ADHD, a student must display for a minimum of six months before age seven at least eight of the characteristics outlined in Figure 10.9.

ADHD is diagnosed more often in boys than in girls and occurs in about 20 percent of all students. About half of the cases are diagnosed before age four. Frequently, the term *attention deficit disorder* (ADD) is used to refer to ADHD, but ADD is a form of learning disorder, whereas ADHD is a behavioral disorder.

∽ **FIGURE 10.9   Types and Characteristics of Attention Deficit Hyperactivity Disorder (ADHD)**

These characteristics of ADHD will help you as you work with school psychologists and other professionals to help appropriately identify children with ADHD. Remember, a primary purpose of identification is to provide appropriate services, instruction, and programs.

Source: Reprinted with permission from the Diagnostic and Statistical Manual of Mental Disorders, *Fourth Edition. Copyright 1994 American Psychiatric Association. [Online:* http://www.cdipage.com/adhd.html].

Attention deficit hyperactivity disorder has several types, including: (1) predominantly inattentive, (2) predominantly impulsive, or (3) combined. Individuals with this condition usually have many (but not all) of the following symptoms:

Inattention
* Often fails to finish what he starts
* Is diagnosis with Attention Deficit Disorder
* Doesn't seem to listen
* Is easily distracted
* Has difficulty concentrating or paying attention
* Doesn't stick with a play activity

Impulsivity
* Often acts without thinking and later feels sorry
* Shifts excessively from one activity to another
* Has difficulty organizing work
* Speaks out loud in class
* Doesn't wait to take turns in games or groups

Hyperactivity
* Runs about or climbs on things excessively
* Can't sit still and is fidgety
* Has difficulty staying in his seat and bothers classmates
* Is excessively active during sleep
* Is always on the "go" and acts as if "driven"

Emotional Instability
* Has angry outbursts
* Is a social loner
* Blames others for problems
* Fights with others quickly
* Is very sensitive to criticism

Strategies for Teaching Children with Disabilities

For more information about inclusion, go to the Companion Website at *http://www. prenhall.com/morrison, select any chapter, then choose Topic 9 of the ECE Supersite module.*

Sound teaching strategies work well for all students, including those with disabilities. You must plan how to create inclusive teaching environments. The ideas shown in Figure 10.10 will help you teach children with disabilities and create inclusive settings that enhance the education of all students. In addition, the "Technology Tie-In: Using Assistive Technology (AT) to Help Children with Disabilities Learn" on page 299 will provide you with tips for ensuring all your students achieve and are successful.

⌾ FIGURE 10.10   Tips for Teaching Children with Disabilities

* Accentuate the positive. One of the most effective strategies is to emphasize what children can do rather than what they cannot do. Children with disabilities have talents and abilities similar to other children, and by exercising professional knowledge and skills you can help these and all children reach their full academic potential.

* Use appropriate assessment, including work samples, cumulative records, and appropriate assessment instruments. Discussions with parents and other professionals who have worked with the individual child are sources of valuable information and contribute to making accurate and appropriate plans for children.

* Use concrete examples and materials.

* Develop and use multisensory approaches to learning.

* Model what children are to do rather than just telling them what to do. Have a child who has mastered a certain task or behavior model it for others. Ask each child to perform a designated skill or task with supervision. Give corrective feedback.

* Let children practice or perform a certain behavior, involving them in their own assessment of that behavior.

* Make the learning environment a pleasant, rewarding place to be.

* Create a dependable classroom schedule. Young children develop a sense of security when daily plans follow a consistent pattern. Allowing for flexibility also is important, however.

* Encourage parents to volunteer at school and to read to their children at home.

* Identify appropriate tasks children can accomplish on their own to create in them an opportunity to become more independent of you and others.

(Continued)

Good teaching is good teaching regardless of where you teach or the children you teach. However, you will want and need to make modifications in your program and curriculum to meet the unique needs of children with disabilities. You will want to identify and use these practices that will help you successfully teach children with disabilities to their fullest potential.

Sources: **J. Burnette, "Including Students with Disabilities in General Education Classrooms: From Policy to Practice,"* The Eric Review 4 *(1996), 2–11.*

† Ibid.

‡ Ibid.

* Use cooperative learning. Cooperative learning enables all students to work together to achieve common goals. Cooperative learning has five components:

  * Positive interdependence. Group members establish mutual goals, divide the prerequisite tasks, share materials and resources, assume shared roles, and receive joint rewards.

  * Face-to-face interaction. Group members encourage and facilitate each other's efforts to complete tasks through direct communication.

  * Individual accountability/personal responsibility. Individual performance is assessed, and results are reported back to both the individual and the group. The group holds each member responsible for completing his or her fair share of responsibility.

  * Interpersonal and small-group skills. Students are responsible for getting to know and trust each other, communicating accurately and clearly, accepting and supporting each other, and resolving conflicts in a constructive manner.

  * Group processing. Group reflection includes describing which contributions of members are helpful or unhelpful in making decisions and which group actions should be continued or changed.

* Use Circle of Friends. This technique helps students develop friendships with their classmates. Classmates volunteer to be part of a student's circle, and the circle meets as a team on a regular basis. The teacher coordinates the circle and helps the group solve problems or concerns that arise. Students in the circle provide friendship and support so that no student is isolated or alone in the class.[*]

* Use Classwide Peer Tutoring (CWPT) Program. CWPT involves whole classrooms of students in tutoring activities that improve achievement and student engagement, particularly for at-risk, low-income students. Having opportunities to teach peers appears to reinforce students' own learning and motivation, according to Charles R. Greenwood, the program developer.[†]

* Develop a peer buddy system. In a peer buddy system, classmates serve as peer buddies (friends, guides, or counselors) to students who are experiencing problems. Variations are to pair an older student with a younger one who is experiencing a problem and to pair two students who are experiencing similar problems.[‡]

Technology Tie-In

USING ASSISTIVE TECHNOLOGY (AT) TO HELP CHILDREN WITH DISABILITIES LEARN

The Individuals with Disabilities Education Act (IDEA) defines assistive technology (AT) as "any item, piece of equipment, or product system, whether acquired commercially off the shelf, modified, or customized, that is used to increase, maintain, or improve functional capabilities of individuals with disabilities."[*]

Assistive technology covers a wide range of products and applications, from battery-operated toys to computer-assisted instruction. Assistive technology should be included as an important tool in your work with children with special needs. As Lou Danielson, director of the U.S. Office of Special Education's Research to Practice Division says, "Children with disabilities should have an opportunity to learn in school what other kids are learning and go on to lead productive adult lives. Technology is one of the key tools to enable that to happen. Assistive technology, including high-tech devices and low-tech devices, undoubtedly has the potential to open the door to literacy and other curricular areas for many of these students."[†]

One of your students with special needs may have trouble holding a pencil. Putting a pencil grip on her pencil makes it easier for her to hold it. The pencil grip is an example of low-tech assistive technology.

Dictionary skills are an important part of language and literacy. If a student has trouble holding and handling a dictionary, an assistive technology solution would be to use an electronic dictionary on the Internet, which also has voice pronunciation.

As this text has stressed, literacy development and learning to read are given a high priority in all grades, pre-K to 3. Children with special needs can learn to read with the help of assistive technology. Here are some programs that can help you achieve this goal.

PHONEMIC AWARENESS/EMERGENT LITERACY SKILLS

Earobics-Cognitive Concepts
Sesame Street Elmo's Reading: Preschool & Kindergarten, The Learning Company

First Phonics, SUNBURST
I Want to Read, DK Family Learning

PHONOLOGICAL DECODING

Curious George Learns Phonics, Houghton Mifflin Interactive
Let's Go Read: 1 & 2, Riverdeep & Edmark
Simon Sounds It Out–Don Johnston
Sound It Out Land Phonics Adventure, 99V

READING COMPREHENSION

Reader Rabbit's Reading Development Library, 3 & 4, The Learning Company
Reading Galaxy, Broderbund
Reading Search, Great Wave Software
Stickybear's Reading Comprehension, Optimum Resource

TALKING STORYBOOKS

Discis Books, Harmony Interactive
Disney's Animated Storybooks, Disney Interactive
EduTales, Milliken

---

[*]Lou Danielson, U.S. Office of Special Education, Research to Practice Division. [Online: http://www.ed.gov/offices/OSERS/Policy/IDEA/].

[†]M. Alexson, "Education as Commodity." www.electronic-school.com Magazine (June 2001): 27.

To locate the products listed and to complete a Technology Tie-In activity, visit the Companion Website at *http://www.prenhall.com/morrison*, select Chapter 10, then choose the Technology Tie-In module.

GIFTED AND TALENTED CHILDREN

In contrast to children with disabilities, children identified as gifted or talented are not covered under IDEA's provisions. Congress has passed other legislation specifically to provide for these children. The Jacob K. Javits Gifted and Talented Students Education Act defines **gifted and talented children** as those who "give evidence of high performance capabilities in areas such as intellectual, creative, artistic, or leadership capacity; or in specific academic fields, and who require services or activities not ordinarily provided by the school in order to fully develop such capabilities."[4] The definition distinguishes between giftedness, characterized by above-average intellectual ability, and talented, referring to individuals who excel in such areas as drama, art, music, athletics, and leadership. Students can have these abilities separately or in combination. A talented five-year-old may be learning disabled, and a student with orthopedic disabilities may be gifted.

For more information about the Gifted and Talented Students Education Act of 1999, go to the Companion Website at *http://www.prenhall.com/ morrison*, select any chapter, then choose Topic 9 of the ECE Supersite module.

Although children may not display all these signs, the presence of several of them can alert parents and early childhood professionals to make appropriate instructional, environmental, and social adjustments.

Educating the Gifted and Talented

Professionals tend to suggest special programs and sometimes schools for meeting the needs of the gifted and talented. Regular classroom teachers can provide for gifted children in their classrooms through enrichment and acceleration. Enrichment provides an opportunity for children to pursue topics in greater depth and in different ways than planned for in the curriculum. Acceleration permits children to progress academically at their own pace.

Many schools have resource rooms for gifted and talented students, in which children can spend a half-day or more every week working with a professional who is interested and trained in working with them. There are seven primary ways to provide for the needs of gifted and talented children:

1. *Enrichment classroom.* The classroom professional conducts a differentiated program of study without the help of outside personnel.
2. *Consultant professional.* A program of differentiated instruction is conducted in the regular classroom with the collaboration of a specially trained consultant.
3. *Resource room pullout.* Gifted students leave the classroom for a short period of time to receive instruction from a specially trained professional.
4. *Community mentor.* Gifted students interact with an adult from the community who has special knowledge in the area of interest.
5. *Independent study.* Students select projects and work on them under the supervision of a qualified professional.

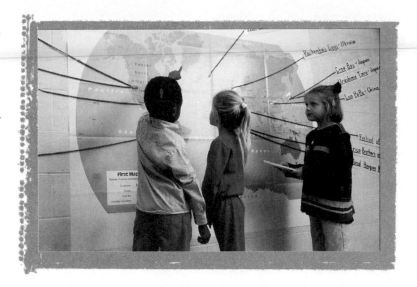

Early childhood educators must consider the diverse needs of students—including gender, ethnicity, race, and socioeconomic factors—when planning learning opportunities for their classes.

6. *Special class.* Gifted students are grouped together during most of the class time and are instructed by a specially trained professional.

7. *Special schools.* Gifted students receive differentiated instruction at a special school with a specially trained staff.[5]

Of these seven methods, the resource room pullout is the most popular. The "Program in Action" on pages 302 and 303, on University Primary School, features a gifted education program for children ages three to seven.

EDUCATION FOR CHILDREN WITH DIVERSE BACKGROUNDS

The population of the United States is changing and will continue to change. For example, projections are that by 2025, almost one-fifth of the population will be Hispanic.

The population of young children in the United States reflects the population at large and represents a number of different cultures and ethnicities. Thus, many cities and school districts have populations that express great ethnic diversity, including Asian Americans, Native Americans, African Americans, and Hispanic Americans. For example, the Dade County, Florida, school district has children from 122 countries, each with its own culture. Table 10–2 shows the proportion of minority students in the nation's ten largest school districts. As a result of changing demographics, more students will require special education, bilingual education, and other special services. Issues of culture and diversity will shape instruction and curriculum. These demographics also have tremendous implications for how you teach and how your children learn.

Program in Action

UNIVERSITY PRIMARY SCHOOL EARLY CHILDHOOD GIFTED EDUCATION PROGRAM

MISSION AND PHILOSOPHY

University Primary School is an early childhood gifted education program serving children ages three to seven. The mission of University Primary School is to provide a site for the individuals at the College of Education of the University of Illinois at Urbana-Champaign to demonstrate, observe, study, and teach best practices in early childhood and gifted education, while at the same time providing a service to the community, especially to families with young children.

The philosophy of University Primary School is that young children are best served by teaching and curriculum practices that strengthen and support their intellectual growth and development, initiate them into basic skills, challenge them to increase their proficiency in academic tasks and intellectual processes, and at the same time foster the development of their social competence.

INSTRUCTIONAL APPROACH AND CURRICULUM

The early childhood program adopted by University Primary School is based on principles of practice derived from the best available knowledge of how children grow, develop, and learn. These principles are generally accepted by the early childhood profession as appropriate to the age groups served. The basic assumption derived from developmental research is that in the early years, children learn best from active rather than passive experiences, from being in interactive rather than receptive roles in the learning context.

The curriculum is child-sensitive and responsive to individual patterns of growth, development, learning, and interests. Children have regular and frequent opportunities to work in informal groups on challenging tasks and to make decisions and choices.

The child's initiative, creativity, and problem solving are encouraged in all areas of the curriculum. By incorporating the Project Approach into the curriculum, children become actively involved in research and inquiry about topics worthy of their time and energy.

UNIQUE FEATURES OF UNIVERSITY PRIMARY SCHOOL

The daily schedule provides time for in-depth study and self-selected activities as well as small-group language arts and math instruction and an individualized reading program.

ACTIVITY TIME AND PROJECT-WORK. Activity Time and Project-Work are highly valued in our curriculum. Activity Time allows students to make choices about their own learning and provides important school time to work in their interest areas. During this

Multicultural Awareness

Multicultural awareness is the appreciation for and understanding of people's cultures, socioeconomic status, and gender. It includes understanding one's own culture. Multicultural awareness programs and activities focus on other cultures while making children aware of the content, nature, and richness of their own. The terms and concepts for describing multicultural education and awareness are shown in Figure 10.11. Review them and learn them so they become a part of your vocabulary. Learning about other cultures concurrently with their own culture enables children to integrate commonalities and appreciate differences without inferring inferiority or superiority of one or the other.

time period, teachers facilitate students' learning by building upon their ideas. Projects present learning to children in real-life contexts and integrate the acquisition and application of basic skills through inquiry modes of learning. Activity Time and Project-Work strive to foster "the love of learning" and provide an opportunity for teachers to engage in the learning with their students.

NUMERATION AND PROBLEM-SOLVING SKILLS. Math is taught with a problem-solving approach, with a focus on relating math to real-life situations using manipulatives and other concrete materials. Teachers facilitate learning in the following areas at the child's individual readiness level: conceptual skills, numeration, computation, measurement, problem solving, and geometry. Many of the student's projects will reflect integration of these mathematical skills.

LANGUAGE ARTS AND LITERACY. This program emphasizes a whole-language approach, where children learn to read by reading and to write by writing. Students are actively involved in both processes throughout the day. Importance is placed on the "making sense" process. They learn within the whole context rather than parts. Early literacy involves three reading cue systems: contextual, grammatical, and phonetic.

Teachers create a literacy-rich environment and model meaningful reading and writing.

ARTS AND AESTHETICS. The arts are integral to children's learning. Teachers guide students toward meaningful experiences in the arts with examples, materials, and cultural artifacts. Teachers promote sensitivity to and an appreciation of the environment.

SOCIAL AND EMOTIONAL GROWTH. Teachers take a proactive role in creating a classroom community that is open, honest, and accepting. To this end, discipline is designed around teachers structuring appropriate choices, students learning how to solve their own problems, and students sharing in the responsibility of developing a caring classroom community. Teachers encourage self-control and strive to develop both intellectual and emotional self-confidence.

Text contributed by Nancy B. Hertzog, Ph.D., director.

 To visit the University Primary School and complete a Program in Action activity, visit the Companion Website at *http://www. prenhall.com/morrison*, select Chapter 10, then choose the Programs in Action module.

Promoting multiculturalism in an early childhood program has implications far beyond your school, classroom, and program. Multiculturalism influences and affects work habits, interpersonal relations, and a child's general outlook on life. Early childhood professionals must take these multicultural influences into consideration when designing curriculum and instructional processes for the impressionable children they will teach. One way to accomplish the primary goal of multicultural education—to positively change the lives of children and their families—is to infuse multiculturalism into early childhood activities and practices. Guam's 2000 Teacher of the Year discusses multiculturalism and inclusion in the "Professionalism in Practice: Multicultural" on page 306.

TABLE 10–2
PROPORTION OF MINORITY STUDENTS IN THE TEN LARGEST PUBLIC SCHOOL DISTRICTS OF THE UNITED STATES

NAME OF REPORTING DISTRICT	STATE OR COMMONWEALTH	PERCENTAGE OF MINORITY STUDENTS
New York City	NY	84.5
Los Angeles Unified	CA	89.5
City of Chicago	IL	89.9
Dade County	FL	87.4
Broward County	FL	55.3
Houston ISD	TX	89.5
Philadelphia City	PA	81.6
Clark County	NV	45.7
Hawaii Department of Education	HI	79.2
Detroit City	MI	95.7

Source: U.S. Department of Education, National Center for Education Statistics, *Digest of Education Statistics 2000* (Washington, DC: Office of Educational Research and Improvement, 2000). [Online: *http://nces.ed.gov/pubs2001/digest*].

Multicultural Infusion

Multicultural infusion means that multicultural education permeates the curriculum to alter or affect the way young children and teachers think about diversity issues. In a larger perspective, infusion strategies are used to ensure that multiculturalism becomes a part of the entire center, school, and home. Infusion processes foster cultural awareness; use appropriate instructional materials, themes, and activities; teach to children's learning styles; and promote parent and community involvement.

Let's look closer at each of these practices.

FOSTER CULTURAL AWARENESS.   As an early childhood professional, keep in mind that you are the key to a multicultural classroom. The following guidelines will help you foster cultural awareness.

*   *Recognize that all children are unique.* Children have special talents, abilities, and styles of learning and relating to others. Make your classroom a place in which children are comfortable being who they are. Always value uniqueness and diversity.
*   *Get to know, appreciate, and respect the cultural backgrounds of your children.* Visit families and community neighborhoods to learn more about cultures and religion and the ways of life they engender.
*   *Infuse children's culture (and other cultures as well) into your teaching.*
*   *Use authentic situations to provide for cultural learning and understanding.* For example, a field trip to a culturally diverse neighborhood of your city or

∾ **FIGURE 10.11   Glossary of Multicultural Terms**

Knowing the terminology of the profession is important. Review these terms, become familiar with them, and use them appropriately.

The following terms will assist you as you provide bias-free and multiculturally appropriate education for your children and families.

Bias-free: Curriculum, programs, materials, language, attitudes, actions, and activities that are free from biased perceptions.

Bilingual education: Education in two languages. Generally, two languages are used for the purpose of academic instruction.

Cultural diversity: The diversity between and within ethnic groups. The extent of group identification by members of ethnic groups varies greatly and is influenced by many factors such as skin color, social class, and professional experience.

Cultural pluralism: The belief that cultural diversity is of positive value.

Culturally fair education: Education that respects and accounts for the cultural backgrounds of all learners.

Diversity: Refers to and describes the relationships among background, socioeconomic status, gender, language, and culture of students, parents, and communities.

English as a Second Language (ESL): Instruction in which students with limited English proficiency attend a special English class.

Infusion: The process of having multiculturalism become an explicit part of the curriculum throughout all the content areas.

Multicultural awareness: Ability to perceive and acknowledge cultural differences among people without making value judgments about these differences.

Multiculturalism: An approach to education based on the premise that all peoples in the United States should receive proportional attention in the curriculum.

town provides children an opportunity for understanding firsthand many of the details about how people live. Such an experience provides wonderful opportunities for involving children in writing, cooking, reading, and dramatic play activities. What about setting up a market in the classroom?

✳ *Use authentic assessment activities to assess fully children's learning and growth.* Portfolios (see Chapter 5) are ideal for assessing children's learning in non-biased and culturally sensitive ways.

✳ *Infuse culture into your lesson planning, teaching, and caregiving.* Use all subject areas—math, science, language arts, literacy, music, art, and social studies—to relate culture to children's cultures.

✳ *Be a role model by accepting, appreciating, and respecting other languages and cultures.* In other words, infuse multiculturalism into your personal and professional lives.

Professionalism in Practice

MULTICULTURALISM

Josh Ledbetter
Guam 2000 Teacher of the Year

As I enter my classroom for the first time each year, I am filled with anticipation. The excitement of meeting a new group of faces and the renewed opportunity to watch them grow, both physically and academically, is what keeps me young and anxious for that first day of school each year. To me, determining the learning style of each of my students is critically important. But just as important, and more exciting, is the discovery of what cultures my students represent. Every year I hope to have at least twenty different cultures represented as I scan my new class list. Sadly, I usually only have about ten! But every child representative of a different culture is another exciting opportunity for all of my students to learn more about the world around them.

In addition to the natural mannerisms and accent that are a part of each child's life, it is rewarding to have a variety of parents who can enhance the learning environment of my classroom by sharing their culture with my students. This sharing accomplishes many things, not the least important of which is the self-importance each child feels as his or her parents share their culture. Children get excited when their parents are the focus of attention for that day, and they quickly recognize that their parents have great respect for school and learning. Only inexperienced teachers will avoid the issue of multiculturalism. Wise teachers look on the variety of cultures in their classroom as multiple learning opportunities.

Children, like ice cream, come in many, many flavors. It is exciting to watch as my students get to sample each of their classmates' cultures and expand their world knowledge.

INCLUSION

Recently, I had the opportunity to discuss the topic of inclusion with a first-year teacher. She expressed concerns about being able to provide for children with disabilities in her classroom. I stressed with her the importance of compliance with the IEP for each student and encouraged her to examine it closely to determine what a child needed and the resources necessary to provide for her educational needs. Once that is assured, it becomes a matter of adjusting your teaching style in order to make provisions for the specific needs of every student, both those with special needs and those students who do not have specific special needs.

You see, every student has special needs. No two children are the same and, consequently, no two students learn the same way or at the same pace. Each student requires a degree of individual attention in order to ensure he or she gets an equal opportunity to learn. That must become the number one responsibility of every teacher. Unless we provide that equality of learning to every student, we are just not doing our job.

It doesn't matter who students are or what "baggage" they bring with them when they enter the classroom. Teachers have spent several years preparing for certification and, as such, have the responsibility to find a place to arrange, store, and use that "baggage" so that every student feels welcome and is fully prepared to learn.

To review the Professional Development Checklist and complete a Professionalism in Practice activity, visit the Companion Website at *http://www.prenhall.com/morrison*, select Chapter 10, then choose the Professional Development module.

All classrooms must be places where people of all cultures, races, socioeconomic backgrounds, religions, and genders are welcomed and accepted. If students learn to embrace diversity within the classroom, they will also embrace diversity outside of it.

* *Use children's experiences to form a basis for planning lessons and developing activities.* This approach makes students feel good about their backgrounds, cultures, families, and experiences.
* *Be knowledgeable about, proud of, and secure in your own culture.* Children will ask about you, and you should be prepared to share your cultural background with them.

USE APPROPRIATE INSTRUCTIONAL MATERIALS. You need to carefully consider and select appropriate instructional materials to support the infusion of multicultural education. The following are some suggestions for achieving this goal.

To review some examples of multicultural literature, go to the Companion Website at *http://www.prenhall.com/morrison*, select Chapter 10, then choose the Resources module.

Multicultural Literature. Choose literature that stresses similarities and differences regarding how children and families live their *whole* lives. Avoid books and stories that note differences or teach only about habits and customs.

Themes. Early childhood professionals may select and teach through thematic units that help strengthen children's understanding of themselves, their culture, and the cultures of others. Some appropriate theme topics are:

* Getting to Know Myself, Getting to Know Others
* What Is Special about You and Me?
* Growing Up in the City
* Growing Up in the Country
* Tell Me about Africa (South America, China, etc.)

Personal Accomplishments.   Add to classroom activities, as appropriate, the accomplishments of people from different cultural groups, women of all cultures, and individuals with disabilities.

When selecting materials for use in a multicultural curriculum for early childhood programs, make sure:

* people of all cultures are represented fairly and accurately;
* to represent people of color, many cultural groups, and people with exceptionalities;
* historical information is accurate and nondiscriminatory;
* materials do not include stereotypical roles and language; and
* there is gender equity—that is, boys and girls are represented equally and in nonstereotypic roles.

TEACH TO CHILDREN'S LEARNING STYLES AND INTELLIGENCES.   Every child has a unique learning style. Although every person's learning style is different, we can cluster learning styles for instructional purposes. The benefits of tailoring education to children's learning styles are exemplified in the "Program in Action: Brightwood Elementary School."

Different Children, Different Learning Styles.   It makes sense to consider students' various **learning styles** and account for them when organizing the environment and developing activities. "Learning style is the way that students of every age are affected by their (1) immediate environment, (2) own emotionality, (3) sociological needs, (4) physical characteristics, and (5) psychological inclinations when concentrating and trying to master and remember new or difficult information or skills."[6]

Learning styles consist of the following elements:

* Environmental—sound, light, temperature, and design
* Emotional—motivation, persistence, responsibility, and the need for either structure or choice
* Sociological—learning alone, with others, or in a variety of ways (perhaps including media)
* Physical—perceptual strengths, intake, time of day or night energy levels, and mobility
* Psychological—global/analytic, hemispheric preference, and impulsive/reflective

Figure 10.12 outlines a learning styles model developed by Rita and Kenneth Dunn, experts on how to teach to children's learning styles. This figure will provide you with many good ideas for how to teach to your children's learning styles. Teaching to children's multiple intelligences is also a good way to infuse multiculturalism into your program. Review now our discussion of multiple intelligences in Chapter 3.

Program in Action

BRIGHTWOOD ELEMENTARY SCHOOL

Brightwood Elementary School (Greensboro, North Carolina) students, who are approximately 55 percent white and 45 percent African American, were scoring in the 30th percentile in mathematics and reading. Principal Roland Andrews decided to test Brightwood's students to determine their preferred learning styles. The results of the Learning Styles Inventory showed that the majority of Brightwood's students were "low auditory" learners and highly tactual and kinesthetic. The students preferred to learn more by touching and doing than by listening.

Teachers were shown how to begin lessons with tactual resources, such as objects to pass, and kinesthetic floor games, such as sentence trains. Later, teachers would reinforce lessons through students' less preferred learning style. Additional preferences considered in the new curriculum were the time of day students learned best, their mobility needs, and their desire to work independently or in cooperative learning groups. Learning style preferences are largely the product of socialization and/or child-rearing patterns, which are strongly influenced by cultural values and practices. For example, socialization patterns for Brightwood's African American students predisposed many of them to learn better in social contexts.

After learning styles were accommodated in teaching, discipline referrals dropped dramatically, from 143 to only 6.

Student scores on the California Achievement Test rose from the 30th percentile in reading and 40th percentile in math to the 74th percentile in reading and the 77th percentile in math. Both African American and white students at Brightwood were scoring in the 93rd percentile on the California Achievement Test. These scores were higher than those of peers in other elementary schools in the district and state.

Brightwood Elementary uses the North Carolina End of Grade Testing Program. According to Sally Voelker, guidance counselor at Brightwood Elementary, students at Brightwood are still scoring at or above the North Carolina state average for elementary students.

Teachers at Brightwood do their planning in teams. As new teachers join the faculty, those who are experienced in the learning styles teaching approach assist their newer colleagues in lesson planning. The school tries to provide learning styles in-service training every three to five years for the entire staff.

The case of Brightwood Elementary indicates that when student's learning styles are taken seriously, assessed, and incorporated into how they are taught, learning improves significantly, along with student satisfaction. This case suggests that when teaching is made more congruent with student learning styles, amazing results may occur.

 To complete a Program in Action activity, visit the Companion Website at *http://www.prenhall.com/morrison*, select Chapter 10, then choose the Programs in Action module.

Howard Gardner maintains that all children possess all nine of the multiple intelligences, although some intelligences may be stronger than others. This accounts for why children have a preferred learning style; different interests, likes, and dislikes; different habits; preferred lifestyles; and preferred career choices.

In the "Professionalism in Practice: Igniting a Variety of Sparks through Brain-Compatible Learning" on pages 312 and 313, an accomplished teacher describes "brain-compatible" learning in the multicultural classrooms of schools on U.S. military bases.

ENVIRONMENTAL STIMULI PREFERENCES

Learning Style Elements

* Sound Preference: This element refers to a student's preference for background sound while learning. To what extent do you prefer silence or background noise or music while concentrating or studying?
* Light Preference: The light element refers to the level of light that is preferred while studying and learning. This element explores the extent to which a student prefers soft, dim, or bright light while concentrating and studying.
* Temperature Preference: What level of temperature do you prefer while involved in studying and/or other learning activities? Preferences on this element may vary from a cool room or a warm room while studying or engaged in various learning activities.
* Design Preference: The design element is associated with the room and furniture arrangements that the student prefers while learning. Do you prefer to study sitting in a traditional desk and chair? Or, do you like a more informal arrangement with different types of furniture, such as a couch, a reclining chair, or pillows and carpet on the floor?

EMOTIONAL STIMULI PREFERENCES

Learning Style Elements

* Motivational Preference: This element deals with the level and/or type of motivation the student has for academic learning, that is, the extent to which a student is interested in school learning. Are you self-motivated (intrinsic), motivated through interest in and contact with peers, or are you primarily motivated by adult feedback and reinforcement?
* Persistence Preference: This element relates to the student's persistence on a learning or instructional task. The persistence preference relates to the student's attention span and ability to, or interest in, staying on one task at a time. Do you have a preference for working on one task until it is finished, or do you prefer to work on a variety of tasks simultaneously?
* Responsibility Preference: To what extent do you prefer to take responsibility for your own academic learning? This element involves the preference to work independently on assignments with little supervision, guidance, or feedback. Do you prefer to work independently without an adult telling you what and how to proceed? Or, do you prefer to have frequent feedback and guidance?

SOCIOLOGICAL STIMULI PREFERENCES

Learning Style Element

* Self-Preference: The "self" element relates to your preference for working on a learning task by yourself. When working on an assignment, do you prefer to work alone or do you prefer working as a member of a group? Some students prefer working on a learning task by themselves. Others may prefer working with someone else. With other students, it may depend on the type of learning task.
* Pair Preference: This element relates to working together with one other student. Do you prefer working together with one other person as opposed to working as a member of a group? Some students may prefer working with one other student, but not with a small group of students or alone.
* Peers/Team Preference: Do you like working as a member of a team, or do you prefer to complete a learning task by yourself? This element helps determine a student's preference for working with a small group of students with a lot of interaction, discussion, and completing the task as a team. At the other end of this element is a preference to work alone.

(Continued)

⟳ FIGURE 10.12   THE DUNN AND DUNN LEARNING STYLES MODEL

* Adult Preference: How do you react to working with an authority figure? Do you like to work together with an adult and/or teacher, or do you react negatively to teacher or adult interaction during a task? This element relates to preference for interactions and guidance from an adult.
* Varied Preference: This element refers to a preference for involvement in a variety of tasks while learning. Do you like routines or patterns, or do you prefer a variety of procedures or activities while learning?

PHYSIOLOGICAL STIMULI PREFERENCES

Learning Style Elements

* Perceptual Preference: Learning by listening, viewing, or touching is the focus of this element. Do you prefer instruction and retain more information when the activities involve visual materials (viewing pictures, maps, or reading), auditory activities (listening to tapes, lectures, or music), or tactile and kinesthetic involvement such as note taking and/or working on projects that involve making things (science projects, storybooks, diaries, model building, etc.)?
* Intake Preference: The intake element is concerned with the need to eat, drink, or chew while engaged in learning activities. Do you prefer to drink something while studying, such as a soft drink or coffee? Do you prefer to chew gum? Does munching on snacks help you concentrate?
* Time Preference: This element is related to the concept of energy level at different times during the day. Do you prefer to work on a task that needs concentration in the early morning, late morning, early afternoon, late afternoon, or evening?
* Mobility Preference: Can you sit still for a long period of time as long as you are interested in what you are doing, or do you prefer to move constantly—standing, walking, changing body position? The mobility element is concerned with the extent to which you prefer to be moving your body, perhaps even unconsciously, while involved in a learning task.

PSYCHOLOGICAL STIMULI PREFERENCES

Learning Style Elements

* Global/Analytic Preference: This element relates to determining whether a student learns best when considering the total topic of study or when approaching the task sequentially—one aspect at a time. Students that have a preference for global learning are concerned with the whole meaning and the end results. They need to start with an overview of the "big picture" before they deal with elements of the whole. Students who prefer an analytic style of learning prefer to learn one detail at a time in a meaningful sequence. Once they know all the parts, they put the parts together and comprehend the "big picture."
* Hemisphericity Preference: The hemisphericity element is associated with left or right brain dominance. Left brain dominance individuals tend to be more analytic or sequential learners, while right brain dominance tends to be associated with simultaneous or global learners. This preference element overlaps with the global/analytic element.
* Impulsive/Reflective Preference: This element relates to the tempo of your thinking. Do you prefer to draw conclusions and make decisions quickly, or do you prefer to take time to think about the various alternatives and evaluate each of the possible alternatives before making a decision?

⊙ **FIGURE 10.12   THE DUNN AND DUNN LEARNING STYLES MODEL** *(Continued)*

Teaching to children's learning styles is a powerful way to enhance and promote achievement. However, it is virtually impossible to teach to all your children's learning styles at the same time. A good approach is to pick the major learning style preference for each of your children and work on ways over the school year to accommodate that style.

Source: Dunn, R. S., and Dunn K. J. (1978). Teaching Students through Their Individual Learning Styles: A Practical Approach. *Needham Heights, MA: Allyn & Bacon.*

Professionalism in Practice

IGNITING A VARIETY OF SPARKS THROUGH BRAIN-COMPATIBLE LEARNING

Millie Harris

2001 Department of Defense Education Activity Teacher of the Year

During my twenty years of teaching culturally diverse students of our nation's soldiers, I have found that children are more alike than they are different. Military schools are truly a colorless society, demonstrating that whether students are Hispanic, Asian, Native American, Caucasian, or African American, they are capable of outstanding achievement when expectations are high and instruction is effective. These students are poorer and more racially diverse than the nation's average. At least half qualify for free or reduced lunches. Two in five are either Hispanic or black, a full 10 percent above the national average. Forty percent finish the school year in a different school than where they started. Although standardized tests are not typically administered to these early childhood students, data that is available on fourth grade and above indicate that they achieve at rates far beyond those of the civilian world. Eighty percent of these students attend college, as compared to 67 percent nationwide.

The outstanding success the military has had in teaching poor, racially diverse, transient students can be attributed to several factors. Effective discipline is maintained through open communication with parents. Parents are actively involved. Technology is integrated into the curriculum. Teachers are provided ongoing training in research-based best teaching practices. Specialists and classroom teachers are also encouraged to engage in regular co-teaching and consultation, creating a community of teacher learners who work together studying, practicing, and refining best teaching practices, particularly brain-compatible learning.

As a specialist in talented and gifted education, one of the most valuable experiences I have had in sharing and learning is co-teaching with regular education teachers. I have extended the critical and creative thinking methods of gifted education into the general curriculum, while learning about effective practices from classroom teachers. Co-teaching is a powerful tool in alleviating the sense of isolation that many teachers feel. It also creates a "win-win" learning environment.

One of the most profound of these win-win experiences was one I had co-teaching with Barbara Culwell, who teaches first and second grade students at Stowers Elementary of the Fort Benning Schools. Mrs. Culwell is a strong proponent of brain-compatible learning, holding teacher training and leading study groups. She served as my mentor in my exploration of teaching children to learn effectively through the extensive neuro-research of the past ten years. I found that whatever children's cultural backgrounds may be, a universal truth is that their brains are wired in essentially the same way.

Classrooms like Mrs. Culwell's that incorporate brain-compatible learning are a far cry from many of the past, when the teacher served as the "drill and kill" dispenser of knowledge. She creates a safe learning environment in which risk taking and original ideas are valued. Her instruction technique includes skillful questioning that elicits higher order thinking. She incorporates varied learning styles and multiple intelligences into her instruction. Mrs. Culwell accommodates the physical needs of students, including water, snacks, and movement to ensure that optimal learning occurs.

Being Teacher of the 2001 Year for the Department of Defense allows me one semester of traveling and learning. I decided to revisit Barbara Culwell, a teacher who played a major role in helping me to grow.

I walk into Barbara Culwell's classroom first thing Monday. The children are working together in groups or in pairs. They seem to know what to do before the teacher gives directions. They are actively going about the business of learning.

A variety of choices, crucial to brain-based learning, are available for all the students who are arriving at different times during the thirty-minute span before the school day officially begins at 8:30. Children are engrossed in different academic computer programs, including, "How to Speak Chinese," since the class is involved in a study of the Chinese New Year. Others are busy reading their favorite books and playing thinking board games. Not a mind is idle.

A parent volunteer works at one computer rotating students testing them on books they had read during the past week. Parents' presence is crucial to classroom management and makes a distinct neural connection, bridging the importance of school and home. It is no secret that parental involvement and school success are positively correlated.

Weekly homework folders are placed on each child's desk. Every day's assignments are neatly typed for students and parents. The few needed worksheets are enclosed in the pocket folder. The children take these home on Monday and return them on Friday. Expectations are clear to every child and parent. Students develop their intrapersonal Intelligence, assessing their own academic growth.

After all the students arrive, Mrs. Culwell instructs them, "Fill up your water bottles." Dehydration is a problem that is connected to weak learning. Since the brain is made up of a higher percentage of water than any other organ, a lack of it causes a loss of attention and increased sluggishness.

The old adage, "To teach it is to learn it," is alive and well in this classroom. Students volunteer to teach others vocabulary words integrating the technology of the InFocus, which projects a computer screen onto the chalkboard, with their spelling lesson. Mrs. Culwell teaches word processing skills through questioning, "How can we make our font really big? How can we change it?" First graders are becoming adept at technology and increasing their vocabularies simultaneously.

Children practice metacognitive skills through making their own rubrics for their writing assignment with the vocabulary words. They agree a smiling face at the end means that they understood what each word means, that they wrote at least three good sentences, using words correctly in these sentences, and that they started each sentence with a capital and ended it with a period. A straight face means that they think they did well, but not perfectly. A frowning face means that they did not try or did not do well.

Mrs. Culwell instructs, "Get your thoughts clear and think of the night sky." As the youngsters begin their writing activity, soft classical Chinese music (Chinese New Year theme) plays in the background. Victoria writes, "I went outside one night. A star blazed across the sky. It was lovely. So now I know how pretty stars can be. I like stars." Use of music is priming the neural pathways so that learning is occurring, as seen in this student's exemplary writing.

After a three-minute stand-up, move-about break and a snack, Mrs. Culwell transforms the spelling, vocabulary, writing lesson into a science lesson about tips for watching the night sky, growing further dendrites for neuron connections. These youngsters are skilled at identifying numerous constellations such as Orion, Taurus, and Leo.

Later, the children practice symmetry, measurement, and following directions by making Chinese lanterns. They use manipulatives to discover the solution to the math problem of the day, displaying their problems on their own PowerPoint slides, and writing journals as to how they arrived at their answers.

At lunchtime I reflect back on a morning well spent in meaningful learning. I witnessed man-made boundaries of race, culture, and economics being broken through nature's common medium—the human brain and a teacher who cares enough to shatter old myths.

Millie Harris is a specialist in talented and gifted education in Fort Benning, Georgia.

 To review the Professional Development Checklist and complete a Professionalism in Practice activity, visit the Companion Website at *http://www.prenhall. com/morrison*, select Chapter 10, then choose the Professional Development module.

PROMOTE PARENT AND COMMUNITY INVOLVEMENT.   You will work with children and families of diverse cultural backgrounds. As such you will need to learn about the cultural background of children and families so that you can respond appropriately to their needs. For example, let's take a look at the Hispanic culture and its implications for parent and family involvement.

Throughout Hispanic culture is a widespread belief in the absolute authority of the school and teachers. In many Latin American countries it is considered rude for a parent to intrude into the life of the school. Parents believe that it is the school's job to educate and the parent's job to nurture and that the two jobs do not mix. A child who is well educated is one who has learned moral and ethical behavior.

Hispanics, as a whole, have strong family ties, believe in family loyalty, and have a collective orientation that supports community life. They have personalized styles of interaction, a relaxed sense of time, and a need for an informal atmosphere for communication. Given these preferences, a culture clash may result when Hispanic students and parents are confronted with the typical task-oriented style of most American teachers.

Whereas an understanding of the general cultural characteristics of Hispanics is helpful, it is important not to overgeneralize. Each family and child is unique, and care should be taken not to assume values and beliefs just because a family speaks Spanish and is from Latin America. It is important that you spend the time to discover the particular values, beliefs, and practices of the families in the community.

In addition to having Hispanic children in your classroom or program, chances are you will also have children from one of the many Asian-American family subgroups. Asian Americans now represent one of the fastest growing minority populations in the United States.

It is always risky to generalize about peoples and their cultures. When we do we make generalizations about ethnic groups that compromise the domain of Asian Americans, we run the risk of assuming that the generalization applies to all groups. It may not. In addition, we always have to consider individual children and families, regardless of their cultural background. With this in mind, some broad generalizations about Asian Americans and values that influence the rearing and education of children include the following: a group orientation as opposed to an individual orientation, the importance of family and family responsibilities, emphasis on self-control and personal discipline, educational achievement, respect for authority, and reverence for the elderly.[7] Think about how you can respond to each of these values as you read the "Program in Action" about the Chinese American International School of San Francisco.

Program in Action

THE SCHOOL: DESCRIPTION AND PHILOSOPHY

The Chinese American International School of San Francisco was established by a multiethnic group of parents, educators, and civic leaders. It remains the nation's only full-time school from prekindergarten through eighth grade offering instruction in English and Mandarin Chinese as equal languages in all subjects.

The school's mission emphasizes fluency in both English and Mandarin Chinese, internationalism, intellectual flexibility, and the development of character, emotional, and social maturity as a foundation for active participation and leadership in the modern world.

No prior Chinese language knowledge is necessary for children to enter the program. Children of every ethnicity are enrolled in the school, with 95 percent of the families speaking no Mandarin Chinese at home.

The program is a 50/50 "foreign language immersion" program whereby all subjects in the curriculum are taught in and through Chinese Mandarin. Chinese Mandarin is an equal language of instruction and communication with English, and not simply the object of study itself, as in traditional foreign language classes.

Parents gravitate to this program for several different reasons: Asian Americans of second, third, or fourth generation seek an education with a link to their cultural and historical heritage; international business professionals want their children to enjoy the advantage of fluency in the language and culture; families who have studied research results send their children to the school for the social and cognitive benefits of bilingual education.

THE PREKINDERGARTEN AND KINDERGARTEN CHILDREN

Entering students in prekindergarten are immediately immersed in both English and Mandarin Chinese so that by the completion of kindergarten they have developed basic proficiency in both languages. Each class is taught by an English teacher and a Chinese teacher with the help of teaching assistants. All teachers are native speakers of the language they use for instruction.

The English kindergarten curriculum uses the Montessori method, allowing careful attention to each child's developmental level and individual learning style. Through lessons and everyday life skill experiences, the children develop a fine sense of order and enhanced ability to concentrate, following a complex sequence of steps. Hands-on learning materials make abstract concepts clear and concrete. Along with the opportunity to explore, it teaches them to be independent, responsible, caring individuals.

The Chinese prekindergarten and kindergarten curriculum provides similar opportunities for the children to grow and learn. It focuses on social interaction skills and respect for others as the children acquire listening and speaking skills in the foreign language. The Chinese immersion curriculum is concrete, multisensory, hands-on, and project oriented. A science class on flotation, for example, would require children to test and record flotation of real objects, enabling them to learn the objects' names as well as to express concepts related to flotation in the Chinese language.

In a typical school day, children will sing dramatized songs, produce art and craft projects, play games, listen to stories, and familiarize themselves with some written characters. The teacher uses Chinese exclusively, making use of movements, facial expressions, voice inflections, pictures, toys, and a myriad of props to ensure comprehension and participation. Children are allowed to demonstrate their understanding in multiple ways.

Together, the Chinese and English teachers in the prekindergarten programs encourage children to organize, hypothesize, explore, invent, discover, and test their experiences. An emphasis is placed on the development of each child's creativity, concentration, initiative, self-confidence, self-discipline, imagination, and love of learning. This lays the foundation for a challenging elementary school curriculum that emphasizes both oral and written communication in the two languages.

THE ELEMENTARY CURRICULUM

In elementary school, science, social studies, language arts, and mathematics share equal prominence in both the English and Chinese classes. In a 50/50 bilingual immersion program, students spend half a day in an English classroom, learning in much the same way as students in a monolingual school would do. Then, in the second part of the day, they will enter a different classroom, filled with Chinese writing and media. They then study subjects from the Chinese teacher, just as they did in the morning, but expressing themselves in Chinese. On the following day, the model reverses itself, beginning with Chinese in the morning and English in the afternoon.

Close coordination between the English and the Chinese teachers allows the development of common themes for study materials and cultural celebrations. Teachers reinforce—but do not repeat or translate—each other's activities. For instance, while the Chinese teacher assumes the responsibility for the celebration of Chinese festivals such as Chinese New Year, the English teacher leads the celebration of American holidays like Thanksgiving. In the course of the celebrations, children can learn language and content simultaneously. Besides immersion in the culture, they acquire second-language vocabulary through cooking, costume designing, and dramatization of events.

PROFESSIONAL DEVELOPMENT

Current enrollment in the new San Francisco Civic Center campus has grown to four hundred students, with most grade levels incorporating multiple sections. The earliest graduates of the Chinese American International School are now enrolled in universities throughout the United States, most continuing their Chinese studies. Alumni in high school regularly serve as counselors and aides during the school's summer session. Summer sessions also serve as training periods for new faculty who work closely with a master/mentor teacher for several years before assuming full curricular responsibility.

The growing interest in teaching Chinese language at all age levels, and in the elementary curriculum in particular, led to the development of a separate unit of the school devoted to teacher training and curricular development. The Institute for Teaching Chinese Language and Culture is supported by two national foundations in its role as the creator of a graduate training program in the CAIS immersion methodology. The elementary school serves as the laboratory practicum for teachers coming for training from throughout the United States and Asia.

Visit the Chinese American International School on the web.

_____

Text contributed by teacher Juliana Carnes and principal Shirley Lee.

 To visit the Chinese American International School and to complete a Program in Action activity, visit the Companion Website at *http://www.prenhall.com/morrison,* **select Chapter 10, then choose the Programs in Action module.**

ACTIVITIES FOR PROFESSIONAL DEVELOPMENT

In this chapter we have stressed the importance of providing for children's special needs, whatever those needs may be. Refer again to the "Professional Development Goal" at the beginning of the chapter, the "Professional Development Checklist" on pages 20 and 21, and the "Professionalism in Practice" features on pages 306, 312, and 313. After you have reviewed these, complete the following exercises.

1. Visit a classroom or program where children with special needs are included, and observe the children during play activities. You can develop an observational checklist based on guidelines provided in Chapter 5. Follow a particular child and note the materials available, the physical arrangement of the environment, and the number of other children involved. Try

to determine whether the child is really engaged in the play activity. Hypothesize about why the child is or is not engaged. Discuss your observations with your colleagues.

2. Visit an early childhood special education classroom and a regular preschool classroom and compare how their methods for guiding children's behavior are similar and different.

3. Visit several public schools and ask to review either IEPs or IFSPs. How are these plans meeting the needs of children and families? What are some services that you think are unique about each plan?

4. How is curriculum and instruction in a class for gifted and talented students different from that in other classes? Get permission to visit and observe such a class. Then compare that class with others you have observed or experienced. On the basis of your observations, describe how you might teach a student who is gifted and talented within your inclusive classroom.

5. How does a teacher modify the classroom environment, classroom routines, learning activities, student groupings, teaching strategies, instructional materials, assessments, and homework assignments to meet all students' special needs? What human and material resources for successful inclusion are available to teachers and to students with special needs? How do students show social acceptance for their classmates with special needs? Visit an inclusive classroom and take notes on what you observe. Compare and discuss your observations with classmates who have visited different settings across all grade levels.

6. Effective educational programs provide children with opportunities to develop an understanding of other persons and cultures. List ways for how you would accomplish the following objectives in your classroom:

   a. Provide children with firsthand, positive experiences with different cultural groups.

   b. Help children reflect on and think about their own cultural group identity.

   c. Help children learn how to obtain accurate information about other cultural groups.

7. Select ten children's books that have multicultural content. Decide how you would use these materials to promote awareness and acceptance of diversity. Read these books to children and get their reactions.

For additional chapter resources and activities, visit the Companion Website at *http://www.prenhall.com/morrison,* select Chapter 10, then choose the Professional Development, Resources, or Linking to Learning modules.

FOCUS QUESTIONS

1. Why is it important to help children guide their own behavior?

2. What are important elements in helping children guide their behavior?

3. Why is developing a philosophy of guiding children's behavior important?

4. What can I do now to develop the knowledge and skills to successfully help children guide their behavior?

chapter 11

Guiding Children's Behavior

HELPING CHILDREN ACT THEIR BEST

To review the chapter focus questions online, go to the Companion Website at *http://www.prenhall.com/ morrison* and select Chapter 11.

PROFESSIONAL DEVELOPMENT GOAL

I understand the principles and importance of behavior guidance. I guide children to be peaceful, cooperative, and in control of their behavior.

A glance at daily newspapers tells volumes about the crises of violence and crime facing children and society. Consider these news headlines:

* "Santee Is Latest Blow to Myth of Suburbia's Safer Schools," *New York Times,* March 9, 2001
* "Violence Is Down, but Some Areas Still Suffer," *New York Times,* January 11, 2001
* "The Columbine Tapes," *Newsweek,* December 20, 1999

These headlines paint a pretty grim picture. Local and national news media underscore public and professional interest in children's behaviors at home, on the streets, and in early childhood programs. The public sees children, at very young ages, being mean and nasty to their peers and adults. Young children are victims of violence and violence is being perpetrated by children at younger ages than ever before.

Who is to blame? Parents receive their share. The public believes parents have the responsibility for rearing their children well and with the manners and morals necessary for civilized living. The public also blames the educational system for allowing and even promoting uncivilized behavior. Schools are accused of not managing children's behavior and not teaching them the manners, morals, and behavior necessary for living in civilized society. Parents and the public look to early childhood professionals for assistance in helping children learn how to live cooperatively and civilly in a democratic society.

HOW TO GUIDE CHILDREN'S BEHAVIOR

Guiding children's behavior is a process of helping children build and use positive behaviors. It involves **behavior guidance,** a process by which all children learn to control and direct their behavior and become independent and self-reliant. In this view, behavior guidance is a process of helping children develop skills useful over a lifetime. They learn to plan, monitor, and guide their own thinking, feeling, and behavior.

To check your understanding of this chapter with the online Study Guide, go to the Companion Website at *http://www.prenhall.com/ morrison,* select Chapter 11, then choose the Study Guide module.

How can professionals achieve these goals? Effective guidance of children's behavior at home and in early childhood programs consists of the twelve essential steps shown in Figure 11.1. Review these twelve steps now as preparation for our discussing each of them. Using these twelve steps will help you become an accomplished professional. Let us now take a closer look at each of these twelve essential steps in guiding children's behavior.

Step 1: Clarify Your Beliefs

The first rule in guiding children's behavior is to know your attitudes about guiding children's behavior. A good way to do this is to develop a philosophy about

FIGURE 11.1 A Twelve-Step Basic Approach to Guiding Children's Behavior

You have a responsibility to help children learn how to become well behaved and responsible. These steps will help you achieve this goal.

Step 1.	Clarify your beliefs about child guidance.
Step 2.	Know developmentally appropriate practice.
Step 3.	Meet children's needs in individually and culturally appropriate ways.
Step 4.	Help children build new behaviors and skills of independence and responsibility.
Step 5.	Establish appropriate expectations.
Step 6.	Arrange and modify the environment so that appropriate, expected behavior and self-control are possible.
Step 7.	Model appropriate behavior.
Step 8.	Avoid creating or encouraging behavior problems.
Step 9.	Develop a partnership with parents, families, and others who are responsible for children.
Step 10.	Recognize, value, and support teachers', parents', and children's basic rights.
Step 11.	Teach cooperative living and learning.
Step 12.	Teach and use conflict management.

Guiding children's behavior consists of essential guidelines, including helping children build new, appropriate behaviors and helping them to be responsible for their behaviors. Why is it important for children to learn to guide their own behavior rather than having teachers and parents always tell them what to do?

what you believe concerning child rearing, guidance, and children. Reviewing the information on how to develop your philosophy of education in Chapter 1 will help you do this. Knowing what you want for your children at home and school helps you decide what to do and how to do it. Knowing what you believe also makes it easier for you to share with parents, help them guide behavior, and counsel them about discipline. Take a few minutes now and write a paragraph titled "My Basic Beliefs about Discipline." This will help you get started on clarifying your beliefs.

Step 2: Know Developmentally Appropriate Practice

The foundation for guiding all children is to know what they are like—how they grow and develop. Knowing child development is the cornerstone of developmentally appropriate practice. Children cannot behave well when adults expect too much or too little of them based on their development or when they expect them to behave in ways inappropriate for them as individuals. Thus, a key for guiding children's behavior is to *really know what they are like.* This is the real meaning of developmentally appropriate practice. You will want to study children's development and observe children's behavior to learn what is appropriate for all children and individual children based on their needs, gender, and culture.

Step 3: Meet Children's Needs

A major reason for knowing children and child development is so that you will be able to meet their needs. Abraham Maslow felt that human growth and development was oriented toward self-actualization, the striving to realize one's potential. Review Maslow's hierarchy in Chapter 3 and consider how children's physical needs, safety and security needs, belonging and affection needs, and self-esteem needs culminate in self-actualization. An example of each of these needs will illustrate how to apply them to your guiding children's behavior.

PHYSICAL NEEDS.   Children's abilities to guide their behaviors depends in part on how well their physical needs are met. Children do their best in school, for example, when they are well nourished. Parents and schools should provide for children's nutritional needs by giving them breakfast. Recent brain research, discussed in Chapter 2, also informs us that the brain needs protein and water to function well. Many teachers encourage children to drink water throughout the day, and they also provide frequent nutritional snacks.

SAFETY AND SECURITY.   Just as teachers can't teach in fear, children can't learn in fear. Children should feel comfortable and secure at home and at school. Consider also the dangers many children face in their neighborhoods, such as crime, drugs, and violence, and the dangers they face at home, such as abuse and neglect. Part of guiding children's behavior includes providing safe and secure communities, neighborhoods, homes, schools, and classrooms. For many children your class-room may be their only haven of safety and security. In addition, you may need to assume a major role of advocacy for safe communities.

BELONGING AND AFFECTION. Children need love and affection. Love and affection needs are satisfied when parents hold, hug, and kiss their children and tell them, "I love you." Teachers meet children's affectional needs when they smile, speak pleasantly, are kind and gentle, treat children with courtesy and respect, and genuinely value each child. Today, many children are starving for affection and recognition. For these children you may be their sole or main source of affectional needs.

SELF-ESTEEM. Children who view themselves as worthy, responsible, and competent feel good about themselves and learn better. Children's views of themselves come from parents and early childhood professionals. Experiencing success gives children feelings of high self-esteem. It is the responsibility of parents and teachers to give all children opportunities for success. Success and achievement are the foundations for self-esteem.

SELF-ACTUALIZATION. Children want to do things for themselves and be independent. Teachers and parents can help children become independent by helping them learn to dress themselves, go to the restroom by themselves, and take care of their environments. They can also help children set achievement and behavior goals ("Tell me what you are going to build with your blocks") and encourage them to evaluate their behavior ("Let's talk about how you cleaned up your room"). Self-actualization is a process of becoming all you can be, and we want this goal for all children. The following "Professionalism in Practice" on pages 324–326 discusses strategies teachers can use to set achievement and behavior goals for gifted students within the regular classroom.

Helping children become more independent by warmly supporting their efforts is one of the most effective forms of guidance. Identify some ways you and other professionals can support children's efforts to do things for themselves.

Professionalism in Practice

HELPING GIFTED CHILDREN THROUGH INTRINSIC MOTIVATION

Susan Winebrenner
Author and Consultant

It may shock you to know that of all the students in mixed-abilities classrooms, those who are at greatest risk of learning the least during a regular school year are those at the top in academic ability. Although this condition has always been present in our schools, it has been greatly exacerbated by the national attention to raising the achievement levels for students scoring below expected standards. Many teachers pay much less attention to students who can easily score well on state and standardized tests or who are getting high grades. It is assumed that those factors indicate that real learning is taking place. If we define learning as one's forward progress during the present year's curriculum, we can appreciate the significant problems faced by gifted students at all grade levels.

Charter schools and home schooling movements have given frustrated parents of high-ability learners affordable options to remove their children from public schools. To prevent a wholesale exodus of gifted students from public schools, teachers should be offering regular opportunities for students who need differentiation to move beyond the curricular parameters. When schools promise that "all kids can learn," gifted students should also be able to reap the benefits of that promise. This vignette summarizes several field-tested, teacher-friendly strategies that all teachers can use to ensure that their gifted students are gaining at least one year in achievement every year they are in school.

LESS PRESSURE ON PERFECTION: CONSISTENT OPPORTUNITIES FOR STRUGGLE AND CHALLENGE

Students who get high grades with little or no effort conclude that smart means easy. The longer their effortless success continues, the more likely they are to resist challenge when it comes because they fear it will send a message that they are not really smart after all. They may conclude from their experience that teachers, parents,

and peers expect them to be perfect at all times. Risk-taking behavior will be diminished.

Teachers and parents must help these students value hard work when learning. Encouragement to try things that do not come easily can help students reconnect with intrinsic motivation. Teachers' willingness to work with these students during their struggle, rather than expecting them to learn all things easily, can give courage to those who may have lost it.

Further, teachers need to recognize that some behavior and productivity problems may reflect a lack of appropriate challenge and/or the fear of not always being the perfect student.

CURRICULUM COMPACTING IS THE ESSENTIAL MOTIVATOR

Compacting describes the process of reducing the amount of time gifted students need to spend on the regular curriculum by allowing them to demonstrate what they already know and providing them with alternate learning activities so they can move forward in their own learning. We can compact the content, and we can compact the pacing.

Gifted students may resist compacting opportunities if they perceive there will be more work for them to do, or that their grades will be lower than if they did the regular class work. Explain to the students how it will be "safe" for them to participate in the compacting.

Teachers may worry that students who are not eligible for compacting may feel badly about that. When all students are doing challenging work, when compacting opportunities are open to everyone, and when all students are encouraged to work on extension activities from time to time, resentment is less likely to occur.

Students who are experiencing compacting are expected to follow what I call the "Three Simple Rules" at all times. When working on something different than other students:

1. Don't bother anyone, including the teacher when she is with other students.
2. Don't call attention to yourself or the fact that you are doing something different than the regular work—it's no big deal.
3. Do the work you choose to do.

COMPACTING THE CONTENT

1. Identify the learning objectives or standards all students must learn in an upcoming chapter or unit.
2. Plan a menu of extension activities related to the content being studied that incorporates more depth and complexity.
3. Ask all students to take a few minutes to examine the upcoming content to assess the degree to which they believe they already know it.
4. Offer a pretest to volunteers who believe they can demonstrate mastery of the upcoming curriculum.
5. Eliminate all review, drill, and practice for students who demonstrate mastery. This includes review work for state tests.
6. On days when you are teaching what students have mastered, allow them to work instead on extension activities they have chosen from the menu you prepared. Always allow room for their independent choices, with your approval.
7. On days when you are teaching what students have not mastered, they are expected to participate in the direct instruction lesson and activities.

COMPACTING STRATEGY: MOST DIFFICULT FIRST

Prepare a menu of extension activities related to the unit concepts but which requires more depth and complexity from the students.

1. Any time you have given a directed lesson and are assigning practice items, decide which five items are the most difficult in the entire set.
2. Tell all class members that any person who completes the most difficult items first (before the other items), and gets no more than one wrong, is done practicing for that day and does not need to continue the practice for homework. The most difficult first should be completed before the end of class. You may correct the work yourself or provide an answer key.
3. Students must maintain an average of 90 percent or higher in this particular subject area to continue to be eligible for most difficult first.

Remember: The grade that is recorded for the student is only what describes their ability with the grade level work. If you grade the extension activities and that leads to lower grades, students will decide to end their participation in these compacting opportunities.

Careful records must be kept of which students experience compacting and on which extension activities they work. By the second half of second grade and up, teachers can show students how to do the record keeping themselves.

COMPACTING THE PACING

When the content cannot be pretested because it is new to students, we can compact the pacing by allowing them to move through the new content at a faster pace than their classmates. This allows them to spend a significant amount of time during the unit to work on topics related to the regular content but which extend the curriculum into areas the teacher does not have time to include for all students. The areas in which this strategy works best are science, social studies, more sophisticated math concepts, and/or thematic integrated units in any subject area.

(Continued)

Professionalism in Practice

1. Prepare two lists of content topics, one containing no more than ten concepts you expect all students to master by the end of the unit. The second list contains topics you would like to include but are unable to for lack of time or other resources.

2. Create a study guide that includes only the key concepts. Gifted students will use that guide to learn the essential concepts of the unit while you are teaching them directly to the other students.

3. Use the second list of topics to create an Extensions Menu. Use a nine-grid Tic-Tac-Toe graphic, and leave the center section open for STUDENT CHOICE.

4. Students who are maintaining a B average or higher, who feel the pace chosen for the class is slowing down their learning, and who enjoy independent study are good candidates for this method. They take the same quizzes and tests on the same date the whole class takes them, but spend part of their unit time becoming a "resident expert" on one topic they have selected from the menu.

5. At the end of the unit, these students share a progress report with their classmates, documenting what they have learned.

6. Although students' grades for the unit could come just from the assessments, they may earn a grade for their independent study as long as the expectations for what they have to do to earn that grade are carefully agreed upon before work begins on the project topic. It's perfectly all right if they don't complete their project; they may wish to continue to work on it during the next unit. Remember that they will receive a

study guide for that unit, so they will be as accountable as all other students for learning the key concepts. It's also all right if the student chooses to change to a new topic for the next unit.

7. Students are expected to sign an Independent Study Agreement that carefully explains the teacher's expectations for work quality and behavior.

8. At regular intervals, invite the whole class to choose topics from the extension menu so they too can do project work that many may enjoy immensely.

INDEPENDENT STUDY ON TOPICS OF PERSONAL INTEREST

Students who always complete their compacted work quickly may be interested in working on an independent study project on a topic in which they have a passionate interest. This topic does not necessarily have to be related to the regular school curriculum. Ask the student and his parents for topic suggestions.

CONCLUSION

In order for gifted students to be challenged in mixed-ability classes, it is imperative for them to spend considerable time working on tasks that provide challenge and interest for them. This vignette has described several strategies teachers can use to facilitate exciting learning for their gifted students.

Reference: Susan Winebrenner, Teaching Gifted Kids in the Regular Classroom *(Minneapolis: Free Spirit Publishers, 2000).*

 To review the Professional Development Checklist and complete a Professionalism in Practice activity, visit the Companion Website at *http://www.prenhall.com/morrison*, select Chapter 11, then choose the Professional Development module.

Step 4: Help Children Build New Behaviors

For strategies preschoolers can use to get along with others, go to the Companion Website at *http://www.prenhall. com/morrison*, select Chapter 11, then choose the Linking to Learning module to connect to the National Network for Child Care site.

Helping children build new behaviors means that you help them learn that they are primarily responsible for their own behavior and that the pleasures and rewards for appropriate behavior are internal, coming from within them as opposed to always coming from outside (i.e., from the approval and praise of others). This concept is known as **locus of control,** the source or place of control. The preferred and recommended locus of control for young children is internal.

The process of developing an internal locus of control begins at birth, continues through the early childhood years, and is a never-ending process throughout life. We want children to control their own behavior. When their locus of control is external, children are controlled by others; they are always told what to do and how to behave. In addition, we want children to take responsibility for their behavior. What we want to avoid is having children blame their behavior on others ("Chandra took my pencil") or on circumstances ("I didn't have time"). Legitimate excuses are appropriate, but always blaming others or external events is not. Learning to do it right and trying again after a failure are other important positive behaviors.

Affirming and acknowledging children's appropriate behaviors is a good way to build new behaviors. Figure 11.2 provides examples on how to do this.

Helping children learn new behaviors and change or modify old behaviors is also an important part of guiding children's behavior. Figure 11.3 outlines some things you can do to help children learn new behaviors that support their efforts to develop and use responsible behaviors.

Responsible choices and support are key ways to help children develop responsible behavior that internalizes their locus of control. Helping children with behavior and emotional problems learn to take control of and guide their own behavior can be a challenge. One source of help is KidTools Support System, which is the focus of this chapter's "Technology Tie-In" on page 329. Review the program now to see how it works.

Step 5: Establish Appropriate Expectations

Expectations set the boundaries for desired behavior. They are the guideposts children use in learning to direct their own behavior. Like everyone, children need guideposts along life's way.

Teachers and parents need to set high and appropriate expectations for children. When children know what to expect, they can better achieve those expectations. Up to a point, the more we expect of children, the more and better they achieve. Generally, we expect too little of children and ourselves.

Verbal (praise)

"I like the way you . . ."	"Wow!"	"Excellent."	"Good job!"
"Great!"	"Way to go."	"Fantastic."	"Tremendous!"
"Right on!"	"Super!"	"Awesome!"	"Beautiful."
"Cool."	"Terrific."	"You're working hard."	

Nonverbal

Facial	*Gestures*	*Proximity*
Smile	Clapping of hands	Standing near someone
Wink	Waving	Shaking hands
Raised eyebrow	Forming an okay sign (thumb + index finger)	Getting down on child's level
	Victory sign	Hugging, touching
	Nodding head	Holding child's arm up
	Shrugging shoulders	

Social (occur in or as a result of social consequences)

Parties

Group approval

Class privileges

∞ **FIGURE 11.2   Ways of Affirming and Acknowledging Children's Behavior**

Everyone likes to be praised and affirmed for a job well done, good efforts, and their best work. Here are some ways you can apply affirmation to your teaching of young children.

---

* *Give children responsibilities.* All children, from an early age, should have responsibilities—that is, tasks that are their job to do and for which they are responsible.

* *Give children choices.* Children like to have choices, and choices help them become independent, confident, and self-disciplined. Learning to make choices early in life lays the foundation for decision making later. Guidelines for giving children choices are as follows:

    * *Give children choices when there are valid choices to make.* When it comes time to clean up the classroom, do not let children choose whether they want to participate, but let them pick between collecting the scissors or the crayons.

    * *Help children make choices.* Rather than say, "What would you like to do today?" say, "Sarah, you have a choice between working in the woodworking center or the computer center. Which would you like to do?" When you do not want children to make a decision, do not offer them a choice.

* *Support children.* Support children in their efforts to be successful. Arrange the environment and make opportunities available for children to be able to do things.

∞ **FIGURE 11.3   Helping Children Build New Behaviors**

Responsibilities, choices, and support are key ways to help children develop responsible behavior that internalizes their locus of control.

Technology Tie-In

HELPING KIDS HELP THEMSELVES—ELECTRONICALLY

Every classroom and early childhood program has children with emotional and behavioral disabilities. Working with these children can be just as challenging as working with children with physical disabilities. One source of help comes from Virtual Resource Center in Behavioral Disorders at the University of Missouri-Columbia. They have developed the KidTools Support System, a three-part software package designed to help children use self-management skills in school settings and take responsibility for their own behavior.

The first program, First Step KidTools for ages seven to ten, consists of tool templates with colorful graphics, text with audio directions, and automatic record-keeping capabilities. Gail Fitzgerald, who helped develop the program, says, "Often teachers attempt to control children's behavior without really involving them in that decision-making process. The focus was to take control from the teachers to children so that they could develop self-control."* You can review information about Kid-Tools online.

*M. Axelson, "Education as Commodity," www.electronic-school. com Magazine, (June 2001): 23.

To review information about KidTools and to complete a Technology Tie-In activity, visit the Companion Website at *http://www.prenhall.com/morrison*, select Chapter 11, then choose the Technology Tie-In module.

For more information about guiding children's behavior, go to the Companion Website at *http://www.prenhall.com/morrison*, select Chapter 11, then choose the Linking to Learning module to connect to the Virginia Cooperative Extension site.

The following are some things you can do to promote appropriate expectations.

SET LIMITS. Setting limits is closely associated with establishing expectations and relates to defining unacceptable behavior. Setting clear limits is important for three reasons:

1. Setting limits helps you clarify in your own mind what you believe is acceptable, based on your knowledge of child development, children, their families, and their culture.
2. Limits help children act with confidence because they know which behaviors are acceptable.
3. Limits provide children with security. Children want and need limits.

As children grow and mature, the limits change and are adjusted to developmental levels, programmatic considerations, and life situations. Knowing what they can and cannot do enables children to guide their own behavior.

DEVELOP CLASSROOM RULES. Plan classroom rules from the first day of class. As the year goes on, you can involve children in establishing classroom rules, but in the beginning, children want and need to know what they can and cannot do. For example, rules might relate to changing groups and bathroom routines. Whatever rules you establish, they should be fair, reasonable, and appropriate to the children's age and maturity. Keep rules to a minimum; the fewer the better.

Classroom environment is one of the most important factors that enables children to develop and use appropriate behavior. The classroom should belong to children, and their ownership and pride in it makes it more likely that they will act responsibly.

Step 6: Arrange and Modify the Environment

Environment plays a key role in children's ability to guide their behavior. Arrange the environment so that it supports the purposes of the program and makes appropriate behavior possible. Appropriate room arrangements signal to children that they are expected to guide and be responsible for their own behavior and enable teachers to observe and provide for children's interests. Also, it is easier to live and work in an attractive and aesthetically pleasing classroom or center. We all want a nice environment—children should have one, too. The guidelines shown in Figure 11.4 can help you think about and arrange your classroom to support children as they guide their own behavior. Figure 11.5 also identifies characteristics of classrooms that support children as they learn how to guide their own behavior.

Step 7: Model Appropriate Behavior

Telling is not teaching. Actions speak louder than words. Children see and remember how other people act. Modeling plays a major role in helping children guide their behavior.

FIGURE 11.4 How to Arrange the Classroom to Support Positive Behavior

Use these guidelines to create a classroom or other environment that will help children do their best and be their best.

* Have an open area in which you and your children can meet as a whole group. This area is essential for story time, general class meetings, and so on. Starting and ending the day with a class meeting provides an opportunity for children to discuss their behaviors and suggest ways they and others can do a better job.

* Create center areas that are well defined and accessible to children and have appropriate and abundant materials. Make center boundaries low enough so that you and others can see over them for proper supervision and observation.

* Provide for all kinds of activities, both quiet and loud. Try to locate quiet areas together (reading area and puzzle area) and loud centers together (woodworking and blocks).

* Locate materials so that children can easily retrieve them. When children have to ask for materials, this promotes dependency and can lead to behavior problems.

* Establish a system so that materials are easily stored, and so that children can easily put them away. A rule of thumb is that there should be a place for everything and everything should be in its place.

* Provide children with guidelines for how to use centers and materials.

* Make the classroom a rewarding place to be. It should be comfortable, safe, and attractive.

* Provide opportunities for children to display their work.

FIGURE 11.5 Basic Features of Classrooms That Support Guidance and Self-Regulation

Classroom arrangement and atmosphere play an important part in supporting children's efforts to control their behavior. Making sure your classroom has these basic features will benefit all children.

* Community and a culture of caring.
* Clear expectations and high expectations.
* Consistent behavior from teachers and staff. They model appropriate behavior and expect it of children.
* Open communication between:
    * children-children;
    * teacher-children;
    * children-teacher;
    * teacher-parents; and
    * parents-teacher.
* Sufficient materials to support learning activities.
* A belief shared by all staff that children can and will learn. The teachers also believe they are good teachers.
* Routines established and maintained.
* A balance between cooperation and independent learning.
* An atmosphere of respect and caring.
* A partnership between teachers and children.

You can use the following techniques to help children learn through modeling:

* *Show.* For example, show children where the block corner is and how and where the blocks are stored.

* *Demonstrate.* Perform a task while students watch. For example, demonstrate the proper way to put the blocks away and how to store them. Extensions of the demonstration method are to have children practice the demonstration while you supervise and to ask a child to demonstrate to other children.

* *Model.* Modeling occurs when you practice the behavior you expect of the children. Also, you can call children's attention to the desired behavior when another child models it.

* *Supervise.* Supervision is a process of reviewing, insisting, maintaining standards, and following up. If children are not performing the desired behavior, you will need to review the behavior. You must be consistent in your expectations of desired behavior. Children will soon learn they do not have to put away their blocks if you allow them not to do it even once. Remember, you are responsible for setting up the environment that enables children's learning to take place.

You can also model and demonstrate social and group-living behaviors, including using simple courtesies (such as saying "please," "thank you," and "you're welcome") and practicing cooperation, sharing, and respect for others.

Step 8: Avoid Problems

It's easy to encourage children's misbehavior. Often teachers expect perfection and adult behavior from children. If you focus on building responsible behavior, there will be less need to solve behavior problems. The "Program in Action" on pages 333–335 profiles the successes of a school employing the positive discipline philosophy.

Ignoring inappropriate behavior is probably one of the most overlooked strategies for guiding children's behavior. Some early childhood professionals feel guilty when they use this strategy. They believe that ignoring undesirable behaviors is not good teaching. Ignoring some inappropriate behavior can be an effective strategy, but it must be combined with positive reinforcement of desirable behavior. Thus, you ignore inappropriate behavior and at the same time reinforce appropriate behavior. A combination of positive reinforcement and ignoring can lead to desired behavior.

When children do something good or are on task, reward them. Use verbal and nonverbal reinforcement and privileges to help ensure that the appropriate behavior will continue. Review the affirmations listed in Figure 11.2. Catch children being good; that is, look for good behavior. This helps improve not only individual behavior, but group behavior as well.

Program in Action

When Grapevine (Texas) Elementary School opened, its staff had a vision. This vision emphasized the desire to encourage all learners to be responsible, intrinsically motivated, and self-directed in an environment of mutual respect. As we looked for a discipline management system that fit this philosophy, we recognized that we needed one that emphasized personal responsibility for behavior and cooperation instead of competition and that focused on developing a community of supportive members. We also discovered that we held several beliefs in common that should be the foundation for our discipline management plan:

1. All human beings have three basic needs: to feel connected (the ability to love and be loved), to feel capable (a sense of "I can" accomplish things), and to feel contributive (I count in the communities in which I belong).
2. Natural and logical consequences for poor choices encourage responsible behavior. Punishment, on the other hand, encourages rebellion and resentment.
3. Children can be creative decision makers and responsible citizens when given opportunities to direct the processes that affect the day-to-day environment in which they live.

Our desire was, and is, to address the needs of the whole child as we educate our children to be responsible citizens.

ADOPTING THE DISCIPLINE PLAN

After much research and deliberation, we, as a faculty and staff, decided to implement "Positive Discipline" as a discipline management system. The training of the staff occurred during the summer before the school opened. As we studied the book *Positive Discipline in the Classroom,* by Jane Nelsen, Lynn Lott, and Stephen Glenn, teachers spontaneously began to discuss several rituals that normally occur in school routines that did not seem to fit the philosophy of the environment we were attempting to create. One of these was the

concept of "rules." Teachers decided to establish a set of "Grapevine Star Responsibilities" in place of the more traditional concept of rules:

* I will be responsible for myself and my learning.
* I will respect others and their property.
* I will listen and follow directions promptly.
* I will complete my classwork and homework in a quality manner.

Furthermore, we decided that rewards—whether in the way of stickers, pencils, or award ceremonies—were not, on the whole, consistent with encouraging intrinsic motivation and the belief that all children should continuously monitor their own learning and behavior. Rather, reward for success should be based on what children find personally significant. Reward should come from within as children and classes celebrate achievement of personal and class goals.

In the summer before school began, teachers discussed the understanding that they should be role models. We understood that the decision to implement Positive Discipline would require a change in thinking and a change in behavior for teachers. Teachers would have to change from the role of arbitrator/referee to mediator; they would become facilitators of decision-making sessions instead of "general in command"; and they would have to consistently challenge themselves to think in terms of consequences instead of punishment. Instead of demanding, they would encourage self-evaluation by students. For example, teachers might ask, "What would responsible second grade behavior look like in this situation?" Teachers knew that the atmosphere of caring they created in their classrooms would determine whether their classrooms would build or hinder the development of community within each class and, in a larger context, the school.

ENGAGING STUDENTS

Throughout the course of the year, students set goals each six-week period (usually one academic goal and one behavioral goal) and conferred with their teachers

(Continued)

Program in Action

at the end of the six weeks to determine the extent of their achievement toward that goal. At the end of our first year, students participated in a celebration of achievement. Each student chose the goal that held the most personal significance and received a certificate that detailed the goal. The principal read each chosen goal in grade-level celebrations as the student walked across the stage and shook hands with the principal. One second grader chose a goal that included developing two new friendships; a third grader chose a goal that reflected learning all of his multiplication facts; a kindergartner expressed delight in overcoming his fear of the class pet, a rat! Teachers, parents, and students all enjoyed this ceremony, which emphasized the worth of each individual and that learning was, and is, the ultimate goal of education and school (as opposed to a grade or series or marks on a report card).

Class meetings are the cornerstone of Positive Discipline. The format of a class meeting is forming a circle, giving compliments, and addressing items that students or teachers have placed on the agenda. In the primary grades, agenda items include problems that students are having with one another or a teacher, decisions the class has to make, and concerns that the teacher might have. Before a class can begin to have meetings, children must begin to develop a basic understanding of the difference between consequences and punishment. Teachers must practice with their students skills such as active listening, the use of "I-messages," and brainstorming solutions to problems.

One of the most amazing and critical parts of a class meeting is the compliment time at the beginning. Children are encouraged to compliment others for specific actions or character traits, not the generic, "I like Joan because she is my friend." In any Grapevine Elementary kindergarten class, one could observe children as they pass a stuffed animal around the circle (whoever holds the stuffed animal is the speaker) and compliment one another with statements such as, "Thanks, Tim, for helping me pick up all the crayons I dropped this morning." If indeed the deepest craving of every soul is the need to be appreciated, this part of the class meeting proves magical. Children beam as their classmates compliment them. We often note that children who normally are left out become the target of compliments by responsible, caring leaders in the class without any prompting from teachers. This part of the class meeting is beneficial in and of itself because it encourages the atmosphere in which children can feel they are connected, capable contributors!

Problems identified by students and teachers are addressed in the meeting's agenda section. Each teacher has his own individualized method for developing a class agenda. In kindergarten, the children draw pictures on a class tablet to remind them of what the problem is; in second grade, children write the problem on a slip of paper and place it in the agenda box. The focus during the agenda section of the class meeting is on addressing problems and finding solutions, not placing blame or punishing. When the school year began, it was not unusual for children to suggest that others be "sent to the principal" for some act of unkindness or lack of responsibility. Gradually, children became extremely creative and often decided on solutions that astounded teachers.

In one third grade class, the children were having a continual problem with one student who was using inappropriate language and embarrassing students. They took turns telling this boy how his language and behavior was making them feel. The boy began to cry quietly. Rather than stopping the process, the children continued. When everyone had a turn at sharing, they each walked by the young boy, touched him gently on the knee or shoulder and told him something they appreciated about him and how glad they were that he was in the class. The boy's behavior changed, and the students were empowered by taking responsibility for communicating respectfully and for helping a fellow classmate.

Irene Boynton, a mixed-age (K–1) teacher, notes that a great deal of teaching and work is required to make class meetings successful. She takes time to brainstorm feeling words because children often get stuck on the words good and bad. Role playing is used successfully in her class meetings to focus on issues such as pushing in line and "bothering" other students. Occasionally, she will purposefully tailor a cooperative learning activity immediately before a class meeting so that everyone can discuss issues of cooperation in the meeting itself while the experiences are fresh in the students' minds. Mrs. Boynton comments that Positive Discipline allows children to experience the rewards of feeling confident and healthy about making respectful, responsible choices because it is the "right" thing to do, not because they will receive something for their choice.

THE BENEFITS

At Grapevine Elementary, it took children a while to move past wanting the teacher to make decisions for them, as had been done in the past, toward an understanding that they had the skills to solve their own problems. Now teachers consistently respond that the use of class meetings encourages children to be responsible for personal problem solving. When asked by a child to referee or arbitrate, they are often able to respond with, "Have you tried to work it out yourselves?" or, "Is this something that you need to place on the class agenda?" Tattling, too, has decreased dramatically as we continue to emphasize the difference between tattling and important telling and the use of "I-Care" language.

Kindergarten teacher Carol Matthews believes that class meetings are an excellent tool for teaching problem solving. Meetings encourage children to talk about their own feelings and to be aware of the feelings of others. For her, seeing children carry skills outside the classroom is exciting. A mother of one of her students once told Mrs. Matthews that her daughter responded in an interesting way when she and some other girls were squabbling over how to accomplish a task during an Indian Princess camp out, declaring, "C'mon you guys, we've got to solve this problem ourselves." The children went off to the side and talked through the problem without help from an adult. The process empowers children!

Teachers at Grapevine Elementary, when asked to comment on Positive Discipline, say such things as, "Is there any other way to teach?" and, "We would never go back to playing referee again!" Students no longer ask, "What am I going to get?" in response to a request to go the extra mile for another student or while working on a project. They are developing respect for themselves and for the rights and needs of others. The skills learned in class meetings extend into academic areas, where we find that students are becoming more thoughtful, introspective, self-motivated, and effective problem solvers. We believe that we are fostering a safe, respectful community where children and adults thrive together in an atmosphere of mutual respect.

Text contributed by Nancy Robinson, Grapevine Elementary, Grapevine, Texas. For more detailed information on implementing positive discipline, refer to Positive Discipline in the Classroom, *by Jane Nelsen, Lynn Lott, and H. Stephen Glenn (Roseville, CA: Prima Publishing, 2000). Our implementation of this program was based on teachers' understanding of the book and other programs, not from direct training from any of the authors.*

 To visit the Grapevine Elementary School and complete a Program in Action activity, visit the Companion Website at *http://www.prenhall.com/morrison,* select Chapter 11, then choose the Program in Action module.

Social relationships play a powerful role in children's and teachers' everyday behaviors. Teachers must promote positive child-child and teacher-child relationships. What are some things you can do to promote positive social relationships in your classroom or program?

Step 9: Develop a Partnership with Parents, Families, and Others

Involving parents and families is a wonderful way to gain invaluable insights about children's behaviors. Some things you can do to collaborate with parents on guiding children's behaviors are these:

For more information about working with families, go to the Companion Website at *http://www.prenhall.com/ morrison*, select any chapter, then choose Topic 10 of the ECE Supersite module.

* Share your philosophy of guiding behavior with parents.
* Share classroom rules and expectations with parents.
* Hold meetings for and with parents and share with them the information in this chapter and how to apply it to their learning how to guide children's behavior in the home.
* Always be available in person or on the phone to discuss with parents questions or concerns they might have about their children's behavior.

Chapter 12 provides many helpful ideas to use in your collaboration with parents.

Step 10: Recognize and Value Basic Rights

Everyone involved in the process of education has basic rights that need to be recognized and honored. When this happens, guiding behavior is easier for everyone. Figure 11.6 lists these basic rights. Consider now how you can and will honor them.

Step 11: Teach Cooperative Living and Learning

You can do a lot to promote cooperative living in which children help each other direct their behavior. Recall from Chapter 3 our discussion of Vygotsky's theory of

FIGURE 11.6 Children's, Teachers', and Parents' Rights That Support Positive Behavior

When everyone's basic rights are respected, it is easier to guide and direct children's behavior. In addition, everyone "wins" in such a process.

Children's Rights

Children have these rights in classrooms designed to promote self-regulation:

✳ To be respected and treated courteously

✳ To be treated fairly in culturally independent and gender-appropriate ways

✳ To learn behaviors necessary for self-guidance

✳ To have teachers who have high expectations for them

✳ To learn and exercise independence

✳ To achieve to their highest levels

✳ To be praised and affirmed for appropriate behaviors and achievements

✳ To learn and practice effective social skills

✳ To learn and apply basic academic skills

Teachers' Rights

✳ To be supported by administration and parents in appropriate efforts to help children guide their behavior

✳ To have a partnership with parents so that they and their children can be successful in developing appropriate behavior

✳ To be treated courteously and professionally by peers and others

Parents' Rights

✳ To share ideas and values of child rearing and discipline with teachers

✳ To be involved in and informed about classroom and school discipline policies

✳ To receive periodic reports and information about their children's behaviors

✳ To be educated and informed about how to guide their children's behavior

social relations. Children are born seeking social interactions, and social relations are necessary for children's learning and development. Peers help each other learn.

Children's natural social groups and play groups are ideal and natural settings in which to help children assist each other in learning new behaviors and being responsible for their own behavior. The classroom as a whole is an important social group. Classroom meetings in which teachers and children talk can serve many useful functions. They can talk about expected behaviors from day to day ("When we are done playing with toys, what do we do with them?"), review with children what they did in a particular center or situation, and help them anticipate what they will do in future situations ("Tomorrow morning when we visit the Senior Citizen Center . . ."). In all these situations, children are cooperatively engaged in thinking about, talking about, and learning how to engage in appropriate behavior.

Program in Action

OVERVIEW AND GOALS OF THE INITIATIVE

Early childhood educators and other helping professionals share a concern over the increasing number of young children who have problems with aggression and out-of-control behaviors. The Early Childhood Mental Health Initiative, a state-of-the-art pilot program funded by a grant in rural southern Ohio, is aimed at helping these youngsters ages three to five to develop appropriate social behaviors and coping skills, such as anger management and problem solving, early on that will serve them well throughout their lives.

By reducing the number of young children who have problems with aggression and out-of-control behaviors, we hope to reduce the risk that these children will eventually be placed in the juvenile justice system or into expensive residential treatment centers. We also hope this program can help decrease the use of medications designed to control young children's behavior.

The Early Childhood Mental Health Initiative is the result of collaboration between the Pickaway County Head Start Program, the Scioto Paint Valley Community Mental Health Center, and the parents and children who participate in the program. We hope this community collaboration model between Head Start programs, mental health center staff, and families can be fostered and adopted elsewhere as standard best practice in the future.

SPECIFIC OBJECTIVES

* To enhance Head Start educators' knowledge and application of family systems theory, an approach that focuses on changing family interaction patterns to help families break out of problem cycles.
* To build partnerships with parents of children who are at risk for the development of early childhood aggression issues and to offer expertise in mental health interventions for very young children and their families.
* To determine what works in the area of prevention and intervention with childhood aggression and out-of-control behaviors.

PROGRAM STRUCTURE

The program has three parts: Head Start teacher training, social skills development for children, and a parent training group. Professionals lead teacher training sessions once a month throughout the school year and are also available to consult with teachers and parents on an as-needed basis. The children meet in a classroom environment to work on social skills once a week for ten consecutive weeks. The parent training group meets once a week for ten consecutive weeks as well.

Parent Group and Children's Group. The parenting group and the social skills classroom consultation for children purposely address the same subject matter. The parenting group is strategically held prior to the children's social skills classroom consultation group. Parents are asked to observe (from behind a two-way mirror in the classroom) mental health consultants in collaboration with Head Start teachers as they educate the children about anger management skills, impulse control techniques, and interpersonal problem-solving skills. Parents are emphatically encouraged to practice the skills they learn in group sessions and to reinforce at home what the consultants and teachers at school are teaching their children.

One particularly successful strategy for reducing impulsive and aggressive behavior in young children and increasing their level of social competence is the use of puppets that engage in interactive role play with the children. Based on the Second Step Pre-K curriculum kit authored by the Committee for Children (1997), these role plays teach problem identification, problem-solving steps, feeling identification, empathy skills, and impulse control. The puppets' names are Impulsive Puppy and Slow Down Snail. An example of teaching impulse control can be seen in Slow Down Snail's regular refrain "slow down, stop, and think." Slow Down Snail's refrain teaches the difference between impulsive actions and thinking through a problem.

An example of a role play that might occur is as follows:

Start with Puppy barking and Snail inside its shell.

Teacher: Impulsive Puppy, why are you barking? I thought you wanted to play with Slow Down. Slow Down won't come out if it's noisy.

Puppy: (Whispers in your ear.)

Teacher: (To class) Impulsive Puppy says he doesn't know how to be quiet. He wants you to teach him. Would you like to teach Impulsive Puppy how to bark more quietly?

(Coach children to bark quietly. Recognize quiet barkers.)

Puppy: Barks quietly like children.

Teacher: (Quietly to class) Do you think Impulsive Puppy is doing a good job? (Children respond.)

Teacher: (Quietly) Look, it's working. Slow Down is coming out.

Snail: Slow down, stop, and think. (Hugs Puppy.)

Puppy: Puppy wags tail and pants with happiness.

Teacher: Very good, Puppy. You deserve a pretend doggy biscuit for that one. (Have children feed Puppy.)

We found that the use of puppets greatly enhances the children's retention of fundamental concepts and strategies.

Teacher Training. Teacher training includes general information about childhood aggression and case studies of specific young children who are exhibiting aggressive and out-of-control behavior in the classroom. We emphasize a family systems approach to assist teachers in forming collaborative partnerships with families, caregivers, and other professionals in the development of intervention and prevention strategies. We also discuss the identification of emotional disorders in early childhood and accessing mental health services.

EARLY RESULTS

Head Start teachers report a reduction in the number of aggressive episodes in the classroom and a stronger sense of partnership between teachers and parents. Head Start parents praised this program and even asked if they could continue the weekly parenting training groups over the summer.

One Head Start parent states, "This program has greatly benefited my daughter and me. My daughter is now able to communicate her feelings and tells me what her problem is rather than impulsively lashing out in frustration."

Contributed by Chris Fraser, Licensed Independent Social Worker (LISW) and Certified Sports Counselor (CSC).

 To complete a Program in Action activity, visit the Companion Website at *http://www.prenhall.com/morrison*, select Chapter 11, then choose the Programs in Action module.

In addition, you can initiate, support, and foster a cooperative, collaborative learning community in the classroom in which children are involved in developing and setting guidelines and devising classroom and, by extension, individual norms of behavior. Teachers "assist" children but do not do things for them, and they ask questions that make children think about their behavior—how it influences the class, themselves, and others. This process of cooperative living occurs daily. Discussions grow out of existing problems, and guidance is provided based on the needs of children and the classroom.

Step 12: Use and Teach Conflict Management

Quite often, conflicts result from children's interactions with others. Increasingly, teachers advocate teaching children ways to manage and resolve their own conflicts.

Teaching conflict resolution strategies is important for several reasons. First, it makes sense to give children the skills they need to handle and resolve their own conflicts. Second, teaching conflict resolution skills to children enables them to use these same skills as adults. Third, the peaceful resolution of interpersonal conflicts contributes, in the long run, to peaceful homes and communities. Children who are involved in efforts to resolve interpersonal behavior problems peacefully and intuitively learn that peace begins with them. The Early Childhood Mental Health Initiative, featured in the "Program in Action" on pages 338 and 339, exemplifies effective methods of teaching young children and their families about anger management and problem solving. Strategies used to teach and model conflict resolution include those in Figure 11.7.

 To review information about KidTools and to complete a Technology Tie-In activity, visit the Companion Website at *http://www.prenhall.com/morrison*, select Chapter 11, then choose the Technology Tie-In module.

As we have emphasized in this and other chapters, cognitive and social development and behavioral characteristics are interconnected. More early childhood teachers recognize that it does not make sense to teach children reading, writing, and arithmetic and not also teach them skills necessary for responsibly guiding their own behavior. The "Technology Tie-In" on page 329 discusses a program for helping children with emotional and behavioral disabilities to learn self-management skills.

ACTIVITIES FOR PROFESSIONAL DEVELOPMENT

In this chapter we have emphasized the twelve steps involved in helping children guide their behavior. Review the "Professional Development Goal" at the beginning of this chapter, the "Professional Development Checklist" on pages 20 and 21, the "Program in Action" on pages 338 and 339, and the "Professionalism in Practice" on pages 324–326. After you have reviewed these for ideas, complete the following exercises.

1. Observe a primary classroom and identify aspects of the physical setting and atmosphere that influence classroom behavior. Can you suggest improvements?

⚭ **FIGURE 11.7 Helping Children Resolve Conflicts**

Peaceful living begins in homes and classrooms. You can share these guidelines with parents so they can support your efforts to help children live and learn in peaceful and loving classrooms.

✳ *Talk it over.* Children can learn that talking about a problem often leads to a resolution and reveals that there are always two sides to an argument. Talking also helps children think about other ways to solve problems. Children should be involved in the solution of their interpersonal problems and classroom and activity problems.

✳ *Model resolutions.* You can model resolutions for children: "Erica, please don't knock over Shantrell's building because she worked hard to build it"; "LaShawn, what is another way (instead of hitting) you can tell Marisel that she is sitting in your chair?"

✳ *Teach children to say, "I'm sorry."* Saying "I'm sorry" is one way to heal and resolve conflicts. It can be a step toward good behavior. Children need to be reared in an environment in which they see and experience others apologizing for their inappropriate actions toward others.

✳ *Do something else.* Teach children to get involved in another activity. Children can learn that they do not always have to play with a toy someone else has. They can get involved in another activity with a different toy. They can do something else now and play with the toy later. Chances are, however, that by getting involved in another activity they will forget about the toy for which they were ready to fight.

✳ *Take turns.* Taking turns is a good way for children to learn that they cannot always be first, have their own way, or do a prized activity. Taking turns brings equality and fairness to interpersonal relations.

✳ *Share.* Sharing is good behavior to promote in any setting. Children have to be taught how to share and how to behave when others do not share. Children can be helped to select another toy rather than hitting or grabbing. Again, keep in mind that during the early years children are egocentric, and acts of sharing are likely to be motivated by expectations of a reward or approval such as being thought of as a "good" boy or girl.

2. In this chapter you learned twelve steps for guiding children's behavior. Although they are all important, rank order the twelve in importance to you. Your first choice will be 1, your second, 2, and so on.

3. List five behaviors you think are desirable in toddlers, five in preschoolers, and five in kindergartners. For each behavior, give two examples of how you would encourage and promote development of that behavior.

4. Interview five parents of young children to determine what they mean when they use the word *discipline*. What implications might these definitions have for you if you were their children's teacher?

For additional chapter resources and activities, visit the Companion Website at *http://www.prenhall.com/morrison*, select Chapter 11, then choose the Professional Development, Resources, or Linking to Learning modules.

FOCUS QUESTIONS

1. Why is collaboration between parents, families, and the community important?

2. What are the benefits of collaborating with parents, families, and the community?

3. How can you encourage and support programs for collaboration with families and communities?

4. How can I conduct an effective parent/family collaboration program?

chapter 12

Cooperation and Collaboration with Parents, Families, and the Community

BUILDING A PARTNERSHIP FOR STUDENT SUCCESS

To review the chapter focus questions online, go to the Companion Website at *http://www.prenhall.com/ morrison* and select Chapter 12.

 # PROFESSIONAL DEVELOPMENT GOAL

COLLABORATING WITH PARENTS AND COMMUNITY

I am an advocate on behalf of children and families. I treat parents with dignity and respect. I involve parents, families, and community members in my program and help and encourage parents in their roles as their children's primary caregivers and teachers.

*O*ne thing we can say with certainty about the educational landscape today is that parents, families, and communities are as much a part of the educational process as are children, teachers, and staff. At no time in U.S. educational history has support for family and community been so high. The involvement of families and communities is critical for student success. For this reason, let's consider some of the reasons why parent, family, and community involvement in education is so important. In addition, we will examine practical and useful ways you can conduct a high-quality, effective program of parent, family, and community involvement.

REDEFINING PARENT INVOLVEMENT

For more information about family-school relations, go to the Companion Website at *http://www.prenhall.com/ morrison*, select any chapter, then choose Topic 10 of the ECE Supersite module.

Current accountability and reform movements that we discussed in Chapter 2 have convinced families that they should no longer be kept out of their children's schools. Families believe their children have a right to effective, high-quality teaching and care. Parents have become more militant in their demands for high-quality education. Schools and other agencies have responded by seeking ways to involve families in this quest for quality. Educators and families realize that mutual cooperation is in everyone's best interest. As a result, parent involvement has changed in these important ways:

* Schools and other agencies are expected to involve and collaborate with parents and families in significant ways. In addition to using traditional ways of involving parents in fund-raising and children's activities, schools are now involving parents in decisions about hiring new teachers, school safety measures, and appropriate curriculum to help ensure that all children learn.

* Today, a major emphasis is on increasing student achievement. One of the best ways to do this is through involving parents in at-home learning activities with their children. As a result, educators expect that parents will be involved in the education of their children both at home and at school. Parent involvement is, now more than ever, a two-way street—from school to home and from home to school.

* Parent involvement may mean that while teachers work with parents to help children learn, they also have to teach parents how to work with their children. Review again our discussion of family-centered teaching in Chapter 1.

* Parents, families, and the community are now viewed as the "owners" of schools. As one parent said to me, "I don't consider myself a visitor at school. I'm an owner!" Teacher Paula McCullough shares how she helps parents take ownership of their children's education in order to increase student achievement. Her "Professionalism in Practice: Home and School: An Unbeatable Team—Together Everyone Achieves More" on pages 346 and 347 will help you get children excited about learning.

Changing Families, Changing Involvement

For more information about changing families, go to the Companion Website at *http://www.prenhall.com/ morrison*, select Chapter 12, then choose the Linking to Learning module.

The family of today is not the family of yesterday, nor will the family of today be the family of tomorrow. More children live in single-family homes than ever before. In addition, more young mothers are entering the workforce. Many children, as early as six weeks, are spending eight hours a day or more in the care of others. Working parents are turning their young children over to others for care and spending less time with their children. Parents and other family members need more help with rearing children. As a result, opportunities have blossomed for child-serving agencies, such as child care centers and preschools, to assist and support parents in their child-rearing efforts. Over the next decade additional programs will provide more parents with child development and child-rearing information and training.

Grandparents as Parents

Since the early 1990s, more grandparents are raising their grandchildren than ever before in American history. Four million children, or 5.5 percent of all children under age eighteen,[1] are living in homes maintained by grandparents. In addition, many of these children are "skipped generation children," meaning that neither of their parents is living with them. Reasons for the increases in the number of children living with grandparents include drug use, divorce, mental and physical illness, teenage pregnancy, child abuse and neglect, and incarceration.

Grandparent parents have all of the parenting responsibilities of parents. This includes providing for their basic needs and care as well as making sure that their

Grandparents acting as parents for their grandchildren are a growing reality in the United States today. What are some things you can do to ensure that grandparents will have the educational assistance and support they need so that their grandchildren will be successful in school?

Professionalism in Practice

HOME AND SCHOOL: AN UNBEATABLE TEAM—TOGETHER EVERYONE ACHIEVES MORE

Paula McCullough

USA Today All-USA Teacher Team 2001

My philosophy of teaching is very simple: it is to teach the whole individual child, not a subject. Each child is unique, with different strengths and weaknesses, different likes and dislikes. To achieve my goal, I must form a partnership with the home. By working together, we can build a team whose mutual goal is the educational success of the child.

My role in this team is to create a school atmosphere where all students can achieve. I believe in using a conservative developmental approach. Education starts with the child's strengths and weaknesses. It is a waste of time and energy and harmful to the child's self-concept to give a child an armful of grade level basals and expect him to perform if he cannot read on grade-level. Therefore, I backtrack and give the child material on his instructional/interest level. Individualized instruction and material are made available to help promote growth of his self-image. A child on the other end of the spectrum also needs to be given material to match her needs. She does not need to be "bored" with education by having to do work that is below her capabilities. To meet these needs, I try to individualize whenever possible.

A strong relationship needs to exist between the school and home in order for the child to get the best education possible. This "unbeatable team" is established through communication. This communication needs to be varied, timely, and honest. Proper communication is the primary tool that allows me to motivate parents to find the necessary time to work with and support their child's education. To this end, I use weekly newsletters, phone calls, notes home, weekly homework bags, parent conferences/meetings, and parent volunteers.

Communication begins with information. I send out a weekly newsletter to inform my parents of "current events" in our classroom. Included in the newsletters are weekly progress reports, a list of spelling words, current areas of study, and special events/dates. I also include helpful tips on learning, such as how to help their child study spelling words, how to encourage reading for enjoyment and comprehension, or what games to play at home to practice reading/math skills.

To encourage a two-way communication between home and school, a place for comments is included in the newsletters. Individual notes are sent home and phone calls made when needed. Sometimes it is necessary to keep parents informed on a daily basis about their child's progress, behavior, and/or work habits. This is done by sending home a daily note that is signed by the parent and returned to school. I have found it helpful to write these notes on a carbonless copy message book so that I always have a copy (for those times when the student conveniently does not make it home with the note). By using different forms of communication that are ongoing and interactive, my parents are well informed of their child's progress, classroom policies/procedures, curriculum goals, and ideas on how best to help their child succeed at school. Honest, two-way communication allows us to work together to resolve problems and concerns.

Homework bags are sent home each week. Each bag contains a worksheet to practice the skills (math/reading) taught in class, a practice reader, a reading activity, and a parent response form. The homework bags become increasingly more difficult as the student advances in abilities.

A variety of reading activities is included to keep students excited about learning. The reading activities are determined by the lesson and the practice reader enclosed in the homework bag. They include games (board games, teacher-made folder games, card games, etc.), art projects (with the materials included), writing projects (a suitcase with a variety of writing materials), and simple cooking recipes.

These homework bags encourage parent-child interaction as they work together on the same skills that are covered at school. The parents have first-hand experience in watching the academic growth of their child and discovering their child's weaknesses and strengths. The child gets to practice needed skills in a safe, warm environment with the added bonus of parental approval.

The parent response form is an interactive communication tool between home and school. Parents can relate problems, successes, and concerns to me. This keeps everyone informed on the child's progress.

The homework bags have been a success. Several parents have told me that the whole family plays the games together, sometimes even an imaginary friend named Sonic. One dad even made a copy of a folder game and changed the cards to help an older sibling who was having difficulty. The games give the parents a fun, nonstressful way to interact with their children while at the same time helping them to succeed at school.

In my district, we encourage parents to visit our school as often as they can. We have regularly scheduled visits with open house and parent-teacher conferences. At these times, I set up a display board outside my classroom to encourage parents to read with their child at home. Handouts and brochures are provided with helpful game ideas for parents to do at home. I also put out books for parents to check out, such as Lee Canter's *What to Do When Your Child Hates to READ: Motivating the Reluctant Reader.* (I have even had parents from other rooms stop by and pick up literature or ask a question.)

At the first of the year, an additional meeting is held for my parents. The purpose of this Parent Night is to explain classroom procedures and how first graders learn to read and solve math problems. The parents are supplied with handouts on activities they can do at home to improve math and reading skills. I do not assume the parents are knowledgeable about how to help their child at home. I conduct a mini-lesson on the parents' role in teaching children to read. I model for them how they should guide their children when reading together by asking predicting questions, discussing cause/effect, using context clues, etc. At the end of the meeting, parents are given the opportunity to ask questions concerning their children's education. This gives me the opportunity to clarify any concepts or activities I had not clearly explained. Usually the questions asked need to be heard by the entire group. Parents realize that everyone has some

of the same concerns: getting a reluctant child to read, homework hassles, improving weak math/reading skills, and challenging high achievers. Parents see that they are not alone in their child's educational journey.

Every year, I recruit parent volunteers to become involved in my class. These "helping hands" are used to encourage my students to develop skills and/or interests. Parents listen to my students read, play games with them, help individual students learn math facts or spelling words, make learning centers, and aid students in creating art projects. The use of parent volunteers helps to strengthen the relationship between school and home. It also makes parents more aware of the importance their role plays in the education of children.

Different ways to bridge the gap between school and family/community need to be found. I started a PALS (People Always Love Stories) program in my classroom. Every Friday a "pal" (parent, grandparent, community leader, etc.) visits my classroom to read a favorite book. Having other adults share their love of reading helps to promote the public's understanding of the importance of reading to children. This also provides an excellent opportunity for children to observe the pleasure that reading gives to other adults, not only their teacher.

Through the use of a variety of activities, I am able to get parents involved in their child's education. If both members of the team—parents and teacher—meet their educational responsibilities, an unbeatable team is formed with the same goal in mind—*children excited about learning.*

Paula McCullough is a transitional first grade teacher at Lakehoma Elementary, Mustang, Oklahoma.

 To review the Professional Development Checklist and complete a Professionalism in Practice activity, visit the Companion Website at *http://www.prenhall.com/morrison*, **select Chapter 12, then choose the Professional Development module.**

grandchildren do well in school. Grandparent parents will need support and educational assistance to achieve this goal. This is where you can help grandparent parents learn to parent all over again. Keep in mind that they are rearing their grandchildren in a whole different generation than the one in which they reared their children.

Given the changes in families today, you can do a number of things as an early childhood professional to ensure that all parents and families are meaningfully involved. These ideas for working with today's changing families are shown in Figure 12.1. Review them now for ideas and background for your work of parent involvement.

Parent/Family Involvement: What Is It?

Parent/family involvement is a process of helping parents and family members use their abilities to benefit themselves, their children, and the early childhood program. Families, children, and the program are all part of the process; consequently, all three parties should benefit from a well-planned program of involvement. Nonetheless, the focus in parent/child/family interactions is the family, and you must work with and through families if you want to be successful.

Education as a Family Affair

For more information about involving families in children's education, go to the Companion Website at *http://www.prenhall. com/morrison*, select Chapter 12, then choose the Linking to Learning module.

Education starts in the home, and what happens there profoundly affects development and learning. The greater the family's involvement in children's learning, the more likely it is that they will receive a high-quality education. Helping parents learn about child development, providing them with activities they can use to teach their children in the home, and supporting parents in their roles as their children's first teachers are powerful ways to help parents and children be successful.

Family-Centered Teaching

Family-centered teaching and learning focuses on meeting the needs of children through the family unit. Family-centered teaching and learning make sense for a number of reasons. First, the family unit has the major responsibility for meeting children's needs. Children's development begins in the family system. The family is a powerful determiner of developmental processes, for better and for worse. What teachers and others want to do is maximize the best and diminish the worst. Therefore, helping parents and other family members meet their children's needs in appropriate ways means that everyone benefits. Helping individuals in the family unit become better parents and family members helps children and consequently promotes their success in school and life.

✳ *Provide support services.* Support can extend from being a "listening ear" to organizing support groups and seminars on single parenting. You can help families link up with other agencies and groups, such as Big Brothers and Big Sisters and Families without Partners. Through newsletters and fliers, professionals can offer families specific advice on how to help children become independent and how to meet the demands of living in single-parent families, stepfamilies, and other family configurations.

✳ *Provide child care.* As more families need child care, you can be an advocate for establishing care where none exists, extending existing services, and helping to arrange cooperative baby-sitting services. Providing child care for parent-teacher conferences and other school-parent/family activities is one way to meet parents' needs and make parent involvement programs successful.

✳ *Avoid criticism.* Be careful not to criticize parents for the jobs they are doing. They may not have extra time to spend with their children or know how to discipline them. Regardless of their circumstances, families need help, not criticism.

✳ *Adjust programs.* Adjust classroom and center activities to account for how particular children cope with their home situations. Children's needs for different kinds of activities depend on their experiences at home. For example, opportunities abound for role playing, and such activities help bring into the open situations that children need to talk about. Use program opportunities to discuss families and the roles they play. Make it a point in the classroom to model, encourage, and teach effective interpersonal skills.

✳ *Be sensitive.* There are specific ways to sensitively approach today's changing family patterns. For example, avoid having children make presents for both parents when it is inappropriate to do so, and do not award prizes for bringing both parents to meetings. Be sensitive to the demands of school in relation to children's home lives.

✳ *Seek training.* Request in-service training to help you work with families. In-service programs can provide information about referral agencies, guidance techniques, ways to help families deal with their problems, and child abuse identification and prevention. Be alert to the signs of all kinds of child abuse, including mental, physical, and sexual abuse.

✳ *Increase parent contacts.* Encourage greater and different kinds of parent involvement through visiting homes; talking to families about children's needs; providing information and opportunities to parents, grandparents, and other family members; gathering information from families (such as through interest inventories); and keeping in touch with parents. Make parent contacts positive.

Second, as is frequently the case, family issues and problems must be addressed first to help children effectively. For instance, helping parents gain access to adequate and affordable health care increases the chances that the whole family, including children, will be healthy.

Third, teachers can do many things concurrently with children and their families that benefit both. Literacy is a good example. Adopting a family approach to literacy means that helping parents learn how to read so they can read aloud to their children helps ensure children's literacy development as well.

For more information on Even Start, go to the Companion Website at *http://www.prenhall.com/morrison*, select Chapter 12, then choose the Linking to Learning module.

Even Start is an example of family-centered teaching. It is a federally funded family literacy program that combines adult literacy and parenting training with early childhood education. Even Start helps parents become full partners in the education of their children, assists children in reaching their full potential, and provides literacy training for parents. Even Start projects are designed to work cooperatively with existing community resources to provide a full range of services and to integrate early childhood education and adult education. For more information on Even Start, go to the Companion Website.

Also, keep in mind the literacy standards and guidelines we discussed in Chapters 7, 8, and 9. In addition to helping you know what children should know and be able to do, they can also provide direction for information and activities you can share with families. For example, providing parents with lists of books to read to their preschoolers is one way to help with family literacy. Collaborating with a local service organization such as Kiwanis could be a good way to raise money necessary to buy books for families. The "Program in Action" on pages 352 and 353 describes the benefits of a family literacy project in an Arizona Head Start classroom.

Two-Generation and Intergenerational Family Programs

Two-generation programs involve parents and their children and are designed to help both generations and strengthen the family unit. Figure 12.2 provides guidelines you can follow to effectively involve all parents and families, including grandparents.

National Standards for Parent Involvement

We have talked about state and national standards, which state what children should know and be able to do. There are also national standards for parent involvement. The National PTA has developed guidelines for improving family and parent involvement, which lead to student success. Figure 12.3 lists these national standards. Review them now and consider how you can use them in your teaching.

Which of these strategies will you need help with as you prepare for your role of involving and collaborating with parents and families?

* Get to know your children's parents and families. Home visits are a good way to do this.

* Ask parents what goals they have for their children. Use these goals to help you in your planning. Encourage parents to have realistically high expectations for their children.

* Build relationships with parents so you may communicate better with them.

* Learn how to best communicate with parents based on their cultural communications preferences. Take into account cultural features that can inhibit collaboration.

* Learn how families rear children and manage their families. Political, social, and moral values of families all have implications for parent participation and ways to teach children.

* Support parents in their roles as first teachers of their children. Support can include information, materials, and help with parenting questions.

* Provide frequent, open communication and feedback on student progress, including good news.

* Educate parents to be mentors, classroom aides, tutors, and homework helpers. Also, communicate guidelines for helping students study for tests.

* Support fathers in their roles as parents. By supporting and encouraging fathers, you support the whole family.

* On the basis of parents' needs, identify resources they can use to help solve family and personal problems.

* Work with and through families. Ask parents to help you in working with and involving them and other parents. Parents respond positively to other parents, so it makes sense to have parents helping families.

⌒⌒   Families continue to change and, as they do, early childhood professionals must adapt and adopt new ways of involving family members and providing for their needs. For example, growing numbers of fathers have sole responsibility for rearing their children. What can professionals do to ensure the involvement of single fathers in their programs?

Program in Action

At first glance it's hard to tell the difference between the two classrooms in the portable building that houses Los Niños Sunnyside Head Start in Tucson, Arizona. Both serve low-income families; both must follow federal standards of safety and cleanliness, being subject to numerous random inspections; both have state-of-the-art books, computers, and exploratory centers where children are actively engaged in learning and play; both have access to the spotless kitchen, which serves all the children two nutritious meals a day; both practice positive discipline and encourage parental involvement in their child's education. And the similarities don't end there.

The difference is that the children in one classroom, along with their parents, are students of Family Literacy. These parents don't go home after dropping their children off at Head Start. They head to Los Niños Elementary School for five hours of adult education (English or GED), vocational education, computers, parent time (parenting and leadership), and, perhaps most critical of all, parents and children together (PACT) time.

PACT time sets Family Literacy apart from other Head Start programs in that parents spend thirty to forty-five minutes every day in the early childhood classroom. Children plan ahead of time where they want to play and send the parent a note with this information. The goal is for parents to dedicate the entire period exclusively to their child, relinquishing control and learning to respect and understand their child's choices in play. To ease this often difficult transition, parents explore how to ask questions of their children to extend play, and they are encouraged to follow the staff's lead in using positive language and discipline.

What is the rest of the children's day like? After they arrive at Head Start, they are served a nourishing,

sugar-free breakfast. They are encouraged to taste everything at least once and to drink their milk. They then do a dry brushing of their teeth. At 9:00 they go outside, and when they return forty-five minutes later, they transition to group activity. At 10:00 they plan for PACT time and then sing and/or play music. Parents arrive for PACT, which takes place between 10:30 and 11:00. During one PACT time a week, parents and children spend fifteen minutes reading together. At the end of PACT, everyone gathers in a circle for Circle Time, where children, parents, and teachers sing or read a story. Afterward, one parent stays to help set the tables and eat lunch with the children while the others go back to their room. After lunch, the children engage in a reading activity, write in their journals, and engage in "Do Time" work. At 12:55 they gather in a circle to review their day, and at 1:00 their parents come to take them home.

As mentioned previously, positive guidance is a fundamental component of Head Start. Because children learn what they live, Head Start staff members guide children to make behavior decisions that are positive and safe for themselves and others. They do this by modeling positive language and actions in the classroom. For example, rules are stated in positive terms: Instead of "Don't run in the classroom!" teachers say, "Ramon, remember, we walk in the classroom. We run outside." Reasons are given: "So you won't hurt yourself and others." A very important rule is "Use your words when you want something." For many children, this is the first time they've experienced a consistently positive and supportive environment.

Head Start also stresses the importance of responsibility. Children have many responsibilities, from putting toys away to setting the table for breakfast and lunch. It's fascinating to watch a four- or five-year-old

352

child set the table! They do it with ease, having no trouble remembering where things go. During lunch children serve themselves and pour their own milk. They are also responsible for bussing their dishes afterward, taking care to put the spoons in one container, the napkins in another, and the cups in another. Parents often comment that after being enrolled in Head Start, their preschoolers carry their dishes to the sink at home and are better at cleaning up after themselves in general.

For many parents, these are things that their children had heretofore been "unable" to do and so were never given the responsibility of doing. But Head Start strongly believes that we create self-esteem in our children by teaching them life skills. The ability to take care of oneself is certainly a skill that can increase a child's sense of competence. And as children become more self-confident, their self-esteem is given the chance to flower and grow.

Here at Los Niños, I have observed the effects of the Head Start/Family Literacy collaboration. Five children who were in the program last year are in kindergarten this year. Their teachers have told me how exceptionally well prepared these children were for kindergarten. Not only could they read and write, but they could also listen and follow rules. Longitudinal studies done by our office have shown that children who attend Family Literacy are consistently successful at school. And approximately 50 percent of former Family Literacy parents surveyed were still involved in their children's education by volunteering in their schools.

What makes Family Literacy stand above many preschool programs is the involvement of the whole family. This is Family Literacy's ninth year at Los Niños. Many lives have been turned around in that time,

though gains are often slow. As the adult educator here, I often ask parents to share something good that's happened to them recently. Just this week one mom said she's yelling less at home now. Another said her fourth grade son, whose classroom she volunteers in two hours a week during her vocational time, told her he was proud of her. Another said that she now feels better able to help her older child with his homework. And the year just got started!

These are the small successes that add up to a program that has changed hundreds of lives. In the words of National Center for Family Literacy President Sharon Darling: "For more than ten years, the NCFL has been at the forefront of efforts to make the most important connection in education—giving parents the tools they need to be their child's first and best teacher. Recognized by academics and policy makers as invaluable to American education and multigenerational empowerment, family literacy . . . improves the lives of children and families like few other efforts." Family Literacy collaborates with other early childhood agencies besides Head Start, so see if there's a Family Literacy program in your area—and if not, start one!

Visit the National Center for Family Literacy on the web.

Text contributed by Emily Creigh, adult educator at Los Niños Sunnyside Head Start.

 To complete a Program in Action activity and visit the National Center for Family Literacy, go to the Companion Website at *http://www.prenhall.com/morrison,* **select Chapter 12, then choose the Programs in Action module.**

Standard 1:	Communicating—Communication between home and school is regular, two-way, and meaningful.
Standard II:	Parenting—Parenting skills are promoted and supported.
Standard III:	Student Learning—Parents play an integral role in assisting student learning.
Standard IV:	Volunteering—Parents are welcome in the school, and their support and assistance are sought.
Standard V:	School Decision Making and Advocacy—Parents are full partners in the decisions that affect children and families.
Standard VI:	Collaborating with Community—Community resources are used to strengthen schools, families, and student learning.

⌐ **FIGURE 12.3   The National PTA's Standards for Parent/Family Involvement Programs**

The National PTA's National Standards for Parent/Family Involvement Programs help schools, communities, and parenting groups implement effective parent involvement programs with the aim of improving students' academic performance. Collaborating with agencies such as the National PTA is an excellent way to enhance and promote your program of parent involvement.

Source: National PTA, "National Standards for Parent/Family Involvement Programs," 2001. Used by permission. Available online at http://www.pta.org.

Activities for Involving Families

Unlimited possibilities exist for family involvement, but a coordinated effort is required to build an effective, meaningful program that can bring about a change in education and benefit all concerned: families, children, professionals, and communities. Figure 12.4 lists some activities you can implement to ensure you will be successful in your parent involvement activities. Using these activities will provide for significant family involvement. As the "Technology Tie-In" on page 358 notes, homework is one example of how early childhood professionals are encouraging parents to play a role in their children's academic success.

Conducting Home Visits

Conducting home visits is becoming more commonplace for many teachers. In fact, California has launched a $15 million initiative to pay teachers overtime for visiting students' homes.[2] Teachers who do home visiting are trained prior to going on the visits. Although not every state or district pays extra for home visits, more schools are building home visits into the school calendar, with a certain number of days being set aside for home visiting. Some districts and programs provide release time for visitation by hiring substitute teachers to enable classroom teachers to make home visits. Figure 12.5 offers guidelines for how you can be successful in your program of home visitation.

Schoolwide Activities

* *Workshops.* Workshops can introduce families to the school's policies, procedures, and programs. Most families want to know what is going on in the school and would do a better job of parenting and educating if they knew how.

* *Family nights, cultural dinners, carnivals, and potluck dinners.* These events can be used to bring families and the community to the school in nonthreatening, social ways.

* *Adult education classes.* Adult education classes provide the community with opportunities to learn about a range of subjects.

* *Training programs.* Training programs can help parents, family members, and others develop skills as classroom aides, club and activity sponsors, curriculum planners, and policy decision makers. When parents, family members, and community persons are viewed as experts, empowerment results.

* *Support services such as car pools and baby-sitting.* Support services make family attendance and involvement possible.

* *Fairs and bazaars.* These can be used to involve families in fund-raising.

Communication Activities

* *Telephone hotlines.* Hotlines staffed by families can help allay fears and provide information relating to child abuse, communicable diseases, and special events. Telephone networks are also used to help children and parents with homework and to monitor latchkey children.

* *Newsletters.* Newsletters planned with parents' help are an excellent way to keep families informed about program events, activities, and curriculum information. Newsletters in parents' native languages help keep language-minority families informed.

* *Home learning materials and activities.* Sending home ideas for learning activities is one good way to help families help their children learn.

Educational Activities

* *Participation in classroom and center activities.* Although not all families can be directly involved in classroom activities, encourage those who can. Those who are involved must have guidance, direction, and training. Involving parents and others as paid aides is also an excellent way to provide employment and training. Many programs, such as Head Start, actively support such a policy.

* *Involvement of families in writing individualized education programs (IEPs) for children with special needs.* Involvement in writing an IEP is not only a legal requirement, but also an excellent learning experience.

Service Activities

* *Classroom and school resource libraries and materials centers.* Families benefit from books and other articles relating to parenting. Some programs furnish resource areas with comfortable chairs to encourage families to use these materials.

(Continued)

FIGURE 12.4 Activities for Parent and Family Involvement

* *Child care.* Families may not be able to attend programs and become involved if they do not have child care for their children. Child care makes their participation possible and more enjoyable.

* *Service exchanges.* Service exchanges operated by early childhood programs and other agencies help families in their needs for services. For example, one parent provided child care in her home in exchange for having her washing machine repaired. The possibilities for such exchanges are endless.

* *Parent support groups.* Parents need support in their roles. Support groups can provide parenting information, community agency information, and speakers.

* *Welcoming committees.* A good way to involve families in any program is to have other families contact them when their children first join a program.

Decision Activities

* *Hiring and policy making.* Parents and community members can and should serve on committees that set policy and hire staff.

* *Curriculum development and review.* Parents' involvement in curriculum planning helps them learn about and understand what constitutes a quality program and what is involved in a developmentally appropriate curriculum. When families know about the curriculum, they are more supportive of it.

∽ **FIGURE 12.4   Activities for Parent and Family Involvement** *(Continued)*

One of the keys to your success as an early childhood teacher will be how well you involve parents and families. Here are eighteen things you can do to ensure that you have an effective program in place to work with the parents and families of young children.

A home visiting program can show that the teachers, principal, and school staff are willing to "go more than halfway" to involve all parents in their children's education. Home visits help teachers demonstrate their interest in students' families and understand their students better by seeing them in their home environment.

These visits should not replace parent-teacher conferences or be used to discuss children's progress. When done early before any school programs can arise, they avoid putting parents on the defensive and signal that teachers are eager to work with all parents. Teachers who have made home visits say they build stronger relationships with parents and their children, and improve attendance and achievement.

Planning

Administrators and teachers must agree to participate in the program and be involved in planning it.

These programs are successful when

* teachers' schedules are adjusted so that they have the necessary time;

* home visits are scheduled during just one month of the school year, preferably early; and

* visits are logged so that teachers and administrators can measure their benefits.

(Continued)

∽ **FIGURE 12.5   Making Successful Home Visits**

Strategies for successful home visits

Who does the visiting? Wherever possible, teachers should visit homes of children in their classes. If this is not possible, the principal should ensure that every home that requests a visit receives one.

If teachers do not speak the parents' language, a translator needs to accompany them.

Scheduling

These suggestions may be helpful:

* Some schools have scheduled home visits in the afternoon right after school. Others have found that early evening is more convenient for parents. Some schedule visits right before a new school year begins. A mix of times may be needed to reach all families.

* Teachers should be given flexibility to schedule their visits during the targeted time period.

* Teachers of siblings may want to visit these children's homes together, but take care not to overwhelm parents.

* Some schools work with community groups (e.g., Boys and Girls Clubs, housing complexes, 4-H, YMCAs, and community centers) to schedule visits in neutral but convenient space.

Making parents feel comfortable

Here are some useful tips:

* Send a letter home to parents explaining the desire to have teachers make informal visits to all students' homes. Include a form that parents can mail back to accept or decline the visit.

* The letter should state clearly that the intent of this fifteen- to thirty-minute visit is only to introduce the teacher and family members to each other, and not to discuss the child's progress.

* The letter might suggest that families think about special things their children would want to share with the teacher.

* The tone of the letter should try to lessen parents' worries. One school included a note to parents that said, "No preparation is required. In fact, our homes need to be vacuumed and all of us are on diets!" This touch of humor and casualness helped to set a friendly and informal tone.

* A phone call to parents who have not responded can explain the plan for home visits and reassure parents that it is to get acquainted and to not evaluate students.

* Enlist community groups, religious organizations, and businesses to help publicize the home visits.

∽ FIGURE 12.5   Making Successful Home Visits *(Continued)*

Successful home visits depend on planning and execution. Review these guidelines and begin to consider how you will use them in your program of home visitation.

Source: Reaching All Families—Creating Family-Friendly Schools, *Office of Educational Research and Improvement, U.S. Department of Education, 1996.*

Technology Tie-In

HOMEWORK HELPERS

Homework assignments for all children are a growing reality in many of today's primary classrooms. Over the past decade homework has increased by 50 percent. First grade teacher Karen Alverez at Aldama Elementary School in Los Angeles assigns her students forty-five minutes of homework every day, Monday through Thursday. Like Karen, teachers are assigning homework in response to higher standards and state tests that begin as early as kindergarten. Many teachers believe homework is one way of helping children learn the knowledge and skills mandated by school districts. Parents not only support homework, but they also expect their children to have homework.

Homework can be a challenge for parents and children. One of the issues parents and children have with homework is how to get the help they need with completing homework assignments. Keep in mind that quite often when you assign homework to children you are also assigning it to parents who are responsible for seeing that their children complete it! Over half of all parents are involved in their children's homework in one way or another.

The Internet is one source of help. B. J. Pinchbeck was nine years old when he founded B. J. Pinchbeck's

Homework Helper which lists more than 700 links to educational sites and is affiliated with the Discovery Channel. Other sources for homework help are

* Education Planet Inc.
* Jeeves for Kids
* Marshall Brain's How Stuff Works
* Yahooligans
* KidsClick!
* Bigchalk

Pick a grade from kindergarten through third and develop a homework assignment for your class. Use these Internet sites to complete it. Develop a set of guidelines for how children can use the Internet to help them with their homework.

To complete this Technology Tie-In and others like it, visit the Companion Website at *http://www.prenhall.com/morrison*, select Chapter 12, then choose the Technology Tie-In module.

Conducting Parent-Teacher Conferences

Significant parent involvement occurs through well-planned and well-conducted conferences between parents and early childhood teachers, informally referred to as parent-teacher conferences. Such conferences are often the first contact many families have with school. Conferences are critical both from a public relations point of view and as a vehicle for helping families and professionals accomplish their goals. The guidelines shown in Figure 12.6 will help you as an early childhood professional prepare for and conduct successful conferences. Principal Jo Murphy at Wilma Fisher Elementary School in Frisco, Texas, believes so much in the importance of parent-teacher conferences that she conducts in-service training for her teachers and models effective conference techniques (personal communication, March 25, 2002). More early childhood programs are going the extra mile to ensure that parent-teacher conferences are a win-win experience for everyone.

∽ **FIGURE 12.6   Conducting Successful Parent Conferences**

With preparation and planning, parent conferences can be successful and rewarding. The primary purpose of parent conferences is to improve home-school communication and increase the educational achievement and possibilities for all children.

✳ Plan ahead. Be sure of the reason for the conference. What are your objectives? What do you want to accomplish? List the points you want to cover and think about what you are going to say.

✳ Get to know the parents. This is not wasted time; the more effectively you establish rapport with parents, the more you will accomplish in the long run.

✳ Avoid an authoritative atmosphere. Do not sit behind your desk while parents sit in children's chairs. Treat parents and others like the adults they are.

✳ Communicate at parents' levels. Do not condescend or patronize. Instead, use familiar words, phrases, and explanations parents understand. Do not use jargon or complicated explanations, and speak in your natural style.

✳ Accentuate the positive. Make every effort to show and tell parents what children are doing well. When you deal with problems, put them in the proper perspective: what a child is able to do, what the goals and purposes of the learning program are, what specific skill or concept you are trying to get the child to learn, and what problems the child is having in achieving the goal or purpose. Most important, explain what you plan to do to help the child achieve and what specific role parents can have in meeting the achievement goals.

✳ Give families a chance to talk. You will not learn much about them if you do all the talking, nor are you likely to achieve your goals. Professionals are often accustomed to dominating a conversation, and many parents will not be as verbal as you, so you will have to encourage families to talk.

✳ Learn to listen. An active listener holds eye contact, uses body language such as head nodding and hand gestures, does not interrupt, avoids arguing, paraphrases as a way of clarifying ideas, and keeps the conversation on track.

✳ Follow up. Ask parents for a definite time for the next conference as you are concluding the current one. Having another conference is the best method of solidifying gains and extending support, but other acceptable means of follow-up are telephone calls, written reports, notes sent with children, and brief visits to the home. Although these types of contacts may appear casual, they should be planned for and conducted as seriously as any regular parent-teacher conference.

✳ Develop an action plan. Never leave parents with a sense of frustration, not knowing what you are doing or what they are to do. Every communication with families should end on a positive note, so that everyone knows what can be done and how to do it.

Telephone Contacts

Making a telephone call is an efficient way to contact families when it is impossible to arrange a face-to-face conference as a follow-up. Here are some tips you can use for your telephone contacts with parents:

* Since you cannot see someone on a telephone, it takes a little longer to build rapport and trust. The time you spend overcoming families' initial fears and apprehensions will pay dividends later.

* Constantly clarify what you are talking about and what you and the families have agreed to do, using such phrases as, "What I heard you say then . . ." and, "So far, we have agreed that . . ."

* Do not act hurried. There is a limit to the amount of time you can spend on the phone, but you may be one of the few people who care about the parent and the child. Your telephone contact may be the major part of the family's support system.

Communicating with Parents over the Internet

The Internet provides another way for you to reach out to parents and keep them informed and involved. Most school districts have a web page that provides general information about the district and individual schools. Many teachers have their own classroom web page. Web pages are excellent ways to give parents and community members general information and let them virtually experience school and classroom events and accomplishments. Before you set up your class web page or begin communicating with parents via e-mail, here are some things to consider:

 For more information about using the Internet to increase communication with parents, go to the Companion Website at *http://www.prenhall. com/morrison*, select Chapter 12, then choose the Linking to Learning module.

* Check with your school or program technology coordinator for guidelines and policies for web page development and communicating electronically with parents.

* Remember that not all parents are connected to the Internet. There is a great "digital divide" in the United States; low-income parents and minorities are less likely to have Internet access. You will have to consider how to provide families without Internet access the same information you provide to families who have Internet service.

Here are some guidelines to follow when you communicate with parents on the Internet:

* Observe all the rules of politeness and courtesy that you would in a face-to-face conversation.

* Observe all the rules of courteous Internet conversations. For example, don't use all capital letters (this is similar to SHOUTING).

* Remember that just like handwritten notes, electronic mail can be saved. In addition, electronic notes are much more easily transferred.

* Be straightforward and concise in your electronic conversations.
* Establish ground rules ahead of time about what you will and will not discuss electronically.

Involving Single-Parent Families

Involving single parents is an important part of making sure that all parents are involved in the educational lives of their children. Figure 12.7 provides you with practical ideas for how to accomplish this goal.

Involving Language-Minority Parents and Families

Language-minority parents are individuals whose English proficiency is minimal and who lack a comprehensive knowledge of the norms and social systems in the United States. Language-minority families often face language and cultural barriers that greatly hamper their ability to become actively involved, although many have a great desire and willingness to participate in their children's education.

Because the culture of language-minority families often differs from the majority in a community, those who seek a truly collaborative community, home, and school involvement must take into account the cultural features that can inhibit collaboration. Traditional styles of child rearing and family organization, attitudes toward schooling, organizations around which families center their lives, life goals and values, political influences, and methods of communication within the cultural group all have implications for parent participation.

Your role as an early childhood professional includes learning how to effectively involve language-minority parents and families of many different cultures. How will you prepare yourself for this important role?

∞ **FIGURE 12.7** Involving
Single and Working Parents

An increasing number of
children live in single-parent
and stepfamilies. Many also
live in foster families and other
nontraditional family forms. In
many two-parent families both
parents work full days, so
children come home to an
empty house. Involving single
and working parents presents
many challenges to schools.

Source: Reaching All Families—
Creating Family-Friendly Schools,
Office of Education Research and
Improvement, U.S. Department of
Education, 1996.

Communication

Communication with single-parent and other nontraditional families will be
more effective if schools do the following:

* Avoid making the assumption that students live with both biological
  parents.
* Avoid the traditional "Dear Parents" greeting in letters and other
  messages, and instead use "Dear Parent," "Dear Family," "Friends," or
  some other form of greeting.
* Develop a system of keeping noncustodial parents informed of their
  children's school progress.
* Demonstrate sensitivity to the rights of noncustodial parents. Inform
  parents that schools may not withhold information from noncustodial
  parents who have the legal right to see their children's records.
* Develop a simple unobtrusive system to keep track of family changes,
  such as these examples:
  * At the beginning of the year, ask for the names and addresses of
    individuals to be informed about each child and involved in school
    activities.
  * At the midyear, send a form to each child's parents or guardians to
    verify that the information is still accurate. Invite parents or
    guardians to indicate any changes.
* Place flyers about school events on bulletin boards of major companies
  in the community that are family-friendly to learning.

These approaches use different and more sensitive ways of
communicating with nontraditional families and do not require much more
material resources.

Involvement

The following practices can make the involvement of single and working
parents in school life more feasible:

* Hold parent-teacher conferences and other school events in the
  evenings.
* Welcome other children at such events, and provide organized
  activities or child care services.
* Provide teachers and counselors with in-service training that sensitizes
  them to special problems faced by children of single and working
  parents and the parents themselves.
* Gather information on whether joint or separate parent conferences
  need to be scheduled with parents.
* Sponsor evening and weekend learning activities at which parents can
  participate and learn with their children.
* Work with local businesses to arrange release time from work so that
  parents can attend conferences, volunteer, or in other ways spend time
  at their child's school when it is in session.

Language-minority families often lack information about the U.S. educational system, including basic school philosophy, practice, and structure, which can result in misconceptions, fear, and a general reluctance to respond to invitations for involvement. Furthermore, this educational system may be quite different from schools with which these families are familiar. Figure 12.8 offers suggestions for working with language-minority families.

∽ **FIGURE 12.8   Culturally Sensitive Family Involvement**

The demographic makeup of America is rapidly changing. Many school districts have student populations in which minorities are the majority. It is not uncommon for schools to have children from almost every country of the world. These guidelines will help you conduct culturally sensitive family involvement.

Source: *J. González-Mena, "Taking a Culturally Sensitive Approach in Infant-Toddler Programs," Young Children 1 (1992): 8–9. Used with permission of the author.*

* Know what each parent in your program wants for his or her child. Find out families' goals. What are their care-giving practices? What concerns do they have about their child? Encourage them to talk about all of this. Encourage them to ask questions. Encourage the conflicts to surface— to come out in the open.

* Be clear about your own values and goals. Know what you believe in. Have a bottom line, but leave space above it to be flexible. When you are clear, you are less likely to present a defensive stance in the face of conflict.

* Become sensitive to your own discomfort. Tune in on those times when something bothers you instead of just ignoring it and hoping it will go away. Work to identify what specific behaviors of others make you uncomfortable. Try to discover exactly what in yourself creates this discomfort. A conflict may be brewing.

* Build relationships. When you do this, you enhance your chances for conflict management or resolution. Be patient. Building relationships takes time, but it enhances communications and understanding. You'll communicate better if you have a relationship, and you'll have a relationship if you learn to communicate.

* Become an effective cross-cultural communicator. It is possible to learn these communication skills. Learn about communication styles that are different from your own. Teach your own communication styles. What you think a person means may not be what he or she really means. Do not make assumptions. Listen carefully. Ask for clarification. Find ways to test for understanding.

* Learn how to create dialogue—how to open communication instead of shutting it down. Often, if you accept and acknowledge the other person's feelings, you encourage him or her to open up. Learn ways to let others know that you are aware of and sensitive to their feelings.

* Use a problem-solving rather than a power approach to conflicts. Be flexible—negotiate when possible. Look at your willingness to share power. Is it a control issue you are dealing with?

* Commit yourself to education—both your own and that of the families. Sometimes lack of information or understanding of each other's perspective is what keeps the conflict going.

Community Involvement

A comprehensive program of involvement would not be complete without community involvement. More early childhood professionals realize that neither they alone nor the limited resources of their programs are sufficient to meet the needs of many children and families. Consequently, early education professionals are seeking ways to link families to community services and resources. Consider the example of the lunch program in the "Video Viewpoint."

 For more information about building stronger bonds between schools and communities, go to the Companion Website at *http://www.prenhall.com/morrison*, select Chapter 12, then choose the Linking to Learning module.

The community offers a vital and rich array of resources for helping you teach better and for helping you meet the needs of parents and their children. Schools and teachers cannot address the many issues facing children and youth without the partnership and collaboration of powerful sectors of society, including community agencies, businesses, and industry.

School-Business Involvement

School-business involvement and partnerships are excellent means of strengthening programs and helping children and families. For their part, businesses are eager to develop the business-school connection in efforts to help schools better educate children.

The challenge to early childhood professionals is quite clear: merely seeking ways to involve parents in school activities is no longer a sufficient program of

Video Viewpoint

FEEDING HUNGRY CHILDREN

 Tired of the conditions she found in her city of Houston, Texas, Carol Porter organized an effort to feed hungry children. Her organization started out with just her family, who spent their life savings to set up Kid Care. Now Carol and her volunteers load up vans and head for Houston's poorest neighborhoods, feeding daily lunches to those who cannot provide for themselves.

REFLECTIVE DISCUSSION QUESTIONS

What effects do hunger and undernourishment have on children's learning? Why is seeing that children are well fed becoming a part of the early childhood curriculum?

REFLECTIVE DECISION MAKING

What can you do to help ensure that the children you teach are properly fed? What community agencies can you work with to help your children receive the food they need?

Community businesses and civic organizations offer many opportunities for collaborative partnerships that can lead to the achievement of common goals for making education better. Begin now to plan for ways that you will reach out to and involve the community in your classroom.

parent involvement. Today, the challenge is to make families the focus of our involvement activities so that their lives and their children's lives are made better. Anything less will not help families and children access and benefit from the opportunities of the twenty-first century.

National Organizations

National organizations dedicated to family involvement are a rich resource for information and support. Some of these are listed here:

* Institute for Responsive Education (IRE), 605 Commonwealth Ave., Boston, MA 02215; 617-353-3309.

* Center on Families, Communities, Schools and Children's Learning, 605 Commonwealth Ave., Boston, MA 02215; 617-353-3309. (The center's address and phone number are the same as IRE's.)

For more information about the Institute for Responsive Education, the National Congress of Parents and Teachers, and other national organizations, go to the Companion Website at *http://www.prenhall.com/morrison,* select Chapter 12, then choose the Linking to Learning module.

* Families United for Better Schools, 31 Maple Wood Mall, Philadelphia, PA 19144; 215-829-0442. This is an organization of families working to help other families work for better schools.

* National Committee for Citizens in Education (NCCE), 900 Second St. NE, Suite 8, Washington, DC 20002-3557; 800-638-9675. This organization seeks to inform families of their rights and to get them involved in public schools.

* The Home and School Institute, 1201 16th St. NW, Washington, DC 20036; 202-466-3633.

* National Congress of Parents and Teachers (National PTA), 700 N. Rush St., Chicago, IL 60611; 312-787-0977.

The Family Involvement Partnership for Learning

For more information about the Family Education Network, Parent Soup, and the National Coalition for Parent Involvement in Education, go to the Companion Website at *http://www.prenhall. com/morrison*, select Chapter 12, then choose the Linking to Learning module.

The mission of the Family Involvement Partnership for Learning is to promote children's learning through the development of family/school/community partnerships. The national Family Involvement Partnership for Learning began as a cooperative effort between the U.S. Department of Education and the National Coalition for Parent Involvement in Education (NCPIE). NCPIE, a coalition of more than 100 national education and advocacy organizations, has been meeting for more than fifteen years to advocate the involvement of families in their children's education and to promote relationships among home, school, and community that can enhance the education of all children and youth. NCPIE represents parents, schools, communities, religious groups, and businesses.[3]

Website Connections

Many websites are available to help parents become more involved in their children's education. For example, the Family Education Network and Parent Soup offer resources and features on a wide array of educational topics.

ACTIVITIES FOR PROFESSIONAL DEVELOPMENT

In this chapter we have stressed the importance of collaboration with parents, families, and community agencies. Refer again to the "Professional Development Goal" at the beginning of the chapter, to the "Professional Development Checklist" on pages 20 and 21, the "Programs in Action" on pages 352 and 353, and the "Professionalism in Practice" on pages 346 and 347. After you have reviewed these ideas, complete the following exercises.

1. Develop a plan for family involvement in a grade in which you plan to teach.
   a. Write objectives for the program.
   b. Develop specific activities for involving families and for providing services to them.
   c. Explain how you would involve fathers, language-minority families, and families of children with disabilities.
2. Visit social services agencies in your area, and list the services they offer.
   a. Describe how early childhood professionals can work with these agencies to meet the needs of children and families.
   b. Invite agency directors to meet with your class to discuss how they and early childhood professionals can work cooperatively to help families and children.

3. As families change, so, too, do the services they need. Interview families in as many settings as possible (e.g., urban, suburban, rural), from as many socioeconomic backgrounds as possible, and from as many kinds of families as possible. Determine what services they believe can help them most, then tell how you as a professional could help provide those services.

For additional chapter resources and activities, visit the Companion Website at *http://www.prenhall.com/morrison*, select Chapter 12, then choose the Professional Development, Resources, or Linking to Learning modules.

THE NAEYC CODE OF ETHICAL CONDUCT

PREAMBLE

NAEYC recognizes that many daily decisions required of those who work with young children are of a moral and ethical nature. The NAEYC Code of Ethical Conduct offers guidelines for responsible behavior and sets forth a common basis for resolving the principal ethical dilemmas encountered in early childhood education. The primary focus is on daily practice with children and their families in programs for children from birth to eight years of age: preschools, child care centers, family day care homes, kindergartens, and primary classrooms. Many of the provisions also apply to specialists who do not work directly with children, including program administrators, parent educators, college professors, and child care licensing specialists.

Standards of ethical behavior in early childhood education are based on commitment to core values that are deeply rooted in the history of our field. We have committed ourselves to:

Appreciating childhood as a unique and valuable stage of the human life cycle

Basing our work with children on knowledge of child development

Appreciating and supporting the close ties between the child and family

Recognizing that children are best understood in the context of family, culture, and society

Respecting the dignity, worth, and uniqueness of each individual (child, family member, and colleague)

Helping children and adults achieve their full potential in the context of relationships that are based on trust, respect, and positive regard

Source: *Code of Ethical Conduct and Statement of Commitment by S. Feeney and K. Kipnis. Copyright ©1997 by the National Association for the Education of Young Children. Reprinted by permission from the National Association for the Education of Young Children.*

The Code sets forth a conception of our professional responsibilities in four sections, each addressing an arena of professional relationships: (1) children, (2) families, (3) colleagues, and (4) community and society. Each section includes an introduction to the primary responsibilities of the early childhood practitioner in that arena, a set of ideals pointing in the direction of exemplary professional practice, and a set of principles defining practices that are required, prohibited, and permitted.

The ideals reflect the aspirations of practitioners. The principles are intended to guide conduct and assist practitioners in resolving ethical dilemmas encountered in the field. There is not necessarily a corresponding principle for each ideal. Both ideals and principles are intended to direct practitioners to those questions which, when responsibly answered, will provide the basis for conscientious decision making. While the Code provides specific direction for addressing some ethical dilemmas, many others will require the practitioner to combine the guidance of the Code with sound professional judgment.

The ideals and principles in this Code present a shared conception of professional responsibility that affirms our commitment to the core values of our field. The Code publicly acknowledges the responsibilities that we in the field have assumed and in so doing supports ethical behavior in our work. Practitioners who face ethical dilemmas are urged to seek guidance in the applicable parts of this Code and in the spirit that informs the whole.

Section I: Ethical Responsibilities to Children

Childhood is a unique and valuable stage in the life cycle. Our paramount responsibility is to provide safe, healthy, nurturing, and responsive settings for children. We are committed to supporting children's development by cherishing individual differences, by helping them learn to live and work cooperatively, and by promoting their self-esteem.

Ideals

I–1.1   To be familiar with the knowledge base of early childhood education and to keep current through continuing education and in-service training.

I–1.2   To base program practices upon current knowledge in the field of child development and related disciplines and upon particular knowledge of each child.

I–1.3   To recognize and respect the uniqueness and the potential of each child.

I–1.4   To appreciate the special vulnerability of children.

I–1.5   To create and maintain safe and healthy settings that foster children's social, emotional, intellectual, and physical development and that respect their dignity and their contributions.

I–1.6   To support the right of children with special needs to participate, consistent with their ability, in regular childhood programs.

Principles

P–1.1   Above all, we shall not harm children. We shall not participate in practices that are disrespectful, degrading, dangerous, exploitative, intimidating, emotionally damaging, or physically harmful to children. *This principle has precedence over all others in this Code.*

P–1.2   We shall not participate in practices that discriminate against children by denying benefits, giving special advantages, or excluding them from programs or activities on the basis of their race, religion, sex, national origin, or the status, behavior, or beliefs of their parents. (This principle does not apply to programs that have a lawful mandate to provide services to a particular population of children.)

P–1.3   We shall involve all of those with relevant knowledge (including staff and parents) in decisions concerning a child.

P–1.4   When, after appropriate efforts have been made with a child and the family, the child still does not appear to be benefitting from a program, we shall communicate our concern to the family in a positive way and offer them assistance in finding a more suitable setting.

P–1.5   We shall be familiar with the symptoms of child abuse and neglect and know and follow community procedures and state laws that protect children against abuse and neglect.

P–1.6   When we have evidence of child abuse or neglect, we shall report the evidence to the appropriate community agency and follow up to ensure that appropriate action has been taken. When possible, parents will be informed that the referral has been made.

P–1.7   When another person tells us of their suspicion that a child is being abused or neglected but we lack evidence, we shall assist that person in taking appropriate action to protect the child.

P–1.8   When a child protective agency fails to provide adequate protection for abused or neglected children, we acknowledge a collective ethical responsibility to work toward improvement of these services.

P–1.9   When we become aware of a practice or situation that endangers the health or safety of children, but has not been previously known to do so, we have an ethical responsibility to inform those who can remedy the situation and who can keep other children from being similarly endangered.

Section II: Ethical Responsibilities to Families

Families are of primary importance in children's development. (The term *family* may include others, besides parents, who are responsibly involved with the child.) Because the family and the early childhood educator have a common interest in the child's welfare, we acknowledge a primary responsibility to bring about collaboration between the home and school in ways that enhance the child's development.

Ideals

I–2.1   To develop relationships of mutual trust with the families we serve.

I–2.2   To acknowledge and build upon strengths and competencies as we support families in their task of nurturing children.

I–2.3   To respect the dignity of each family and its culture, customs, and beliefs.

I–2.4   To respect families' childrearing values and their right to make decisions for their children.

I–2.5   To interpret each child's progress to parents within the framework of a developmental perspective and to help families understand and appreciate the value of developmentally appropriate early childhood programs.

I–2.6   To help family members improve their understanding of their children and to enhance their skills as parents.

I–2.7   To participate in building support networks for families by providing them with opportunities to interact with program staff and families.

Principles

P–2.1   We shall not deny family members access to their child's classroom or program setting.

P–2.2   We shall inform families of program philosophy, policies, and personnel qualifications, and explain why we teach as we do.

P–2.3   We shall inform families of and, when appropriate, involve them in policy decisions.

P–2.4   We shall inform families of and, when appropriate, involve them in significant decisions affecting their child.

P–2.5   We shall inform the family of accidents involving their child, of risks such as exposures to contagious disease that may result in infection, and of events that might result in psychological damage.

P–2.6   We shall not permit or participate in research that could in any way hinder the education or development of the children in our programs. Families shall be fully informed of any proposed research projects involving their children and shall have the opportunity to give or withhold consent.

P–2.7   We shall not engage in or support exploitation of families. We shall not use our relationship with a family for private advantage or personal gain, or enter into relationships with family members that might impair our effectiveness in working with children.

P–2.8   We shall develop written policies for the protection of confidentiality and the disclosure of children's records. The policy documents shall be made available to all program personnel and families. Disclosure of children's records beyond family members, program personnel, and consultants having an obligation of confidentiality shall require familial consent (except in cases of abuse or neglect).

P–2.9   We shall maintain confidentiality and shall respect the family's right to privacy, refraining from disclosure of confidential information and intrusion into family life. However, when we are concerned about a child's welfare, it is permissible to reveal confidential information to agencies and individuals who may be able to act in the child's interest.

P–2.10   In cases where family members are in conflict we shall work openly, sharing our observations of the child, to help all parties involved make informed decisions. We shall refrain from becoming an advocate for one party.

P–2.11   We shall be familiar with and appropriately use community resources and professional services that support families. After a referral has been made, we shall follow up to ensure that services have been adequately provided.

Section III: Ethical Responsibilities to Colleagues

In a caring, cooperative work place human dignity is respected, professional satisfaction is promoted, and positive relationships are modeled. Our primary responsibility in this arena is to establish and maintain settings and relationships that support productive work and meet professional needs.

A—Responsibilities to Co-workers: Ideals

I–3A.1   To establish and maintain relationships of trust and cooperation with co-workers.

I–3A.2   To share resources and information with co-workers.

I–3A.3   To support co-workers in meeting their professional needs and in their professional development.

I–3A.4   To accord co-workers due recognition of professional achievement.

Principles

P–3A.1   When we have concern about the professional behavior of a co-worker, we shall first let that person know of our concern and attempt to resolve the matter collegially.

P–3A.2   We shall exercise care in expressing views regarding the personal attributes or professional conduct of co-workers. Statements should be based on firsthand knowledge and relevant to the interests of children and programs.

B—Responsibilities to Employers: Ideals

I–3B.1   To assist the program in providing the highest quality of service.

I–3B.2   To maintain loyalty to the program and uphold its reputation.

Principles

P–3B.1   When we do not agree with program policies, we shall first attempt to effect change through constructive action within the organization.

P–3B.2   We shall speak or act on behalf of an organization only when authorized. We shall take care to note when we are speaking for the organization and when we are expressing a personal judgment.

C—Responsibilities to Employees: Ideals

I–3C.1   To promote policies and working conditions that foster competence, well-being, and self-esteem in staff members.

I–3C.2   To create a climate of trust and candor that will enable staff to speak and act in the best interests of children, families, and the field of early childhood education.

I–3C.3   To strive to secure an adequate livelihood for those who work with or on behalf of young children.

Principles

P–3C.1   In decisions concerning children and programs, we shall appropriately utilize the training, experience, and expertise of staff members.

P–3C.2   We shall provide staff members with working conditions that permit them to carry out their responsibilities, timely and nonthreatening evaluation procedures, written grievance procedures, constructive feedback, and opportunities for continuing professional development and advancement.

P–3C.3   We shall develop and maintain comprehensive written personnel policies that define program standards and, when applicable, that specify the extent to which employees are accountable for their conduct outside the work place. These policies shall be given to new staff members and shall be available for review by all staff members.

P–3C.4   Employees who do not meet program standards shall be informed of areas of concern and, when possible, assisted in improving their performance.

P–3C.5   Employees who are dismissed shall be informed of the reasons for the termination. When a dismissal is for cause, justification must be based on evidence of inadequate or inappropriate behavior that is accurately documented, current, and available for the employee to review.

P–3C.6   In making evaluations and recommendations, judgments shall be based on fact and relevant to the interests of children and programs.

P–3C.7   Hiring and promotion shall be based solely on a person's record of accomplishment and ability to carry out the responsibilities of the position.

P–3C.8   In hiring, promotion, and provision of training, we shall not participate in any form of discrimination based on race, religion, sex, national origin, handicap, age, or sexual preference. We shall be familiar with laws and regulations that pertain to employment discrimination.

Section IV: Ethical Responsibilities to Community and Society

Early childhood programs operate within a context of an immediate community made up of families and other institutions concerned with children's welfare. Our responsibilities to the community are to provide programs that meet its needs and to cooperate with agencies and professions that share responsibility for children. Because the larger society has a measure of responsibility for the welfare and protection of children, and because of our specialized expertise in child development, we acknowledge an obligation to serve as a voice for children everywhere.

Ideals

I–4.1   To provide the community with high-quality, culturally sensitive programs and services.

I–4.2   To promote cooperation among agencies and professions concerned with the welfare of young children, their families, and their teachers.

I–4.3   To work, through education, research, and advocacy, toward an environmentally safe world in which all children are adequately fed, sheltered, and nurtured.

I–4.4   To work, through education, research, and advocacy, toward a society in which all young children have access to quality programs.

I–4.5   To promote knowledge and understanding of young children and their needs. To work toward greater social acknowledgement of children's rights and greater social acceptance of responsibility for their well-being.

I–4.6   To support policies and laws that promote the well-being of children and families. To oppose those that impair their well-being. To cooperate with other individuals and groups in these efforts.

I–4.7   To further the professional development of the field of early childhood education and to strengthen its commitment to realizing its core values as reflected in this Code.

Principles

P–4.1   We shall communicate openly and truthfully about the nature and extent of services that we provide.

P–4.2   We shall not accept or continue to work in positions for which we are personally unsuited or professionally unqualified. We shall not offer services that we do not have the competence, qualifications, or resources to provide.

P–4.3   We shall be objective and accurate in reporting the knowledge upon which we base our program practices.

P–4.4   We shall cooperate with other professionals who work with children and their families.

P–4.5   We shall not hire or recommend for employment any person who is unsuited for a position with respect to competence, qualifications, or character.

P–4.6   We shall report the unethical or incompetent behavior of a colleague to a supervisor when informal resolution is not effective.

P–4.7   We shall be familiar with laws and regulations that serve to protect the children in our programs.

P–4.8   We shall not participate in practices which are in violation of laws and regulations that protect the children in our programs.

P–4.9   When we have evidence that an early childhood program is violating laws or regulations protecting children, we shall report it to persons responsible for the program. If compliance is not accomplished within a reasonable time, we will report the violation to appropriate authorities who can be expected to remedy the situation.

P–4.10   When we have evidence that an agency or a professional charged with providing services to children, families, or teachers is failing to meet its obligations, we acknowledge a collective ethical responsibility to report the problem to appropriate authorities or to the public.

P–4.11   When a program violates or requires its employees to violate this Code, it is permissible, after fair assessment of the evidence, to disclose the identity of that program.

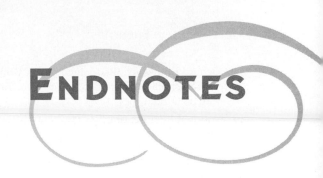

ENDNOTES

CHAPTER 1

1. Carol Brunson Phillips, *Field Advisor's Guide for the CDA Professional Preparation Program* (Washington, DC: Council for Early Childhood Professional Recognition, 1991), 2.

2. National Association for the Education of Young Children, *Early Childhood Teacher Education Guidelines* (Washington, DC: Author, 1982), xii.

CHAPTER 2

1. Marian W. Edelman, "A Voice for Children." Children's Defense Fund: Online Archives. November 1998. [Online: http://www.childrens defense.org/voice1198.htm].

2. Margaret G. Radford, "Just Don't Call Them 'Mr. Mom.'" Family.com: Stay-at-Home Dads. [Online: http://family2.go.com/features/family_1997_06/denv/denv67dad/denv67dad.html].

3. Stephanie J. Ventura and Christine A. Bachrach, "Nonmarital Childbearing in the United States, 1940–99," *National Vital Statistics Reports*, vol. 48, no. 16. (Hyattsville, Md: National Center for Health Statistics, October 18, 2000). [Online: http://www.cdc.gov/nchs/releases/00facts/nonmarit.htm].

4. S. J. Ventura, J. A. Martin, S. C. Curtin, F. Menacker, and B. E. Hamilton, "Births: Final Data for 1999," *National Vital Statistics Reports*, vol. 49, no. 1. (Hyattsville, Md: National Center for Health Statistics, 2001). [Online: http://www.cdc.gov/nchs/data/nvsr/nvsr49/nvsr49_01.pdf].

5. Healthy Child Publications, "How Asthma-Friendly Is Your Childcare Setting?," *Asthma Resources* (Harbor Springs, Mich.: Author). [Online: http://www.healthychild.net/Articles/Asthma9. html].

6. Richard Rothstein, "Reducing Poverty Could Increase School Achievement," *New York Times*, 7 March 2001, p. A18.

7. J. Dalaker and M. Naifeh, *U.S. Bureau of the Census*, Current Population Reports, Series P60-201, "Poverty in the United States: 1997" (Washington, DC: U.S. Government Printing Office, 1998), Table 2.

8. Rhode Island Department of Attorney General, "A. G. Whitehouse Sues Lead Paint Industry." Press release, October 13, 1999. [Online: http://www.riag.state.ri.us/press/Oct99/101399.html].

9. U.S. Bureau of the Census, *Current Population Survey*, March 1998.

10. National Center for Education Statistics, *The Condition of Education 1994* (Washington, DC: U.S. Department of Education, 1994).

11. National Center for Education Statistics, *The Condition of Education 1994* (Washington, DC: U.S. Department of Education, 1994), 1.

12. U.S. General Accounting Office, *Health Insurance for Children: Many Remain Uninsured Despite Medicaid Expansion* (Washington, DC: Author, 1995), 18.

13. Jennifer Ehrle and K. Moore, *Children's Environment and Behavior: Behavioral and Emotional Problems in Children* (Washington, DC: Urban Institute, 1999). [Online: http://newfederalism.urban. org/nsaf/children_c6.html].

14. Richard Rothstein, "Reducing Poverty Could Increase School Achievement," *New York Times*, 7 March 2001, p. A18.

15. National Institute of Child Health and Development, *The NICHD Study of Early Child Care* (Washington, DC: Author, 1999).

16. H. Chugani, "Functional Brain Reorganization in Children," *Brain and Development* 18 (1996): 347–56.

17. M. Lamb and J. Campos, *Development in Infancy* (New York: Random House, 1982).

18. National Education Goals Panel, "Promising Practices: Progress Toward the Goals 2000" (Washington, DC: Author, 2001). [Online: http://www.negp.gov/promprac/promprac00/promprac00.pdf].

19. H. Chugani, "Functional Brain Reorganization in Children," *Brain and Development* 18 (1996): 347–56.

CHAPTER 3

1. U.S. Department of Education, *Ready to Read, Ready to Learn: First Lady Laura Bush's Education Initiatives.* [Online: http://www.ed.gov/inits/rrrl/index.html].

2. John Amos Comenius, *The Great Didactic of John Amos Comenius,* ed. and trans. M. W. Keating (New York: Russell & Russell, 1967), 58.

3. Jean-Jacques Rousseau, *Émile, Or Education,* trans. Barbara Foxley (New York: Dutton, Everyman's Library, 1933), 5.

4. Maria Montessori, *The Discovery of the Child,* trans. M. J. Costelloe (Notre Dame, Ind.: Fides, 1967), 22.

5. Reginald D. Archambault, ed., *John Dewey on Education—Selected Writings* (New York: Random House, 1964), 430.

6. David M. Brodizinsky, Irving E. Sigel, and Roberta M. Golinkoff, "New Dimensions in Piagetian Theory and Research: An Integrative Perspective, *New Directions in Piagetian Theory and Practice,* eds. Irving E. Sigel, David M. Brodizinsky, and Roberta M. Golinkoff (Hillsdale, NJ: Erlbaum, 1981), 5.

7. P. G. Richmond, *An Introduction to Piaget* (New York: Basic Books, 1970), 68.

8. L. S. Vygotsky, *Mind in Society* (Cambridge, Mass.: Harvard University Press, 1978), 244.

9. Jonathan R. H. Tudge, "Processes and Consequences of Peer Collaboration: A Vygotskian Analysis," *Child Development* 63 (1992): 1365.

CHAPTER 4

1. National Academy of Early Childhood Programs, Accreditation. [Online: http://www.naeyc.org/accreditation/faq_0.htm].

2. Jodi Wilgoren, "Quality Day Care, Early, Is Tied to Achievements as an Adult," *New York Times,* 22 October 1999, A16.

3. Children's Defense Fund, "Why Quality Child Care and Early Education Matters," *The Children of the Cost, Quality, and Outcomes Study Go to School: Executive Summary.* [Online: http://www.childrensdefensefund.org/childcare/cc_quality matters. html].

4. Ibid.

5. Ibid.

6. Ibid.

7. Linda Jacobson, "Study: High-Quality Child Care Pays Off," *Education Week,* 28 April 1999, 9.

8. High/Scope Education Research Foundation, *The High/Scope K–3 Curriculum: An Introduction* (Ypsilanti, Mich.: Author, 1989), 1.

9. Ibid.

10. Maria Montessori, *Dr. Montessori's Own Handbook* (New York: Schocken Books, 1965), 131.

11. Administration for Children and Families, *Project Head Start Statistical Fact Sheet 1999* (Washington, DC: Author, 1999). [Online: http://www2.acf.dhhs.gov/programs/hsb/research/99_hsfs.htm].

12. U.S. Department of Health and Human Services, *Head Start Program Performance Standards,* 45 CFR §1304 (Washington, DC: U.S. Government Printing Office, November 1984), 8–9.

13. Ibid.

CHAPTER 6

1. P. Kuhl, *Early Language Acquisition: The Brain Comes Prepared* (St. Louis, Mo.: Parents as Teachers National Center, 1996).

2. E. L. Newport, "Mother, I'd Rather Do It Myself: Some Effects and Non-Effects on Maternal Speech Style," in C. E. Snow and C. A. Ferguson, eds., *Talking to Children* (Cambridge, England: Cambridge University Press), 112–29.

3. S. Bredekamp and C. Copple, eds., *Developmentally Appropriate Practice in Early Childhood Programs* (Washington, DC: National Association for the Education of Young Children, 1997), 9.

CHAPTER 7

1. National Association for the Education of Young Children, "NAEYC Position Statement on School Readiness," *Young Children* 46 (1), 21.

CHAPTER 8

1. Literacy Volunteers of America, *Facts on Literacy* (Syracuse, NY: Author, 1994).

2. M. J. Adams, *Beginning to Read: Thinking and Learning About Print* (Urbana, Ill.: The Reading Research and Education Center, 1990), 36–38.

3. Ibid., 8.

4. K. L. Maxwell and S. K. Elder, "Children's Transition to Kindergarten," *Young Children* 49 (6), 56–63.

CHAPTER 9

1. Frank Bruni, "Bush Emphasizes Teaching of Values to Children," *The New York Times*. 15 August 2001, A21.

2. School-to-Work Initiative. [Online: http://www.stw.ed.gov/expsrch.cfm].

3. National Council of Teachers of Mathematics, [Online: http://standards.nctm.org/document/chapter4/comm. htm#ee45].

CHAPTER 10

1. Public Law 105-17, 1997.

2. Ibid.

3. A. Turnbull, H. Turnbull III, M. Shank, and D. Leal, *Exceptional Lives: Special Education in Today's Schools*, 2nd ed. (Upper Saddle River, NJ: Merrill/Prentice Hall, 1995), 64–71.

4. Jacob K. Javits Gifted and Talented Students Education Act of 1988.

5. J. Gallagher, P. Weiss, K. Oglesby, and T. Thomas, *The Status of Gifted/Talented Education: United States Survey of Needs, Practices, and Policies* (Los Angeles: National/State Leadership Training Institute on the Gifted and Talented, 1983).

6. Marie Cabo, Rita Dunn, and Kenneth Dunn, *Teaching Students to Read Through Their Individual Learning Styles* (Boston: Allyn & Bacon, 1991), 2.

7. Hilderbrand, V., Phenice, L. A., Grey, M. M., and Hines, R. P., *Knowing and Serving Diverse Families* (Columbus, Ohio: Merrill/Prentice Hall, 2000), 107.

CHAPTER 12

1. U.S. Census Bureau. *Coresident Grandparents and Children* (1999). [Online: http://www.census.gov/prod/99pubs/p23-198.pdf].

2. Office of Educational Research and Improvement, U.S. Department of Education. Reaching All Families—Creating Family Friendly Schools (1996).

3. Family Involvement Partnership for Learning, Community Update #23 (Washington, DC: Author, April 1995).

GLOSSARY

Aide Assists the teacher and teacher assistant when requested; usually considered an entry-level position.

Adaptive education Modifying programs, environments, curricula, and activities to provide learning experiences that help all students achieve desired education goals.

Alphabetic knowledge The knowledge that letters have names and shapes and that letters can represent sounds in language.

Alphabetic principle Awareness that each speech sound or phoneme in a language has its own distinctive graphic representation and an understanding that letters go together in patterns to represent sounds.

Assessment The process of collecting information about children's development, learning, health, behavior, academic progress, and need for special services, in order to plan and implement curriculum and instruction.

Attention deficit hyperactivity disorder (ADHD) A behavioral disorder in which children display cognitive delays as a result of difficulties with attention, impulse control, and hyperactivity.

Authentic assessment Evaluation of the actual learning and instructional activities in which children are involved.

Before- and after-school care Provides care for children of school age, generally Pre-K–6, before and after school hours.

Behavior guidance A process by which teachers help all children learn to control and direct their behavior and become independent and self-reliant.

Bias-free Curriculum, programs, materials, language, attitudes, actions, and activities that are free from biased perceptions.

Bilingual education Education in two languages. Generally, two languages are used for the purpose of academic instruction.

Caregiver Provides care, education, and protection for the very young in or outside the home; includes parents, relatives, child care workers, and early childhood teachers.

Child and Family Resource Program Delivers Head Start services to families; birth to eight years.

Child care Play/socialization; baby-sitting; physical care; provides parents opportunities to work; cognitive development; full-quality care; birth to six years.

Child development associate Has completed a CDA assessment and received the CDA credential of the National Credentialing Program, Child Development Associate Assessment System and Competency Standards.

Children with disabilities Children who need special education and related services because of mental retardation, hearing impairments, speech or language impairments, serious emotional disturbances, orthopedic impairments, autism, traumatic brain injury, other health impairments, or specific learning disabilities.

Circular response Developmental reaction that typically begins to develop in early infancy in which infants' actions cause them to react or when another person prompts an infant to try to repeat the original action; similar to a stimulus-response or cause-and-effect relationship.

381

Cognitive theory Jean Piaget's proposition that children develop intelligence through direct experiences with the physical world. In this sense, learning is an internal (mental) process involving children's adapting new knowledge to what they already know.

Comprehension In reading, the basic understanding of the words and the content or meaning contained within printed material.

Constructivist process The continuous mental organizing, structuring, and restructuring of experiences in relation to schemes of thought, or mental images, which result in cognitive growth.

Co-teaching The process by which a regular classroom professional and a special educator or a person trained in exceptional student education team teach, in the same classroom, a group of regular and mainstreamed children.

Cultural diversity The diversity between and within ethnic groups. The extent of group identification by members of ethnic groups varies greatly and is influenced by many factors such as skin color, social class, and professional experience.

Cultural literacy Based on the theory of E. D. Hirsch, Jr., emphasizes a knowledge of the facts and ideas that make up the "common core" that forms the basis of American civilization and culture.

Culturally fair education Education that respects and accounts for the cultural backgrounds of all learners.

Cultural pluralism The belief that cultural diversity is of positive value.

Decoding The process whereby children identify words through context or letter-sound associations. Decoding is frequently used synonymously with phonics.

Department of Children, Youth, and Families A multipurpose agency of many state and county governments; usually provides such services as administration of state and federal monies, child care licensing, and protective services for children of all ages.

Developmental kindergarten Same as regular kindergarten; often enrolls children ages five and six who have completed one or more years in an early childhood special education program.

Developmentally appropriate practice Teaching based on how children grow and develop.

Director Develops and implements a center or school program; supervises all staff; may teach a group of children.

Diversity Refers to and describes the relationships among background, socioeconomic status, gender, language, and culture of students, parents, and communities.

Drop-off child care centers Provides care for infants, toddlers, and young children for short periods of time while parents shop, exercise, or have appointments.

Dual-age classroom An organizational plan in which children from two grade levels are grouped together; maintains reasonable student-teacher ratios; another term for multi-age grouping; variable ages.

Early childhood assistant teacher Assists the teacher in conducting a developmentally and educationally appropriate program for a group or classroom; frequently acts as a co-teacher but may lack education or training to be classified as a teacher (many people who have teacher qualifications serve as an assistant teacher because they enjoy the program or because the position of teacher is not available); usually has a high school diploma or associate degree and is involved in professional development.

Early childhood associate teacher Plans and implements activities with children; has an associate degree and/or the CDA credential; may also be responsible for care and education of a group of children.

Early childhood educator Works with young children and has committed to self-development by participating in specialized training and programs to extend professional knowledge and competence.

Early childhood professional This is the preferred title for anyone who works with young children in any capacity. The designation reflects the growing belief of the early childhood profession that people who work with children at any level are professionals and as such are worthy of the respect, remuneration, and responsibilities that go with being a professional.

Early childhood program Multipurpose; birth to grade three.

Early childhood teacher Responsible for planning and conducting a developmentally and educationally appropriate program for a group or classroom of children; supervises an assistant teacher or aide; usually has a bachelor's degree in early childhood, elementary education, or child development.

Early Head Start   Federally funded, community-based program for low-income pregnant women and families with infants and toddlers. Promotes healthy births and enhances the development of very young children.

Early intervention   Providing services to children and families as early in the child's life as possible to prevent or help with a special need or needs.

English as a Second Language (ESL)   Instruction in which students with limited English proficiency attend a special English class.

Employer/corporate child care   Different settings for meeting child care needs; variable ages, usually as early as six weeks to the beginning of school.

Even Start   Federally funded family literacy program that combines adult literacy and parenting training with early childhood education.

Exceptional student education   Replaces the term *special education;* refers to the education of children with special needs.

Expressive language   A preschooler's developing ability to talk fluently and articulately with teacher and peers, the ability to express oneself in the language of the school, and the ability to communicate needs and ideas.

Family day care   Provides care for a group of children in a home setting; generally custodial and educational in nature; variable ages.

Fatherhood Project   National research and education program that examines the future of fatherhood and supports men's involvement in child rearing.

Follow Through   Extended Head Start services to grades one, two, and three.

Full inclusion   The mainstreaming or inclusion of all children with disabilities into natural environments such as playgrounds, family day care centers, child care centers, preschool, kindergarten, and primary grades.

Gifted and talented children   As defined by federal law, children who demonstrate the potential for high performance in intellectual, creative, artistic, or leadership capacities.

Head Start   Federally funded program for children ages two to six, involving play/socialization, academic learning, and comprehensive social and health services; program prepares children for kindergarten and first grade.

Health and Human Services   Same as Department of Children, Youth, and Families; all ages.

Health and Social Services   Same as Department of Children, Youth, and Families; all ages.

High school child care programs   Provides child care for children of high school students, especially unwed parents; serves as an incentive for student-parents to finish high school and as a training program in child care and parenting skills; programs are for children six weeks to five years.

High/Scope   A constructivist educational approach based on Piaget's cognitive development theory. High/Scope promotes the constructivist process of learning and broadens the child's emerging intellectual and social skills.

High-stakes testing   Using standardized and other tests to make important, often life-influencing, decisions about children, such as admissions to a program, grade advancement or failure, and removal from a program.

Holophrases   One-word sentences toddlers use to communicate.

Home Start   Provides Head Start services in the home setting; birth to six or seven years.

Home visitor   Conducts a home-based child development/education program; works with children, families, and staff members.

Impulse control   The ability to stay on task, pay attention to a learning activity, work cooperatively with others, and not hit or interfere with the work of other children.

Independence   The ability to work alone on a task, take care of oneself, and initiate projects without always being told what to do.

Individualized education program (IEP)   A plan created to specify instruction for children with disabilities.

Individualized family service plan (IFSP)   A plan created for infants and toddlers with disabilities and their families, specifying what services they will receive to help them reach their goals.

Infant stimulation programs (also called parent/ infant stimulation)   Programs for enhancing sensory and cognitive development of infants and young toddlers through exercise and play; activities include general sensory stimulation for children and educational information and advice for parents; three months to two years.

Integration The education of children with disabilities along with typically developing children. This education can occur in mainstream, reverse mainstream, and full-inclusion programs.

Interim first grade Provides children with an additional year of kindergarten and readiness activities prior to and as preparation for first grade; five and six years.

Interpersonal skills The ability to get along and work with both peers and adults.

Junior first grade Preparation for first grade; five and six years.

Junior kindergarten Prekindergarten program, primarily for four-year-olds.

Kindergarten Preparation for first grade; developmentally appropriate activities for children ages four and a half to six; increasingly viewed as the grade before the first grade and a regular part of the public school program.

Laboratory school Provides demonstration programs for preservice teacher; and conducts research; variable ages, birth through senior high.

Language experience approach A reading instruction method that links oral and written language. Based on the premise that what is thought can be said, what is said can be written, and what is written can be read.

Learning Acquisition of knowledge, behaviors, skills, and attitudes.

Learning families Another name for multi-age grouping; however, the emphasis is on practices that create a family atmosphere and encourage living and learning as a family; the term was commonly used in open educational programs; its revival signifies the reemergence of progressive and child-centered approaches; variable ages.

Learning style The way a child is affected by his or her environment, emotions, sociological needs, physical characteristics, and psychological inclinations as he or she works to master new or difficult information or skills.

Least restrictive environment (LRE) Children with disabilities are educated with children who have no disabilities. Special classes, separate schooling, or other removal of children with disabilities from the regular educational environment occurs only when the nature or severity of the disability is such that education in regular classes with the use of supplementary aids and services cannot be achieved satisfactorily.

Lekotek Resource center for families who have children with special needs; sometimes referred to as a toy library or play library (*lekotek* is a Scandinavian word that means "play library"); birth through primary years.

Limited English proficiency (LEP) Describes children who have limited English skills.

Locus of control The source or place of control; the goal of behavioral guidance is to help children learn that their locus of control is internal, that they are responsible for their behavior, and that the rewards for good behavior come from within themselves.

Looping Assigning teachers to spend two or more years with the same group of same-age children.

Magnet school Specializes in subjects and curriculum designed to attract students; usually has a theme (e.g., performing arts); designed to give parents choices and to integrate schools; five to eighteen years.

Montessori school (preschool and grade school) Provides programs that use the philosophy, procedures, and materials developed by Maria Montessori (see Chapter 4); one to eight years.

Multi-age grades or groups Groups of classes of children of various ages; generally spanning two to three years per group; variable ages.

Multicultural awareness Appreciation for and understanding of people's cultures, socioeconomic status, and gender.

Multicultural infusion Permeating the curriculum with multicultural education to influence the way young children and teachers think about diversity issues.

Multiculturalism An approach to education based on the premise that all peoples in the United States should receive proportional attention in the curriculum.

Multiple intelligences Howard Gardner's concept that people are "smart" in many ways; those intelligences include linguistic, musical, logical-mathematical, spatial, bodily-kinesthetic, interpersonal, intrapersonal, naturalistic, and existentialist.

Natural environment   Any environment in which it is natural for any child to be, such as home, child care center, preschool, kindergarten, and primary grades.

Nursery school (public or private)   Play/socialization; cognitive development; two to four years.

Object permanence   The concept that things out of sight continue to exist; this intellectual milestone typically begins to develop at four to eight months.

Observation   The intentional, systematic act of looking at the behavior of a child or children in a particular setting, program, or situation.

Onset-rime   The onset is any consonants that precede the vowel, and the rime is the vowel plus any succeeding consonants. In *pig*, *p* is the onset and *ig* is the rime.

Operation   A reversible mental action.

Orthographic awareness   Familiarity with written symbols and an understanding of the relationships between these symbols and the sounds they represent.

Parent   Provides the child with basic care, direction, support, protection, and guidance.

Parent cooperative preschool   Play/socialization; preparation for kindergarten and first grade; baby-sitting; cognitive development; two to five years. Many of these programs require or encourage parent participation.

Parent/family involvement   Process of helping parents and family members use their abilities to benefit themselves, their children, and the early childhood program.

Philosophy of education   Set of beliefs about how children develop and learn and what and how they should be taught.

Phoneme   The smallest unit of speech that makes a difference to meaning.

Phonemic awareness   The ability to deal explicitly and segmentally with sound units smaller than the syllable.

Phonics   The learning of alphabetic principles of language and knowledge of letter-sound relationships. Children learn to associate letters with the phonemes (basic speech sounds) to help break the alphabetic code.

Phonics instruction   Emphasizes teaching letter-sound correspondence so children can learn to combine sounds into words.

Phonological awareness   The ability to manipulate language at the levels of syllables, rhymes, and individual speech sounds.

Portfolios   A purposeful compilation of children's work samples, products, and teacher observations collected over time.

Pre-first grade   Preparation for first grade; often for students who "failed" or did not do well in kindergarten; five and six years.

Prekindergarten   Program that emphasizes play/socialization and preparation for kindergarten; three and a half to five years.

Preprimary   Preparation for first grade; five and six years.

Preschool (public or private)   Program that focuses on play/socialization and cognitive development; two and a half to five years.

Primary grades   Refers to first, second, and third grades.

Print awareness   The recognition of conventions and characteristics of a written language.

Proprietary care   Provides care and/or education to children; designed to make a profit; six weeks to entrance into first grade.

Psychosocial development   Erik H. Erikson's theory that contends that cognitive and social development must occur simultaneously.

Readiness   Being ready to learn; possessing the knowledge, skills, and abilities necessary for learning and for success in school.

Receptive language   Skills that toddlers and preschoolers develop, such as listening to the teacher and following directions.

Reflective practice   Professionals employ a reflective practice cycle to improve their work: they think about what and how they will teach before they teach, think about their teaching as they teach, and think about what they taught after they teach.

Reggio Emilia   An educational program named for a town in Italy where it originated. This early education method emphasizes the child's relations with family, peers, teachers, and the wider community; small-group interaction; schedules set by the child's personal rhythms; and visual arts programs coordinated by a specially trained atelierista.

Reverse mainstreaming   The process by which typically developing children are placed in programs for children with disabilities. In reverse mainstreaming, children with disabilities are in the majority.

Scaffolding Assistance or support of some kind from a teacher, parent, caregiver, or peer to help children complete tasks they cannot complete independently.

Screening procedures Initial evaluations and information gathering to create a broad picture of children's abilities and physical and emotional status.

Self-actualization Abraham Maslow's theory of motivation based on the satisfaction of needs; Maslow maintained that children cannot achieve self-actualization until certain basic needs, including food, shelter, safety, and love, are met.

Sight word approach Also called *whole-word* or *look-say*, the approach involves presenting children with whole words so they develop a "sight vocabulary" that enables them to begin reading and writing.

Sociocultural theory Lev Vygotsky's suggestion that children's mental, language, and social development is supported and enhanced through social interactions with other children, older peers, and adults.

Split class Teaches basic academic and social skills of grades involved; variable ages, but usually primary ages.

Standards Statements of what pre-K–12 students should know and be able to do.

Sustained instruction Assigning an early childhood professional to teach the same group of children over several years.

Symbolic language Knowing the names of people, places, and things, words for concepts, and adjectives and prepositions.

Symbolic representation The understanding, that develops at about age two, that something else can stand for a mental image; for example, a word can represent real objects, something not present, and concepts.

Synaptogenesis The formation of connections, or synapses, among neurons; this process of brain development begins before birth and continues until age ten.

Telegraphic speech Two-word sentences, such as "Go out" or "All gone," used by toddlers.

Title I A federal program designed to improve the basic skills (reading and mathematics) of low-ability children from low-income families.

Toy lending libraries Provide children and parents with games, toys, and other materials that can be used for learning purposes; housed in libraries, vans, or early childhood centers; birth through primary years.

Transitional kindergarten Extended learning of kindergarten; preparation for first grade; variable ages.

Typically developing children Children who are developing according to and within the boundaries of normal growth and development.

Volunteers Contribute time, services, and talents to support staff. Usually are parents, retired persons, grandparents, and university, college, or high school students.

Whole language approach Philosophy of literacy development that advocates the use of real literature—reading, writing, listening, and speaking—to help children become motivated to read and write.

Zero to Three A national program promoting the healthy development of infants and toddlers.

Zone of proximal development That area of development into which a child can be led by a more competent partner. Also, the range of tasks that children cannot do independently but which they can learn with the help of a more competent other.

INDEX